YOU COULD HELP, YOU KNOW!
YOU MUST HAVE LEARNED SOMETHING AFTER ALL THOSE YEARS IN DETECTIVE COMICS!
BATMAN

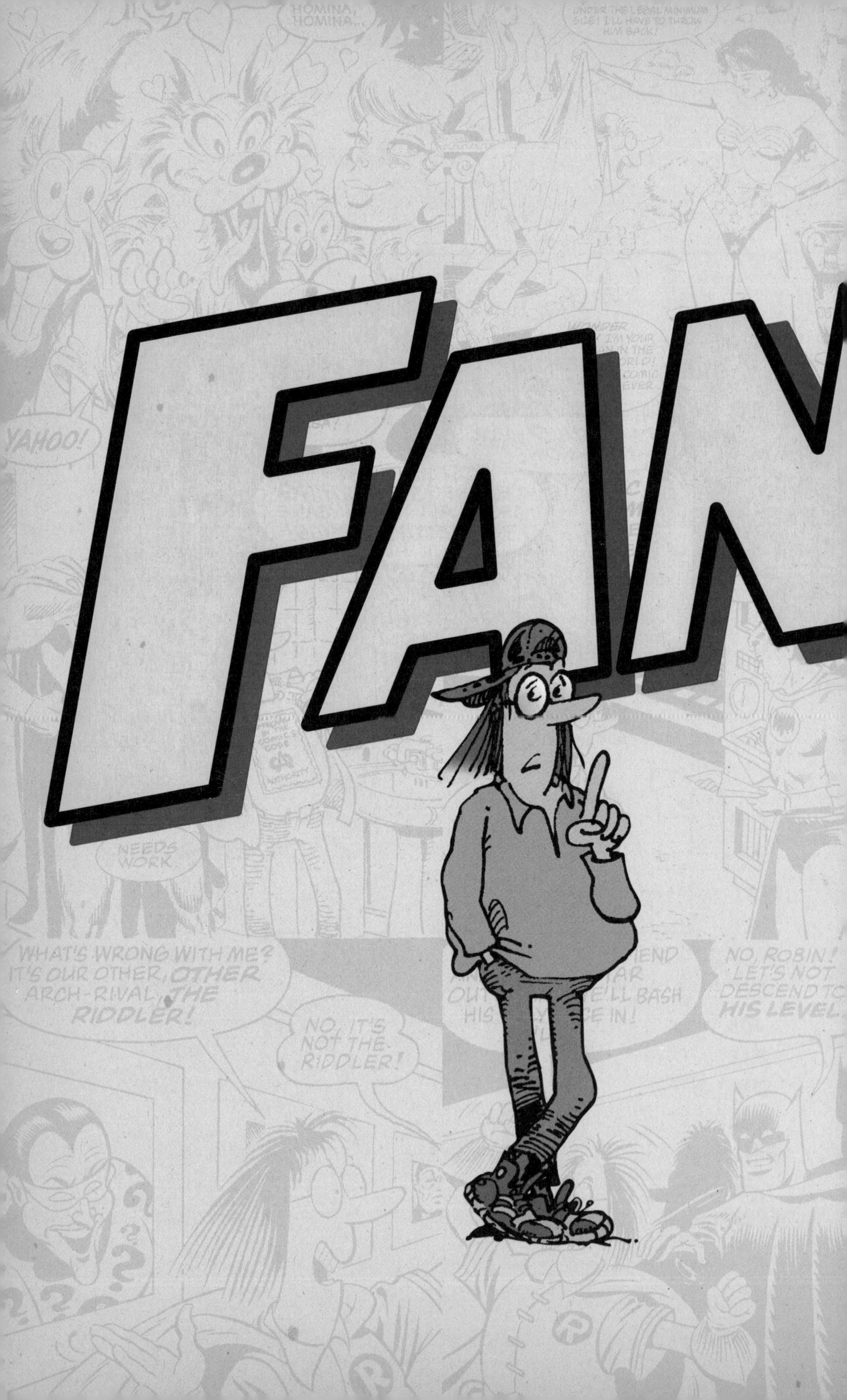
HOMINA, HOMINA...
UNDER THE LEGAL MINIMUM SIZE! I'LL HAVE TO THROW HIM BACK!
FAN
YAHOO!
NEEDS WORK.
WHAT'S WRONG WITH ME? IT'S OUR OTHER, OTHER ARCH-RIVAL, THE RIDDLER!
NO, IT'S NOT THE RIDDLER!
NO, ROBIN! LET'S NOT DESCEND TO HIS LEVEL!

BOY

by **MARK EVANIER**
and **SERGIO ARAGONÉS**

With additional art by:

NEAL ADAMS	JIM MOONEY
BRENT ANDERSON	KEVIN NOWLAN
JORDI BERNET	JERRY ORDWAY
WILL BLYBERG	WENDY PINI
DAVE GIBBONS	STEVE RUDE
JOE GIELLA	MARIE SEVERIN
MIKE GRELL	BILL SIENKIEWICZ
MATT HALEY	TOM SIMMONS
RUSS HEATH	DAN SPIEGLE
PHIL JIMENEZ	DICK SPRANG
GIL KANE	BRUCE TIMM
FRANK MILLER	BERNIE WRIGHTSON

Original covers by:

SERGIO ARAGONÉS
JERRY ORDWAY
GIL KANE
KEVIN MAGUIRE
MARLO ALQUIZA
JOE KUBERT
BOB KANE
BRIAN BOLLAND

Coloring by
TOM LUTH

Lettering by
TODD KLEIN

FANBOY created by MARK EVANIER and SERGIO ARAGONÉS

DC Comics

Jenette Kahn
President & Editor-in-Chief

Paul Levitz
Executive Vice President & Publisher

Mike Carlin
Executive Editor

Tony Bedard
Editor-original series

Scott Nybakken
Editor-collected edition

Nick J. Napolitano
Associate Editor-collected edition

Georg Brewer
Design Director

Robbin Brosterman
Art Director

Richard Bruning
VP-Creative Director

Patrick Caldon
Senior VP-Finance & Operations

Dorothy Crouch
VP-Licensed Publishing

Terri Cunningham
VP-Managing Editor

Joel Ehrlich
Senior VP-Advertising & Promotions

Alison Gill
Executive Director-Manufacturing

Lillian Laserson
VP & General Counsel

Jim Lee
Editorial Director-WildStorm

John Nee
VP & General Manager-WildStorm

Cheryl Rubin
VP-Licensing & Merchandising

Bob Wayne
VP-Sales & Marketing

Published by DC Comics.
Cover, compilation and introduction © 2001 Horse Feathers, Inc. and Sergio Aragonés.
All Rights Reserved.

Originally published in single magazine form as FANBOY 1-6.
Copyright © 1999 Horse Feathers, Inc. and Sergio Aragonés.
All Rights Reserved. Except for DC characters, all characters, their distinctive likenesses,
and all related indicia featured in this publication
are trademarks of Horse Feathers, Inc. and Sergio Aragonés.
DC characters are trademarks of DC Comics. The stories, characters, and
incidents featured in this publication are entirely fictional.

DC Comics, 1700 Broadway, New York, NY 10019
A division of Warner Bros. - An AOL Time Warner Company
Printed in Canada. First Printing.
ISBN: 1-56389-724-5
Cover illustration by Sergio Aragonés.

Special thanks to Carolyn Kelly

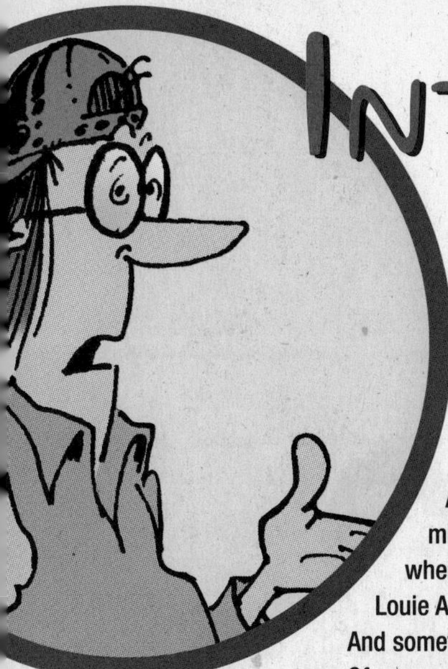

INTRODUCTION

Hello. I'm Finster, and so, in a way, are you.

You know, I've been reading DC comics all my life. I never thought I'd be one.

But last year, I don't know how it happened. One day, I was working in a comic shop, selling the things. And the next, I was in one of them, sharing my world with all of you, unburdening my four-color soul, getting to be drawn by some of the field's best artists.

It's an amazing experience, one I hope you all experience some day. At times, when I read it, I wasn't sure if I was looking at a comic book or a mirror. If it was a mirror, then sometimes it was one of those Fun House kinds where the image is all distorted and as you move, you go from looking like Louie Anderson to Magic Johnson and then back again to Louie Anderson.

And sometimes, it was a little *too* accurate, if you know what I mean.

Of course you know what I mean. You're a comics fan. You must be if you picked up this collection. You didn't just wander into Barnes & Noble searching for a copy of *Root Canal for Dummies* and wind up with *Fanboy.* You bought me because you live as I live, in a couple of worlds, at least one of which is filled with super-heroes and monsters and outer space creatures and ladies who look like Wonder Woman as drawn by Brian Bolland and Steve Rude. Sigh.

You don't live there every moment. At least, I hope you don't. But you visit there all the time, just to see what it's like, just to see your old friends, or just to see the bad guys lose when they're supposed to. In some ways, the more time you spend in that world, the more you learn about this one — the one where you just paid good money for my book, thank you — and about your role in it.

A lot of unenlightened people who don't read comics think we spend all our time in that world and can't tell the difference between that one and this one. In the book you're about to read, unless they've accidentally placed this at the end, there may be points where it seems like I'm getting them confused.

This is not so. I can absolutely tell the difference between reality and fantasy.

Fantasy is what happens when you're surrounded by unearthly creatures and cosmic-powered heroes. Reality is when you're drawn by Sergio Aragonés.

As I said, I was honored to be drawn by some of the best artists in comics. Two of them, sadly, have passed away since they drew me, and I hope not because of it.

Gil Kane will forever be the Green Lantern artist for me, just as Hal Jordan will forever be Green Lantern. Yes, I know other guys got to fly around with the ring. If you're older than me, Alan Scott is your Green Lantern. If you're younger, it's Guy Gardner. And if you're really young, it's Kyle Rayner.

That's another of the great things about comics. You can have your Green Lantern and I can have mine.

Mine was masterfully drawn by the great Gil Kane, who made everything he touched exciting and interesting. I really miss not being able to unpack the new comics when they come into the store and find a Gil Kane story I've never seen before.

I don't have just one favorite Batman artist. Too many great talents have drawn him, and some of them are in this very book. However, Dick Sprang was one of the best. He almost never got his name on the wonderful stories he drew. I was proud to see all those wonderful artists' names on my comic book, but that one was really special.

I hope, when you get your own comic book, you have a similar thrill. Let me know so I can order a copy.

Your pal,

Finster

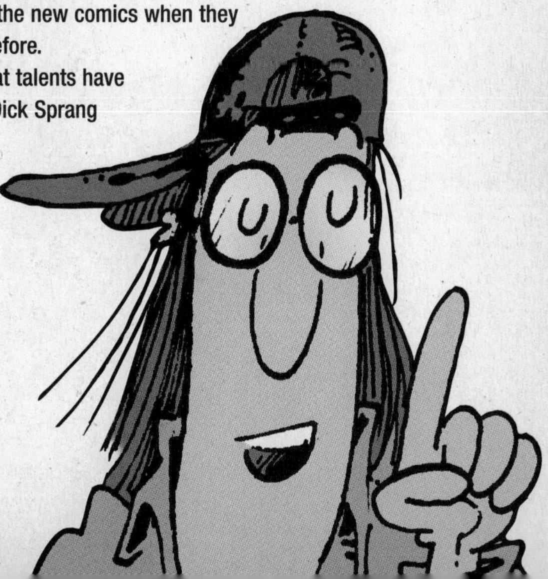

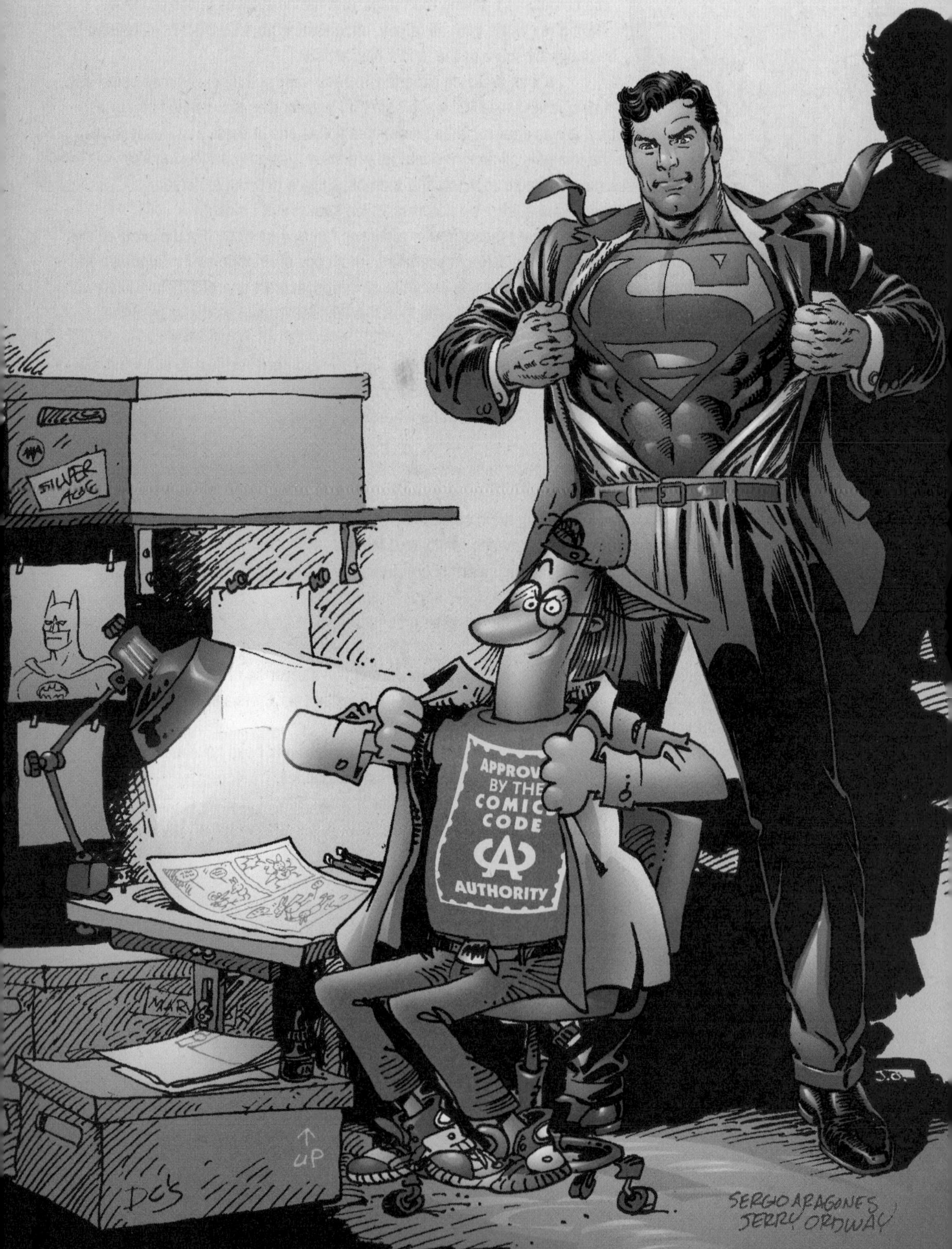
SILVER AGE
APPROV
BY THE
COMIC
CODE
AUTHORITY
UP
DC'S
J.O.
SERGIO ARAGONES
JERRY ORDWAY

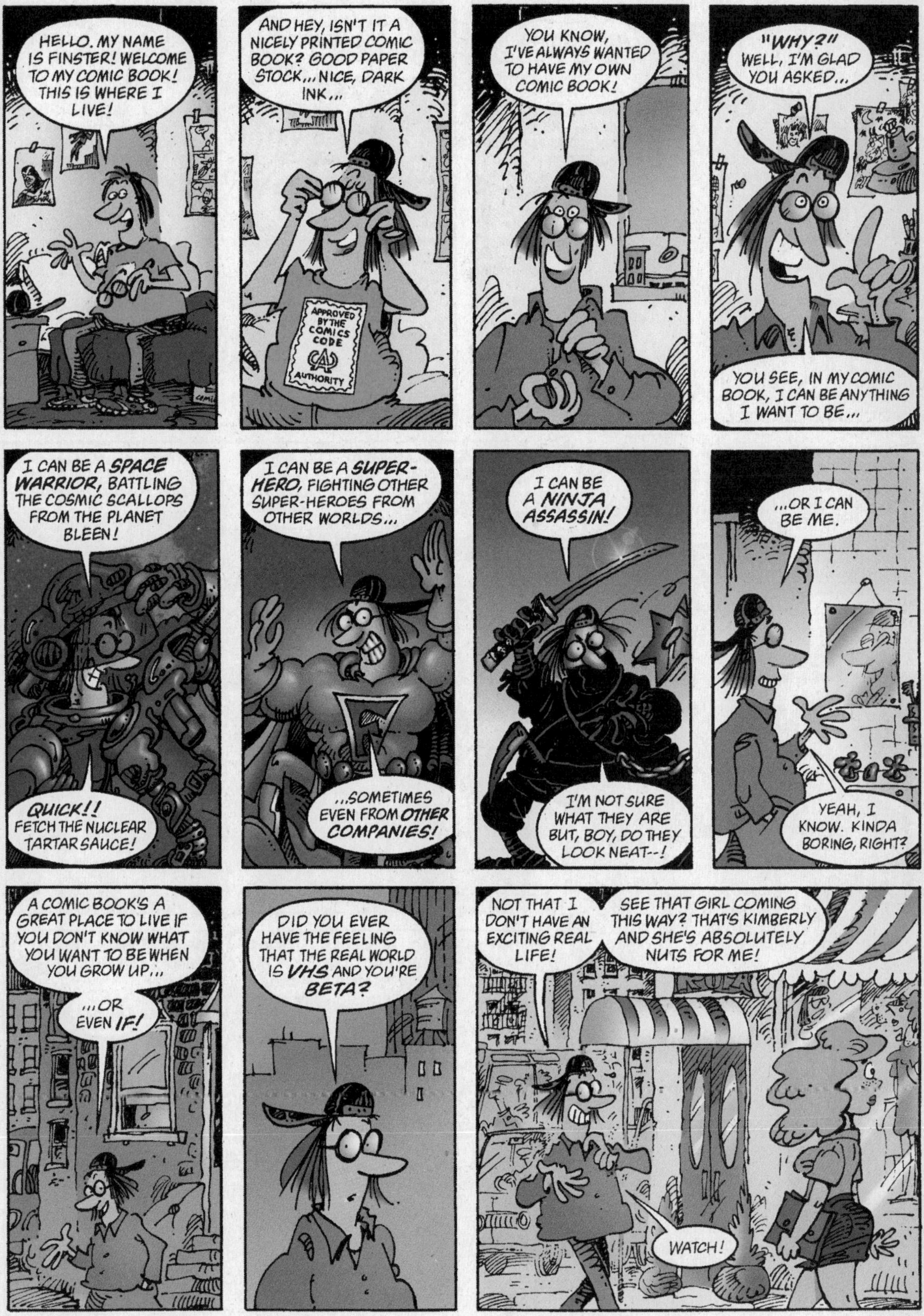
HELLO. MY NAME IS FINSTER! WELCOME TO MY COMIC BOOK! THIS IS WHERE I LIVE!
AND HEY, ISN'T IT A NICELY PRINTED COMIC BOOK? GOOD PAPER STOCK... NICE, DARK INK...
APPROVED BY THE COMICS CODE AUTHORITY
YOU KNOW, I'VE ALWAYS WANTED TO HAVE MY OWN COMIC BOOK!
"WHY?" WELL, I'M GLAD YOU ASKED...
YOU SEE, IN MY COMIC BOOK, I CAN BE ANYTHING I WANT TO BE...
I CAN BE A SPACE WARRIOR, BATTLING THE COSMIC SCALLOPS FROM THE PLANET BLEEN!
QUICK!! FETCH THE NUCLEAR TARTAR SAUCE!
I CAN BE A SUPER-HERO, FIGHTING OTHER SUPER-HEROES FROM OTHER WORLDS...
...SOMETIMES EVEN FROM OTHER COMPANIES!
I CAN BE A NINJA ASSASSIN!
I'M NOT SURE WHAT THEY ARE BUT, BOY, DO THEY LOOK NEAT--!
...OR I CAN BE ME.
YEAH, I KNOW. KINDA BORING, RIGHT?
A COMIC BOOK'S A GREAT PLACE TO LIVE IF YOU DON'T KNOW WHAT YOU WANT TO BE WHEN YOU GROW UP...
...OR EVEN IF!
DID YOU EVER HAVE THE FEELING THAT THE REAL WORLD IS VHS AND YOU'RE BETA?
NOT THAT I DON'T HAVE AN EXCITING REAL LIFE!
SEE THAT GIRL COMING THIS WAY? THAT'S KIMBERLY AND SHE'S ABSOLUTELY NUTS FOR ME!
WATCH!

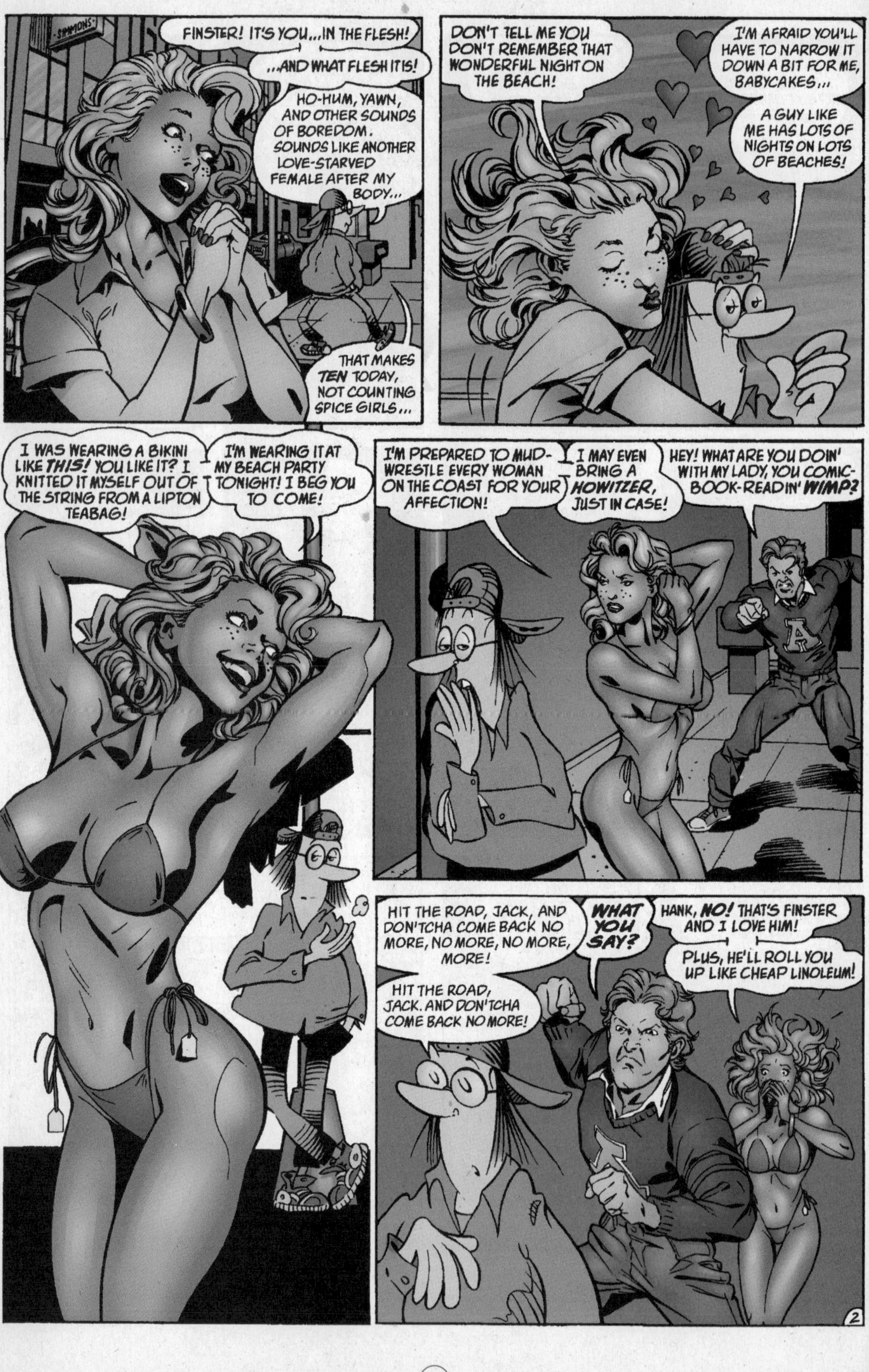
SIMMONS
FINSTER! IT'S YOU...IN THE FLESH!
...AND WHAT FLESH IT IS!
HO-HUM, YAWN, AND OTHER SOUNDS OF BOREDOM. SOUNDS LIKE ANOTHER LOVE-STARVED FEMALE AFTER MY BODY...
THAT MAKES TEN TODAY, NOT COUNTING SPICE GIRLS...
DON'T TELL ME YOU DON'T REMEMBER THAT WONDERFUL NIGHT ON THE BEACH!
I'M AFRAID YOU'LL HAVE TO NARROW IT DOWN A BIT FOR ME, BABYCAKES...
A GUY LIKE ME HAS LOTS OF NIGHTS ON LOTS OF BEACHES!
I WAS WEARING A BIKINI LIKE THIS! YOU LIKE IT? I KNITTED IT MYSELF OUT OF THE STRING FROM A LIPTON TEABAG!
I'M WEARING IT AT MY BEACH PARTY TONIGHT! I BEG YOU TO COME!
I'M PREPARED TO MUD-WRESTLE EVERY WOMAN ON THE COAST FOR YOUR AFFECTION!
I MAY EVEN BRING A HOWITZER, JUST IN CASE!
HEY! WHAT ARE YOU DOIN' WITH MY LADY, YOU COMIC-BOOK-READIN' WIMP?
HIT THE ROAD, JACK, AND DON'TCHA COME BACK NO MORE, NO MORE, NO MORE, MORE!
HIT THE ROAD, JACK. AND DON'TCHA COME BACK NO MORE!
WHAT YOU SAY?
HANK, NO! THAT'S FINSTER AND I LOVE HIM!
PLUS, HE'LL ROLL YOU UP LIKE CHEAP LINOLEUM!
2

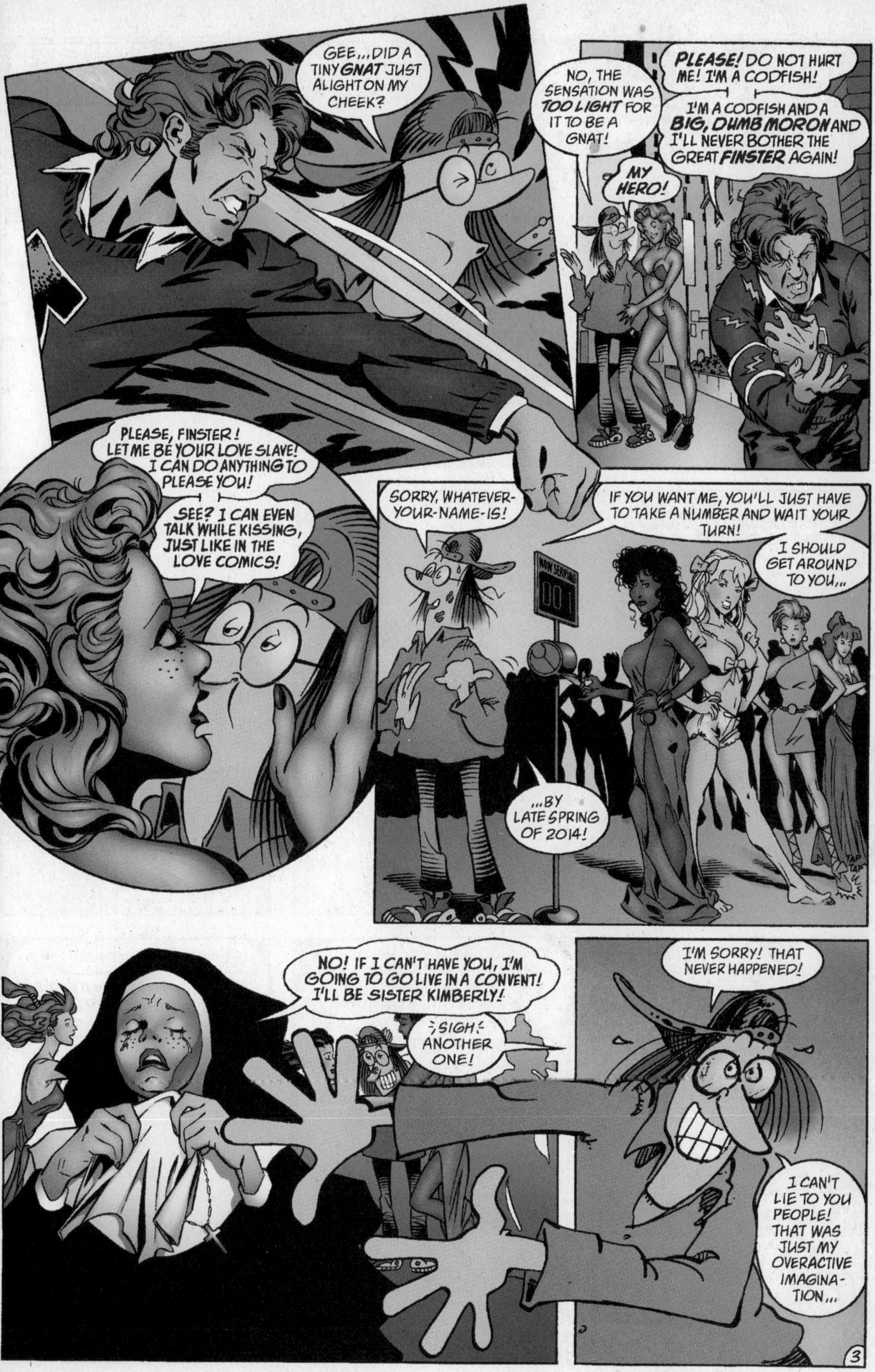
GEE...DID A TINY GNAT JUST ALIGHT ON MY CHEEK?
NO, THE SENSATION WAS TOO LIGHT FOR IT TO BE A GNAT!
PLEASE! DO NOT HURT ME! I'M A CODFISH!
I'M A CODFISH AND A BIG, DUMB MORON AND I'LL NEVER BOTHER THE GREAT FINSTER AGAIN!
MY HERO!
PLEASE, FINSTER! LET ME BE YOUR LOVE SLAVE! I CAN DO ANYTHING TO PLEASE YOU!
SEE? I CAN EVEN TALK WHILE KISSING, JUST LIKE IN THE LOVE COMICS!
SORRY, WHATEVER-YOUR-NAME-IS!
IF YOU WANT ME, YOU'LL JUST HAVE TO TAKE A NUMBER AND WAIT YOUR TURN!
I SHOULD GET AROUND TO YOU...
...BY LATE SPRING OF 2014!
NOW SERVING
001
TAP TAP
NO! IF I CAN'T HAVE YOU, I'M GOING TO GO LIVE IN A CONVENT! I'LL BE SISTER KIMBERLY!
SIGH ANOTHER ONE!
I'M SORRY! THAT NEVER HAPPENED!
I CAN'T LIE TO YOU PEOPLE! THAT WAS JUST MY OVERACTIVE IMAGINATION...
3

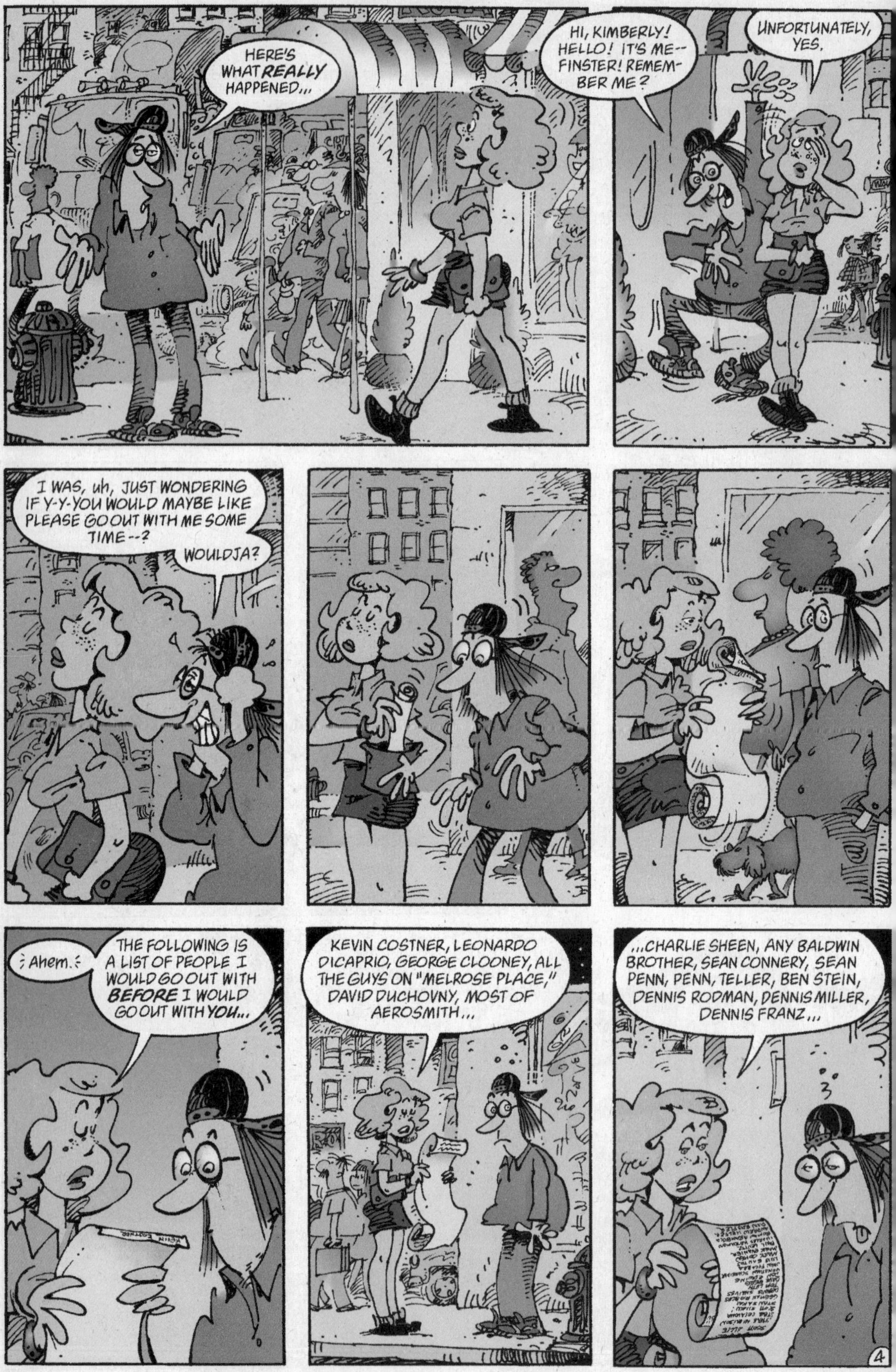
HERE'S WHAT REALLY HAPPENED...
HI, KIMBERLY! HELLO! IT'S ME-- FINSTER! REMEMBER ME?
UNFORTUNATELY, YES.
I WAS, uh, JUST WONDERING IF Y-Y-YOU WOULD MAYBE LIKE PLEASE GO OUT WITH ME SOME TIME--?
WOULDJA?
Ahem.
THE FOLLOWING IS A LIST OF PEOPLE I WOULD GO OUT WITH BEFORE I WOULD GO OUT WITH YOU...
KEVIN COSTNER, LEONARDO DICAPRIO, GEORGE CLOONEY, ALL THE GUYS ON "MELROSE PLACE," DAVID DUCHOVNY, MOST OF AEROSMITH...
...CHARLIE SHEEN, ANY BALDWIN BROTHER, SEAN CONNERY, SEAN PENN, PENN, TELLER, BEN STEIN, DENNIS RODMAN, DENNIS MILLER, DENNIS FRANZ...

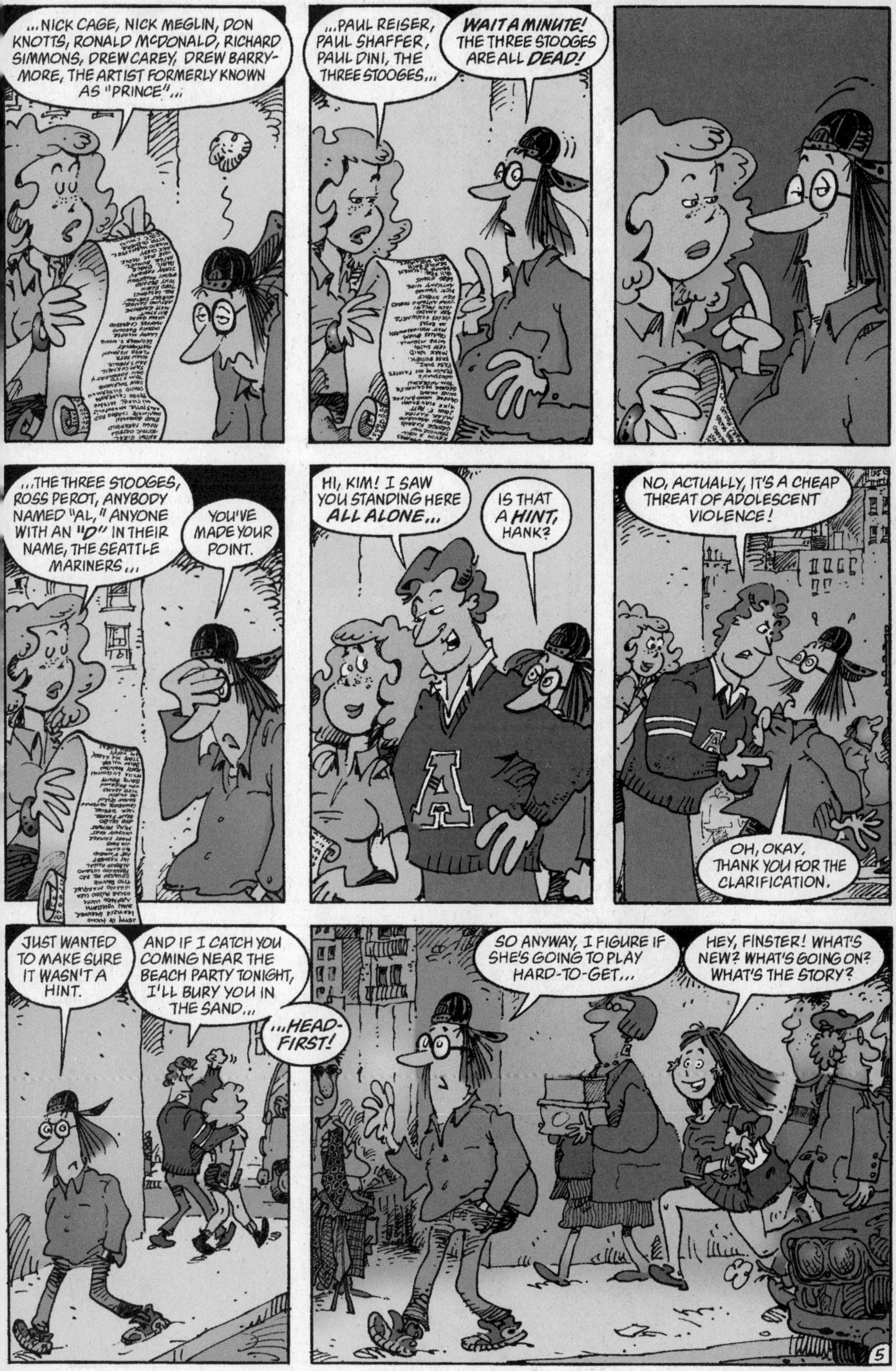
...NICK CAGE, NICK MEGLIN, DON KNOTTS, RONALD McDONALD, RICHARD SIMMONS, DREW CAREY, DREW BARRY-MORE, THE ARTIST FORMERLY KNOWN AS "PRINCE"...
...PAUL REISER, PAUL SHAFFER, PAUL DINI, THE THREE STOOGES...
WAIT A MINUTE! THE THREE STOOGES ARE ALL DEAD!
...THE THREE STOOGES, ROSS PEROT, ANYBODY NAMED "AL," ANYONE WITH AN "D" IN THEIR NAME, THE SEATTLE MARINERS...
YOU'VE MADE YOUR POINT.
HI, KIM! I SAW YOU STANDING HERE ALL ALONE...
IS THAT A HINT, HANK?
NO, ACTUALLY, IT'S A CHEAP THREAT OF ADOLESCENT VIOLENCE!
OH, OKAY. THANK YOU FOR THE CLARIFICATION.
JUST WANTED TO MAKE SURE IT WASN'T A HINT.
AND IF I CATCH YOU COMING NEAR THE BEACH PARTY TONIGHT, I'LL BURY YOU IN THE SAND...
...HEAD-FIRST!
SO ANYWAY, I FIGURE IF SHE'S GOING TO PLAY HARD-TO-GET...
HEY, FINSTER! WHAT'S NEW? WHAT'S GOING ON? WHAT'S THE STORY?
5

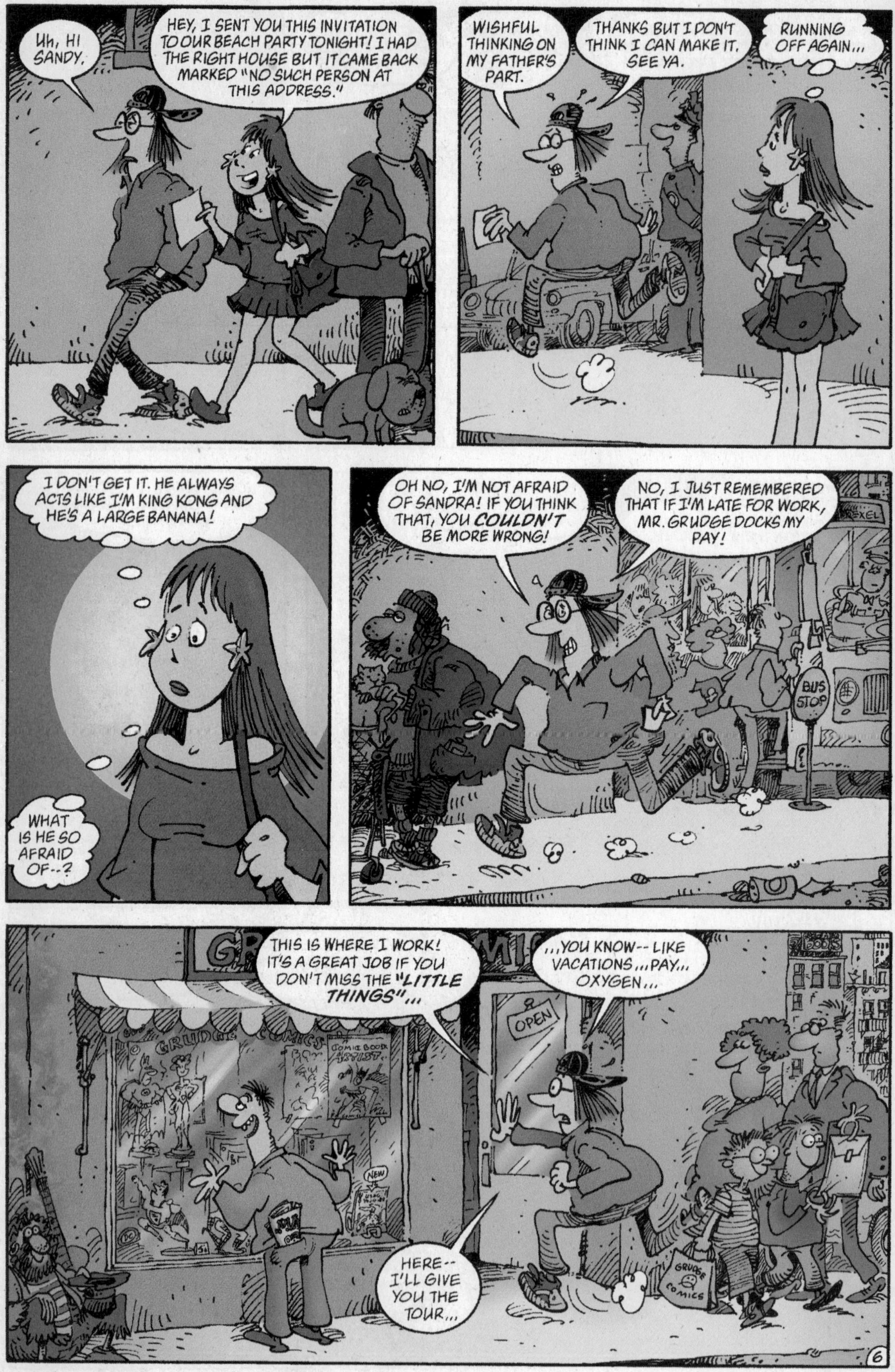
Uh, HI SANDY.
HEY, I SENT YOU THIS INVITATION TO OUR BEACH PARTY TONIGHT! I HAD THE RIGHT HOUSE BUT IT CAME BACK MARKED "NO SUCH PERSON AT THIS ADDRESS."
WISHFUL THINKING ON MY FATHER'S PART.
THANKS BUT I DON'T THINK I CAN MAKE IT. SEE YA.
RUNNING OFF AGAIN...
I DON'T GET IT. HE ALWAYS ACTS LIKE I'M KING KONG AND HE'S A LARGE BANANA!
WHAT IS HE SO AFRAID OF--?
OH NO, I'M NOT AFRAID OF SANDRA! IF YOU THINK THAT, YOU COULDN'T BE MORE WRONG!
NO, I JUST REMEMBERED THAT IF I'M LATE FOR WORK, MR. GRUDGE DOCKS MY PAY!
BUS STOP
THIS IS WHERE I WORK! IT'S A GREAT JOB IF YOU DON'T MISS THE "LITTLE THINGS"...
...YOU KNOW-- LIKE VACATIONS... PAY... OXYGEN...
OPEN
GRUDGE COMICS
HERE-- I'LL GIVE YOU THE TOUR...
6

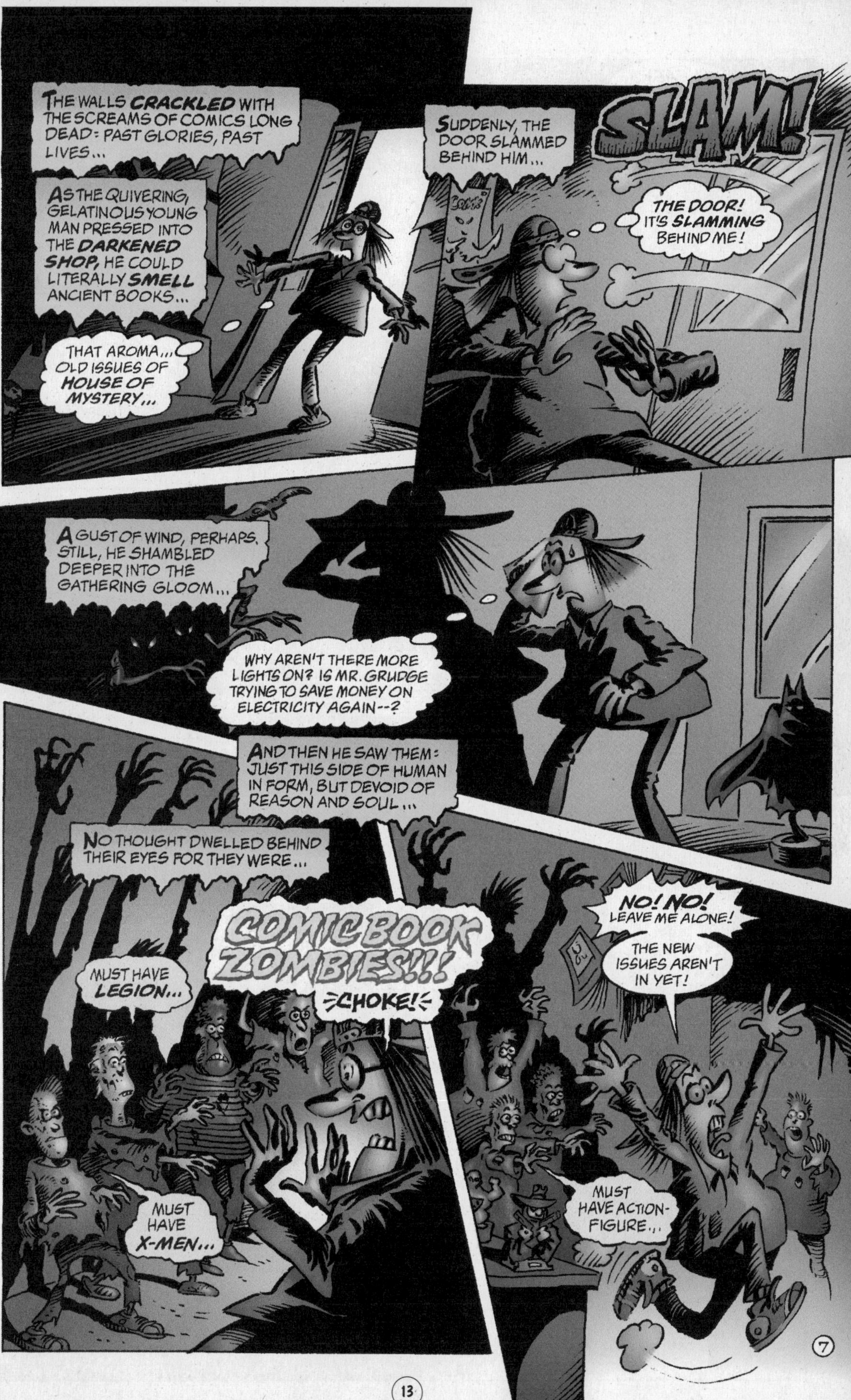
THE WALLS CRACKLED WITH THE SCREAMS OF COMICS LONG DEAD: PAST GLORIES, PAST LIVES...
AS THE QUIVERING, GELATINOUS YOUNG MAN PRESSED INTO THE DARKENED SHOP, HE COULD LITERALLY SMELL ANCIENT BOOKS...
THAT AROMA... OLD ISSUES OF HOUSE OF MYSTERY...
SUDDENLY, THE DOOR SLAMMED BEHIND HIM...
SLAM!
THE DOOR! IT'S SLAMMING BEHIND ME!
A GUST OF WIND, PERHAPS. STILL, HE SHAMBLED DEEPER INTO THE GATHERING GLOOM...
WHY AREN'T THERE MORE LIGHTS ON? IS MR. GRUDGE TRYING TO SAVE MONEY ON ELECTRICITY AGAIN--?
AND THEN HE SAW THEM: JUST THIS SIDE OF HUMAN IN FORM, BUT DEVOID OF REASON AND SOUL...
NO THOUGHT DWELLED BEHIND THEIR EYES FOR THEY WERE...
COMIC BOOK ZOMBIES!!!
CHOKE!
MUST HAVE LEGION...
MUST HAVE X-MEN...
NO! NO! LEAVE ME ALONE!
THE NEW ISSUES AREN'T IN YET!
MUST HAVE ACTION-FIGURE...
7

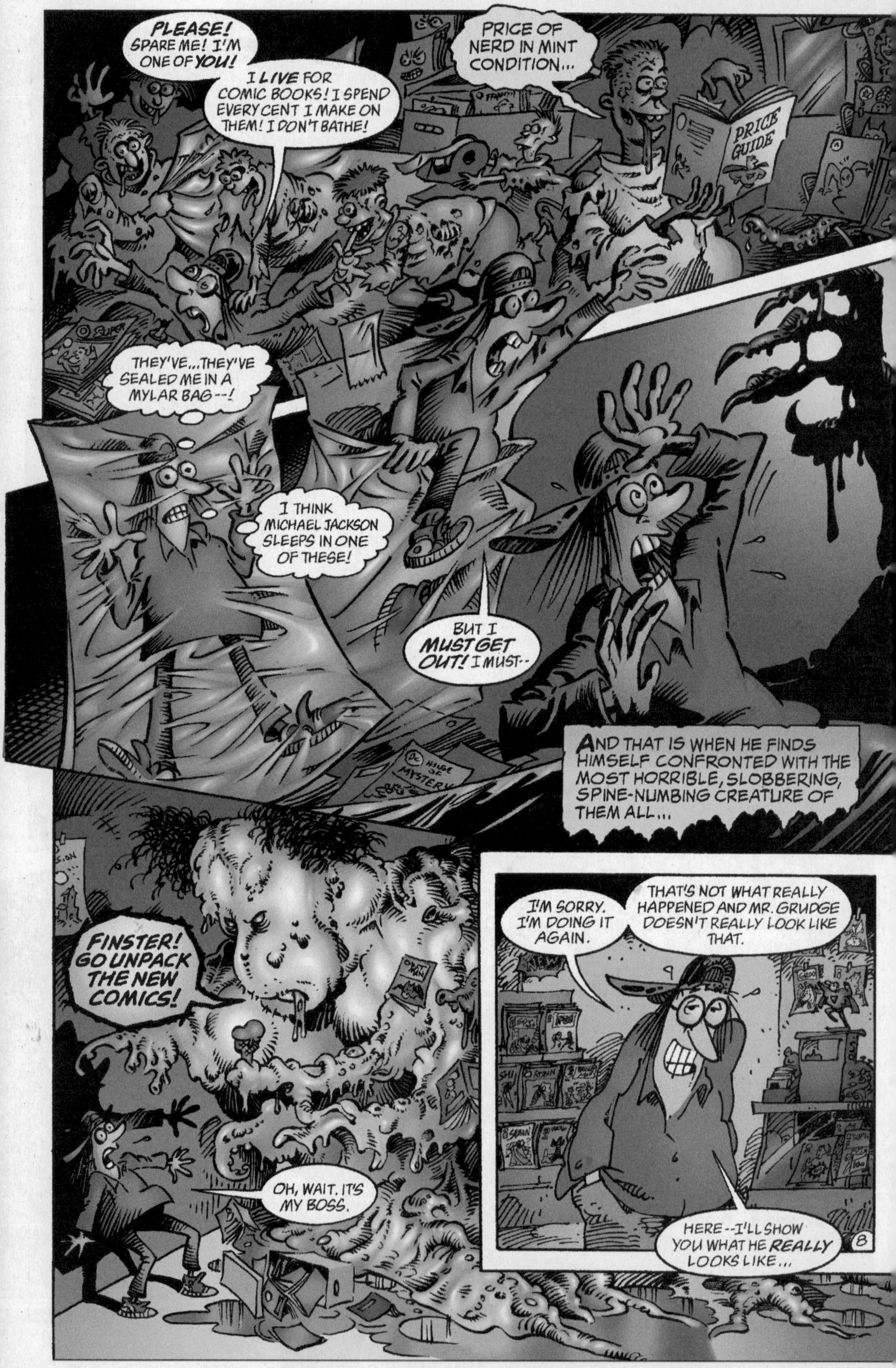
PLEASE! SPARE ME! I'M ONE OF YOU!
I LIVE FOR COMIC BOOKS! I SPEND EVERY CENT I MAKE ON THEM! I DON'T BATHE!
PRICE OF NERD IN MINT CONDITION...
PRICE GUIDE
THEY'VE...THEY'VE SEALED ME IN A MYLAR BAG--!
I THINK MICHAEL JACKSON SLEEPS IN ONE OF THESE!
BUT I MUST GET OUT! I MUST--
AND THAT IS WHEN HE FINDS HIMSELF CONFRONTED WITH THE MOST HORRIBLE, SLOBBERING, SPINE-NUMBING CREATURE OF THEM ALL...
FINSTER! GO UNPACK THE NEW COMICS!
OH, WAIT. IT'S MY BOSS.
I'M SORRY. I'M DOING IT AGAIN.
THAT'S NOT WHAT REALLY HAPPENED AND MR. GRUDGE DOESN'T REALLY LOOK LIKE THAT.
HERE--I'LL SHOW YOU WHAT HE REALLY LOOKS LIKE...
8

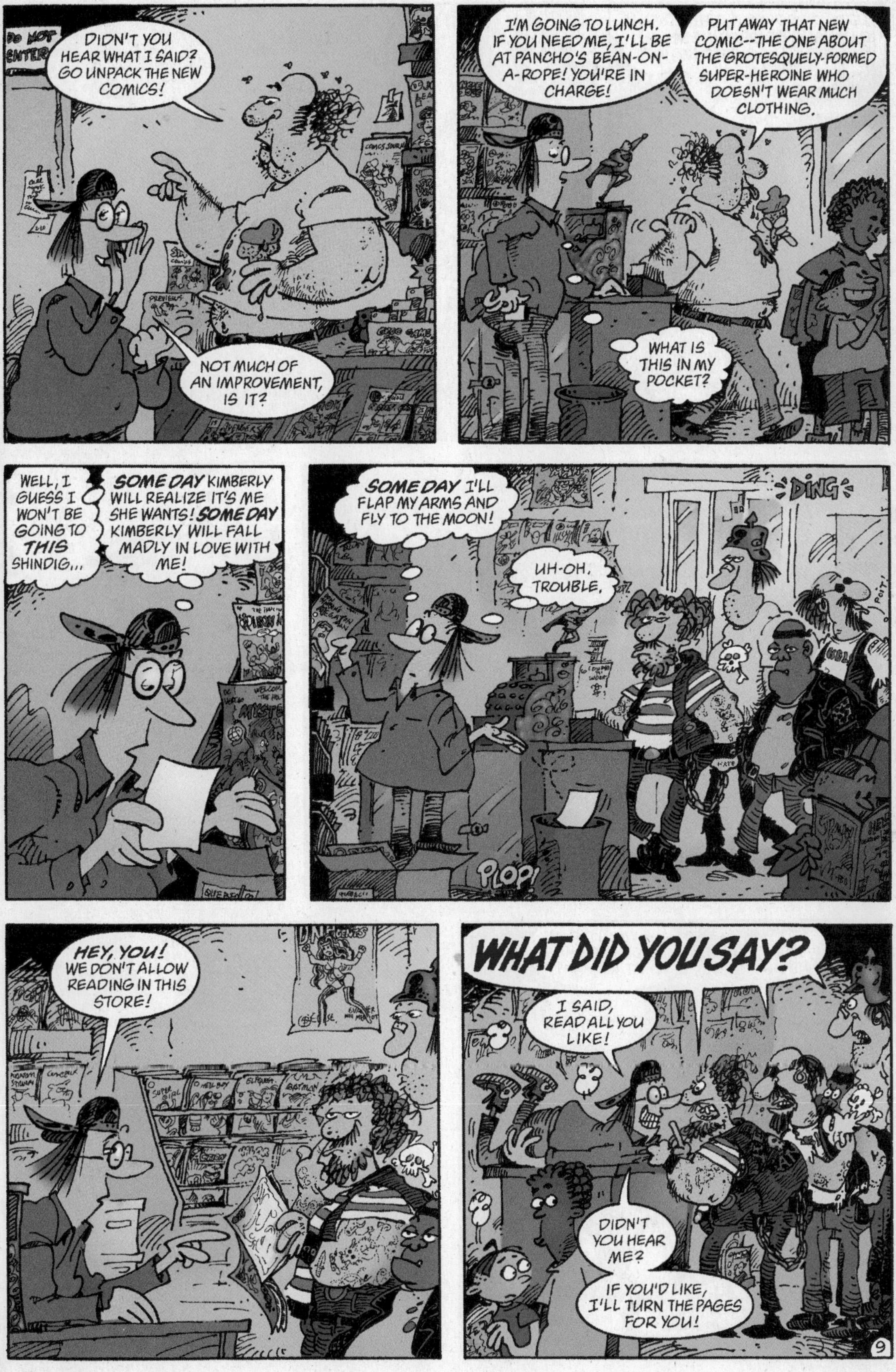
DO NOT ENTER
DIDN'T YOU HEAR WHAT I SAID? GO UNPACK THE NEW COMICS!
NOT MUCH OF AN IMPROVEMENT, IS IT?
I'M GOING TO LUNCH. IF YOU NEED ME, I'LL BE AT PANCHO'S BEAN-ON-A-ROPE! YOU'RE IN CHARGE!
PUT AWAY THAT NEW COMIC--THE ONE ABOUT THE GROTESQUELY-FORMED SUPER-HEROINE WHO DOESN'T WEAR MUCH CLOTHING.
WHAT IS THIS IN MY POCKET?
WELL, I GUESS I WON'T BE GOING TO THIS SHINDIG...
SOME DAY KIMBERLY WILL REALIZE IT'S ME SHE WANTS! SOME DAY KIMBERLY WILL FALL MADLY IN LOVE WITH ME!
SOME DAY I'LL FLAP MY ARMS AND FLY TO THE MOON!
DING
UH-OH. TROUBLE.
PLOP!
HEY, YOU! WE DON'T ALLOW READING IN THIS STORE!
WHAT DID YOU SAY?
I SAID, READ ALL YOU LIKE!
DIDN'T YOU HEAR ME?
IF YOU'D LIKE, I'LL TURN THE PAGES FOR YOU!
9

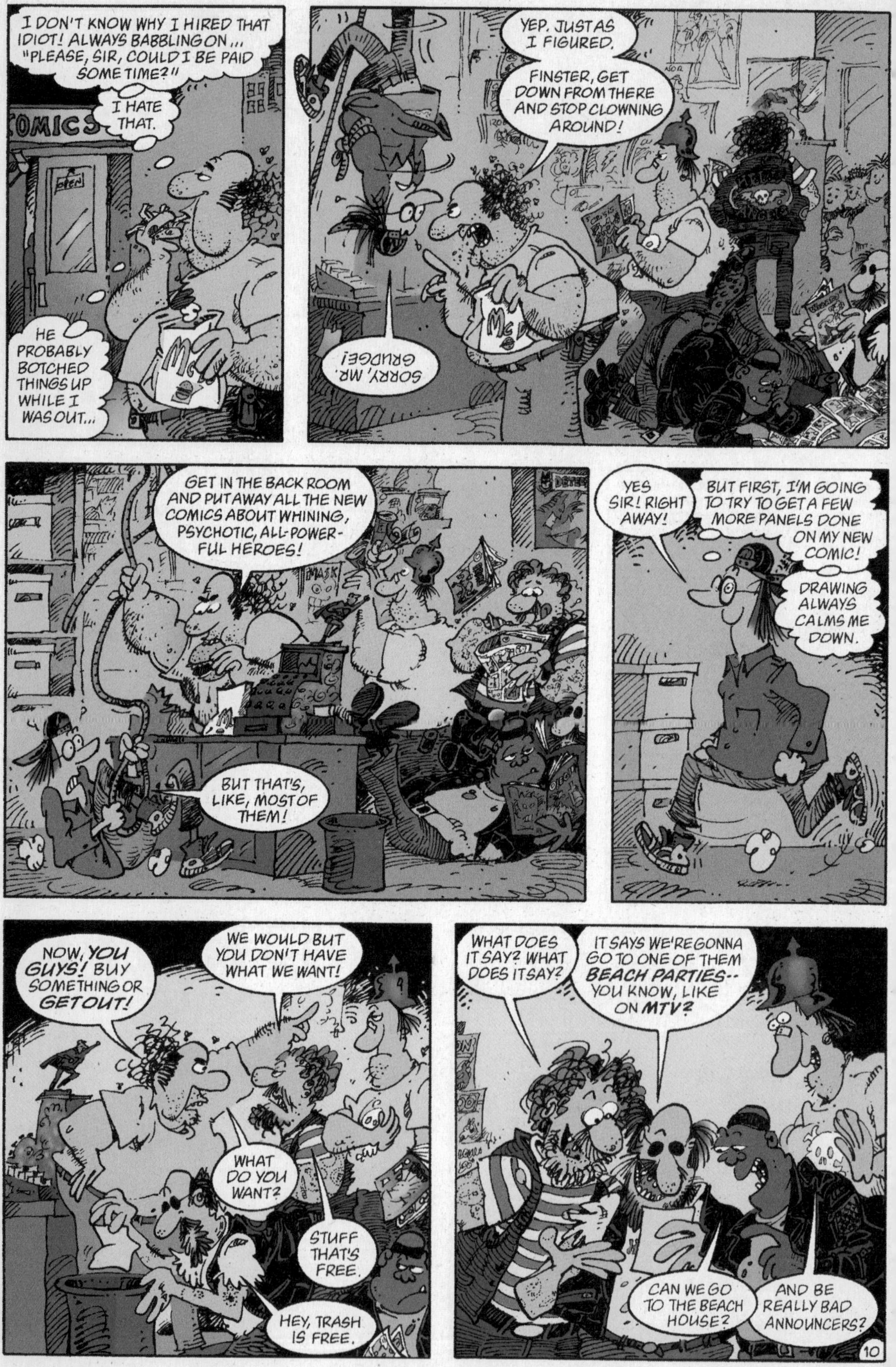
I DON'T KNOW WHY I HIRED THAT IDIOT! ALWAYS BABBLING ON... "PLEASE, SIR, COULD I BE PAID SOME TIME?"
I HATE THAT.
COMICS
HE PROBABLY BOTCHED THINGS UP WHILE I WAS OUT...
YEP. JUST AS I FIGURED.
FINSTER, GET DOWN FROM THERE AND STOP CLOWNING AROUND!
SORRY, MR. GRUDGE!
GET IN THE BACK ROOM AND PUT AWAY ALL THE NEW COMICS ABOUT WHINING, PSYCHOTIC, ALL-POWERFUL HEROES!
BUT THAT'S, LIKE, MOST OF THEM!
YES SIR! RIGHT AWAY!
BUT FIRST, I'M GOING TO TRY TO GET A FEW MORE PANELS DONE ON MY NEW COMIC!
DRAWING ALWAYS CALMS ME DOWN.
NOW, YOU GUYS! BUY SOMETHING OR GET OUT!
WE WOULD BUT YOU DON'T HAVE WHAT WE WANT!
WHAT DO YOU WANT?
STUFF THAT'S FREE.
HEY, TRASH IS FREE.
WHAT DOES IT SAY? WHAT DOES IT SAY?
IT SAYS WE'RE GONNA GO TO ONE OF THEM BEACH PARTIES-- YOU KNOW, LIKE ON MTV?
CAN WE GO TO THE BEACH HOUSE?
AND BE REALLY BAD ANNOUNCERS?
10

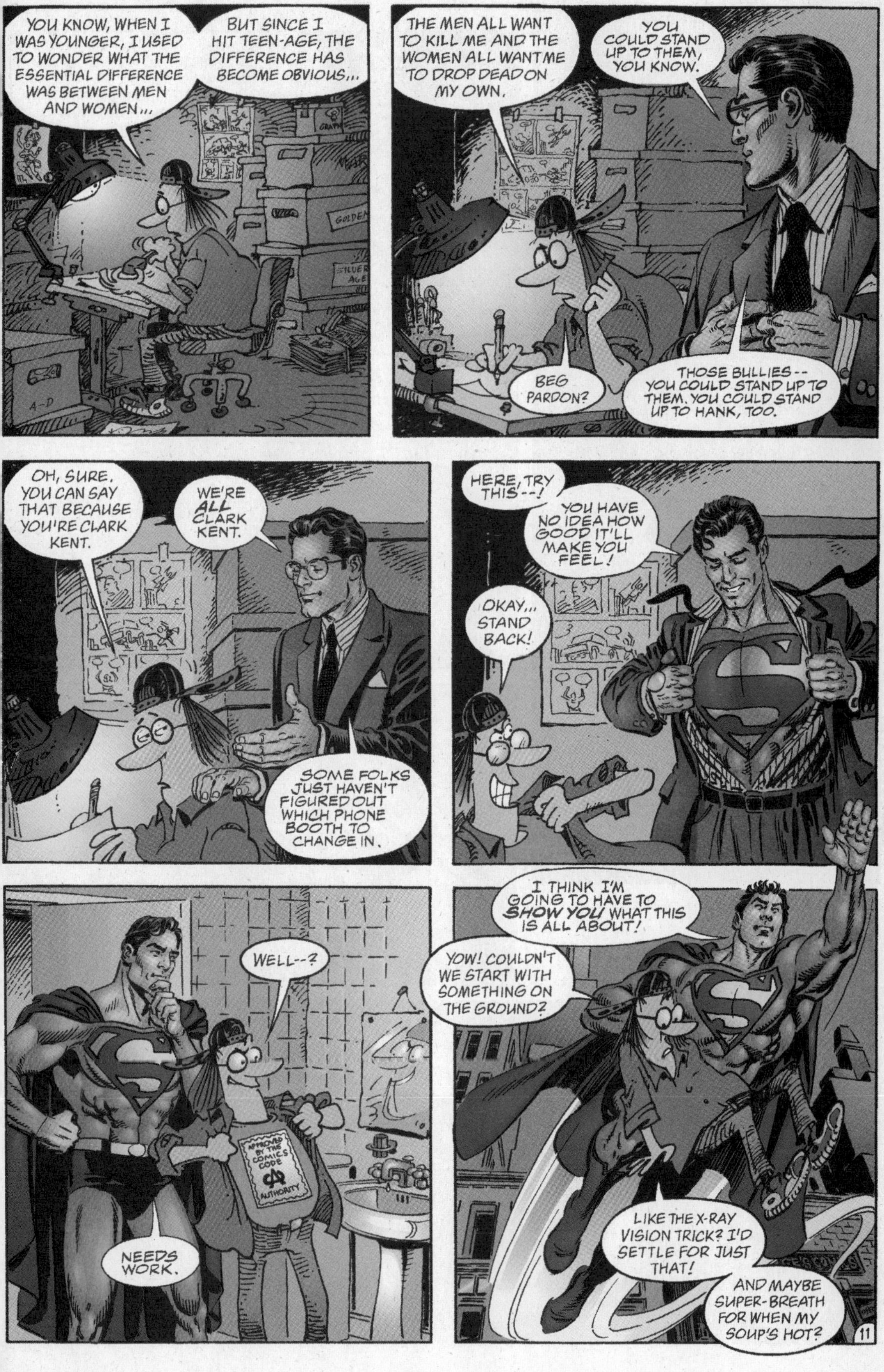
YOU KNOW, WHEN I WAS YOUNGER, I USED TO WONDER WHAT THE ESSENTIAL DIFFERENCE WAS BETWEEN MEN AND WOMEN...
BUT SINCE I HIT TEEN-AGE, THE DIFFERENCE HAS BECOME OBVIOUS...
THE MEN ALL WANT TO KILL ME AND THE WOMEN ALL WANT ME TO DROP DEAD ON MY OWN.
YOU COULD STAND UP TO THEM, YOU KNOW.
BEG PARDON?
THOSE BULLIES-- YOU COULD STAND UP TO THEM. YOU COULD STAND UP TO HANK, TOO.
OH, SURE. YOU CAN SAY THAT BECAUSE YOU'RE CLARK KENT.
WE'RE ALL CLARK KENT.
SOME FOLKS JUST HAVEN'T FIGURED OUT WHICH PHONE BOOTH TO CHANGE IN.
HERE, TRY THIS--!
YOU HAVE NO IDEA HOW GOOD IT'LL MAKE YOU FEEL!
OKAY... STAND BACK!
WELL--?
NEEDS WORK.
APPROVED BY THE COMICS CODE AUTHORITY
I THINK I'M GOING TO HAVE TO SHOW YOU WHAT THIS IS ALL ABOUT!
YOW! COULDN'T WE START WITH SOMETHING ON THE GROUND?
LIKE THE X-RAY VISION TRICK? I'D SETTLE FOR JUST THAT!
AND MAYBE SUPER-BREATH FOR WHEN MY SOUP'S HOT?
11

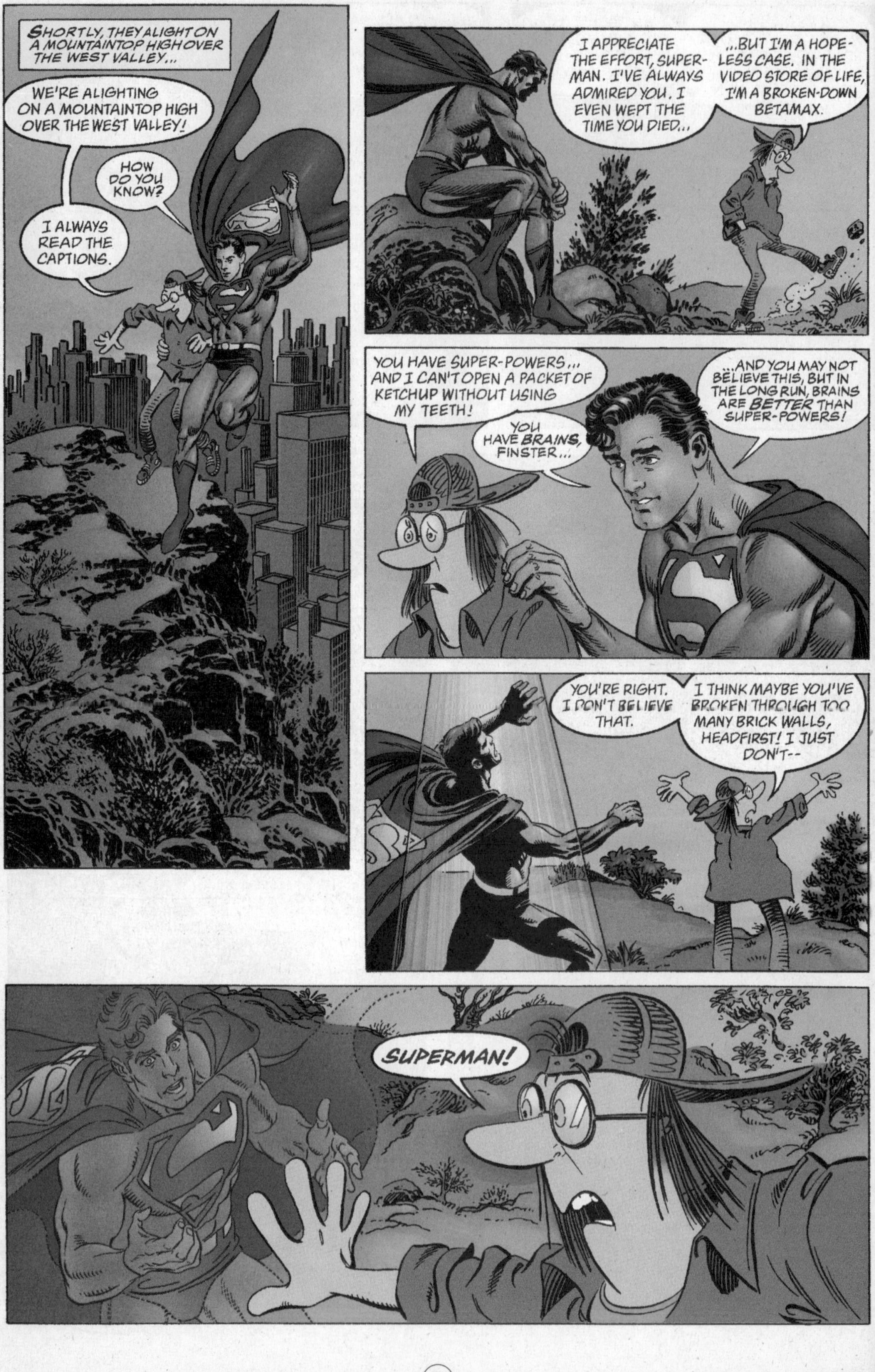
SHORTLY, THEY ALIGHT ON A MOUNTAINTOP HIGH OVER THE WEST VALLEY...
WE'RE ALIGHTING ON A MOUNTAINTOP HIGH OVER THE WEST VALLEY!
HOW DO YOU KNOW?
I ALWAYS READ THE CAPTIONS.
I APPRECIATE THE EFFORT, SUPERMAN. I'VE ALWAYS ADMIRED YOU. I EVEN WEPT THE TIME YOU DIED...
...BUT I'M A HOPELESS CASE. IN THE VIDEO STORE OF LIFE, I'M A BROKEN-DOWN BETAMAX.
YOU HAVE SUPER-POWERS... AND I CAN'T OPEN A PACKET OF KETCHUP WITHOUT USING MY TEETH!
YOU HAVE BRAINS, FINSTER...
...AND YOU MAY NOT BELIEVE THIS, BUT IN THE LONG RUN, BRAINS ARE BETTER THAN SUPER-POWERS!
YOU'RE RIGHT. I DON'T BELIEVE THAT.
I THINK MAYBE YOU'VE BROKEN THROUGH TOO MANY BRICK WALLS, HEADFIRST! I JUST DON'T--
SUPERMAN!

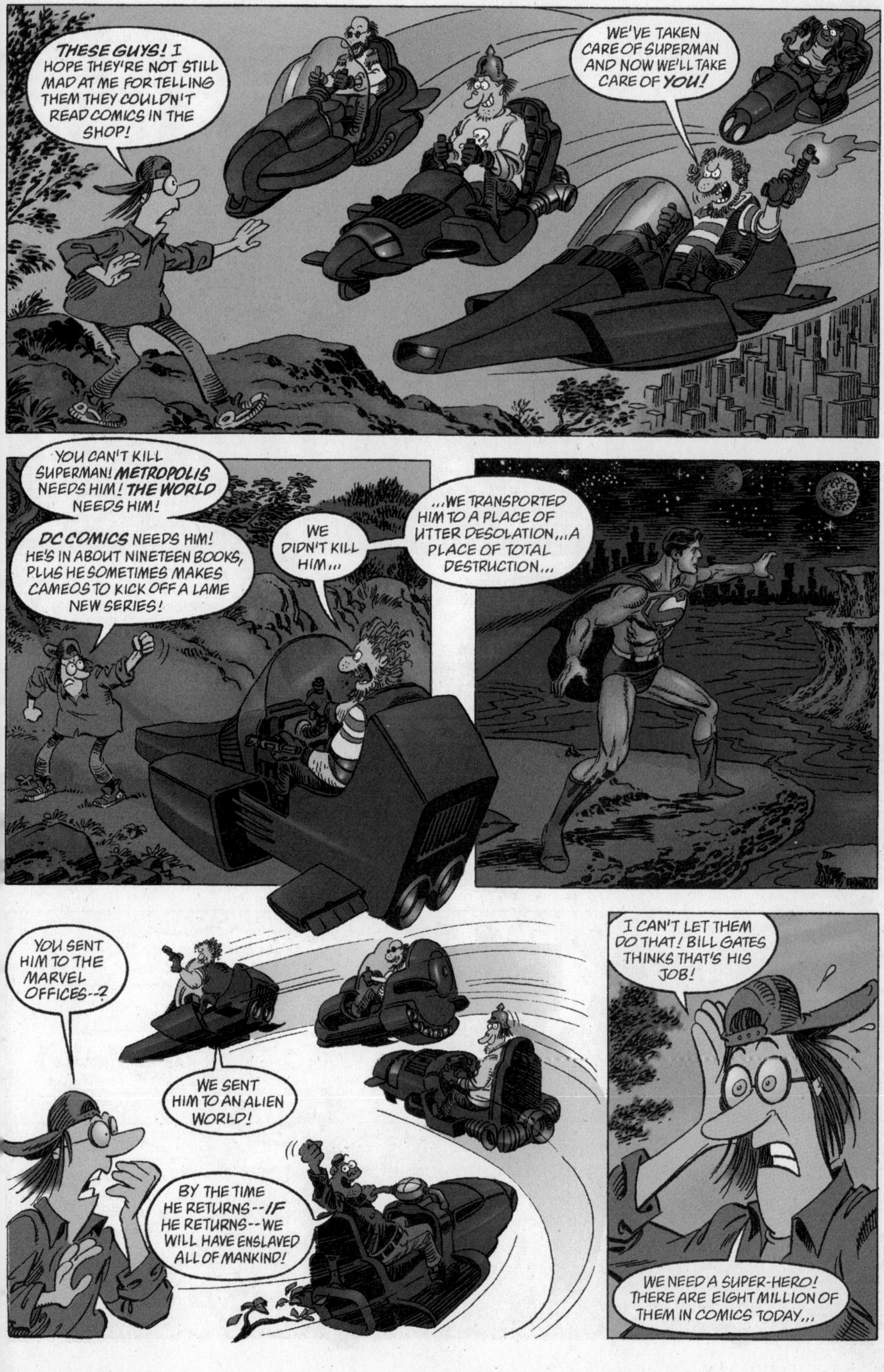
THESE GUYS! I HOPE THEY'RE NOT STILL MAD AT ME FOR TELLING THEM THEY COULDN'T READ COMICS IN THE SHOP!
WE'VE TAKEN CARE OF SUPERMAN AND NOW WE'LL TAKE CARE OF YOU!
YOU CAN'T KILL SUPERMAN! METROPOLIS NEEDS HIM! THE WORLD NEEDS HIM!
DC COMICS NEEDS HIM! HE'S IN ABOUT NINETEEN BOOKS, PLUS HE SOMETIMES MAKES CAMEOS TO KICK OFF A LAME NEW SERIES!
WE DIDN'T KILL HIM...
...WE TRANSPORTED HIM TO A PLACE OF UTTER DESOLATION... A PLACE OF TOTAL DESTRUCTION...
YOU SENT HIM TO THE MARVEL OFFICES--?
WE SENT HIM TO AN ALIEN WORLD!
BY THE TIME HE RETURNS--IF HE RETURNS--WE WILL HAVE ENSLAVED ALL OF MANKIND!
I CAN'T LET THEM DO THAT! BILL GATES THINKS THAT'S HIS JOB!
WE NEED A SUPER-HERO! THERE ARE EIGHT MILLION OF THEM IN COMICS TODAY...

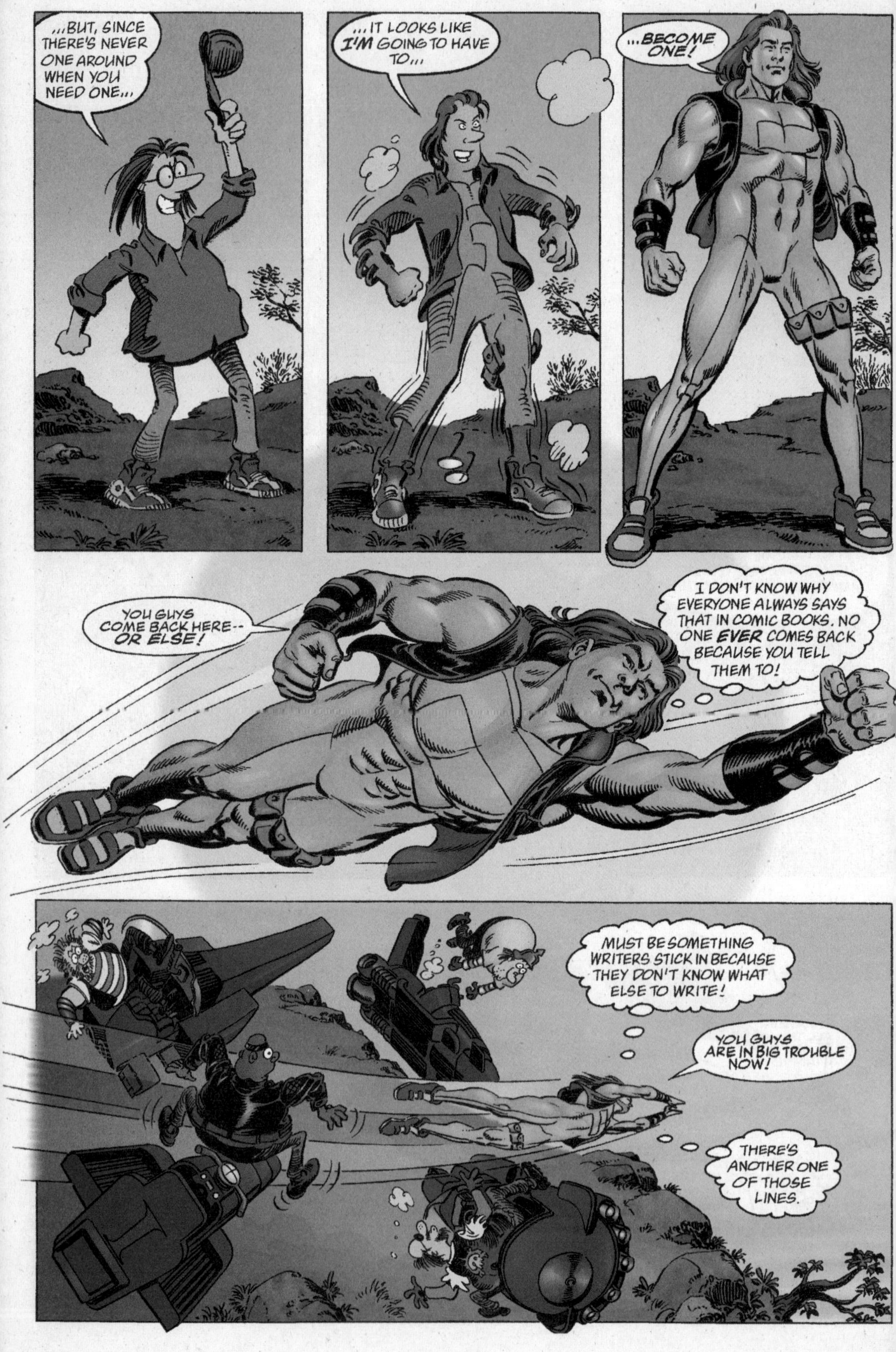
...BUT, SINCE THERE'S NEVER ONE AROUND WHEN YOU NEED ONE...
...IT LOOKS LIKE I'M GOING TO HAVE TO...
...BECOME ONE!
YOU GUYS COME BACK HERE-- OR ELSE!
I DON'T KNOW WHY EVERYONE ALWAYS SAYS THAT IN COMIC BOOKS. NO ONE EVER COMES BACK BECAUSE YOU TELL THEM TO!
MUST BE SOMETHING WRITERS STICK IN BECAUSE THEY DON'T KNOW WHAT ELSE TO WRITE!
YOU GUYS ARE IN BIG TROUBLE NOW!
THERE'S ANOTHER ONE OF THOSE LINES.

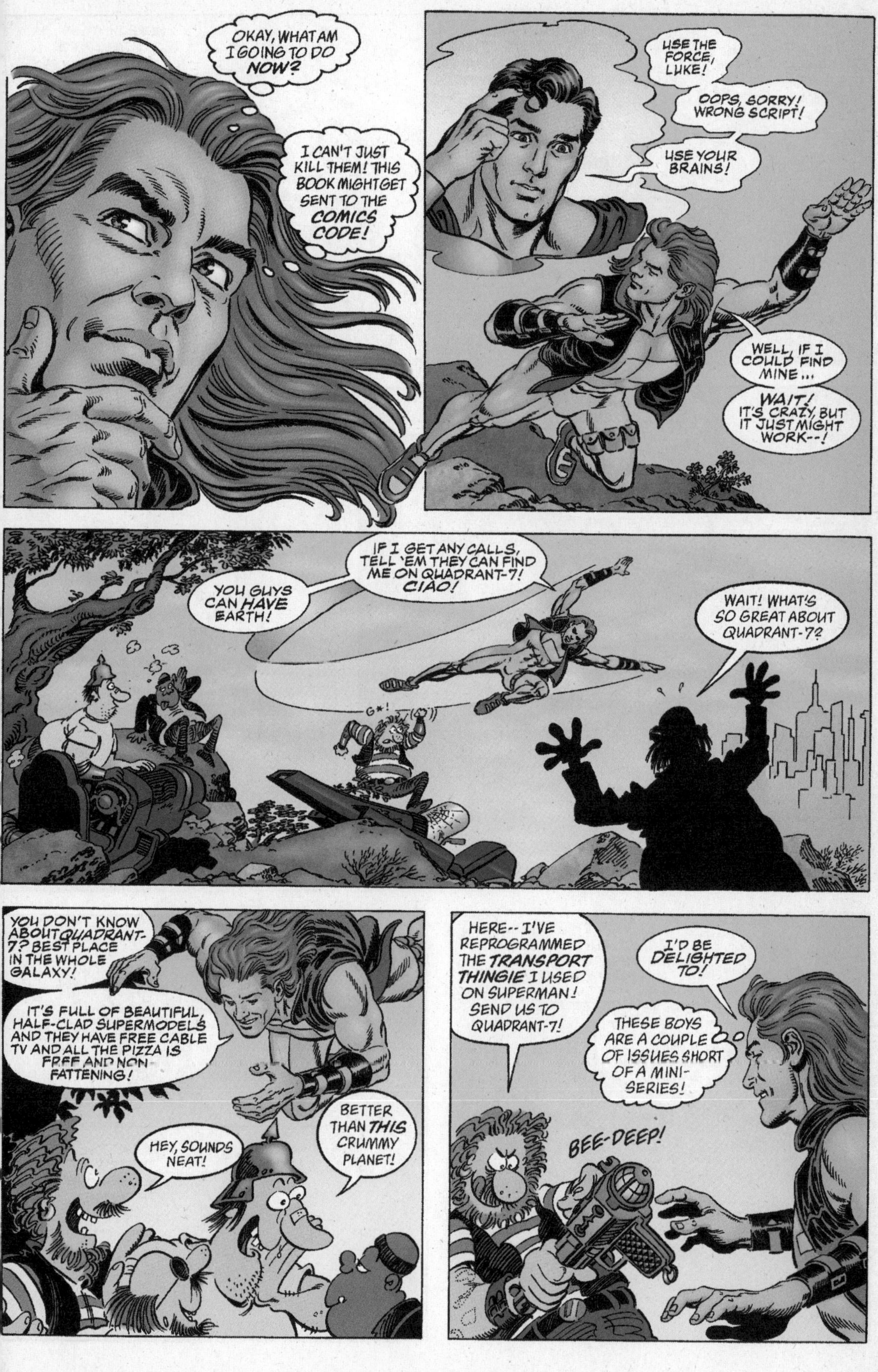
OKAY, WHAT AM I GOING TO DO NOW?
I CAN'T JUST KILL THEM! THIS BOOK MIGHT GET SENT TO THE COMICS CODE!
USE THE FORCE, LUKE!
OOPS, SORRY! WRONG SCRIPT!
USE YOUR BRAINS!
WELL, IF I COULD FIND MINE...
WAIT! IT'S CRAZY, BUT IT JUST MIGHT WORK--!
YOU GUYS CAN HAVE EARTH!
IF I GET ANY CALLS, TELL 'EM THEY CAN FIND ME ON QUADRANT-7! CIAO!
WAIT! WHAT'S SO GREAT ABOUT QUADRANT-7?
YOU DON'T KNOW ABOUT QUADRANT-7? BEST PLACE IN THE WHOLE GALAXY!
IT'S FULL OF BEAUTIFUL, HALF-CLAD SUPERMODELS AND THEY HAVE FREE CABLE TV AND ALL THE PIZZA IS FREE AND NON-FATTENING!
HEY, SOUNDS NEAT!
BETTER THAN THIS CRUMMY PLANET!
HERE-- I'VE REPROGRAMMED THE TRANSPORT THINGIE I USED ON SUPERMAN! SEND US TO QUADRANT-7!
I'D BE DELIGHTED TO!
THESE BOYS ARE A COUPLE OF ISSUES SHORT OF A MINI-SERIES!
BEE-DEEP!

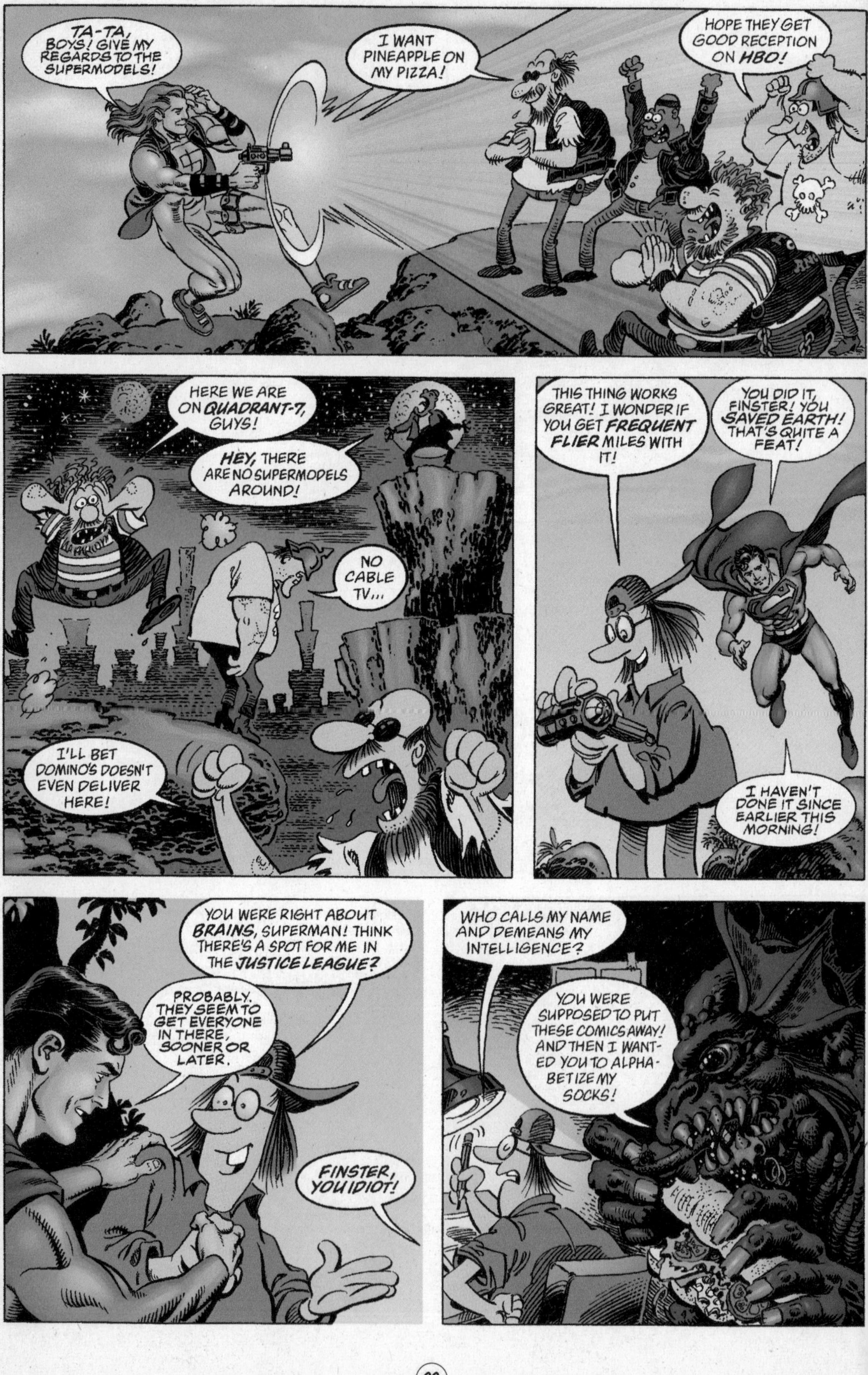
TA-TA, BOYS! GIVE MY REGARDS TO THE SUPERMODELS!
I WANT PINEAPPLE ON MY PIZZA!
HOPE THEY GET GOOD RECEPTION ON HBO!
HERE WE ARE ON QUADRANT-7, GUYS!
HEY, THERE ARE NO SUPERMODELS AROUND!
NO CABLE TV...
I'LL BET DOMINO'S DOESN'T EVEN DELIVER HERE!
THIS THING WORKS GREAT! I WONDER IF YOU GET FREQUENT FLIER MILES WITH IT!
YOU DID IT, FINSTER! YOU SAVED EARTH! THAT'S QUITE A FEAT!
I HAVEN'T DONE IT SINCE EARLIER THIS MORNING!
YOU WERE RIGHT ABOUT BRAINS, SUPERMAN! THINK THERE'S A SPOT FOR ME IN THE JUSTICE LEAGUE?
PROBABLY. THEY SEEM TO GET EVERYONE IN THERE, SOONER OR LATER.
FINSTER, YOU IDIOT!
WHO CALLS MY NAME AND DEMEANS MY INTELLIGENCE?
YOU WERE SUPPOSED TO PUT THESE COMICS AWAY! AND THEN I WANT-ED YOU TO ALPHA-BETIZE MY SOCKS!

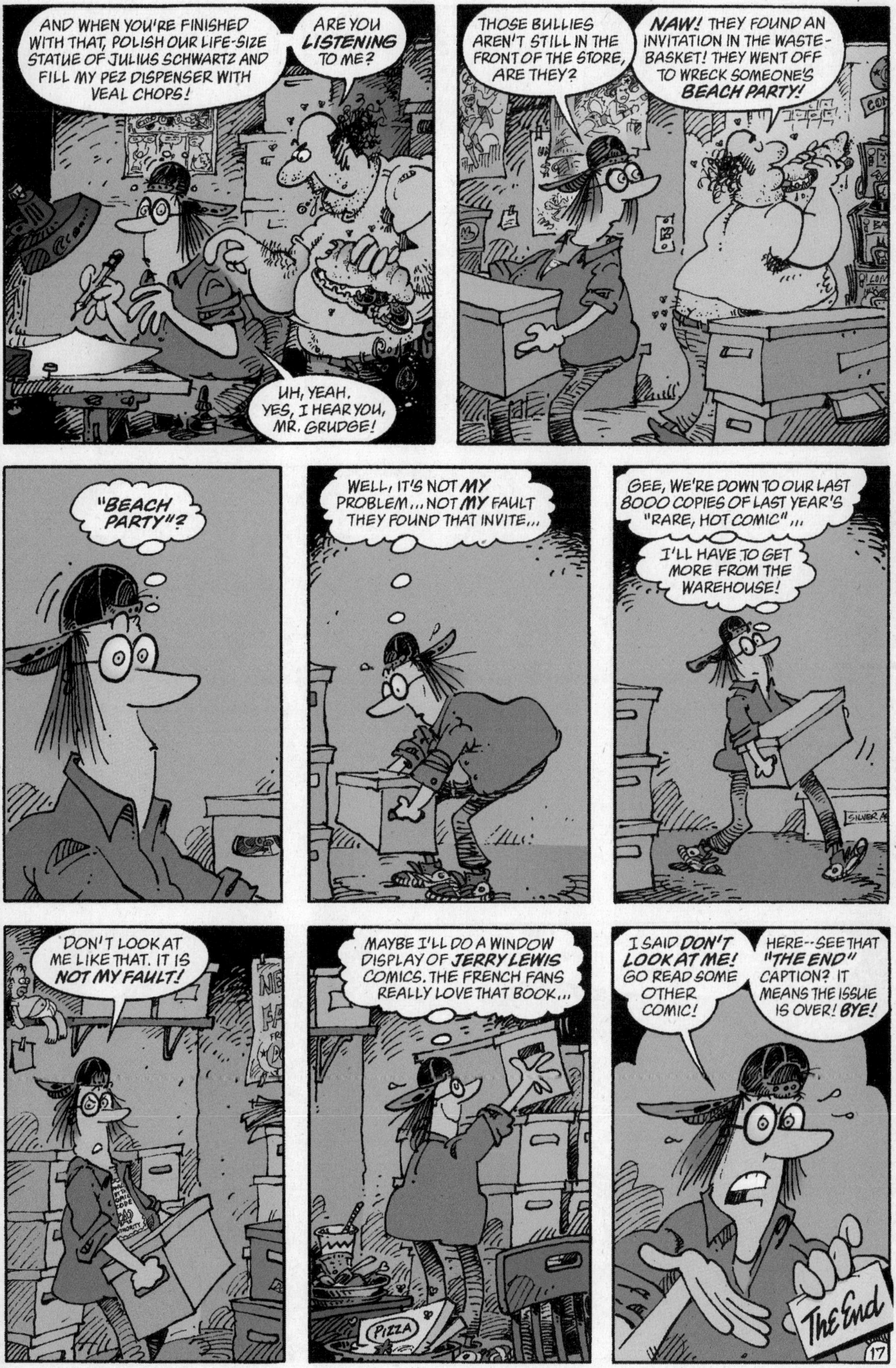

AND WHEN YOU'RE FINISHED WITH THAT, POLISH OUR LIFE-SIZE STATUE OF JULIUS SCHWARTZ AND FILL MY PEZ DISPENSER WITH VEAL CHOPS!
ARE YOU LISTENING TO ME?
UH, YEAH. YES, I HEAR YOU, MR. GRUDGE!
THOSE BULLIES AREN'T STILL IN THE FRONT OF THE STORE, ARE THEY?
NAW! THEY FOUND AN INVITATION IN THE WASTE-BASKET! THEY WENT OFF TO WRECK SOMEONE'S BEACH PARTY!
"BEACH PARTY"?
WELL, IT'S NOT MY PROBLEM... NOT MY FAULT THEY FOUND THAT INVITE...
GEE, WE'RE DOWN TO OUR LAST 8000 COPIES OF LAST YEAR'S "RARE, HOT COMIC"...
I'LL HAVE TO GET MORE FROM THE WAREHOUSE!
SILVER AGE
DON'T LOOK AT ME LIKE THAT. IT IS NOT MY FAULT!
MAYBE I'LL DO A WINDOW DISPLAY OF JERRY LEWIS COMICS. THE FRENCH FANS REALLY LOVE THAT BOOK...
PIZZA
I SAID DON'T LOOK AT ME! GO READ SOME OTHER COMIC!
HERE--SEE THAT "THE END" CAPTION? IT MEANS THE ISSUE IS OVER! BYE!
THE End
17

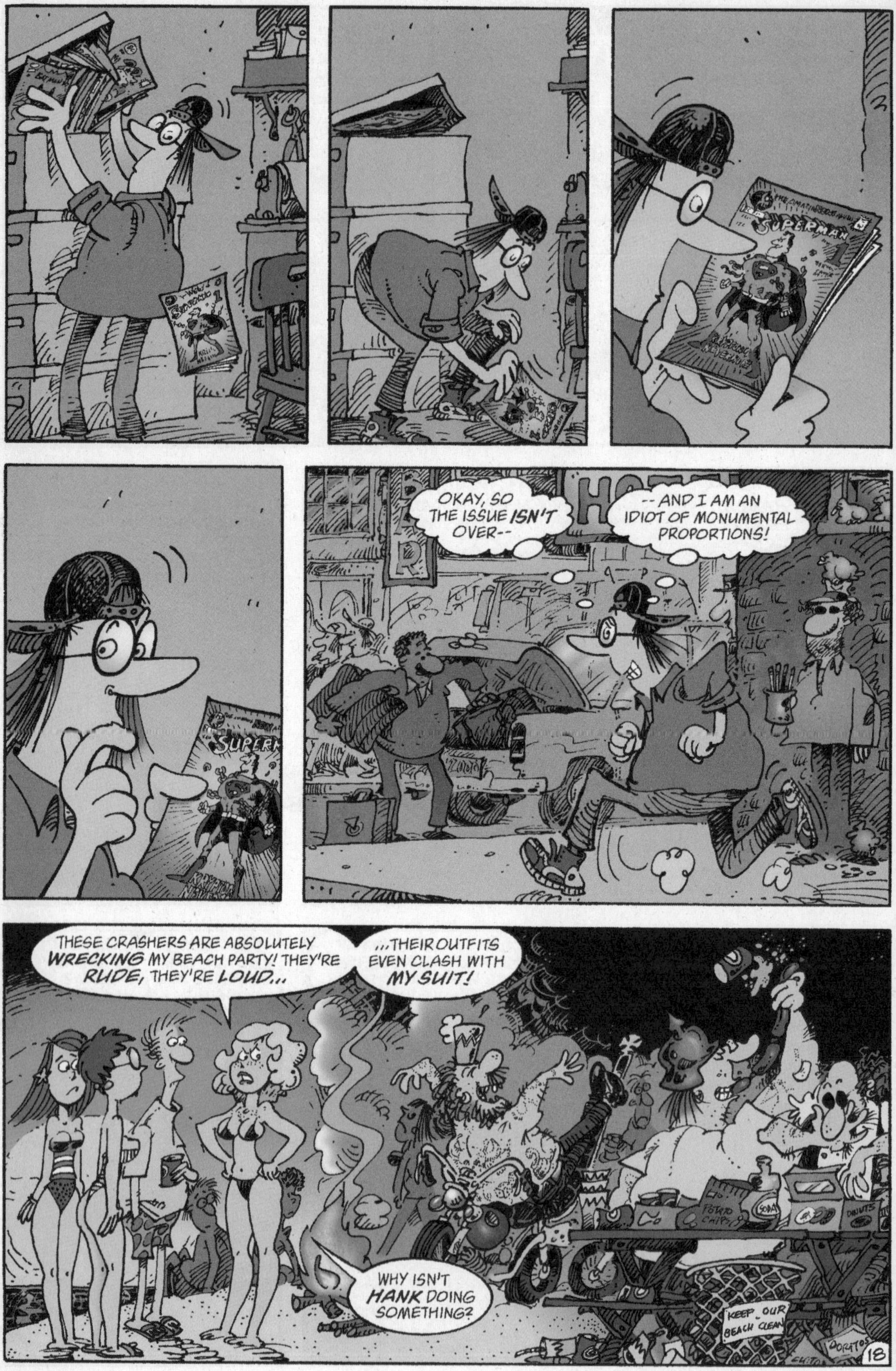
SUPERMAN
OKAY, SO THE ISSUE ISN'T OVER--
-- AND I AM AN IDIOT OF MONUMENTAL PROPORTIONS!
THESE CRASHERS ARE ABSOLUTELY WRECKING MY BEACH PARTY! THEY'RE RUDE, THEY'RE LOUD...
...THEIR OUTFITS EVEN CLASH WITH MY SUIT!
WHY ISN'T HANK DOING SOMETHING?
POTATO CHIPS
SODA
DONUTS
KEEP OUR BEACH CLEAN
DORITOS
18

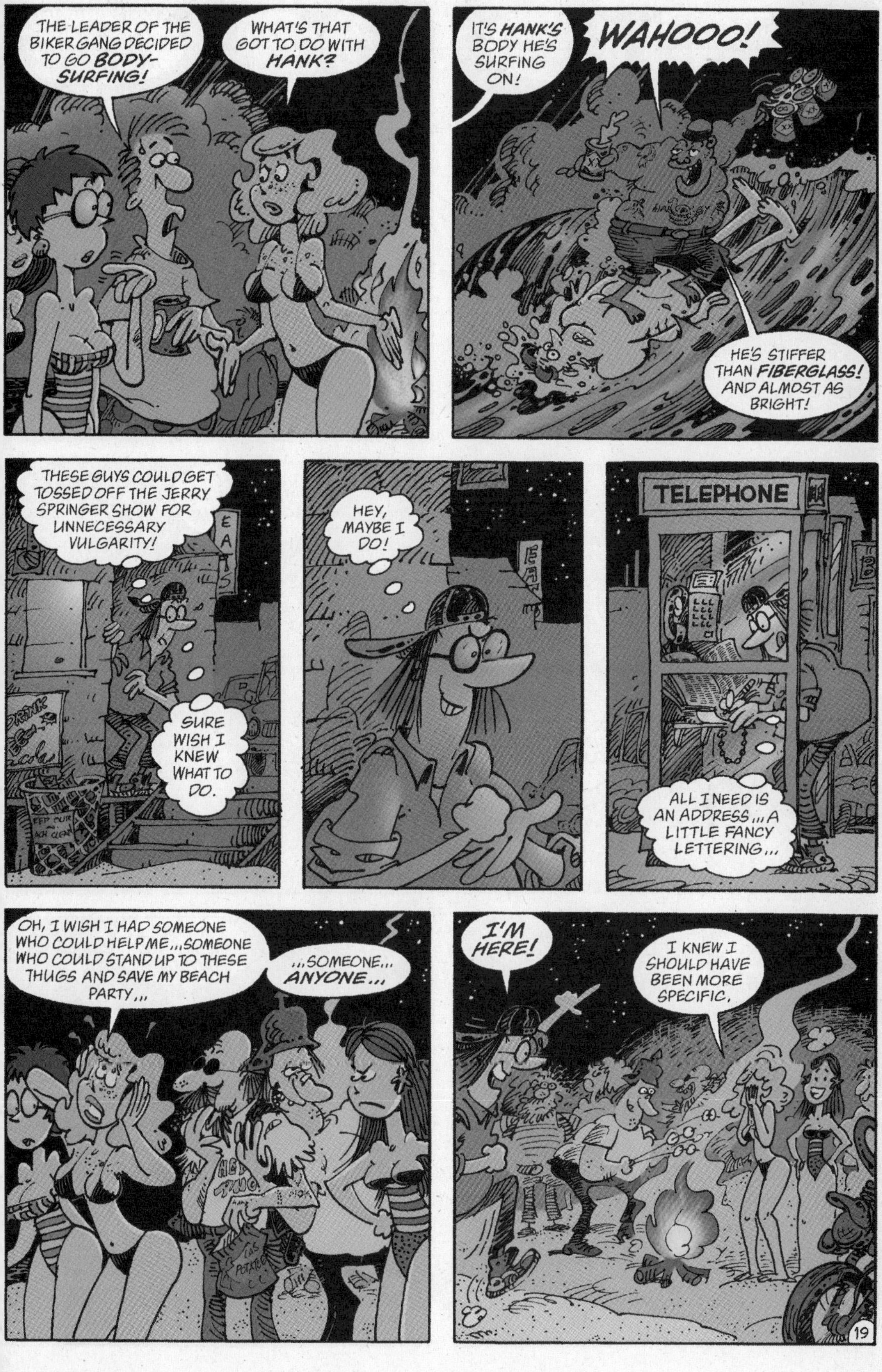
THE LEADER OF THE BIKER GANG DECIDED TO GO BODY-SURFING!
WHAT'S THAT GOT TO DO WITH HANK?
IT'S HANK'S BODY HE'S SURFING ON!
WAHOOO!
HE'S STIFFER THAN FIBERGLASS! AND ALMOST AS BRIGHT!
THESE GUYS COULD GET TOSSED OFF THE JERRY SPRINGER SHOW FOR UNNECESSARY VULGARITY!
SURE WISH I KNEW WHAT TO DO.
HEY, MAYBE I DO!
TELEPHONE
ALL I NEED IS AN ADDRESS... A LITTLE FANCY LETTERING...
OH, I WISH I HAD SOMEONE WHO COULD HELP ME... SOMEONE WHO COULD STAND UP TO THESE THUGS AND SAVE MY BEACH PARTY...
...SOMEONE... ANYONE...
I'M HERE!
I KNEW I SHOULD HAVE BEEN MORE SPECIFIC.
19

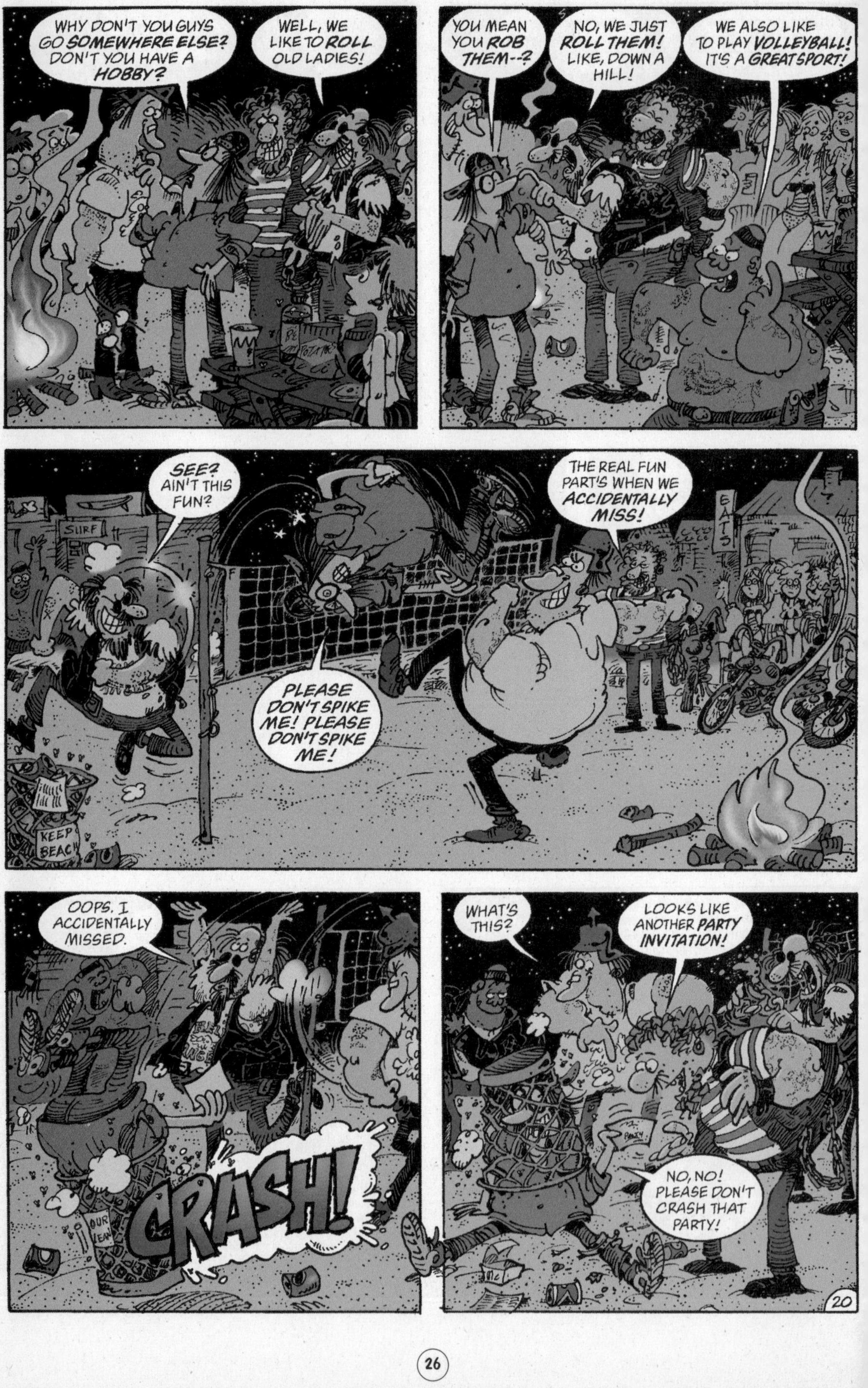
WHY DON'T YOU GUYS GO **SOMEWHERE ELSE?** DON'T YOU HAVE A **HOBBY?**
WELL, WE LIKE TO **ROLL** OLD LADIES!
YOU MEAN YOU **ROB THEM--?**
NO, WE JUST **ROLL THEM!** LIKE, DOWN A HILL!
WE ALSO LIKE TO PLAY **VOLLEYBALL!** IT'S A **GREAT SPORT!**
SEE? AIN'T THIS FUN?
SURF
EATS
THE REAL FUN PART'S WHEN WE **ACCIDENTALLY MISS!**
PLEASE DON'T SPIKE ME! PLEASE DON'T SPIKE ME!
KEEP BEAC
OOPS. I ACCIDENTALLY MISSED.
CRASH!
WHAT'S THIS?
LOOKS LIKE ANOTHER **PARTY INVITATION!**
NO, NO! PLEASE DON'T CRASH THAT PARTY!
20

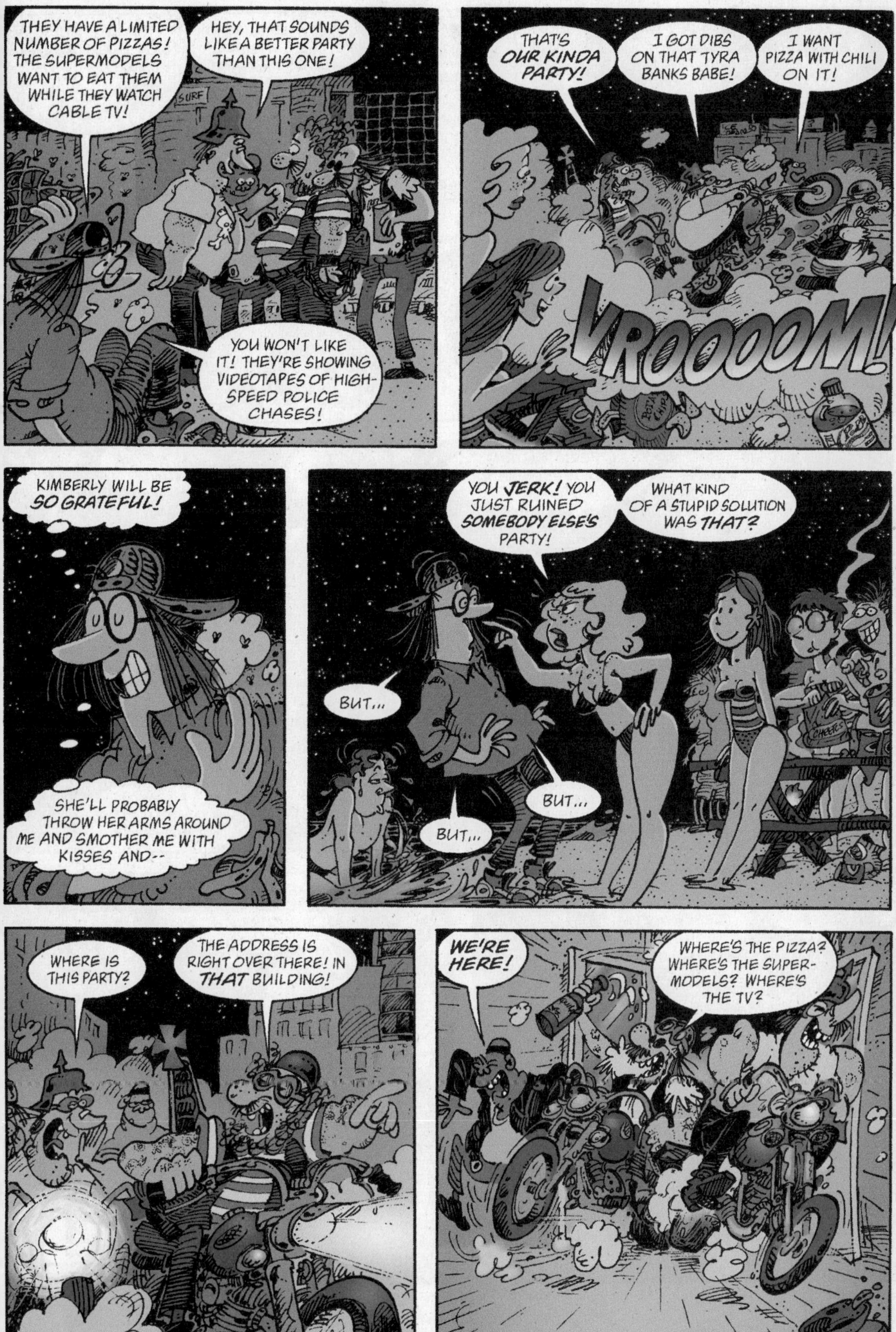
THEY HAVE A LIMITED NUMBER OF PIZZAS! THE SUPERMODELS WANT TO EAT THEM WHILE THEY WATCH CABLE TV!
HEY, THAT SOUNDS LIKE A BETTER PARTY THAN THIS ONE!
YOU WON'T LIKE IT! THEY'RE SHOWING VIDEOTAPES OF HIGH-SPEED POLICE CHASES!
THAT'S OUR KINDA PARTY!
I GOT DIBS ON THAT TYRA BANKS BABE!
I WANT PIZZA WITH CHILI ON IT!
VROOOOM!
KIMBERLY WILL BE SO GRATEFUL!
SHE'LL PROBABLY THROW HER ARMS AROUND ME AND SMOTHER ME WITH KISSES AND--
YOU JERK! YOU JUST RUINED SOMEBODY ELSE'S PARTY!
WHAT KIND OF A STUPID SOLUTION WAS THAT?
BUT...
BUT...
BUT...
WHERE IS THIS PARTY?
THE ADDRESS IS RIGHT OVER THERE! IN THAT BUILDING!
WE'RE HERE!
WHERE'S THE PIZZA? WHERE'S THE SUPER-MODELS? WHERE'S THE TV?
21

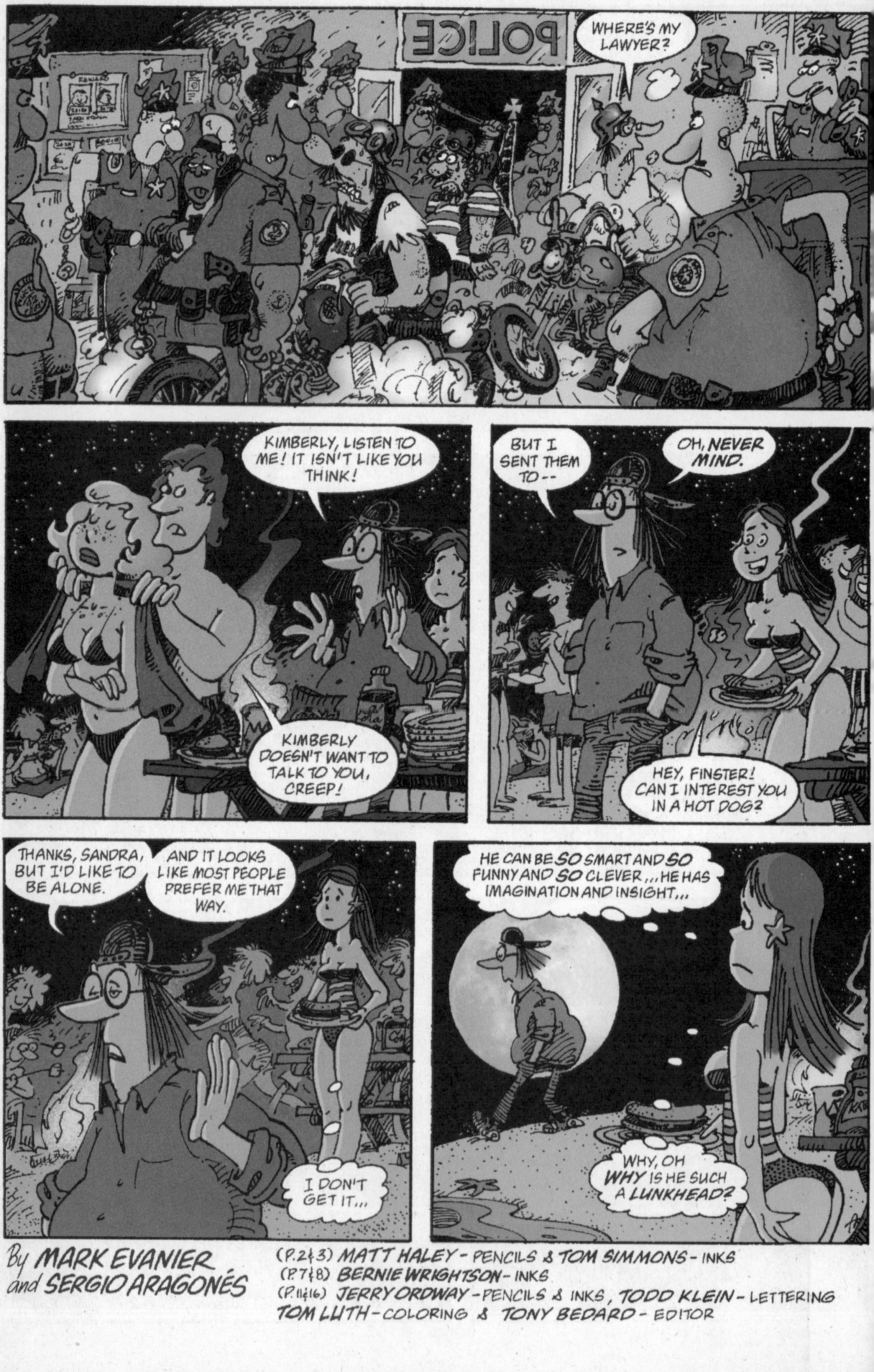
POLICE
WHERE'S MY LAWYER?
KIMBERLY, LISTEN TO ME! IT ISN'T LIKE YOU THINK!
KIMBERLY DOESN'T WANT TO TALK TO YOU, CREEP!
BUT I SENT THEM TO --
OH, NEVER MIND.
HEY, FINSTER! CAN I INTEREST YOU IN A HOT DOG?
THANKS, SANDRA, BUT I'D LIKE TO BE ALONE.
AND IT LOOKS LIKE MOST PEOPLE PREFER ME THAT WAY.
I DON'T GET IT...
HE CAN BE SO SMART AND SO FUNNY AND SO CLEVER... HE HAS IMAGINATION AND INSIGHT...
WHY, OH WHY IS HE SUCH A LUNKHEAD?

By MARK EVANIER and SERGIO ARAGONÉS

(P.2&3) MATT HALEY - PENCILS & TOM SIMMONS - INKS
(P.7&8) BERNIE WRIGHTSON - INKS
(P.11&16) JERRY ORDWAY - PENCILS & INKS, TODD KLEIN - LETTERING
TOM LUTH - COLORING & TONY BEDARD - EDITOR

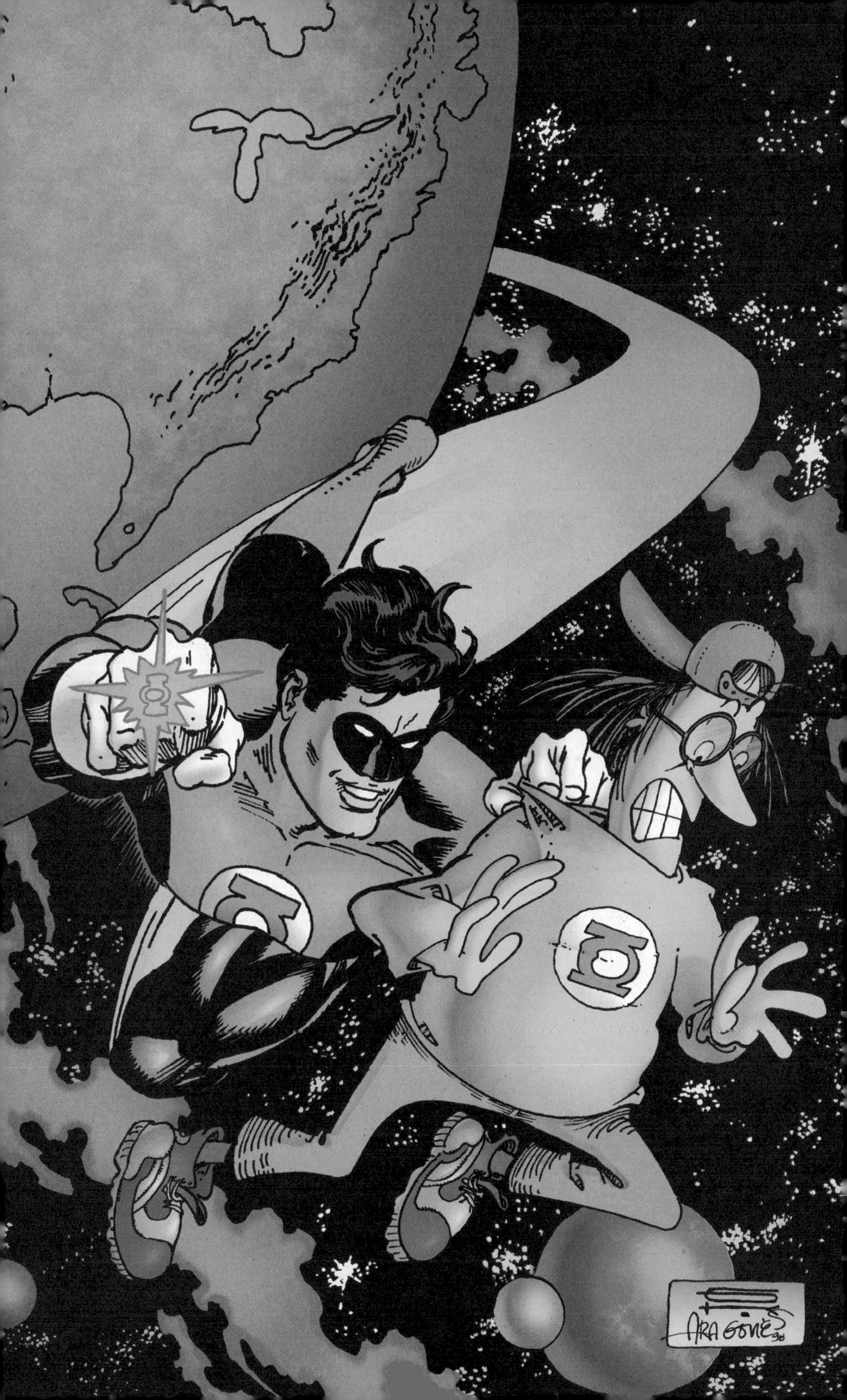
ARAGONÉS 98

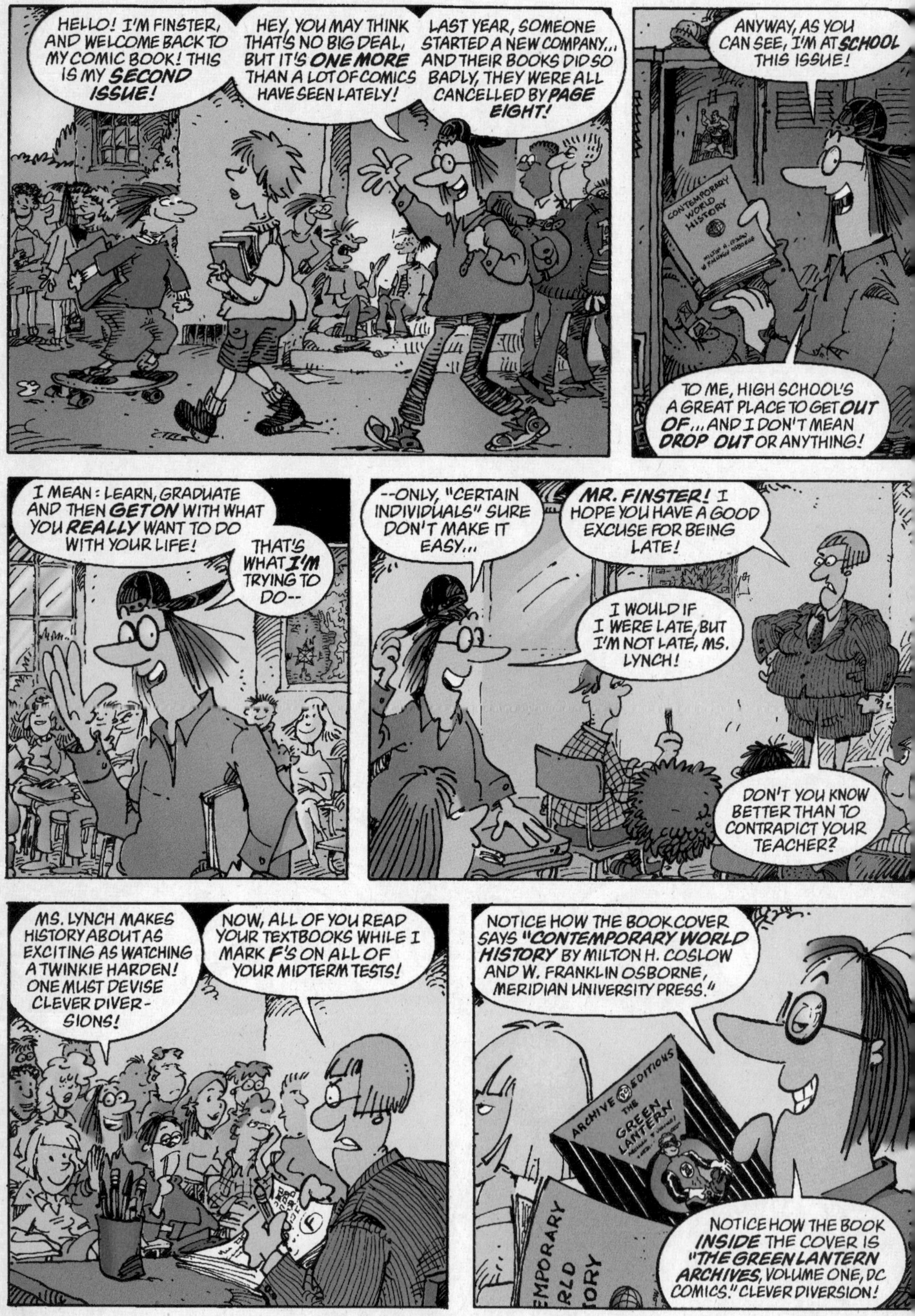
HELLO! I'M FINSTER, AND WELCOME BACK TO MY COMIC BOOK! THIS IS MY SECOND ISSUE!
HEY, YOU MAY THINK THAT'S NO BIG DEAL, BUT IT'S ONE MORE THAN A LOT OF COMICS HAVE SEEN LATELY!
LAST YEAR, SOMEONE STARTED A NEW COMPANY... AND THEIR BOOKS DID SO BADLY, THEY WERE ALL CANCELLED BY PAGE EIGHT!
ANYWAY, AS YOU CAN SEE, I'M AT SCHOOL THIS ISSUE!
CONTEMPORARY WORLD HISTORY
TO ME, HIGH SCHOOL'S A GREAT PLACE TO GET OUT OF... AND I DON'T MEAN DROP OUT OR ANYTHING!
I MEAN: LEARN, GRADUATE AND THEN GET ON WITH WHAT YOU REALLY WANT TO DO WITH YOUR LIFE!
THAT'S WHAT I'M TRYING TO DO--
--ONLY, "CERTAIN INDIVIDUALS" SURE DON'T MAKE IT EASY...
MR. FINSTER! I HOPE YOU HAVE A GOOD EXCUSE FOR BEING LATE!
I WOULD IF I WERE LATE, BUT I'M NOT LATE, MS. LYNCH!
DON'T YOU KNOW BETTER THAN TO CONTRADICT YOUR TEACHER?
MS. LYNCH MAKES HISTORY ABOUT AS EXCITING AS WATCHING A TWINKIE HARDEN! ONE MUST DEVISE CLEVER DIVERSIONS!
NOW, ALL OF YOU READ YOUR TEXTBOOKS WHILE I MARK F'S ON ALL OF YOUR MIDTERM TESTS!
NOTICE HOW THE BOOK COVER SAYS "CONTEMPORARY WORLD HISTORY BY MILTON H. COSLOW AND W. FRANKLIN OSBORNE, MERIDIAN UNIVERSITY PRESS."
ARCHIVE EDITIONS THE GREEN LANTERN
NOTICE HOW THE BOOK INSIDE THE COVER IS "THE GREEN LANTERN ARCHIVES, VOLUME ONE, DC COMICS." CLEVER DIVERSION!

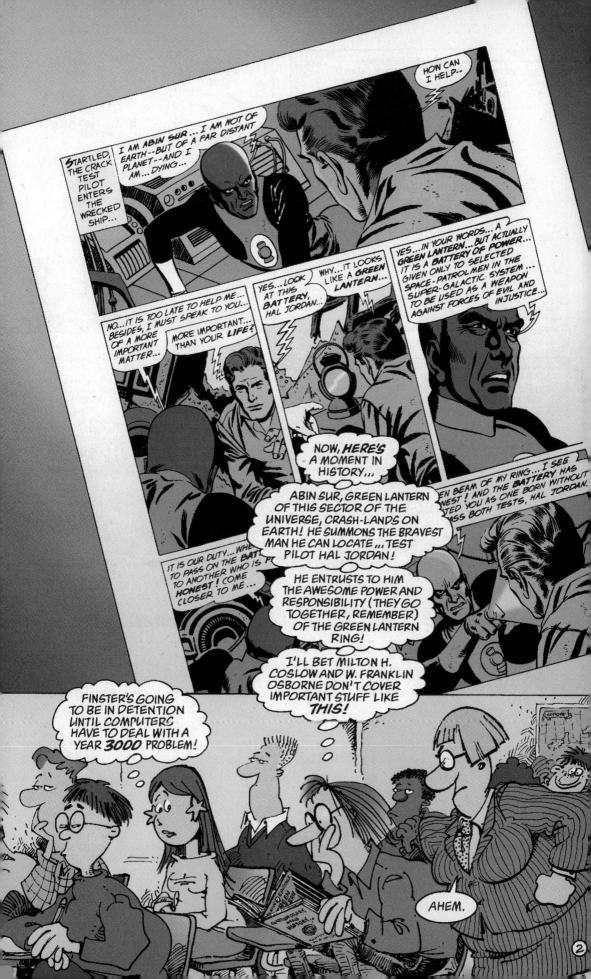

STARTLED, THE CRACK TEST PILOT ENTERS THE WRECKED SHIP...

I AM ABIN SUR... I AM NOT OF A FAR DISTANT EARTH--BUT OF A FAR DISTANT PLANET--AND I AM... DYING...

HOW CAN I HELP--

NO... IT IS TOO LATE TO HELP ME... BESIDES, I MUST SPEAK TO YOU... OF A MORE IMPORTANT MATTER...

MORE IMPORTANT... THAN YOUR LIFE?

YES... LOOK AT THIS BATTERY, HAL JORDAN...

WHY... IT LOOKS LIKE A GREEN LANTERN...

YES... IN YOUR WORDS... A GREEN LANTERN... BUT ACTUALLY IT IS A BATTERY OF POWER... GIVEN ONLY TO SELECTED SPACE-PATROLMEN IN THE SUPER-GALACTIC SYSTEM... TO BE USED AS A WEAPON AGAINST FORCES OF EVIL AND INJUSTICE...

NOW, HERE'S A MOMENT IN HISTORY...

ABIN SUR, GREEN LANTERN OF THIS SECTOR OF THE UNIVERSE, CRASH-LANDS ON EARTH! HE SUMMONS THE BRAVEST MAN HE CAN LOCATE... TEST PILOT HAL JORDAN!

HE ENTRUSTS TO HIM THE AWESOME POWER AND RESPONSIBILITY (THEY GO TOGETHER, REMEMBER) OF THE GREEN LANTERN RING!

I'LL BET MILTON H. COSLOW AND W. FRANKLIN OSBORNE DON'T COVER IMPORTANT STUFF LIKE THIS!

IT IS OUR DUTY... WHE TO PASS ON THE BAT TO ANOTHER WHO IS F HONEST! COME CLOSER TO ME...

EN BEAM OF MY RING... I SEE NEST! AND THE BATTERY HAS TED YOU AS ONE BORN WITHOUT ASS BOTH TESTS, HAL JORDAN.

FINSTER'S GOING TO BE IN DETENTION UNTIL COMPUTERS HAVE TO DEAL WITH A YEAR 3000 PROBLEM!

AHEM.

2

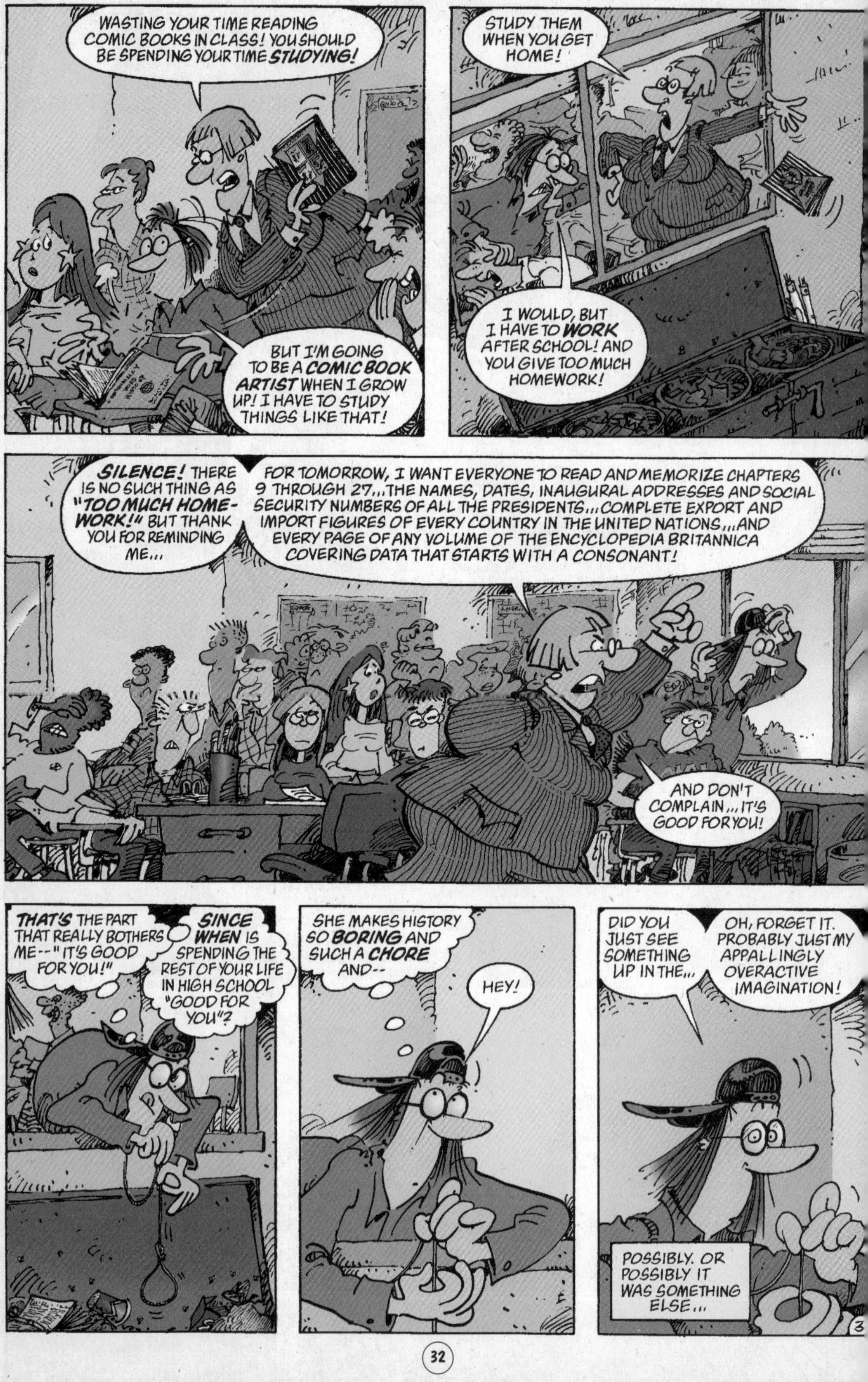
WASTING YOUR TIME READING COMIC BOOKS IN CLASS! YOU SHOULD BE SPENDING YOUR TIME **STUDYING!**
BUT I'M GOING TO BE A **COMIC BOOK ARTIST** WHEN I GROW UP! I HAVE TO STUDY THINGS LIKE THAT!
STUDY THEM WHEN YOU GET HOME!
I WOULD, BUT I HAVE TO **WORK** AFTER SCHOOL! AND YOU GIVE TOO MUCH HOMEWORK!
SILENCE! THERE IS NO SUCH THING AS **"TOO MUCH HOME-WORK!"** BUT THANK YOU FOR REMINDING ME...
FOR TOMORROW, I WANT EVERYONE TO READ AND MEMORIZE CHAPTERS 9 THROUGH 27... THE NAMES, DATES, INAUGURAL ADDRESSES AND SOCIAL SECURITY NUMBERS OF ALL THE PRESIDENTS... COMPLETE EXPORT AND IMPORT FIGURES OF EVERY COUNTRY IN THE UNITED NATIONS... AND EVERY PAGE OF ANY VOLUME OF THE ENCYCLOPEDIA BRITANNICA COVERING DATA THAT STARTS WITH A CONSONANT!
AND DON'T COMPLAIN... IT'S GOOD FOR YOU!
THAT'S THE PART THAT REALLY BOTHERS ME-- "IT'S GOOD FOR YOU!"
SINCE WHEN IS SPENDING THE REST OF YOUR LIFE IN HIGH SCHOOL "GOOD FOR YOU"?
SHE MAKES HISTORY SO **BORING** AND SUCH A **CHORE** AND--
HEY!
DID YOU JUST SEE SOMETHING UP IN THE...
OH, FORGET IT. PROBABLY JUST MY APPALLINGLY OVERACTIVE IMAGINATION!
POSSIBLY. OR POSSIBLY IT WAS SOMETHING ELSE...
3

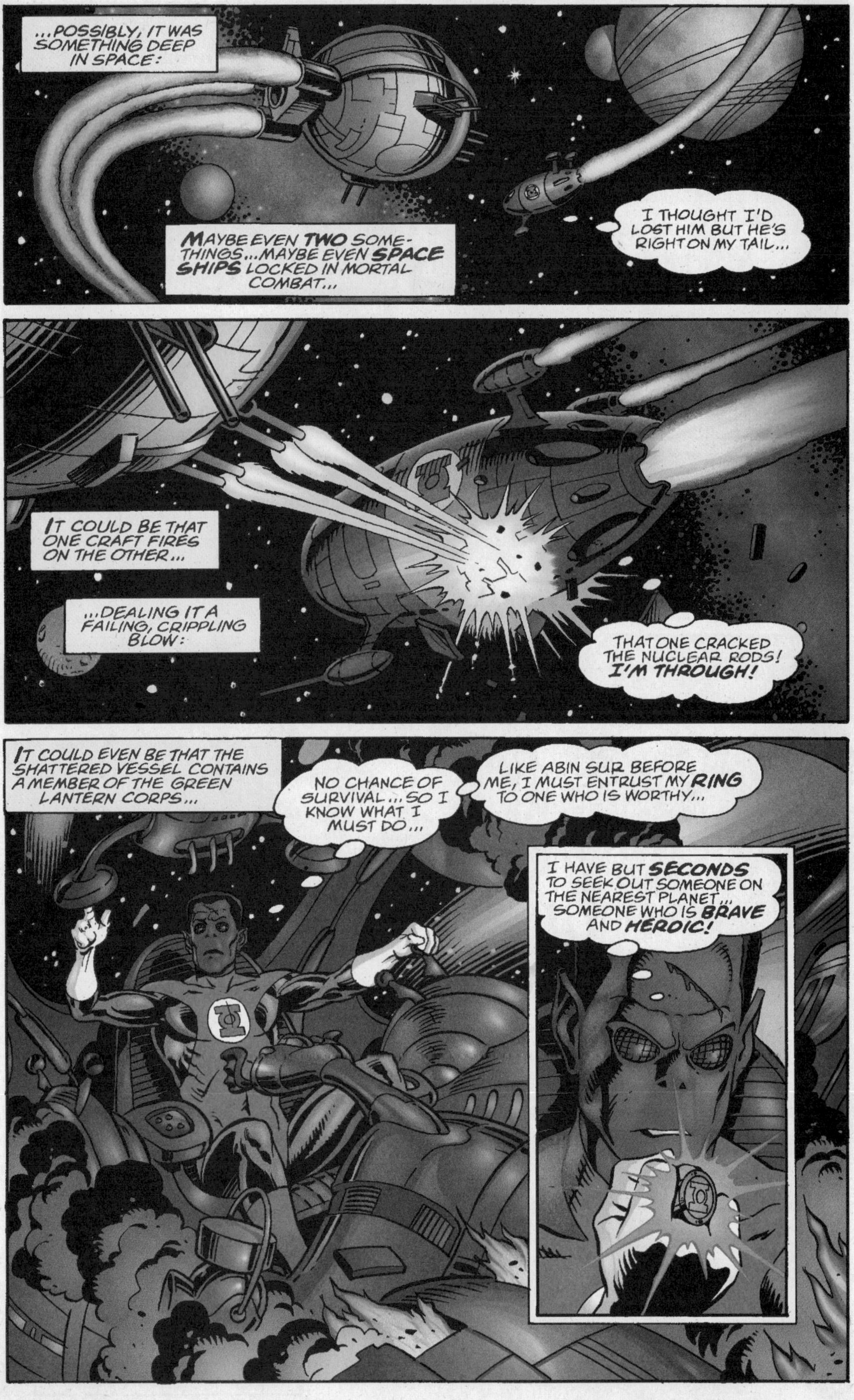

...POSSIBLY, IT WAS SOMETHING DEEP IN SPACE:
MAYBE EVEN TWO SOME-THINGS...MAYBE EVEN SPACE SHIPS LOCKED IN MORTAL COMBAT...
I THOUGHT I'D LOST HIM BUT HE'S RIGHT ON MY TAIL...
IT COULD BE THAT ONE CRAFT FIRES ON THE OTHER...
...DEALING IT A FAILING, CRIPPLING BLOW:
THAT ONE CRACKED THE NUCLEAR RODS! I'M THROUGH!
IT COULD EVEN BE THAT THE SHATTERED VESSEL CONTAINS A MEMBER OF THE GREEN LANTERN CORPS...
NO CHANCE OF SURVIVAL... SO I KNOW WHAT I MUST DO...
LIKE ABIN SUR BEFORE ME, I MUST ENTRUST MY RING TO ONE WHO IS WORTHY...
I HAVE BUT SECONDS TO SEEK OUT SOMEONE ON THE NEAREST PLANET... SOMEONE WHO IS BRAVE AND HEROIC!

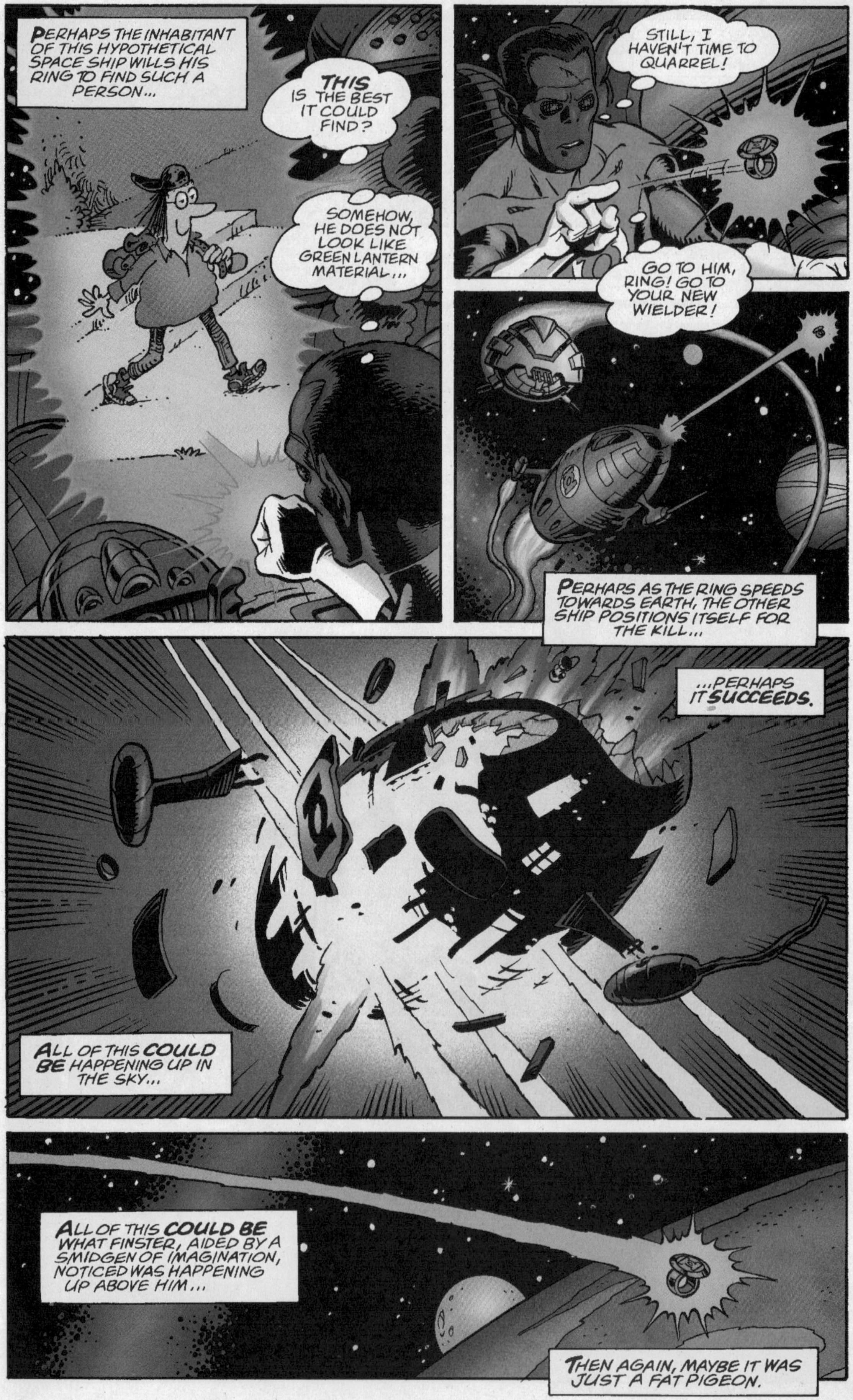
PERHAPS THE INHABITANT OF THIS HYPOTHETICAL SPACE SHIP WILLS HIS RING TO FIND SUCH A PERSON...
THIS IS THE BEST IT COULD FIND?
SOMEHOW, HE DOES NOT LOOK LIKE GREEN LANTERN MATERIAL...
STILL, I HAVEN'T TIME TO QUARREL!
GO TO HIM, RING! GO TO YOUR NEW WIELDER!
PERHAPS AS THE RING SPEEDS TOWARDS EARTH, THE OTHER SHIP POSITIONS ITSELF FOR THE KILL...
...PERHAPS IT SUCCEEDS.
ALL OF THIS COULD BE HAPPENING UP IN THE SKY...
ALL OF THIS COULD BE WHAT FINSTER, AIDED BY A SMIDGEN OF IMAGINATION, NOTICED WAS HAPPENING UP ABOVE HIM...
THEN AGAIN, MAYBE IT WAS JUST A FAT PIGEON.

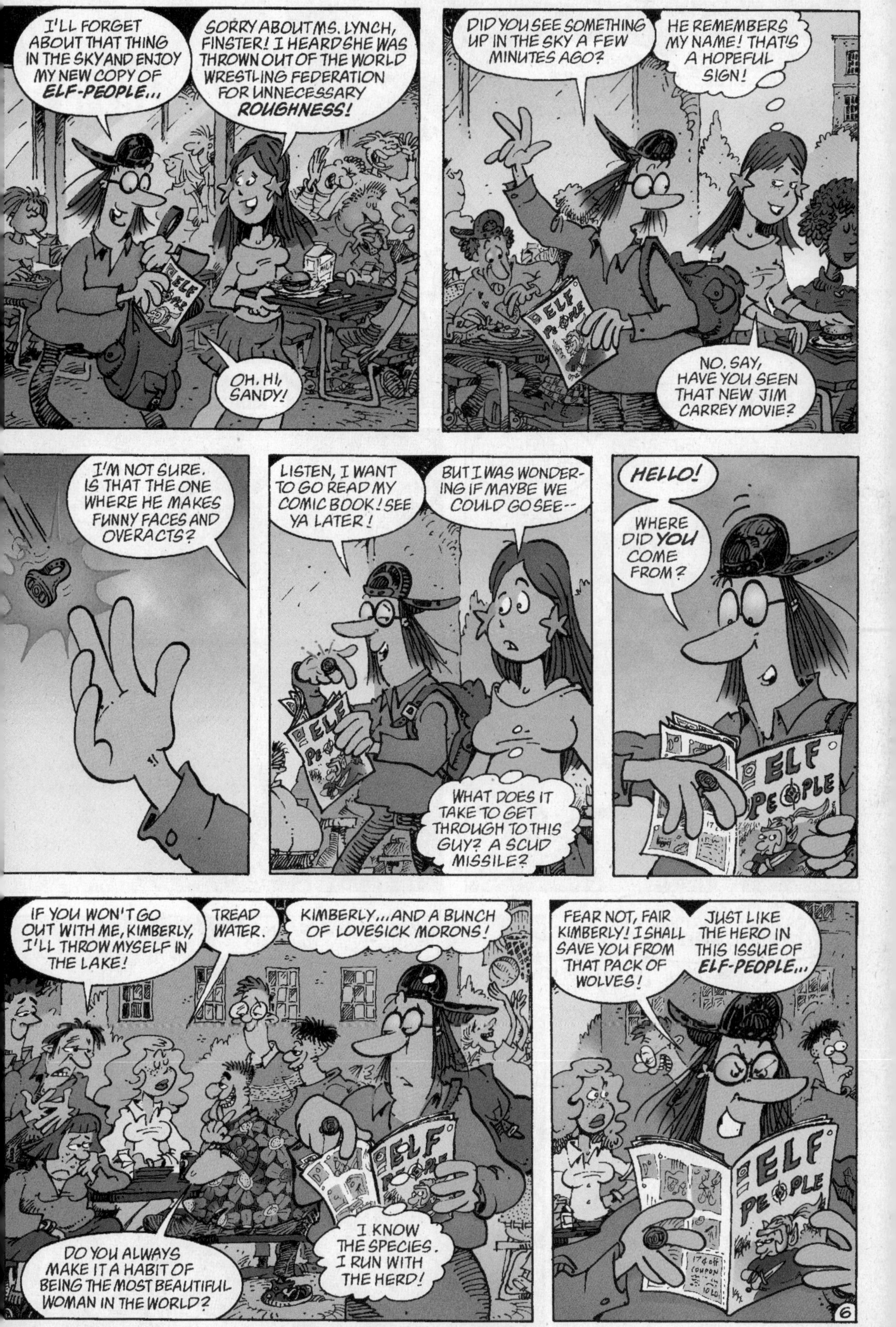
I'LL FORGET ABOUT THAT THING IN THE SKY AND ENJOY MY NEW COPY OF ELF-PEOPLE...
SORRY ABOUT MS. LYNCH, FINSTER! I HEARD SHE WAS THROWN OUT OF THE WORLD WRESTLING FEDERATION FOR UNNECESSARY ROUGHNESS!
OH. HI, SANDY!
DID YOU SEE SOMETHING UP IN THE SKY A FEW MINUTES AGO?
HE REMEMBERS MY NAME! THAT'S A HOPEFUL SIGN!
NO. SAY, HAVE YOU SEEN THAT NEW JIM CARREY MOVIE?
I'M NOT SURE. IS THAT THE ONE WHERE HE MAKES FUNNY FACES AND OVERACTS?
LISTEN, I WANT TO GO READ MY COMIC BOOK! SEE YA LATER!
BUT I WAS WONDERING IF MAYBE WE COULD GO SEE--
WHAT DOES IT TAKE TO GET THROUGH TO THIS GUY? A SCUD MISSILE?
HELLO!
WHERE DID YOU COME FROM?
IF YOU WON'T GO OUT WITH ME, KIMBERLY, I'LL THROW MYSELF IN THE LAKE!
TREAD WATER.
KIMBERLY... AND A BUNCH OF LOVESICK MORONS!
DO YOU ALWAYS MAKE IT A HABIT OF BEING THE MOST BEAUTIFUL WOMAN IN THE WORLD?
I KNOW THE SPECIES. I RUN WITH THE HERD!
FEAR NOT, FAIR KIMBERLY! I SHALL SAVE YOU FROM THAT PACK OF WOLVES!
JUST LIKE THE HERO IN THIS ISSUE OF ELF-PEOPLE...
6

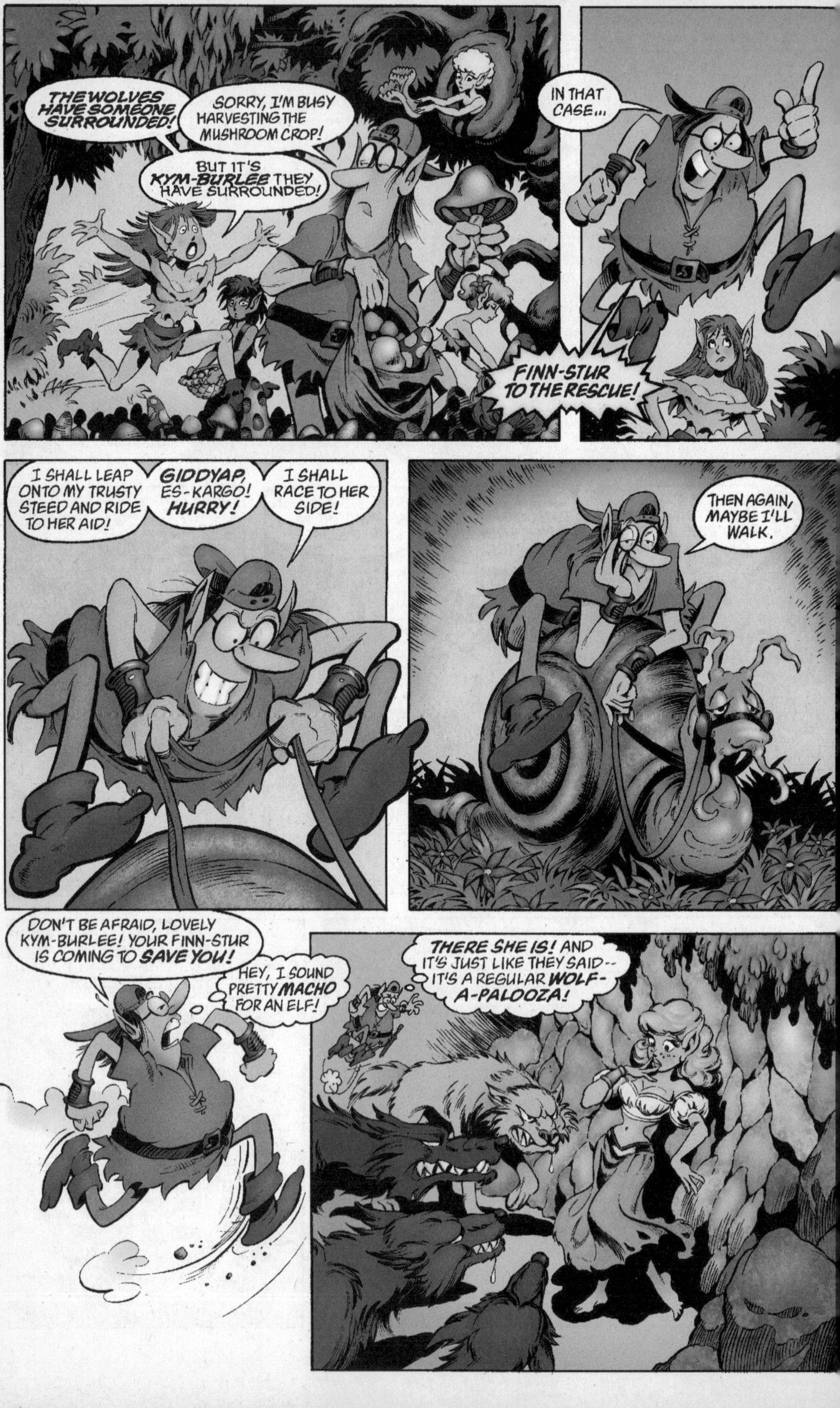

THE WOLVES HAVE SOMEONE SURROUNDED!
SORRY, I'M BUSY HARVESTING THE MUSHROOM CROP!
BUT IT'S KYM-BURLEE THEY HAVE SURROUNDED!
IN THAT CASE...
FINN-STUR TO THE RESCUE!
I SHALL LEAP ONTO MY TRUSTY STEED AND RIDE TO HER AID!
GIDDYAP, ES-KARGO! HURRY!
I SHALL RACE TO HER SIDE!
THEN AGAIN, MAYBE I'LL WALK.
DON'T BE AFRAID, LOVELY KYM-BURLEE! YOUR FINN-STUR IS COMING TO SAVE YOU!
HEY, I SOUND PRETTY MACHO FOR AN ELF!
THERE SHE IS! AND IT'S JUST LIKE THEY SAID-- IT'S A REGULAR WOLF-A-PALOOZA!

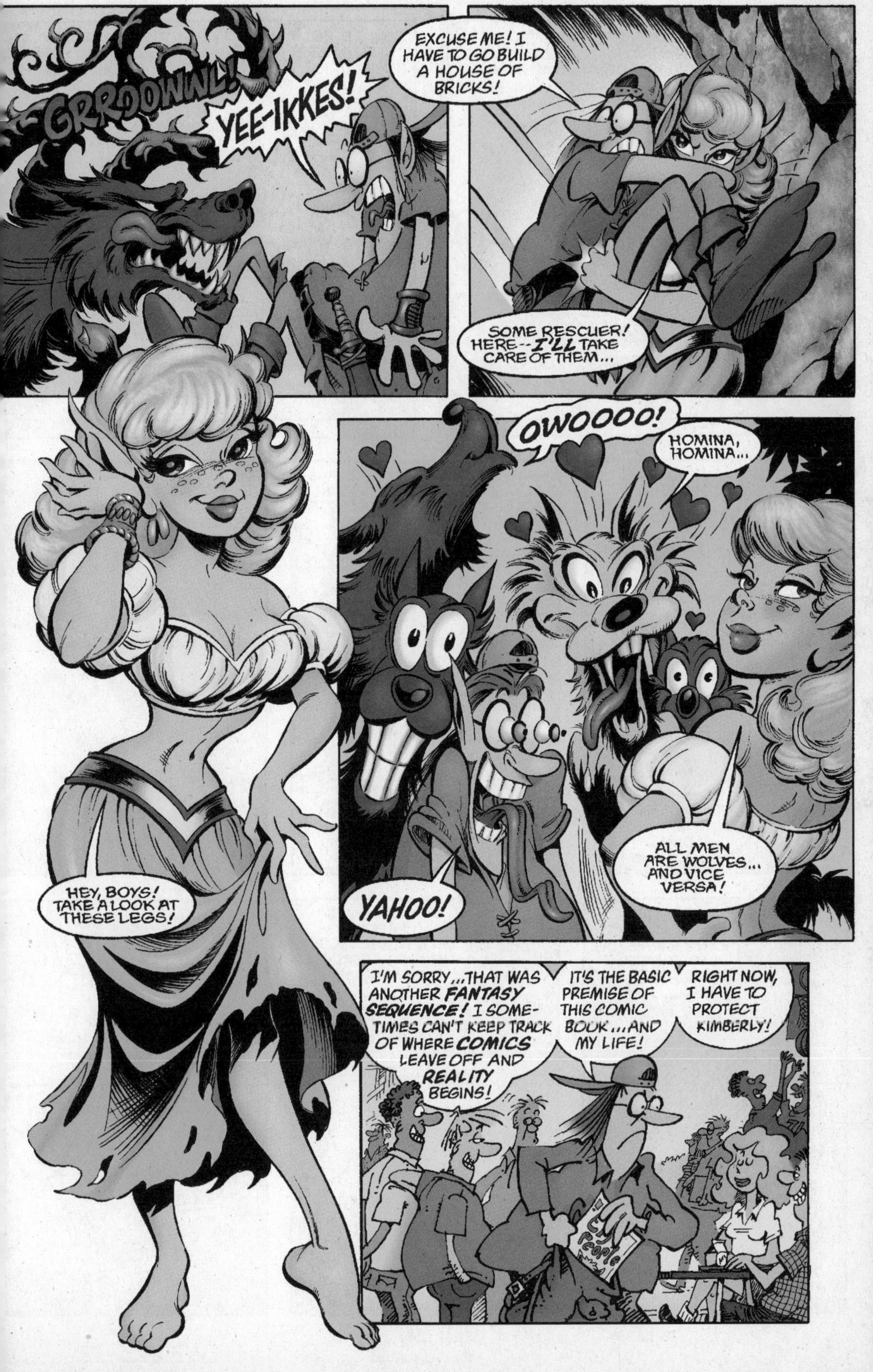
GRRDOWWL!
YEE-IKKES!
EXCUSE ME! I HAVE TO GO BUILD A HOUSE OF BRICKS!
SOME RESCUER! HERE--I'LL TAKE CARE OF THEM...
HEY, BOYS! TAKE A LOOK AT THESE LEGS!
OWOOOO!
HOMINA, HOMINA...
ALL MEN ARE WOLVES... AND VICE VERSA!
YAHOO!
I'M SORRY...THAT WAS ANOTHER FANTASY SEQUENCE! I SOMETIMES CAN'T KEEP TRACK OF WHERE COMICS LEAVE OFF AND REALITY BEGINS!
IT'S THE BASIC PREMISE OF THIS COMIC BOOK... AND MY LIFE!
RIGHT NOW, I HAVE TO PROTECT KIMBERLY!

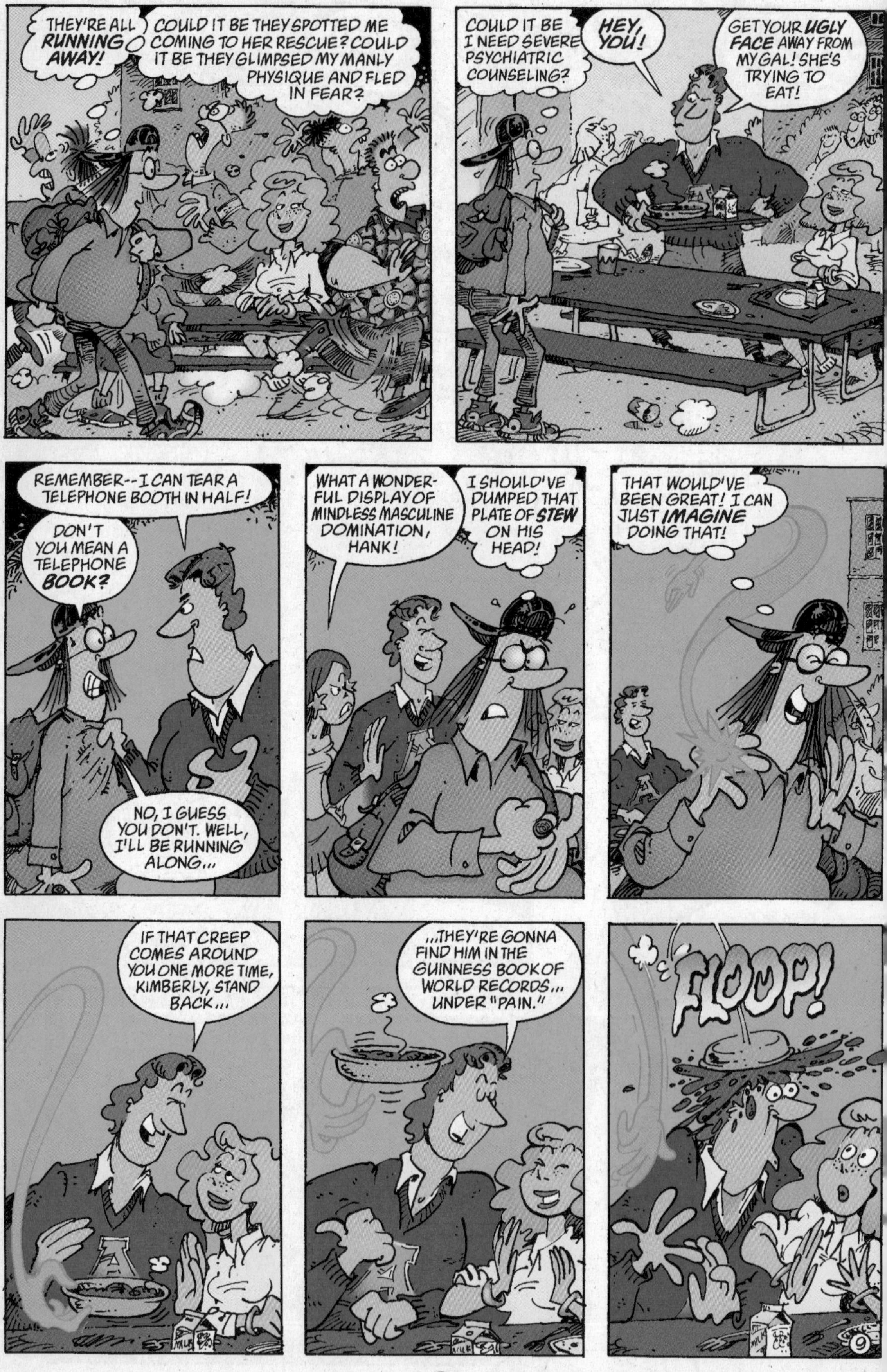
THEY'RE ALL RUNNING AWAY!
COULD IT BE THEY SPOTTED ME COMING TO HER RESCUE? COULD IT BE THEY GLIMPSED MY MANLY PHYSIQUE AND FLED IN FEAR?
COULD IT BE I NEED SEVERE PSYCHIATRIC COUNSELING?
HEY, YOU!
GET YOUR UGLY FACE AWAY FROM MY GAL! SHE'S TRYING TO EAT!
REMEMBER--I CAN TEAR A TELEPHONE BOOTH IN HALF!
DON'T YOU MEAN A TELEPHONE BOOK?
NO, I GUESS YOU DON'T. WELL, I'LL BE RUNNING ALONG...
WHAT A WONDERFUL DISPLAY OF MINDLESS MASCULINE DOMINATION, HANK!
I SHOULD'VE DUMPED THAT PLATE OF STEW ON HIS HEAD!
THAT WOULD'VE BEEN GREAT! I CAN JUST IMAGINE DOING THAT!
IF THAT CREEP COMES AROUND YOU ONE MORE TIME, KIMBERLY, STAND BACK...
...THEY'RE GONNA FIND HIM IN THE GUINNESS BOOK OF WORLD RECORDS... UNDER "PAIN."
FLOOP!
9

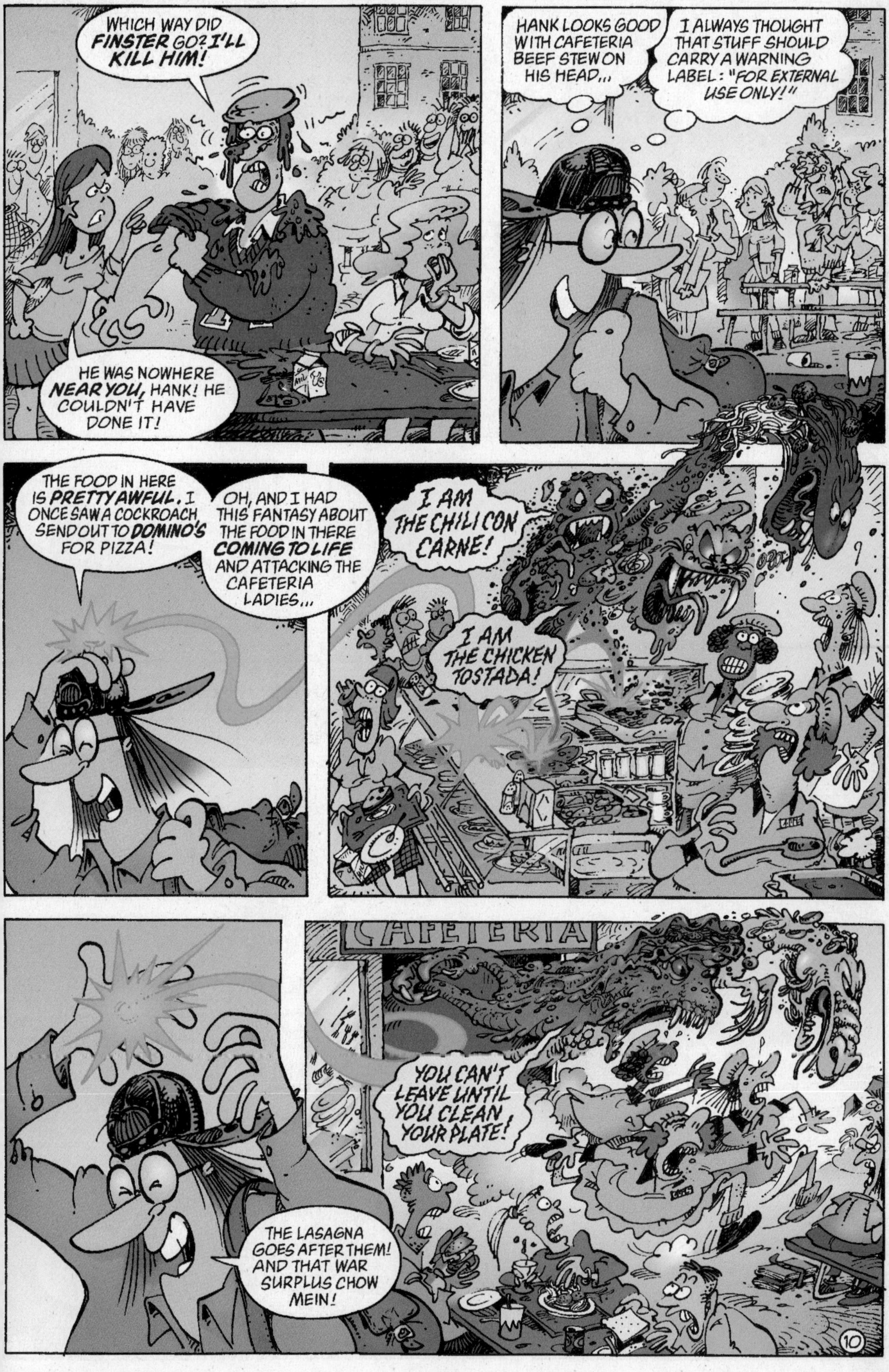
WHICH WAY DID FINSTER GO? I'LL KILL HIM!
HE WAS NOWHERE NEAR YOU, HANK! HE COULDN'T HAVE DONE IT!
HANK LOOKS GOOD WITH CAFETERIA BEEF STEW ON HIS HEAD...
I ALWAYS THOUGHT THAT STUFF SHOULD CARRY A WARNING LABEL: "FOR EXTERNAL USE ONLY!"
THE FOOD IN HERE IS PRETTY AWFUL. I ONCE SAW A COCKROACH SEND OUT TO DOMINO'S FOR PIZZA!
OH, AND I HAD THIS FANTASY ABOUT THE FOOD IN THERE COMING TO LIFE AND ATTACKING THE CAFETERIA LADIES...
I AM THE CHILI CON CARNE!
I AM THE CHICKEN TOSTADA!
CAFETERIA
YOU CAN'T LEAVE UNTIL YOU CLEAN YOUR PLATE!
THE LASAGNA GOES AFTER THEM! AND THAT WAR SURPLUS CHOW MEIN!
10

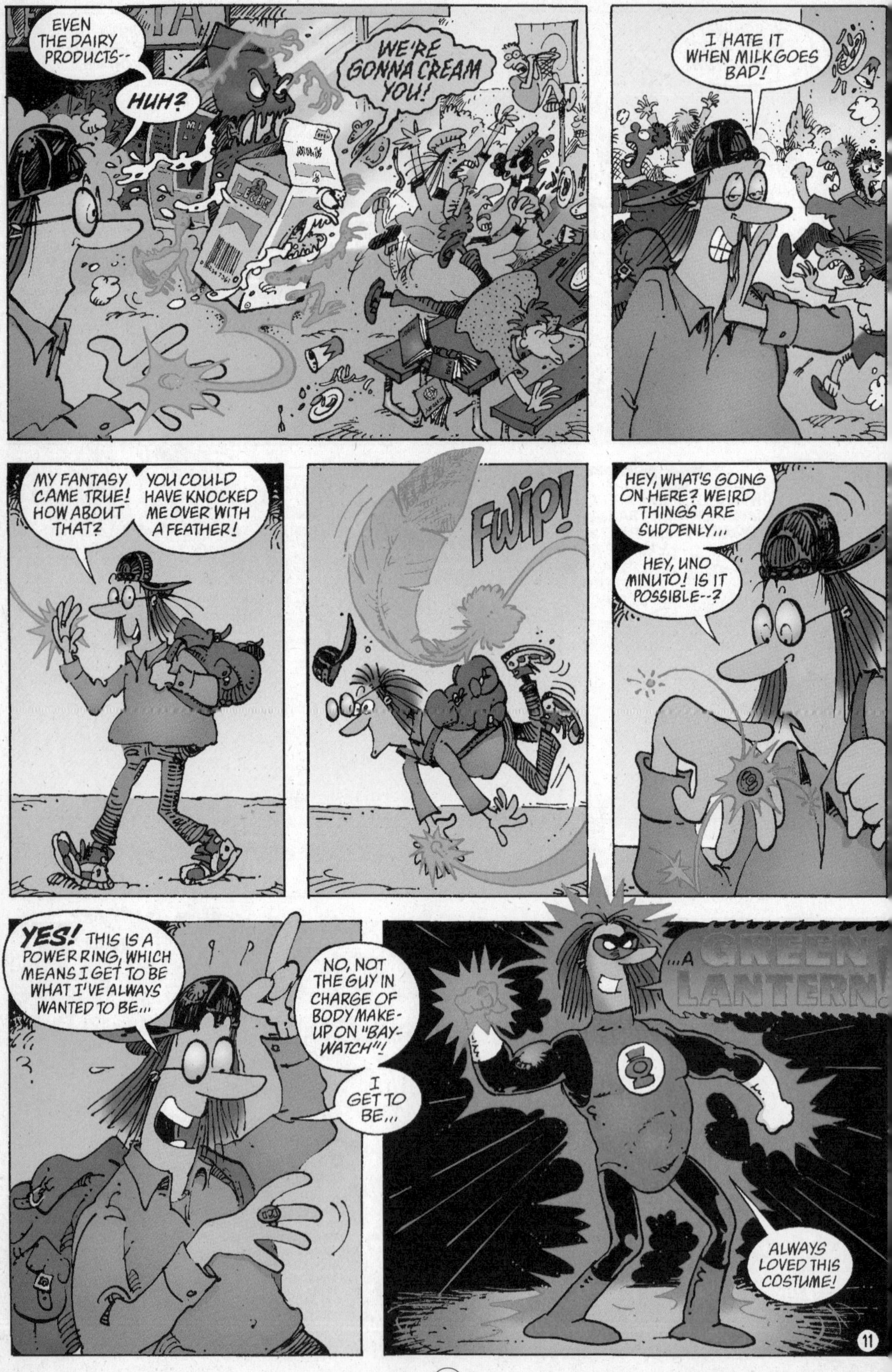
EVEN THE DAIRY PRODUCTS--
HUH?
WE'RE GONNA CREAM YOU!
I HATE IT WHEN MILK GOES BAD!
MY FANTASY CAME TRUE! HOW ABOUT THAT?
YOU COULD HAVE KNOCKED ME OVER WITH A FEATHER!
FWIP!
HEY, WHAT'S GOING ON HERE? WEIRD THINGS ARE SUDDENLY...
HEY, UNO MINUTO! IS IT POSSIBLE--?
YES! THIS IS A POWER RING, WHICH MEANS I GET TO BE WHAT I'VE ALWAYS WANTED TO BE...
NO, NOT THE GUY IN CHARGE OF BODY MAKE-UP ON "BAYWATCH"!
I GET TO BE...
...A GREEN LANTERN!
ALWAYS LOVED THIS COSTUME!
11

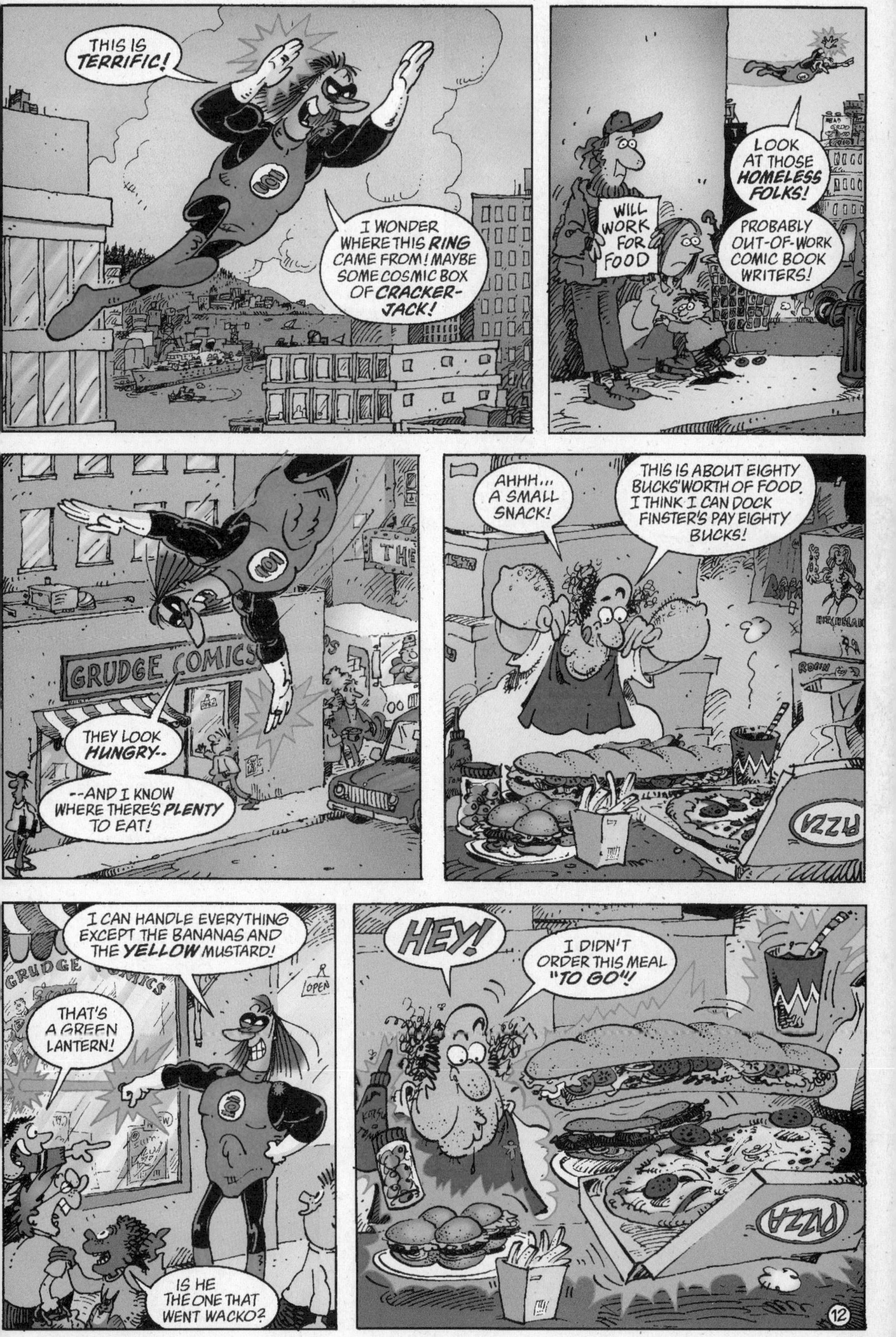
THIS IS TERRIFIC!
I WONDER WHERE THIS RING CAME FROM! MAYBE SOME COSMIC BOX OF CRACKER-JACK!
LOOK AT THOSE HOMELESS FOLKS!
PROBABLY OUT-OF-WORK COMIC BOOK WRITERS!
WILL WORK FOR FOOD
GRUDGE COMICS
THEY LOOK HUNGRY--
--AND I KNOW WHERE THERE'S PLENTY TO EAT!
AHHH... A SMALL SNACK!
THIS IS ABOUT EIGHTY BUCKS' WORTH OF FOOD. I THINK I CAN DOCK FINSTER'S PAY EIGHTY BUCKS!
PIZZA
I CAN HANDLE EVERYTHING EXCEPT THE BANANAS AND THE YELLOW MUSTARD!
GRUDGE COMICS
OPEN
THAT'S A GREEN LANTERN!
IS HE THE ONE THAT WENT WACKO?
HEY!
I DIDN'T ORDER THIS MEAL "TO GO"!
PIZZA
12

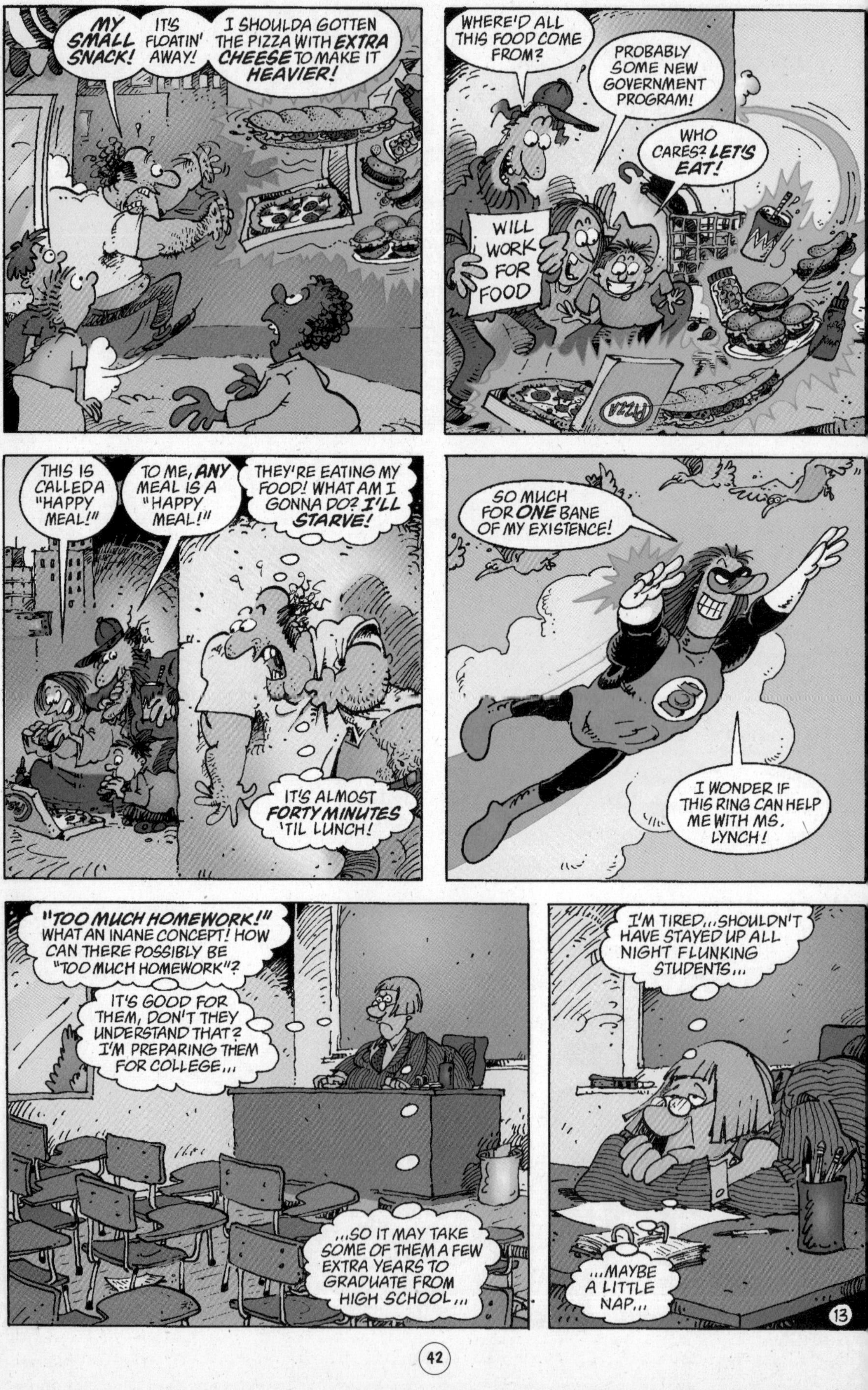
MY SMALL SNACK!
IT'S FLOATIN' AWAY!
I SHOULDA GOTTEN THE PIZZA WITH EXTRA CHEESE TO MAKE IT HEAVIER!
WHERE'D ALL THIS FOOD COME FROM?
PROBABLY SOME NEW GOVERNMENT PROGRAM!
WHO CARES? LET'S EAT!
WILL WORK FOR FOOD
PIZZA
THIS IS CALLED A "HAPPY MEAL!"
TO ME, ANY MEAL IS A "HAPPY MEAL!"
THEY'RE EATING MY FOOD! WHAT AM I GONNA DO? I'LL STARVE!
IT'S ALMOST FORTY MINUTES 'TIL LUNCH!
SO MUCH FOR ONE BANE OF MY EXISTENCE!
I WONDER IF THIS RING CAN HELP ME WITH MS. LYNCH!
"TOO MUCH HOMEWORK!" WHAT AN INANE CONCEPT! HOW CAN THERE POSSIBLY BE "TOO MUCH HOMEWORK"?
IT'S GOOD FOR THEM, DON'T THEY UNDERSTAND THAT? I'M PREPARING THEM FOR COLLEGE...
...SO IT MAY TAKE SOME OF THEM A FEW EXTRA YEARS TO GRADUATE FROM HIGH SCHOOL...
I'M TIRED... SHOULDN'T HAVE STAYED UP ALL NIGHT FLUNKING STUDENTS...
...MAYBE A LITTLE NAP...
13

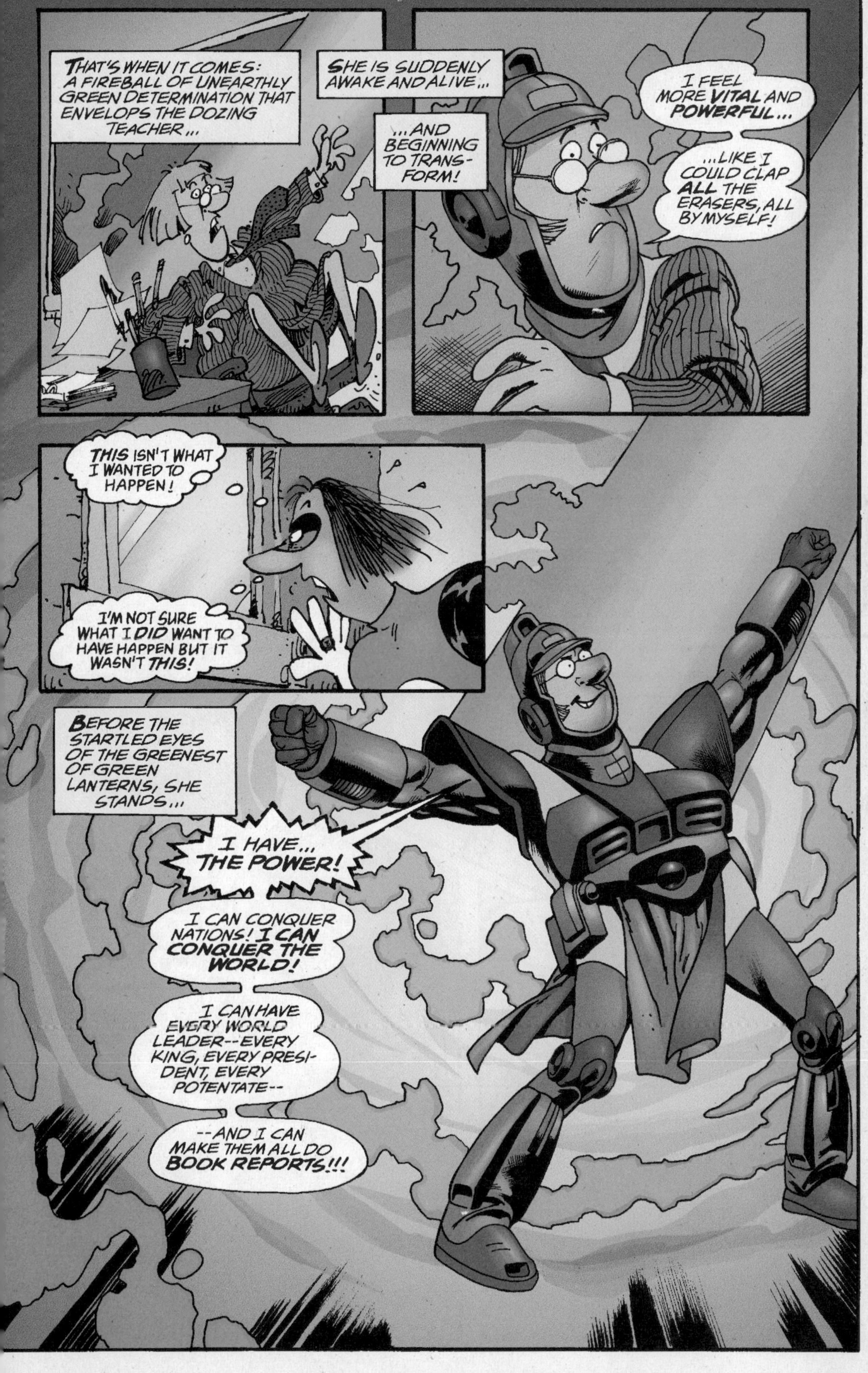
THAT'S WHEN IT COMES: A FIREBALL OF UNEARTHLY GREEN DETERMINATION THAT ENVELOPS THE DOZING TEACHER...
SHE IS SUDDENLY AWAKE AND ALIVE...
...AND BEGINNING TO TRANS-FORM!
I FEEL MORE VITAL AND POWERFUL...
...LIKE I COULD CLAP ALL THE ERASERS, ALL BY MYSELF!
THIS ISN'T WHAT I WANTED TO HAPPEN!
I'M NOT SURE WHAT I DID WANT TO HAVE HAPPEN BUT IT WASN'T THIS!
BEFORE THE STARTLED EYES OF THE GREENEST OF GREEN LANTERNS, SHE STANDS...
I HAVE... THE POWER!
I CAN CONQUER NATIONS! I CAN CONQUER THE WORLD!
I CAN HAVE EVERY WORLD LEADER--EVERY KING, EVERY PRESI-DENT, EVERY POTENTATE--
--AND I CAN MAKE THEM ALL DO BOOK REPORTS!!!

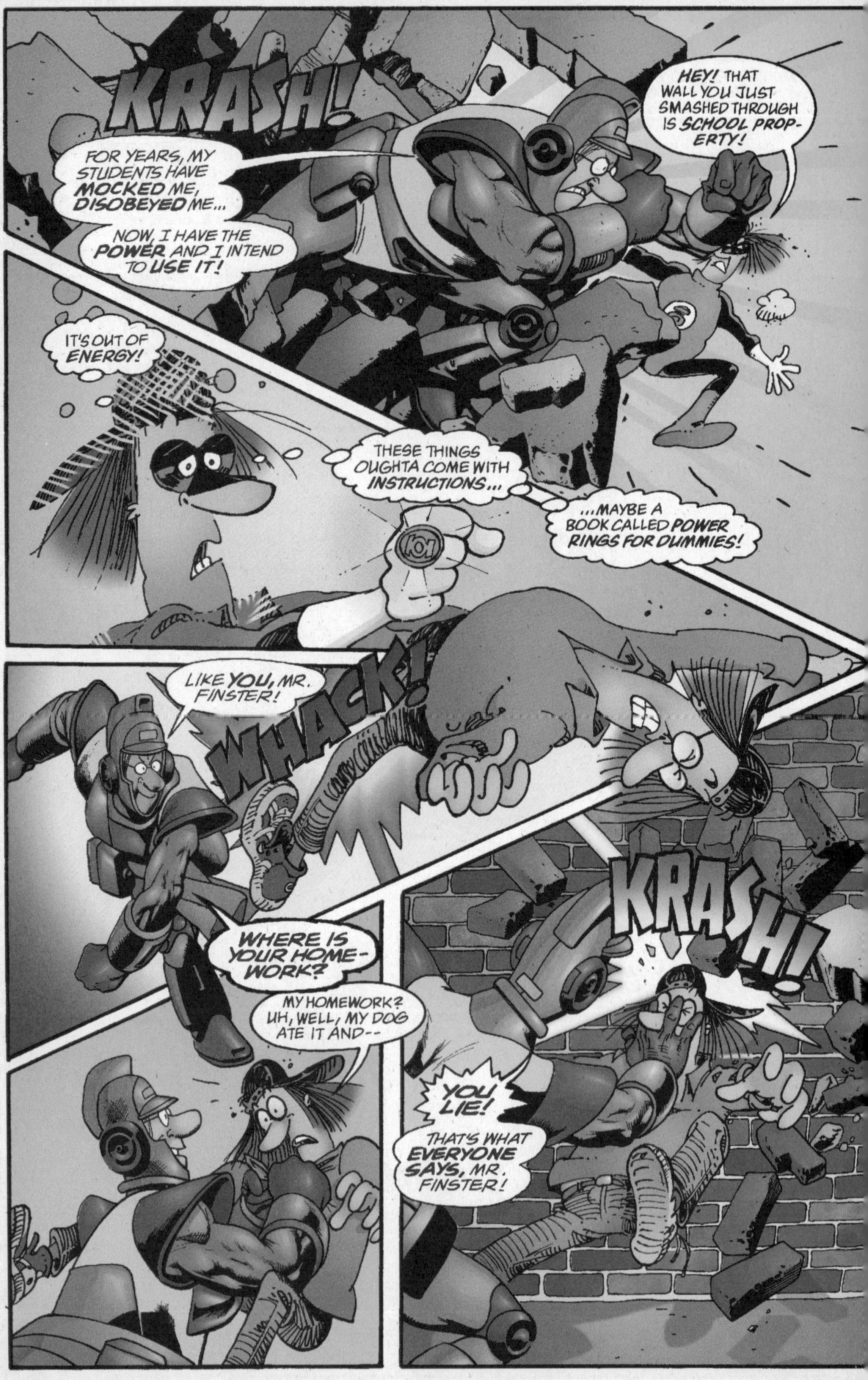
KRASH!
FOR YEARS, MY STUDENTS HAVE MOCKED ME, DISOBEYED ME...
NOW, I HAVE THE POWER AND I INTEND TO USE IT!
HEY! THAT WALL YOU JUST SMASHED THROUGH IS SCHOOL PROPERTY!
IT'S OUT OF ENERGY!
THESE THINGS OUGHTA COME WITH INSTRUCTIONS...
...MAYBE A BOOK CALLED POWER RINGS FOR DUMMIES!
LIKE YOU, MR. FINSTER!
WHACK!
KRASH!
WHERE IS YOUR HOME-WORK?
MY HOMEWORK? UH, WELL, MY DOG ATE IT AND--
YOU LIE!
THAT'S WHAT EVERYONE SAYS, MR. FINSTER!

IF EVERYONE'S TELLING THE TRUTH, **ALPO** SHOULD PUT OUT A HOMEWORK-FLAVORED DOG FOOD!
YOU MUST BE **PUNISHED!** I'LL TAKE YOU TO MY SECRET, OUTER SPACE **PUNISHMENT PLACE!**
SOON, IN HER SECRET, OUTER SPACE **PUNISHMENT PLACE...**
WH-WHERE AM I?
YOU AREN'T PAYING ATTENTION, MR. FINSTER! YOU'RE IN MY (SAY IT WITH ME:) SECRET, OUTER SPACE **PUNISHMENT PLACE!**
YOU **NEVER** PAY ATTENTION! THAT'S WHY YOU'RE **HERE!**
YOU STUDENTS... WASTING YOUR TIME DOING THINGS OTHER THAN STUDYING... YOU **SICKEN ME!**
THAT'S WHY I BROUGHT YOU ALL HERE! THIS MACHINE WILL DRILL THE INFORMATION INTO YOU IN THE BEST POSSIBLE WAY...
...WITHOUT CONTEXT OR COMPREHENSION!
UH, JUST **WHEN** DID YOU SET THIS UP? YOU'VE BEEN A SUPER-VILLAIN FOR ABOUT TEN MINUTES...
SHUT UP! AS YOU CAN SEE, THEY ARE BEING FILLED WITH FACTS...
LOUISIANA PURCHASE
MONITOR
LINCOLN-DOUGLAS DEBATES
JIM CROW DECISION
MERRIMAC
ANDREW JOHNSON
CALVIN COOLIDGE
PANAMA CANAL
STAMP ACT
CONTINENTAL CONGRESS
EMANCIPATION PROCLAMATION

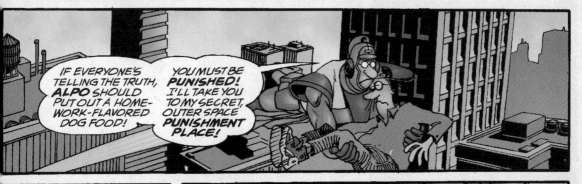

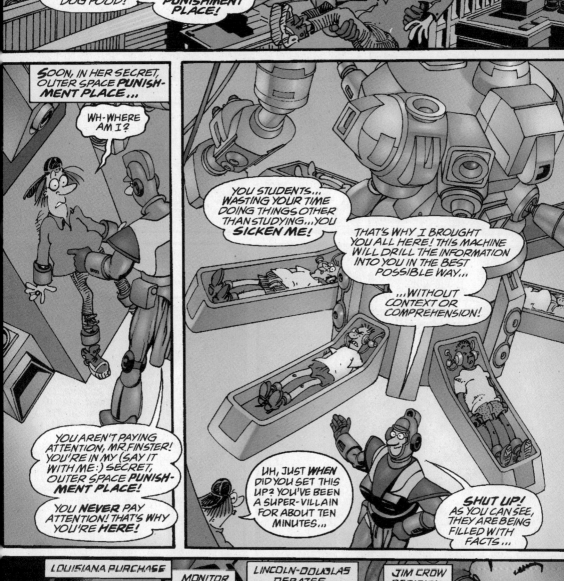

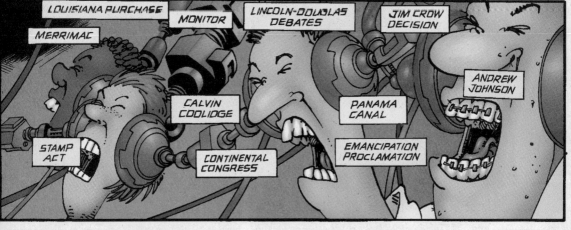

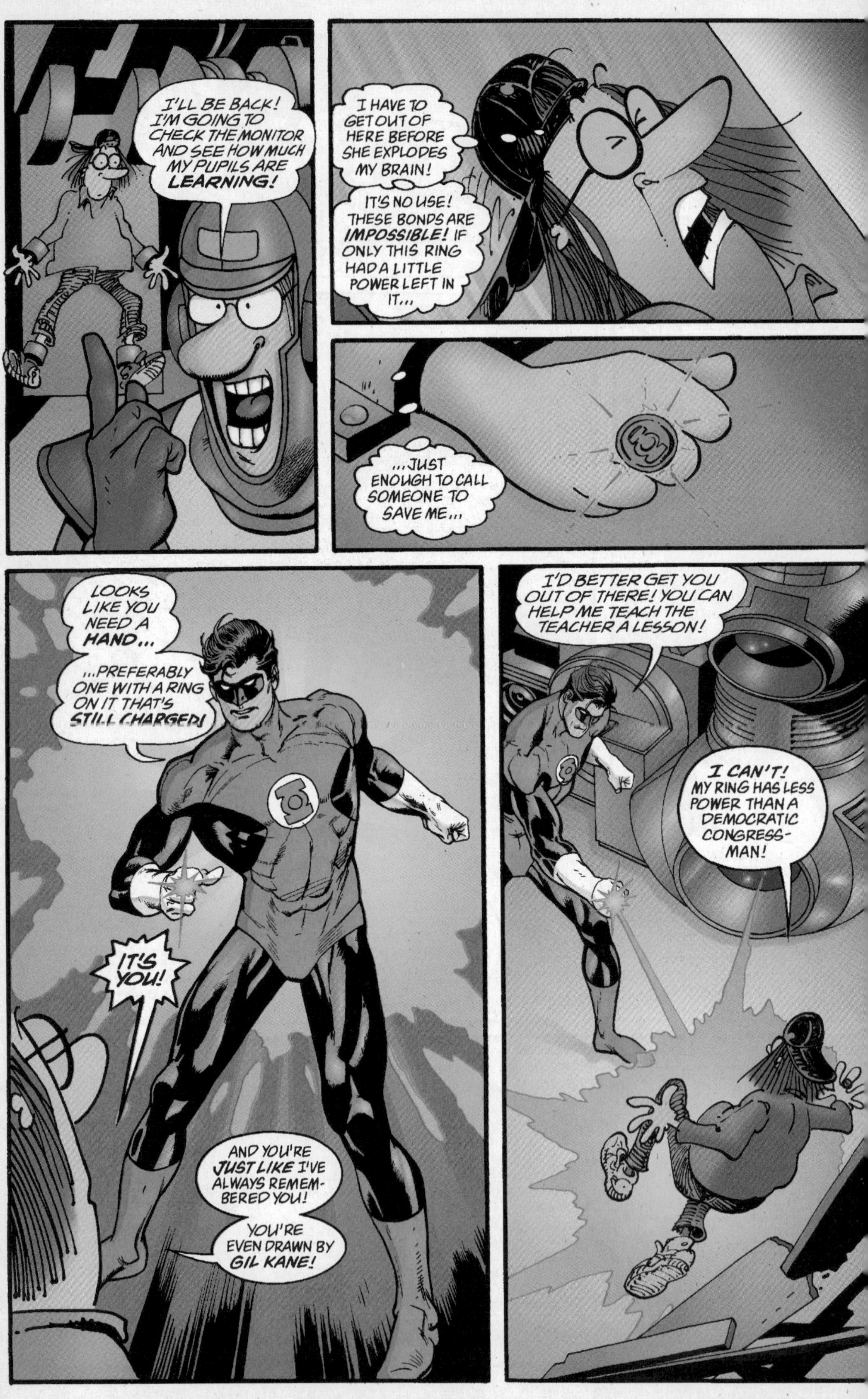
I'LL BE BACK! I'M GOING TO CHECK THE MONITOR AND SEE HOW MUCH MY PUPILS ARE LEARNING!
I HAVE TO GET OUT OF HERE BEFORE SHE EXPLODES MY BRAIN!
IT'S NO USE! THESE BONDS ARE IMPOSSIBLE! IF ONLY THIS RING HAD A LITTLE POWER LEFT IN IT...
...JUST ENOUGH TO CALL SOMEONE TO SAVE ME...
LOOKS LIKE YOU NEED A HAND...
...PREFERABLY ONE WITH A RING ON IT THAT'S STILL CHARGED!
IT'S YOU!
AND YOU'RE JUST LIKE I'VE ALWAYS REMEMBERED YOU!
YOU'RE EVEN DRAWN BY GIL KANE!
I'D BETTER GET YOU OUT OF THERE! YOU CAN HELP ME TEACH THE TEACHER A LESSON!
I CAN'T! MY RING HAS LESS POWER THAN A DEMOCRATIC CONGRESSMAN!

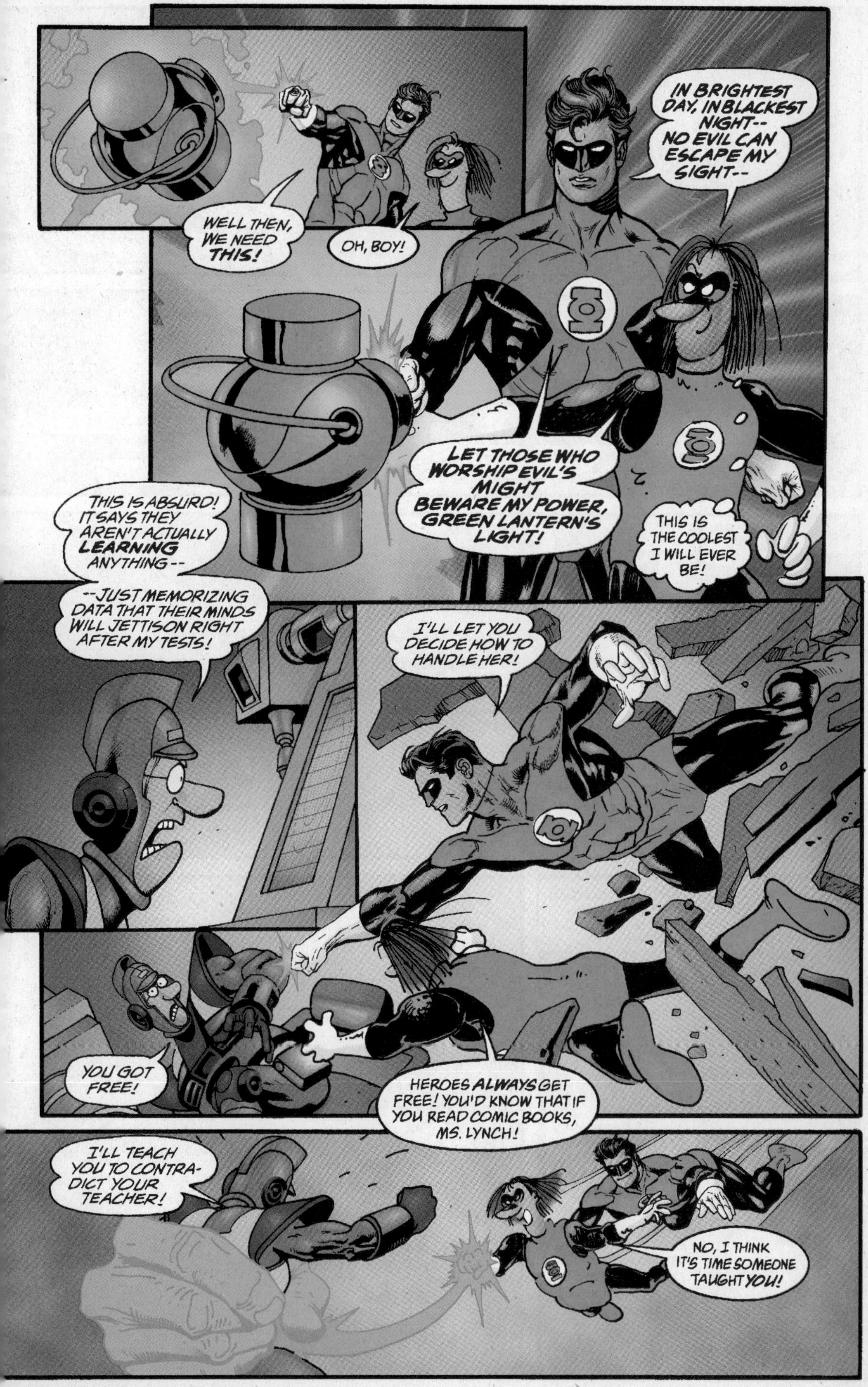
WELL THEN, WE NEED THIS!
OH, BOY!
IN BRIGHTEST DAY, IN BLACKEST NIGHT-- NO EVIL CAN ESCAPE MY SIGHT--
LET THOSE WHO WORSHIP EVIL'S MIGHT BEWARE MY POWER, GREEN LANTERN'S LIGHT!
THIS IS THE COOLEST I WILL EVER BE!
THIS IS ABSURD! IT SAYS THEY AREN'T ACTUALLY LEARNING ANYTHING--
--JUST MEMORIZING DATA THAT THEIR MINDS WILL JETTISON RIGHT AFTER MY TESTS!
I'LL LET YOU DECIDE HOW TO HANDLE HER!
YOU GOT FREE!
HEROES ALWAYS GET FREE! YOU'D KNOW THAT IF YOU READ COMIC BOOKS, MS. LYNCH!
I'LL TEACH YOU TO CONTRA-DICT YOUR TEACHER!
NO, I THINK IT'S TIME SOMEONE TAUGHT YOU!

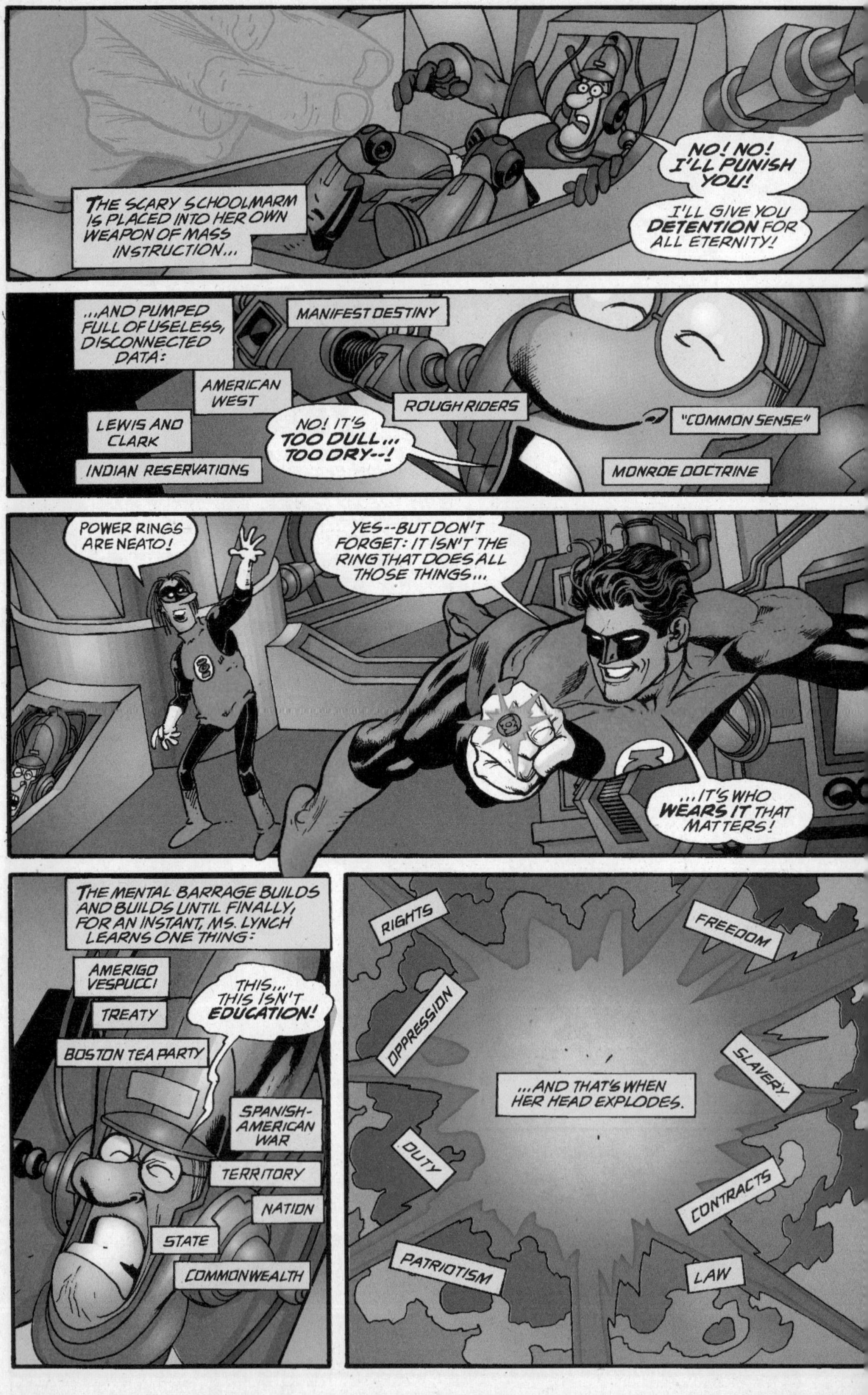
THE SCARY SCHOOLMARM IS PLACED INTO HER OWN WEAPON OF MASS INSTRUCTION...
NO! NO! I'LL PUNISH YOU!
I'LL GIVE YOU **DETENTION** FOR ALL ETERNITY!
...AND PUMPED FULL OF USELESS, DISCONNECTED DATA:
MANIFEST DESTINY
AMERICAN WEST
LEWIS AND CLARK
INDIAN RESERVATIONS
NO! IT'S **TOO DULL... TOO DRY--!**
ROUGH RIDERS
"COMMON SENSE"
MONROE DOCTRINE
POWER RINGS ARE NEATO!
YES--BUT DON'T FORGET: IT ISN'T THE RING THAT DOES ALL THOSE THINGS...
...IT'S WHO **WEARS IT** THAT MATTERS!
THE MENTAL BARRAGE BUILDS AND BUILDS UNTIL FINALLY, FOR AN INSTANT, MS. LYNCH LEARNS ONE THING:
AMERIGO VESPUCCI
TREATY
THIS... THIS ISN'T **EDUCATION!**
BOSTON TEA PARTY
SPANISH-AMERICAN WAR
TERRITORY
NATION
STATE
COMMONWEALTH
RIGHTS
FREEDOM
OPPRESSION
SLAVERY
...AND THAT'S WHEN HER HEAD EXPLODES.
DUTY
CONTRACTS
PATRIOTISM
LAW

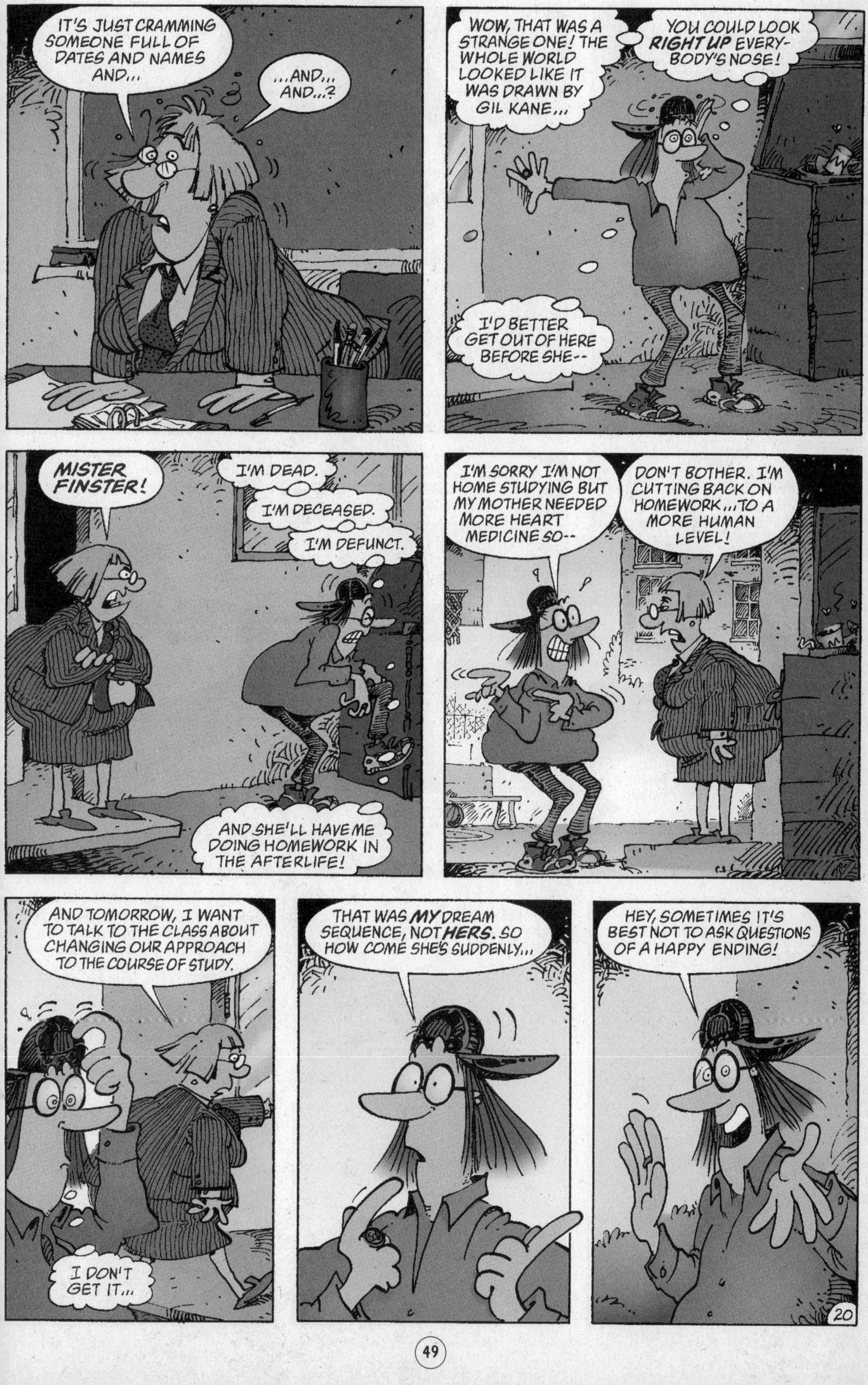
IT'S JUST CRAMMING SOMEONE FULL OF DATES AND NAMES AND...
...AND... AND...?
WOW, THAT WAS A STRANGE ONE! THE WHOLE WORLD LOOKED LIKE IT WAS DRAWN BY GIL KANE...
YOU COULD LOOK RIGHT UP EVERY-BODY'S NOSE!
I'D BETTER GET OUT OF HERE BEFORE SHE--
MISTER FINSTER!
I'M DEAD.
I'M DECEASED.
I'M DEFUNCT.
AND SHE'LL HAVE ME DOING HOMEWORK IN THE AFTERLIFE!
I'M SORRY I'M NOT HOME STUDYING BUT MY MOTHER NEEDED MORE HEART MEDICINE SO--
DON'T BOTHER. I'M CUTTING BACK ON HOMEWORK...TO A MORE HUMAN LEVEL!
AND TOMORROW, I WANT TO TALK TO THE CLASS ABOUT CHANGING OUR APPROACH TO THE COURSE OF STUDY.
I DON'T GET IT...
THAT WAS MY DREAM SEQUENCE, NOT HERS. SO HOW COME SHE'S SUDDENLY...
HEY, SOMETIMES IT'S BEST NOT TO ASK QUESTIONS OF A HAPPY ENDING!
20

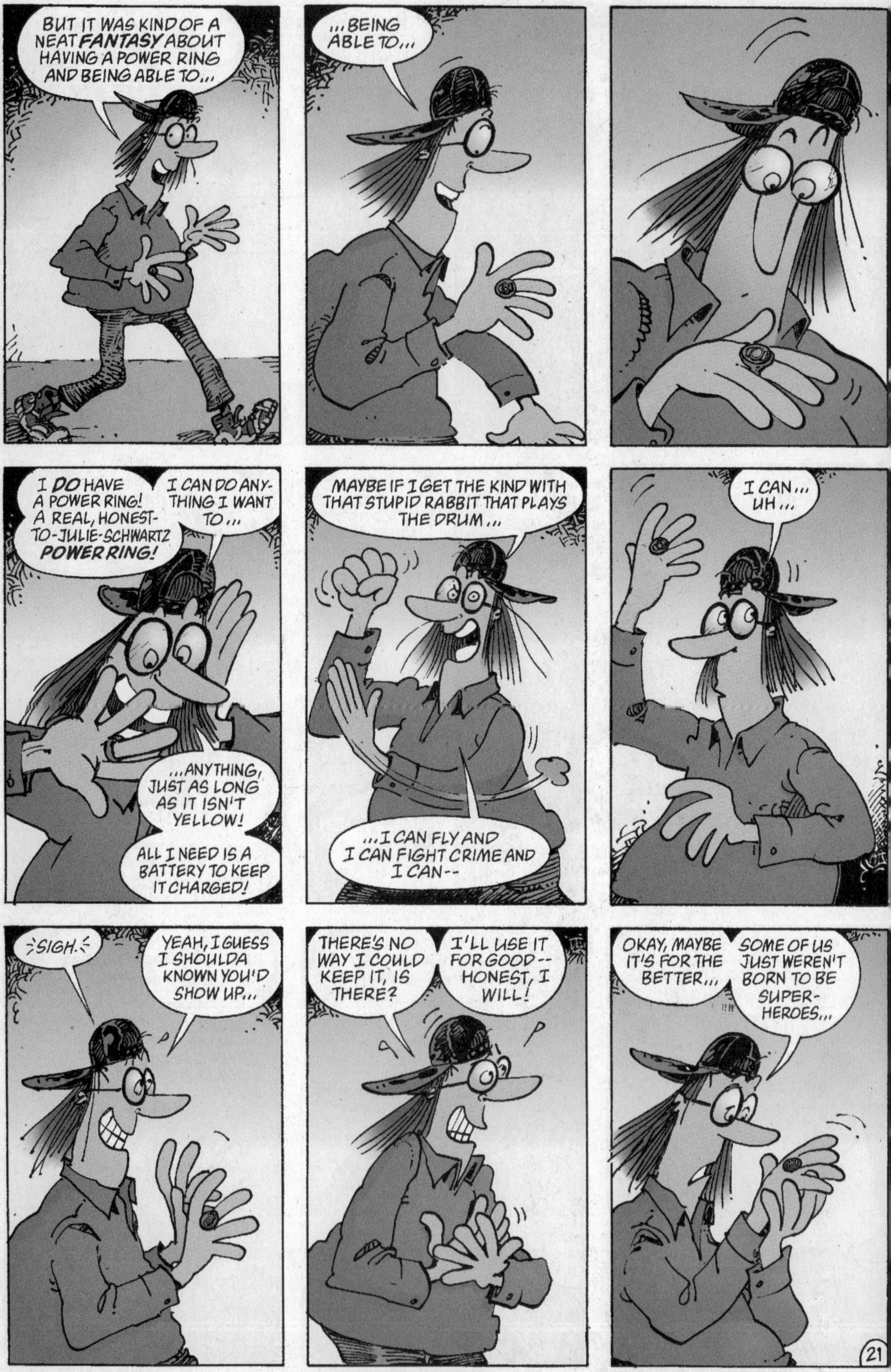

BUT IT WAS KIND OF A NEAT FANTASY ABOUT HAVING A POWER RING AND BEING ABLE TO...
...BEING ABLE TO...
I DO HAVE A POWER RING! A REAL, HONEST-TO-JULIE-SCHWARTZ POWER RING!
I CAN DO ANYTHING I WANT TO...
...ANYTHING, JUST AS LONG AS IT ISN'T YELLOW!
ALL I NEED IS A BATTERY TO KEEP IT CHARGED!
MAYBE IF I GET THE KIND WITH THAT STUPID RABBIT THAT PLAYS THE DRUM...
...I CAN FLY AND I CAN FIGHT CRIME AND I CAN--
I CAN... UH...
SIGH.
YEAH, I GUESS I SHOULDA KNOWN YOU'D SHOW UP...
THERE'S NO WAY I COULD KEEP IT, IS THERE?
I'LL USE IT FOR GOOD-- HONEST, I WILL!
OKAY, MAYBE IT'S FOR THE BETTER...
SOME OF US JUST WEREN'T BORN TO BE SUPER-HEROES...
21

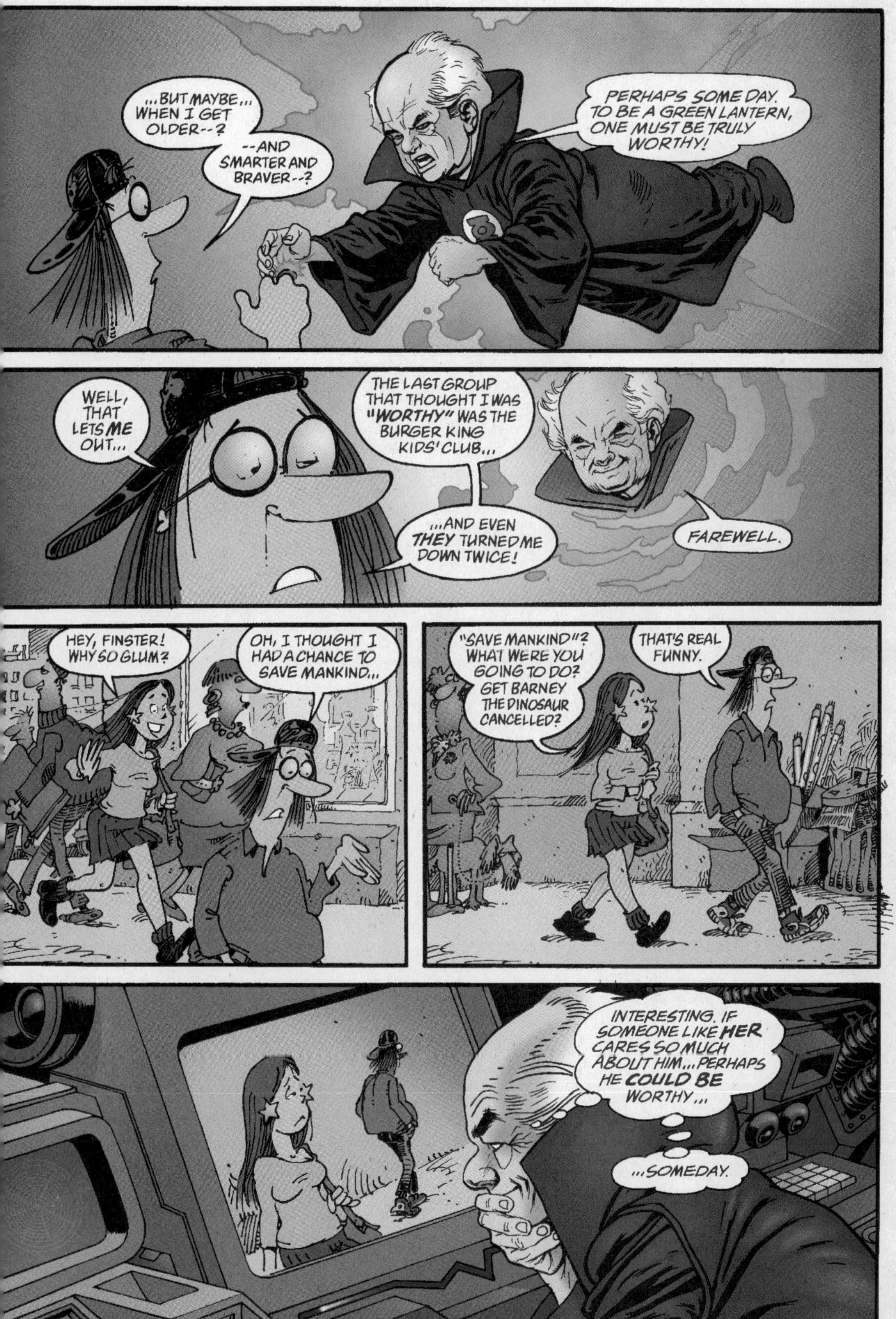
...BUT MAYBE... WHEN I GET OLDER--?
--AND SMARTER AND BRAVER--?
PERHAPS SOME DAY. TO BE A GREEN LANTERN, ONE MUST BE TRULY WORTHY!
WELL, THAT LETS ME OUT...
THE LAST GROUP THAT THOUGHT I WAS "WORTHY" WAS THE BURGER KING KIDS' CLUB...
...AND EVEN THEY TURNED ME DOWN TWICE!
FAREWELL.
HEY, FINSTER! WHY SO GLUM?
OH, I THOUGHT I HAD A CHANCE TO SAVE MANKIND...
"SAVE MANKIND"? WHAT WERE YOU GOING TO DO? GET BARNEY THE DINOSAUR CANCELLED?
THAT'S REAL FUNNY.
INTERESTING. IF SOMEONE LIKE HER CARES SO MUCH ABOUT HIM... PERHAPS HE COULD BE WORTHY...
...SOMEDAY.

By **MARK EVANIER** and **SERGIO ARAGONES**

(p.4 & 5) **DAVE GIBBONS** - PENCILS & INKS • **TODD KLEIN** - LETTERS
(p.7 & 8) **WENDY PINI** - PENCILS, **WILL BLYBERG** - INKS • **TOM LUTH** - COLORS
(p.14-19 & 22) **GIL KANE** - PENCILS, **KEVIN NOWLAN** - INKS • **TONY BEDARD** - EDITS

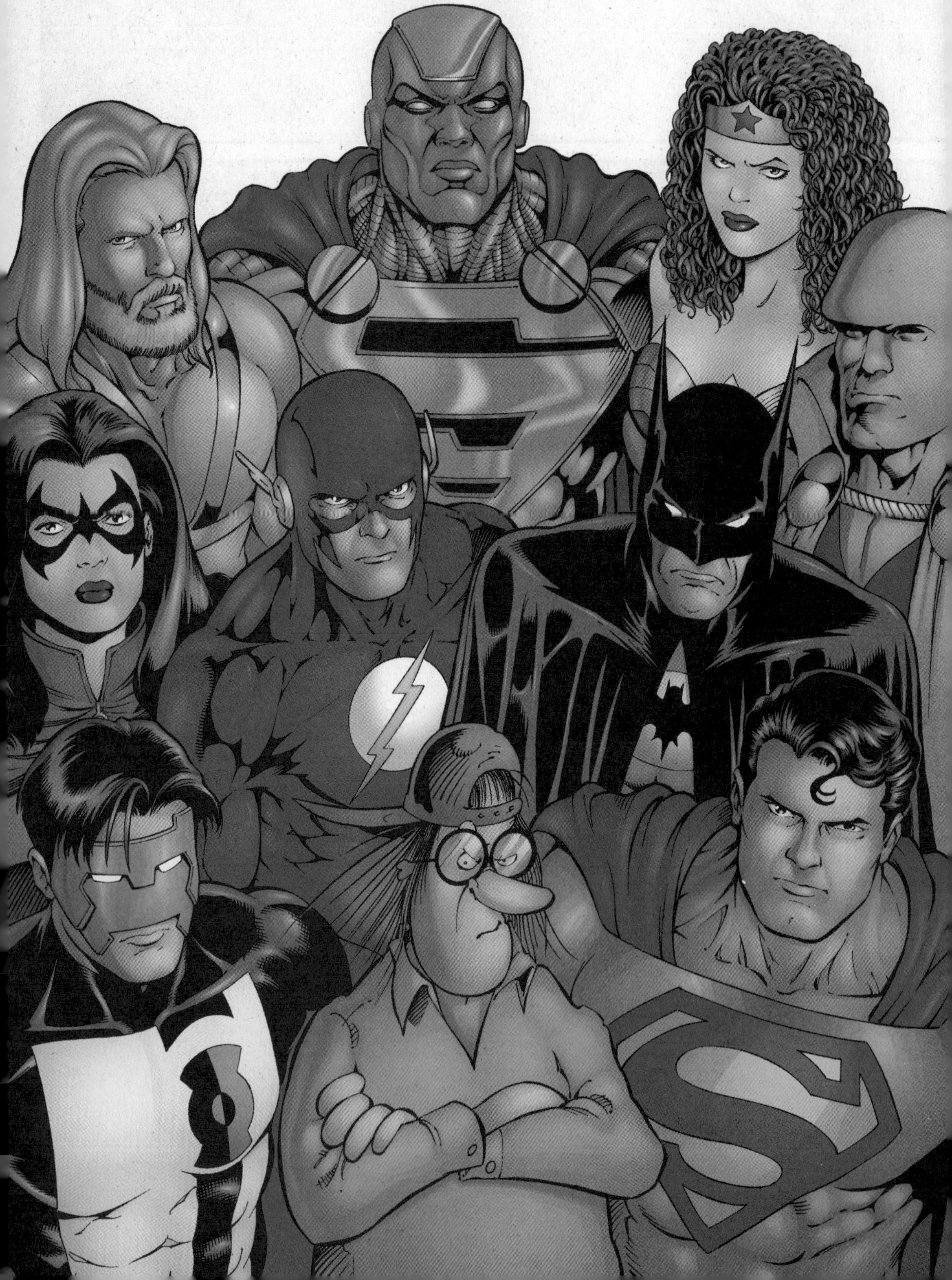

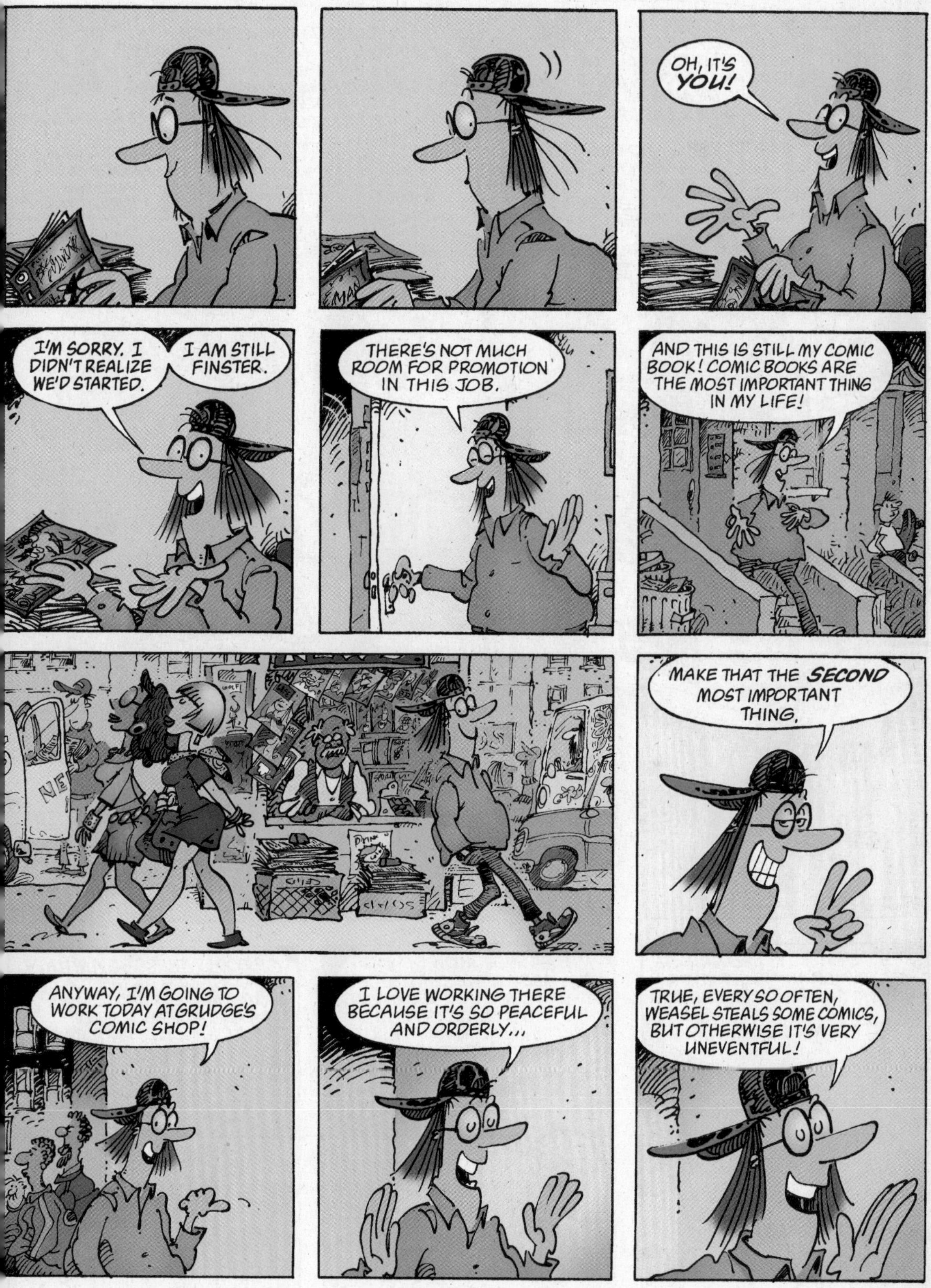

OH, IT'S YOU!
I'M SORRY. I DIDN'T REALIZE WE'D STARTED.
I AM STILL FINSTER.
THERE'S NOT MUCH ROOM FOR PROMOTION IN THIS JOB.
AND THIS IS STILL MY COMIC BOOK! COMIC BOOKS ARE THE MOST IMPORTANT THING IN MY LIFE!
MAKE THAT THE SECOND MOST IMPORTANT THING.
ANYWAY, I'M GOING TO WORK TODAY AT GRUDGE'S COMIC SHOP!
I LOVE WORKING THERE BECAUSE IT'S SO PEACEFUL AND ORDERLY...
TRUE, EVERY SO OFTEN, WEASEL STEALS SOME COMICS, BUT OTHERWISE IT'S VERY UNEVENTFUL!

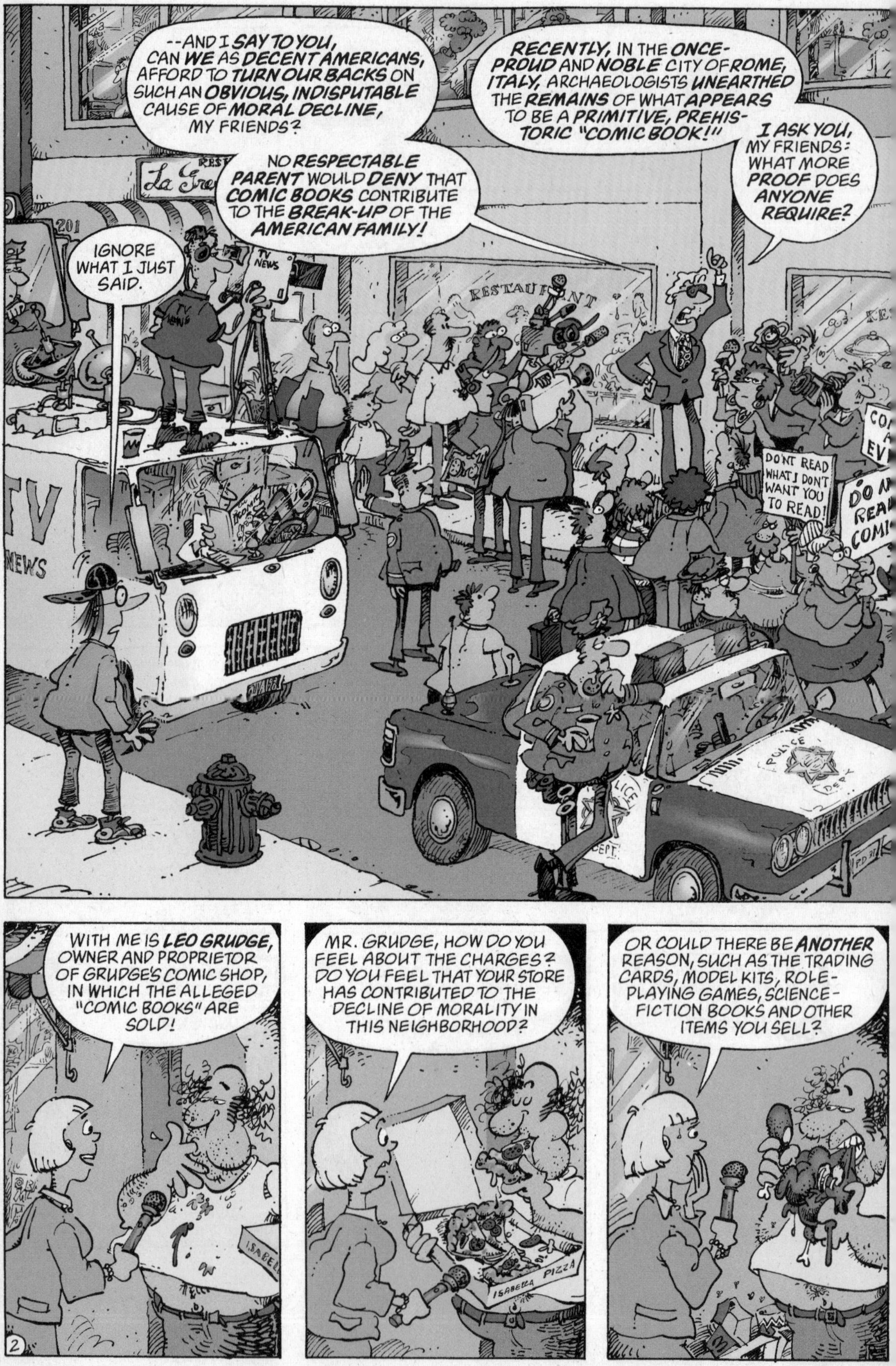
--AND I SAY TO YOU, CAN WE AS DECENT AMERICANS, AFFORD TO TURN OUR BACKS ON SUCH AN OBVIOUS, INDISPUTABLE CAUSE OF MORAL DECLINE, MY FRIENDS?
NO RESPECTABLE PARENT WOULD DENY THAT COMIC BOOKS CONTRIBUTE TO THE BREAK-UP OF THE AMERICAN FAMILY!
RECENTLY, IN THE ONCE-PROUD AND NOBLE CITY OF ROME, ITALY, ARCHAEOLOGISTS UNEARTHED THE REMAINS OF WHAT APPEARS TO BE A PRIMITIVE, PREHISTORIC "COMIC BOOK!"
I ASK YOU, MY FRIENDS: WHAT MORE PROOF DOES ANYONE REQUIRE?
IGNORE WHAT I JUST SAID.
TV NEWS
DON'T READ WHAT I DON'T WANT YOU TO READ!
POLICE DEPT.
WITH ME IS LEO GRUDGE, OWNER AND PROPRIETOR OF GRUDGE'S COMIC SHOP, IN WHICH THE ALLEGED "COMIC BOOKS" ARE SOLD!
MR. GRUDGE, HOW DO YOU FEEL ABOUT THE CHARGES? DO YOU FEEL THAT YOUR STORE HAS CONTRIBUTED TO THE DECLINE OF MORALITY IN THIS NEIGHBORHOOD?
ISABELLA PIZZA
OR COULD THERE BE ANOTHER REASON, SUCH AS THE TRADING CARDS, MODEL KITS, ROLE-PLAYING GAMES, SCIENCE-FICTION BOOKS AND OTHER ITEMS YOU SELL?

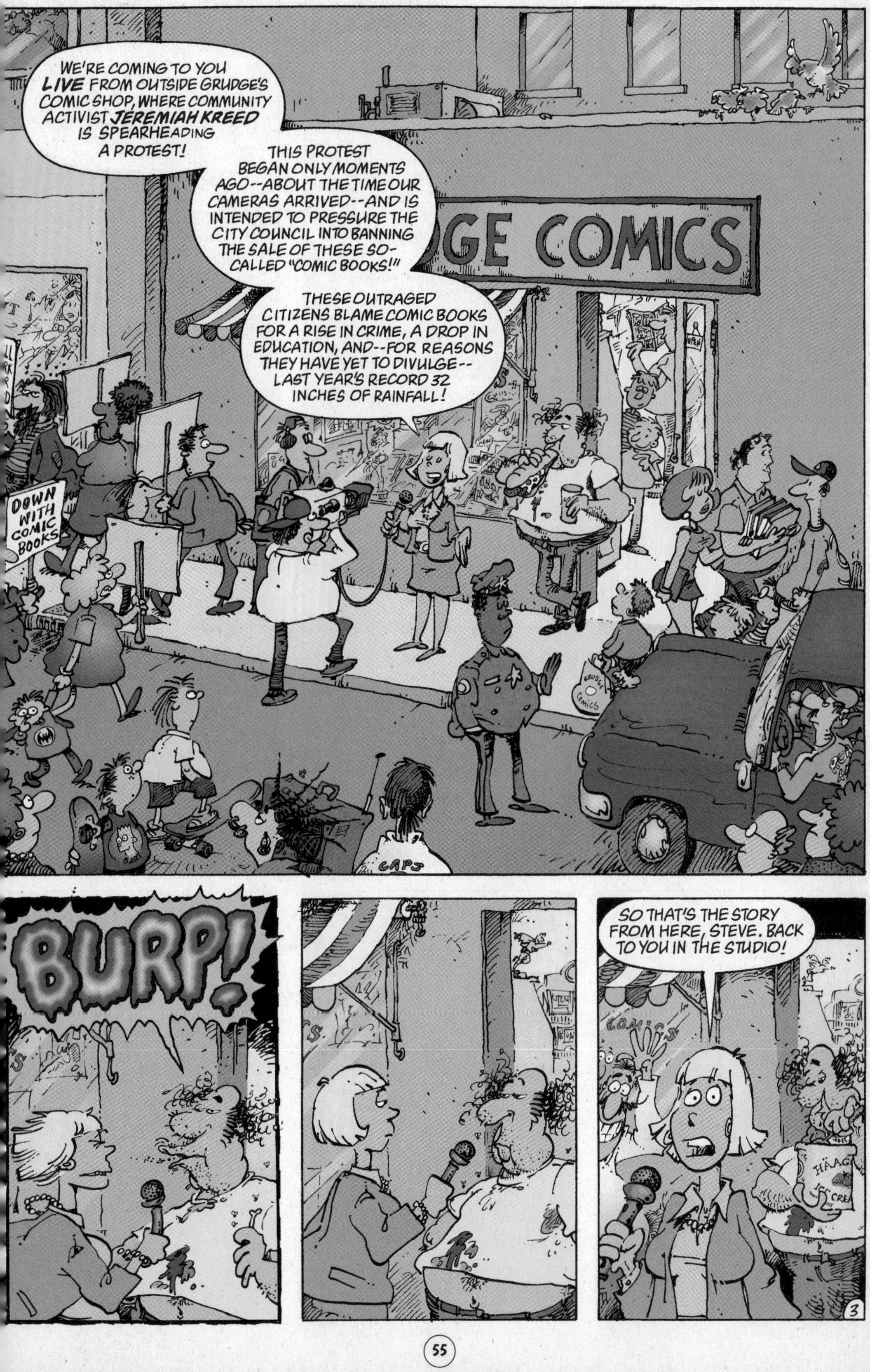
WE'RE COMING TO YOU LIVE FROM OUTSIDE GRUDGE'S COMIC SHOP, WHERE COMMUNITY ACTIVIST JEREMIAH KREED IS SPEARHEADING A PROTEST!
THIS PROTEST BEGAN ONLY MOMENTS AGO--ABOUT THE TIME OUR CAMERAS ARRIVED--AND IS INTENDED TO PRESSURE THE CITY COUNCIL INTO BANNING THE SALE OF THESE SO-CALLED "COMIC BOOKS!"
THESE OUTRAGED CITIZENS BLAME COMIC BOOKS FOR A RISE IN CRIME, A DROP IN EDUCATION, AND--FOR REASONS THEY HAVE YET TO DIVULGE--LAST YEAR'S RECORD 32 INCHES OF RAINFALL!
DOWN WITH COMIC BOOKS
BURP!
SO THAT'S THE STORY FROM HERE, STEVE. BACK TO YOU IN THE STUDIO!

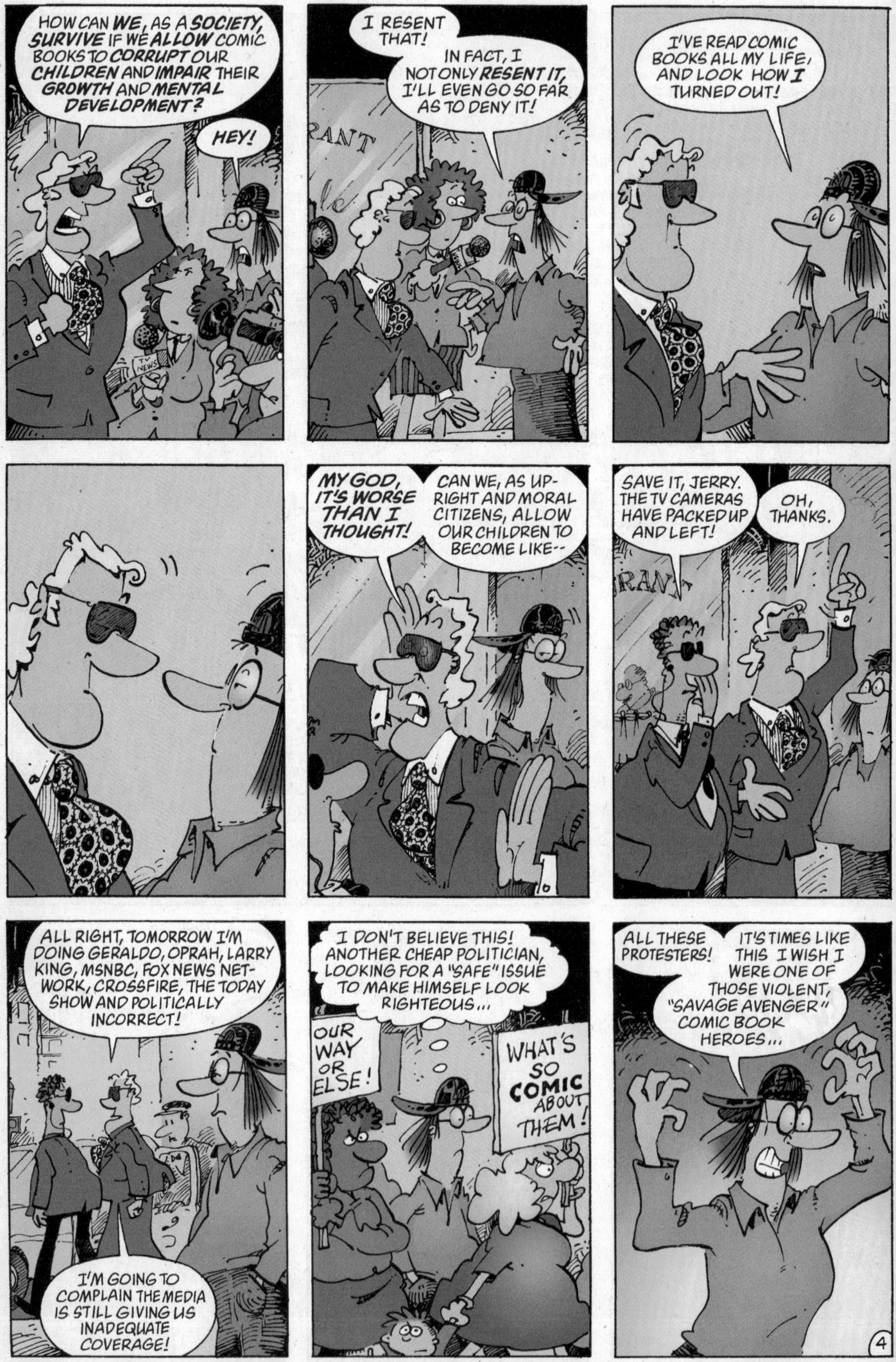
HOW CAN WE, AS A SOCIETY, SURVIVE IF WE ALLOW COMIC BOOKS TO CORRUPT OUR CHILDREN AND IMPAIR THEIR GROWTH AND MENTAL DEVELOPMENT?
HEY!
TV NEWS
I RESENT THAT!
IN FACT, I NOT ONLY RESENT IT, I'LL EVEN GO SO FAR AS TO DENY IT!
RANT
I'VE READ COMIC BOOKS ALL MY LIFE, AND LOOK HOW I TURNED OUT!
MY GOD, IT'S WORSE THAN I THOUGHT!
CAN WE, AS UP-RIGHT AND MORAL CITIZENS, ALLOW OUR CHILDREN TO BECOME LIKE--
SAVE IT, JERRY. THE TV CAMERAS HAVE PACKED UP AND LEFT!
OH, THANKS.
RANT
ALL RIGHT, TOMORROW I'M DOING GERALDO, OPRAH, LARRY KING, MSNBC, FOX NEWS NET-WORK, CROSSFIRE, THE TODAY SHOW AND POLITICALLY INCORRECT!
I'M GOING TO COMPLAIN THE MEDIA IS STILL GIVING US INADEQUATE COVERAGE!
I DON'T BELIEVE THIS! ANOTHER CHEAP POLITICIAN, LOOKING FOR A "SAFE" ISSUE TO MAKE HIMSELF LOOK RIGHTEOUS...
OUR WAY OR ELSE!
WHAT'S SO COMIC ABOUT THEM!
ALL THESE PROTESTERS!
IT'S TIMES LIKE THIS I WISH I WERE ONE OF THOSE VIOLENT, "SAVAGE AVENGER" COMIC BOOK HEROES...
4

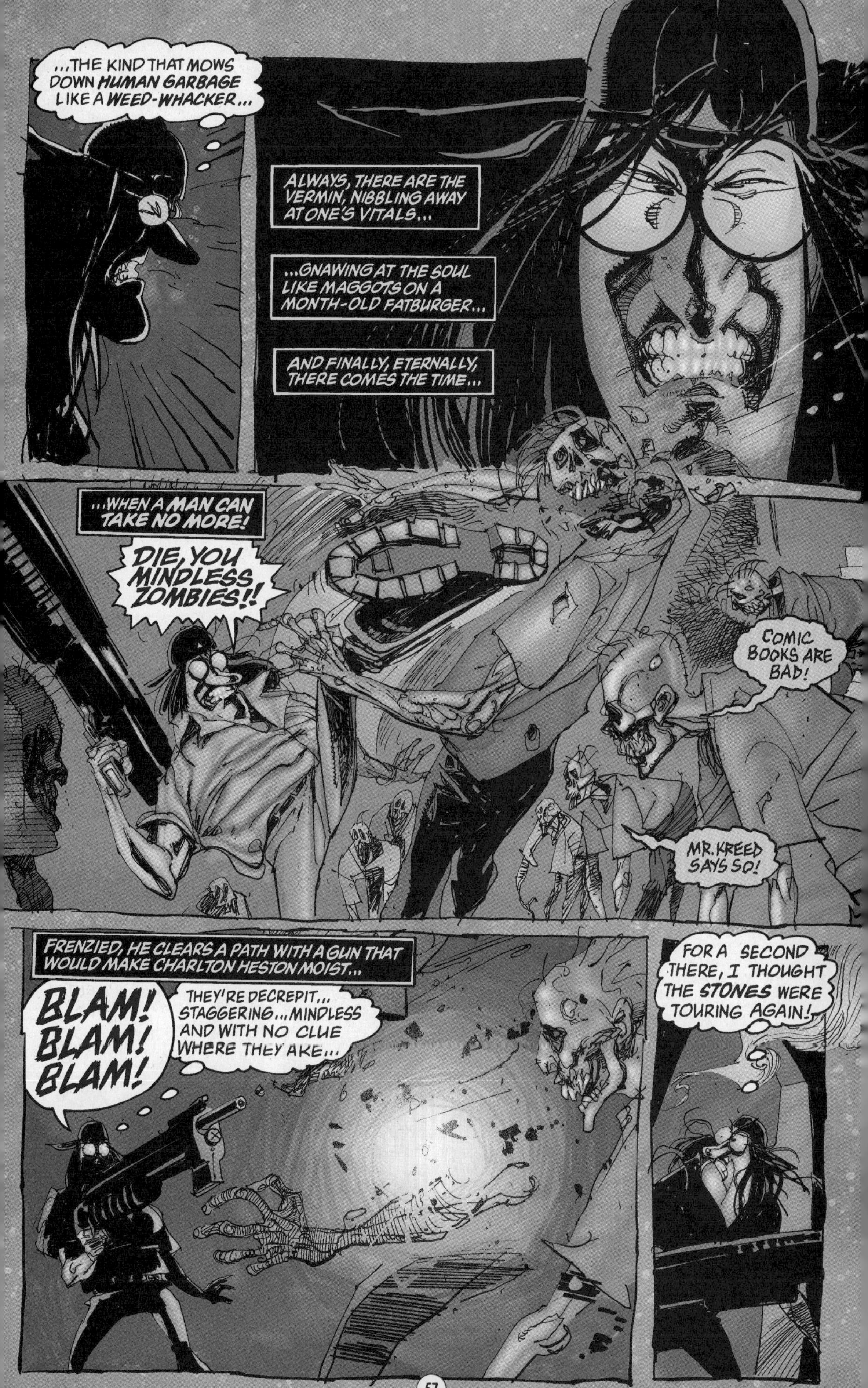

...THE KIND THAT MOWS DOWN HUMAN GARBAGE LIKE A WEED-WHACKER...
ALWAYS, THERE ARE THE VERMIN, NIBBLING AWAY AT ONE'S VITALS...
...GNAWING AT THE SOUL LIKE MAGGOTS ON A MONTH-OLD FATBURGER...
AND FINALLY, ETERNALLY, THERE COMES THE TIME...
...WHEN A MAN CAN TAKE NO MORE!
DIE, YOU MINDLESS ZOMBIES!!
COMIC BOOKS ARE BAD!
MR. KREED SAYS SO!
FRENZIED, HE CLEARS A PATH WITH A GUN THAT WOULD MAKE CHARLTON HESTON MOIST...
BLAM! BLAM! BLAM!
THEY'RE DECREPIT... STAGGERING... MINDLESS AND WITH NO CLUE WHERE THEY ARE...
FOR A SECOND THERE, I THOUGHT THE STONES WERE TOURING AGAIN!

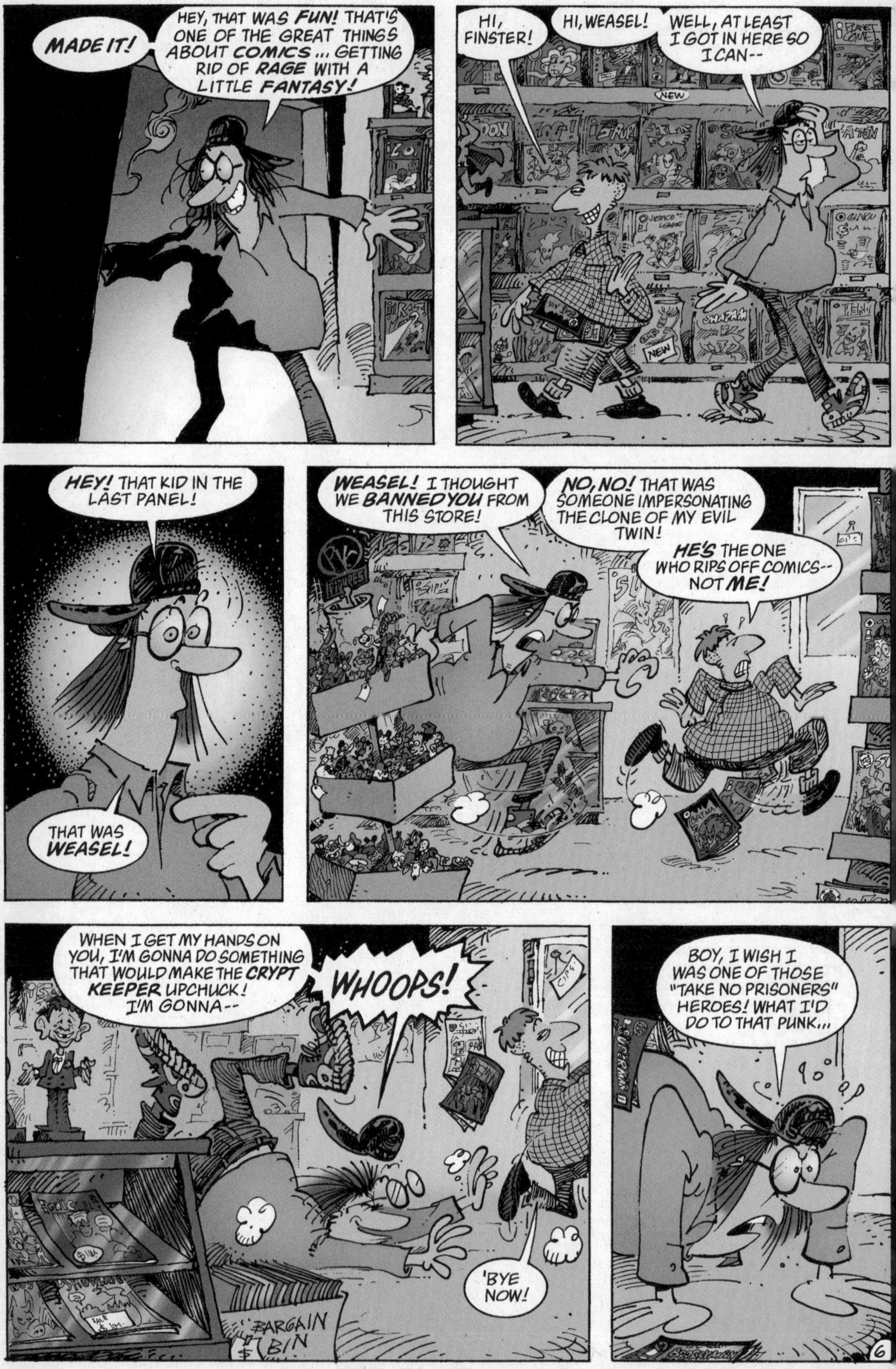
MADE IT!
HEY, THAT WAS FUN! THAT'S ONE OF THE GREAT THINGS ABOUT COMICS ... GETTING RID OF RAGE WITH A LITTLE FANTASY!
HI, FINSTER!
HI, WEASEL!
WELL, AT LEAST I GOT IN HERE SO I CAN--
HEY! THAT KID IN THE LAST PANEL!
THAT WAS WEASEL!
WEASEL! I THOUGHT WE BANNED YOU FROM THIS STORE!
NO, NO! THAT WAS SOMEONE IMPERSONATING THE CLONE OF MY EVIL TWIN!
HE'S THE ONE WHO RIPS OFF COMICS-- NOT ME!
WHEN I GET MY HANDS ON YOU, I'M GONNA DO SOMETHING THAT WOULD MAKE THE CRYPT KEEPER UPCHUCK! I'M GONNA--
WHOOPS!
'BYE NOW!
BARGAIN BIN
BOY, I WISH I WAS ONE OF THOSE "TAKE NO PRISONERS" HEROES! WHAT I'D DO TO THAT PUNK...
6

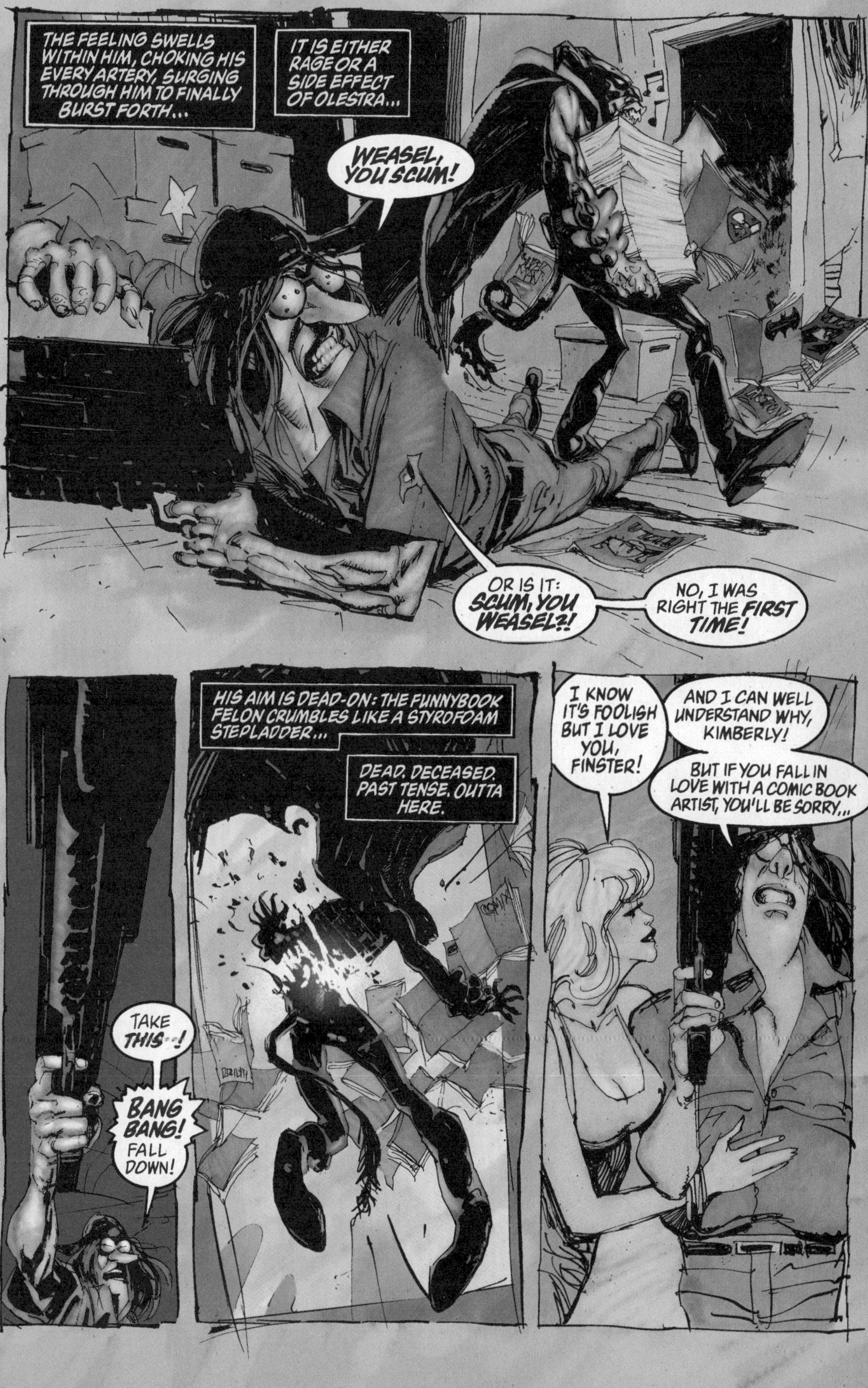
THE FEELING SWELLS WITHIN HIM, CHOKING HIS EVERY ARTERY, SURGING THROUGH HIM TO FINALLY BURST FORTH...
IT IS EITHER RAGE OR A SIDE EFFECT OF OLESTRA...
WEASEL, YOU SCUM!
OR IS IT: SCUM, YOU WEASEL?!
NO, I WAS RIGHT THE FIRST TIME!
TAKE THIS--!
BANG BANG! FALL DOWN!
HIS AIM IS DEAD-ON: THE FUNNYBOOK FELON CRUMBLES LIKE A STYROFOAM STEPLADDER...
DEAD. DECEASED. PAST TENSE. OUTTA HERE.
I KNOW IT'S FOOLISH BUT I LOVE YOU, FINSTER!
AND I CAN WELL UNDERSTAND WHY, KIMBERLY!
BUT IF YOU FALL IN LOVE WITH A COMIC BOOK ARTIST, YOU'LL BE SORRY...

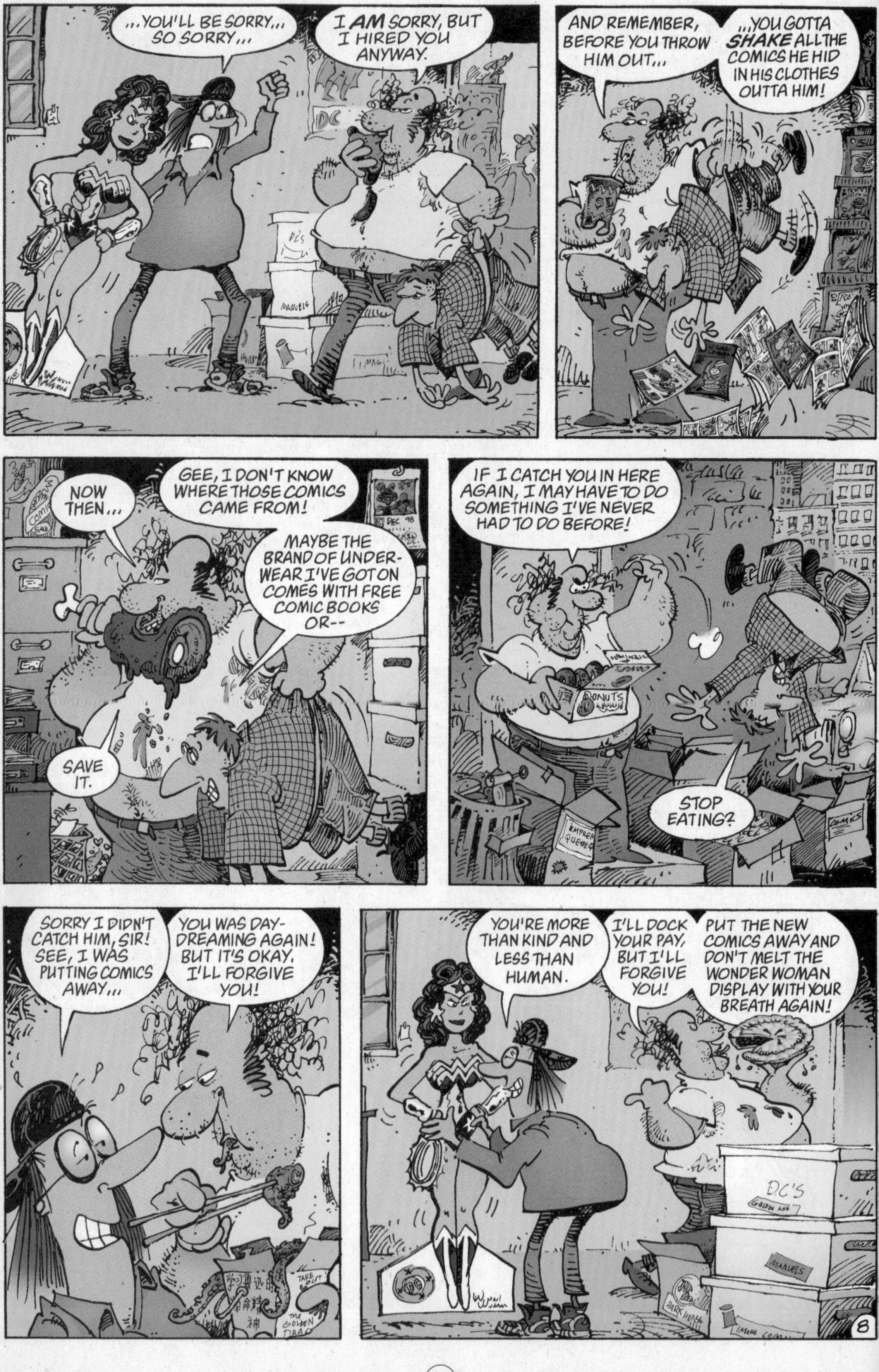
...YOU'LL BE SORRY... SO SORRY...
I AM SORRY, BUT I HIRED YOU ANYWAY.
DC
AND REMEMBER, BEFORE YOU THROW HIM OUT...
...YOU GOTTA SHAKE ALL THE COMICS HE HID IN HIS CLOTHES OUTTA HIM!
NOW THEN...
GEE, I DON'T KNOW WHERE THOSE COMICS CAME FROM!
MAYBE THE BRAND OF UNDER-WEAR I'VE GOT ON COMES WITH FREE COMIC BOOKS OR--
SAVE IT.
IF I CATCH YOU IN HERE AGAIN, I MAY HAVE TO DO SOMETHING I'VE NEVER HAD TO DO BEFORE!
DONUTS
STOP EATING?
SORRY I DIDN'T CATCH HIM, SIR! SEE, I WAS PUTTING COMICS AWAY...
YOU WAS DAY-DREAMING AGAIN! BUT IT'S OKAY. I'LL FORGIVE YOU!
TAKE OUT
THE GOLDEN DRAG
YOU'RE MORE THAN KIND AND LESS THAN HUMAN.
I'LL DOCK YOUR PAY, BUT I'LL FORGIVE YOU!
PUT THE NEW COMICS AWAY AND DON'T MELT THE WONDER WOMAN DISPLAY WITH YOUR BREATH AGAIN!
DC'S
MARVELS
DARK HORSE
8

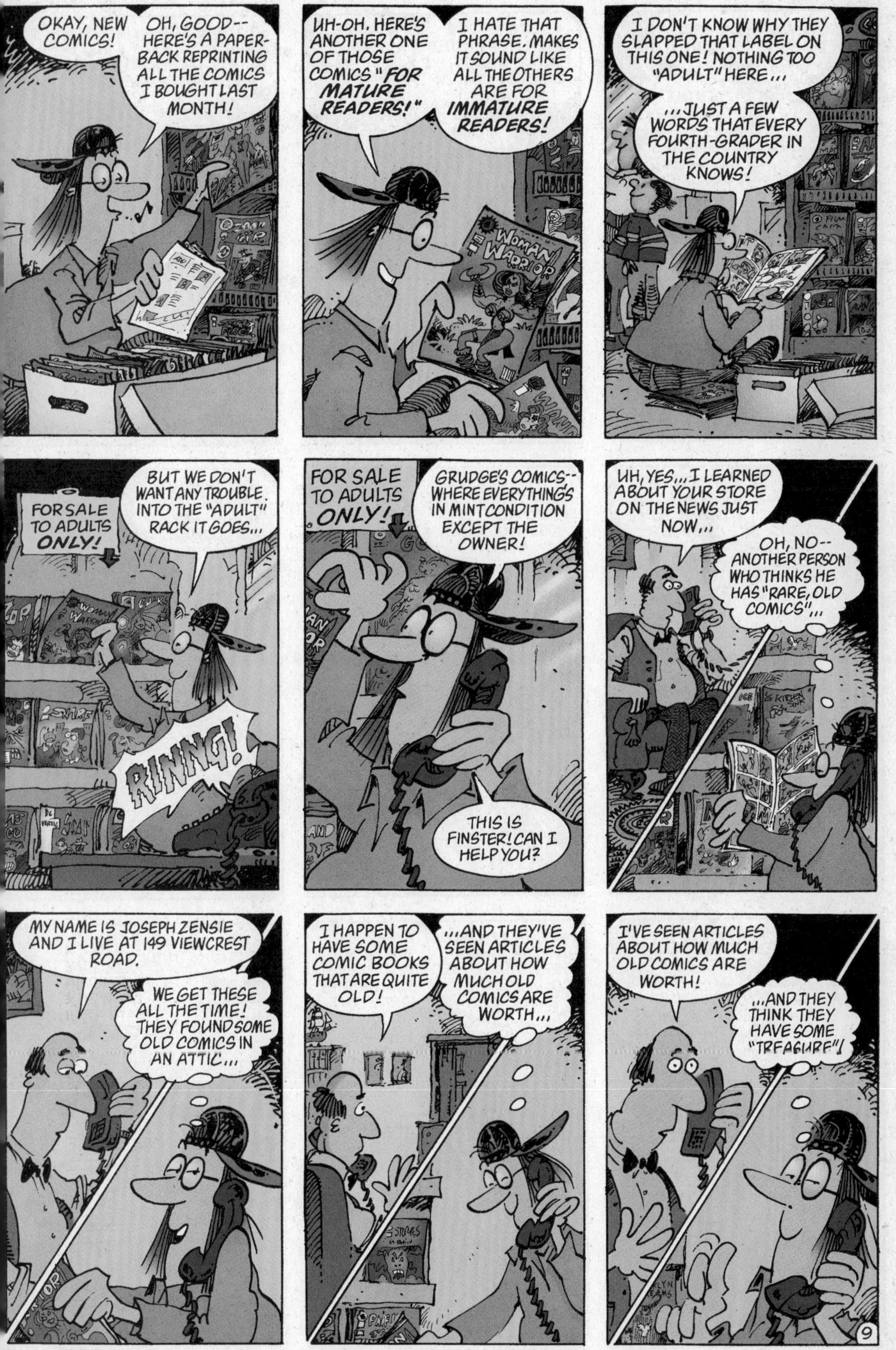
OKAY, NEW COMICS!
OH, GOOD-- HERE'S A PAPER-BACK REPRINTING ALL THE COMICS I BOUGHT LAST MONTH!
UH-OH. HERE'S ANOTHER ONE OF THOSE COMICS "FOR MATURE READERS!"
I HATE THAT PHRASE. MAKES IT SOUND LIKE ALL THE OTHERS ARE FOR IMMATURE READERS!
WOMAN WARRIOR
I DON'T KNOW WHY THEY SLAPPED THAT LABEL ON THIS ONE! NOTHING TOO "ADULT" HERE...
...JUST A FEW WORDS THAT EVERY FOURTH-GRADER IN THE COUNTRY KNOWS!
FOR SALE TO ADULTS ONLY!
BUT WE DON'T WANT ANY TROUBLE. INTO THE "ADULT" RACK IT GOES...
RINNG!
FOR SALE TO ADULTS ONLY!
GRUDGE'S COMICS-- WHERE EVERYTHING'S IN MINT CONDITION EXCEPT THE OWNER!
THIS IS FINSTER! CAN I HELP YOU?
UH, YES... I LEARNED ABOUT YOUR STORE ON THE NEWS JUST NOW...
OH, NO-- ANOTHER PERSON WHO THINKS HE HAS "RARE, OLD COMICS"...
MY NAME IS JOSEPH ZENSIE AND I LIVE AT 149 VIEWCREST ROAD.
WE GET THESE ALL THE TIME! THEY FOUND SOME OLD COMICS IN AN ATTIC...
I HAPPEN TO HAVE SOME COMIC BOOKS THAT ARE QUITE OLD!
...AND THEY'VE SEEN ARTICLES ABOUT HOW MUCH OLD COMICS ARE WORTH...
I'VE SEEN ARTICLES ABOUT HOW MUCH OLD COMICS ARE WORTH!
...AND THEY THINK THEY HAVE SOME "TREASURE"!
9

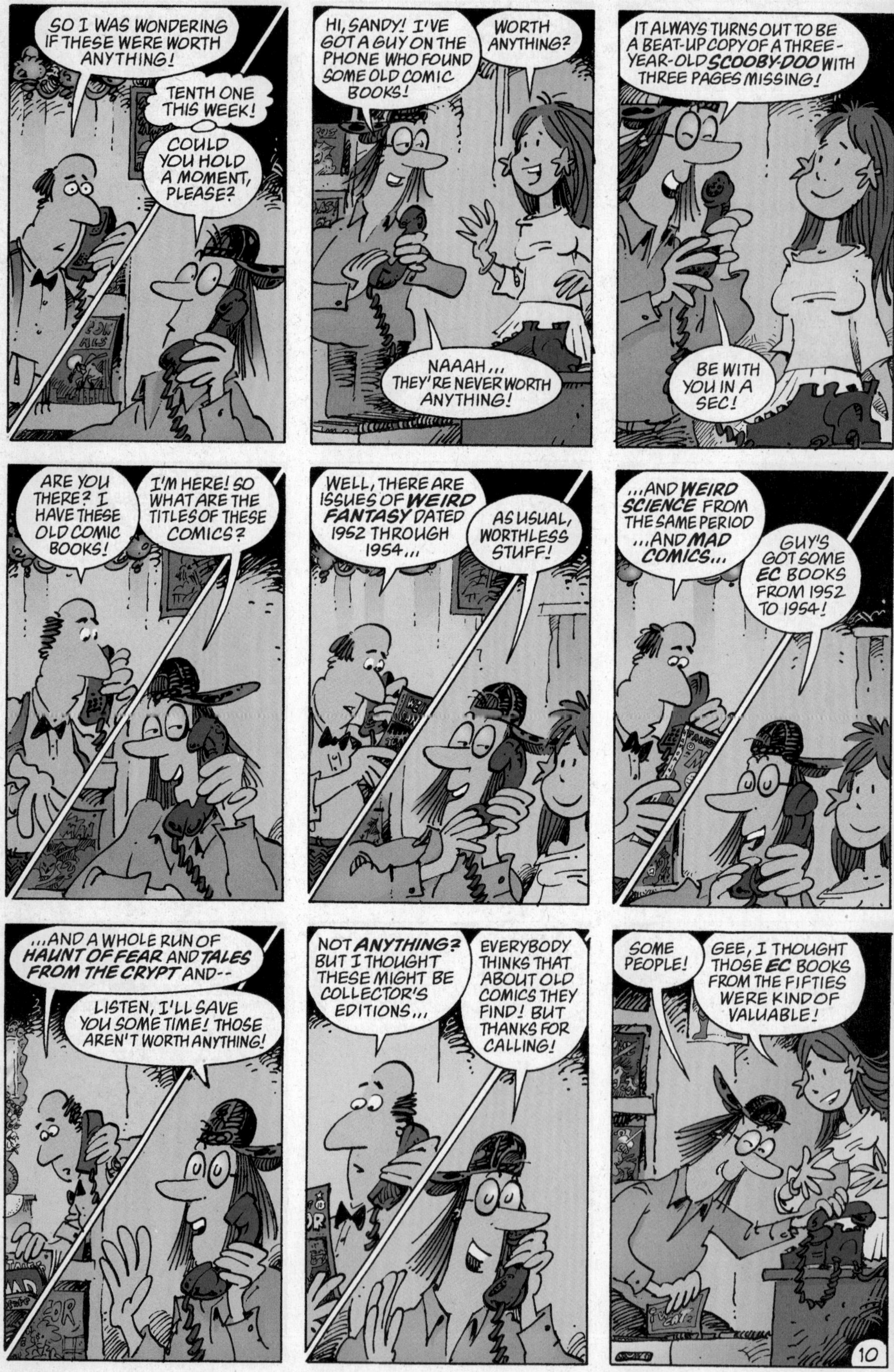
SO I WAS WONDERING IF THESE WERE WORTH ANYTHING!
TENTH ONE THIS WEEK!
COULD YOU HOLD A MOMENT, PLEASE?
HI, SANDY! I'VE GOT A GUY ON THE PHONE WHO FOUND SOME OLD COMIC BOOKS!
WORTH ANYTHING?
NAAAH... THEY'RE NEVER WORTH ANYTHING!
IT ALWAYS TURNS OUT TO BE A BEAT-UP COPY OF A THREE-YEAR-OLD SCOOBY-DOO WITH THREE PAGES MISSING!
BE WITH YOU IN A SEC!
ARE YOU THERE? I HAVE THESE OLD COMIC BOOKS!
I'M HERE! SO WHAT ARE THE TITLES OF THESE COMICS?
WELL, THERE ARE ISSUES OF WEIRD FANTASY DATED 1952 THROUGH 1954...
AS USUAL, WORTHLESS STUFF!
...AND WEIRD SCIENCE FROM THE SAME PERIOD ...AND MAD COMICS...
GUY'S GOT SOME EC BOOKS FROM 1952 TO 1954!
...AND A WHOLE RUN OF HAUNT OF FEAR AND TALES FROM THE CRYPT AND--
LISTEN, I'LL SAVE YOU SOME TIME! THOSE AREN'T WORTH ANYTHING!
NOT ANYTHING? BUT I THOUGHT THESE MIGHT BE COLLECTOR'S EDITIONS...
EVERYBODY THINKS THAT ABOUT OLD COMICS THEY FIND! BUT THANKS FOR CALLING!
SOME PEOPLE!
GEE, I THOUGHT THOSE EC BOOKS FROM THE FIFTIES WERE KIND OF VALUABLE!
10

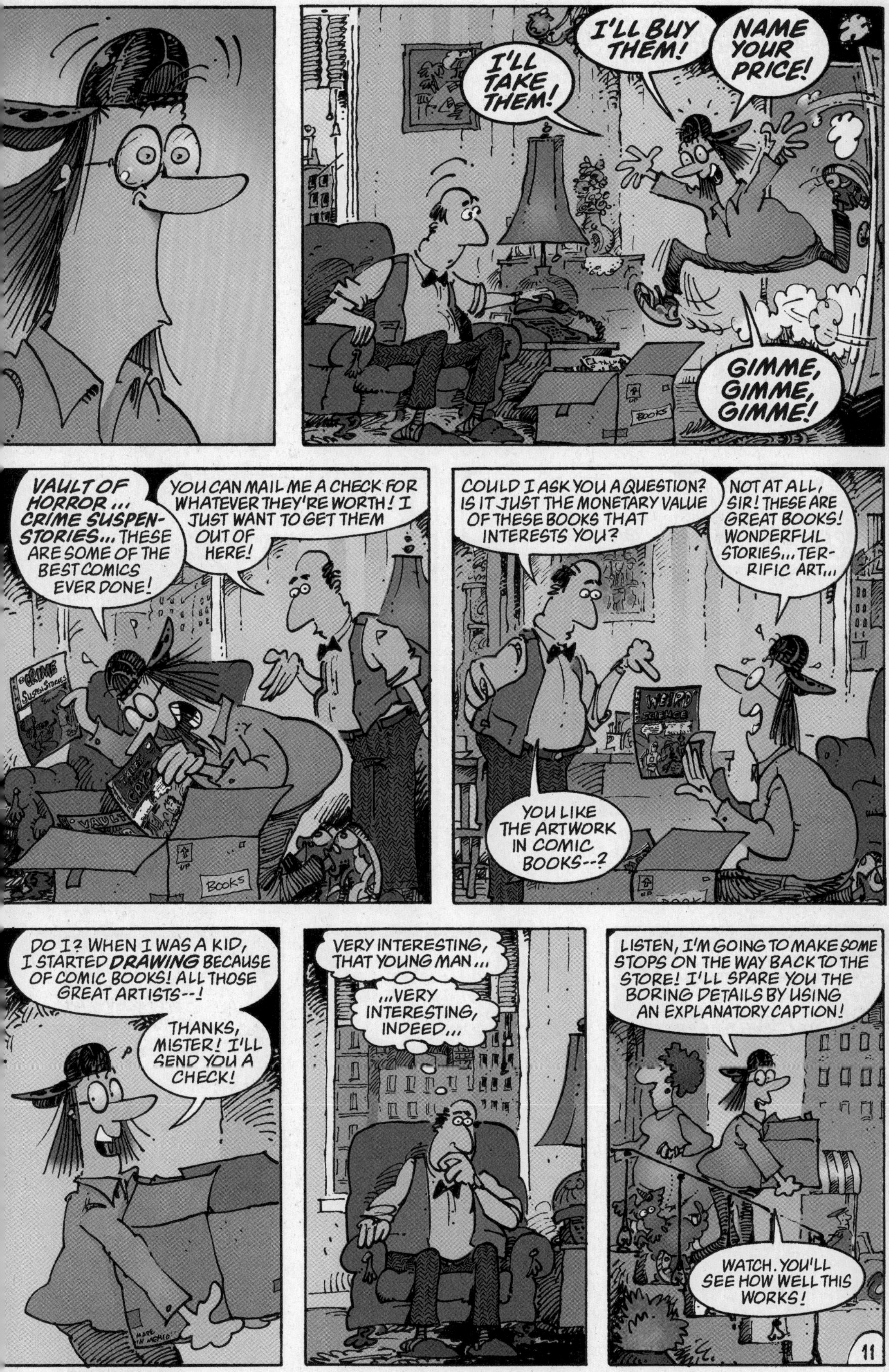
I'LL TAKE THEM!
I'LL BUY THEM!
NAME YOUR PRICE!
GIMME, GIMME, GIMME!
VAULT OF HORROR... CRIME SUSPENSTORIES... THESE ARE SOME OF THE BEST COMICS EVER DONE!
YOU CAN MAIL ME A CHECK FOR WHATEVER THEY'RE WORTH! I JUST WANT TO GET THEM OUT OF HERE!
BOOKS
COULD I ASK YOU A QUESTION? IS IT JUST THE MONETARY VALUE OF THESE BOOKS THAT INTERESTS YOU?
NOT AT ALL, SIR! THESE ARE GREAT BOOKS! WONDERFUL STORIES... TERRIFIC ART...
YOU LIKE THE ARTWORK IN COMIC BOOKS--?
DO I? WHEN I WAS A KID, I STARTED DRAWING BECAUSE OF COMIC BOOKS! ALL THOSE GREAT ARTISTS--!
THANKS, MISTER! I'LL SEND YOU A CHECK!
VERY INTERESTING, THAT YOUNG MAN...
...VERY INTERESTING, INDEED...
LISTEN, I'M GOING TO MAKE SOME STOPS ON THE WAY BACK TO THE STORE! I'LL SPARE YOU THE BORING DETAILS BY USING AN EXPLANATORY CAPTION!
WATCH. YOU'LL SEE HOW WELL THIS WORKS!
11

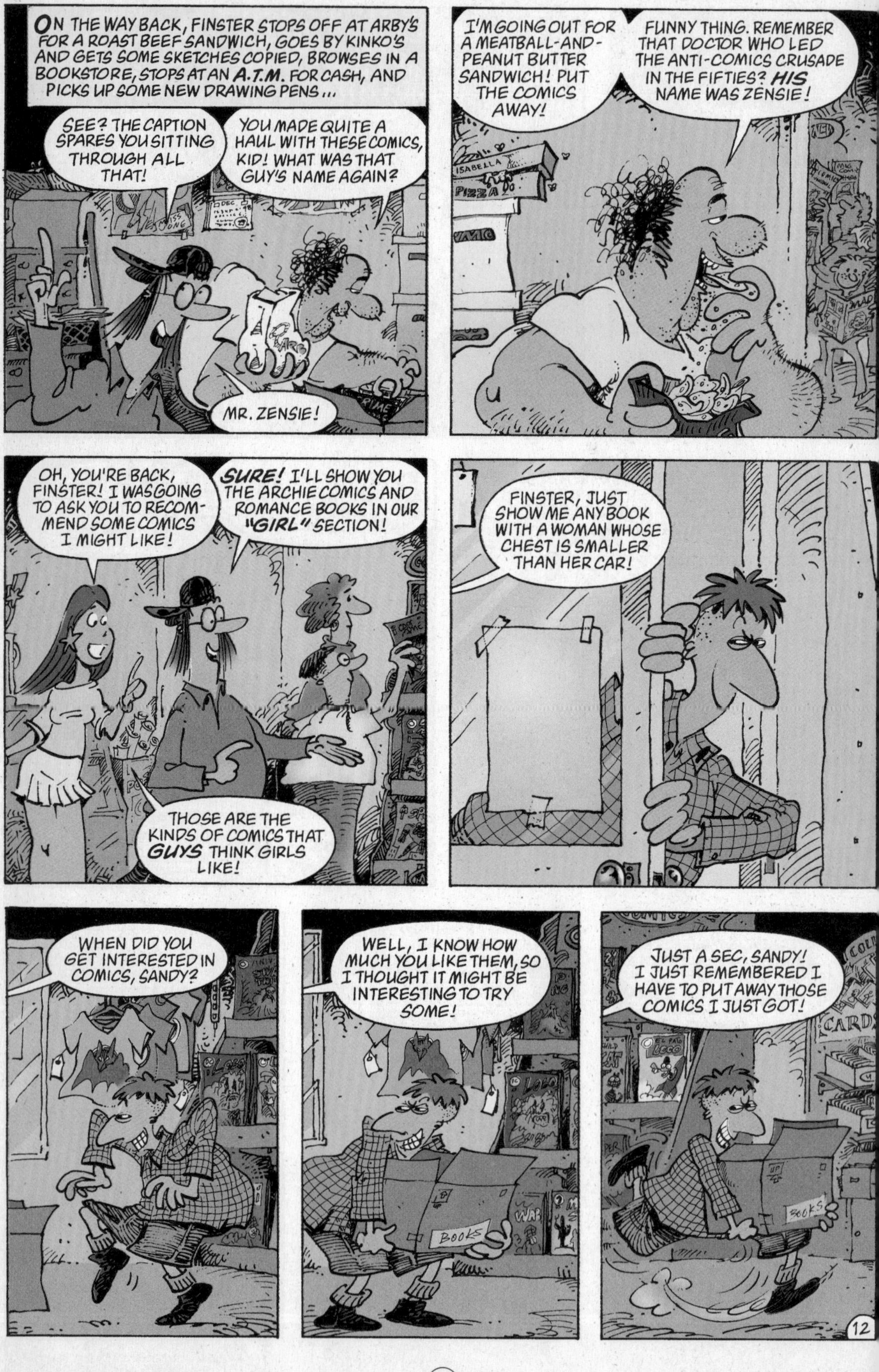
ON THE WAY BACK, FINSTER STOPS OFF AT ARBY'S FOR A ROAST BEEF SANDWICH, GOES BY KINKO'S AND GETS SOME SKETCHES COPIED, BROWSES IN A BOOKSTORE, STOPS AT AN A.T.M. FOR CASH, AND PICKS UP SOME NEW DRAWING PENS...
SEE? THE CAPTION SPARES YOU SITTING THROUGH ALL THAT!
YOU MADE QUITE A HAUL WITH THESE COMICS, KID! WHAT WAS THAT GUY'S NAME AGAIN?
MR. ZENSIE!
I'M GOING OUT FOR A MEATBALL-AND-PEANUT BUTTER SANDWICH! PUT THE COMICS AWAY!
FUNNY THING. REMEMBER THAT DOCTOR WHO LED THE ANTI-COMICS CRUSADE IN THE FIFTIES? HIS NAME WAS ZENSIE!
ISABELLA PIZZA
OH, YOU'RE BACK, FINSTER! I WAS GOING TO ASK YOU TO RECOMMEND SOME COMICS I MIGHT LIKE!
SURE! I'LL SHOW YOU THE ARCHIE COMICS AND ROMANCE BOOKS IN OUR "GIRL" SECTION!
THOSE ARE THE KINDS OF COMICS THAT GUYS THINK GIRLS LIKE!
FINSTER, JUST SHOW ME ANY BOOK WITH A WOMAN WHOSE CHEST IS SMALLER THAN HER CAR!
WHEN DID YOU GET INTERESTED IN COMICS, SANDY?
WELL, I KNOW HOW MUCH YOU LIKE THEM, SO I THOUGHT IT MIGHT BE INTERESTING TO TRY SOME!
BOOKS
JUST A SEC, SANDY! I JUST REMEMBERED I HAVE TO PUT AWAY THOSE COMICS I JUST GOT!
CARDS
BOOKS
12

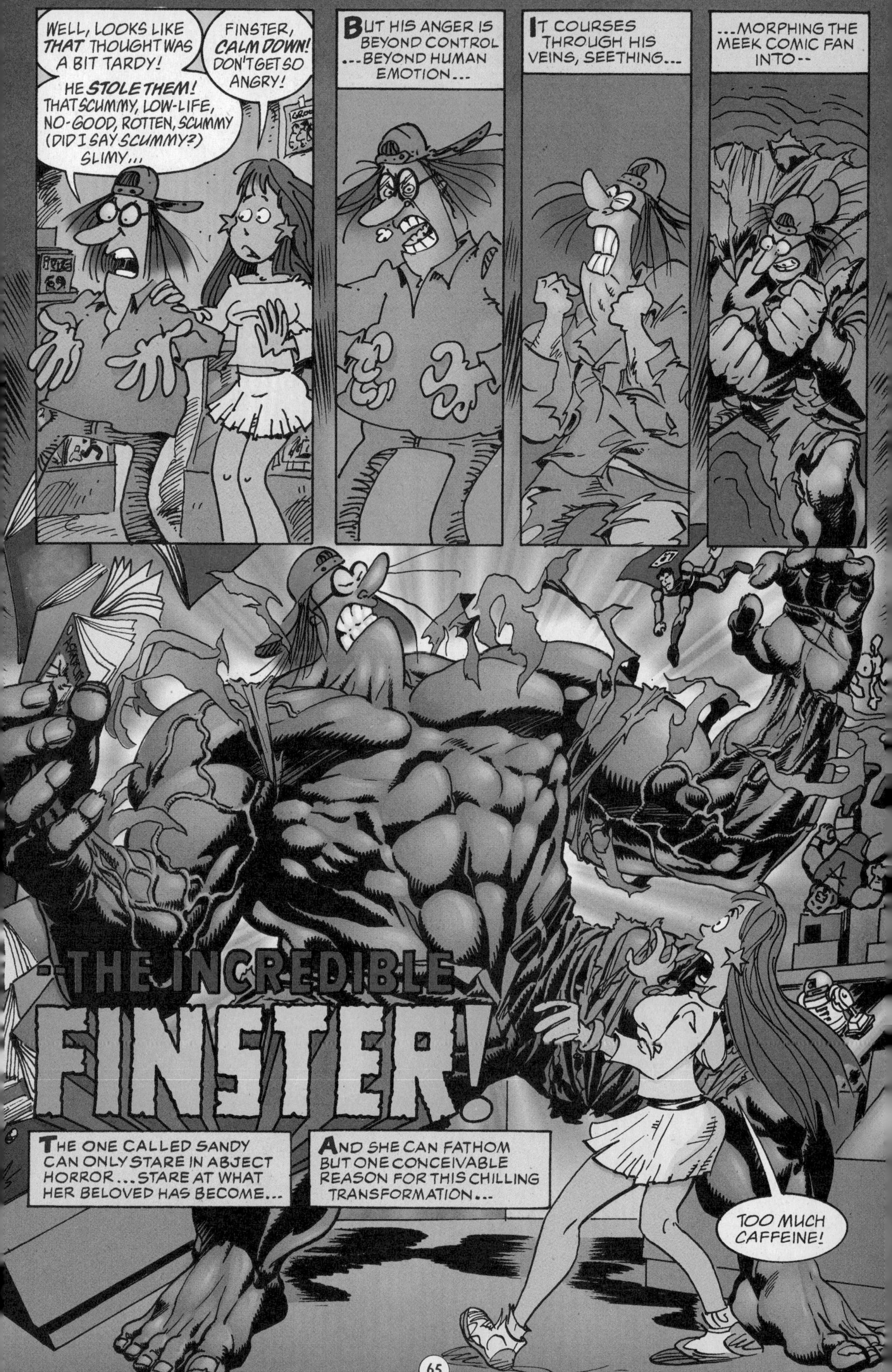

WELL, LOOKS LIKE THAT THOUGHT WAS A BIT TARDY!
HE STOLE THEM! THAT SCUMMY, LOW-LIFE, NO-GOOD, ROTTEN, SCUMMY (DID I SAY SCUMMY?) SLIMY...
FINSTER, CALM DOWN! DON'T GET SO ANGRY!
BUT HIS ANGER IS BEYOND CONTROL ...BEYOND HUMAN EMOTION...
IT COURSES THROUGH HIS VEINS, SEETHING...
...MORPHING THE MEEK COMIC FAN INTO--
--THE INCREDIBLE
FINSTER!
THE ONE CALLED SANDY CAN ONLY STARE IN ABJECT HORROR ... STARE AT WHAT HER BELOVED HAS BECOME...
AND SHE CAN FATHOM BUT ONE CONCEIVABLE REASON FOR THIS CHILLING TRANSFORMATION...
TOO MUCH CAFFEINE!

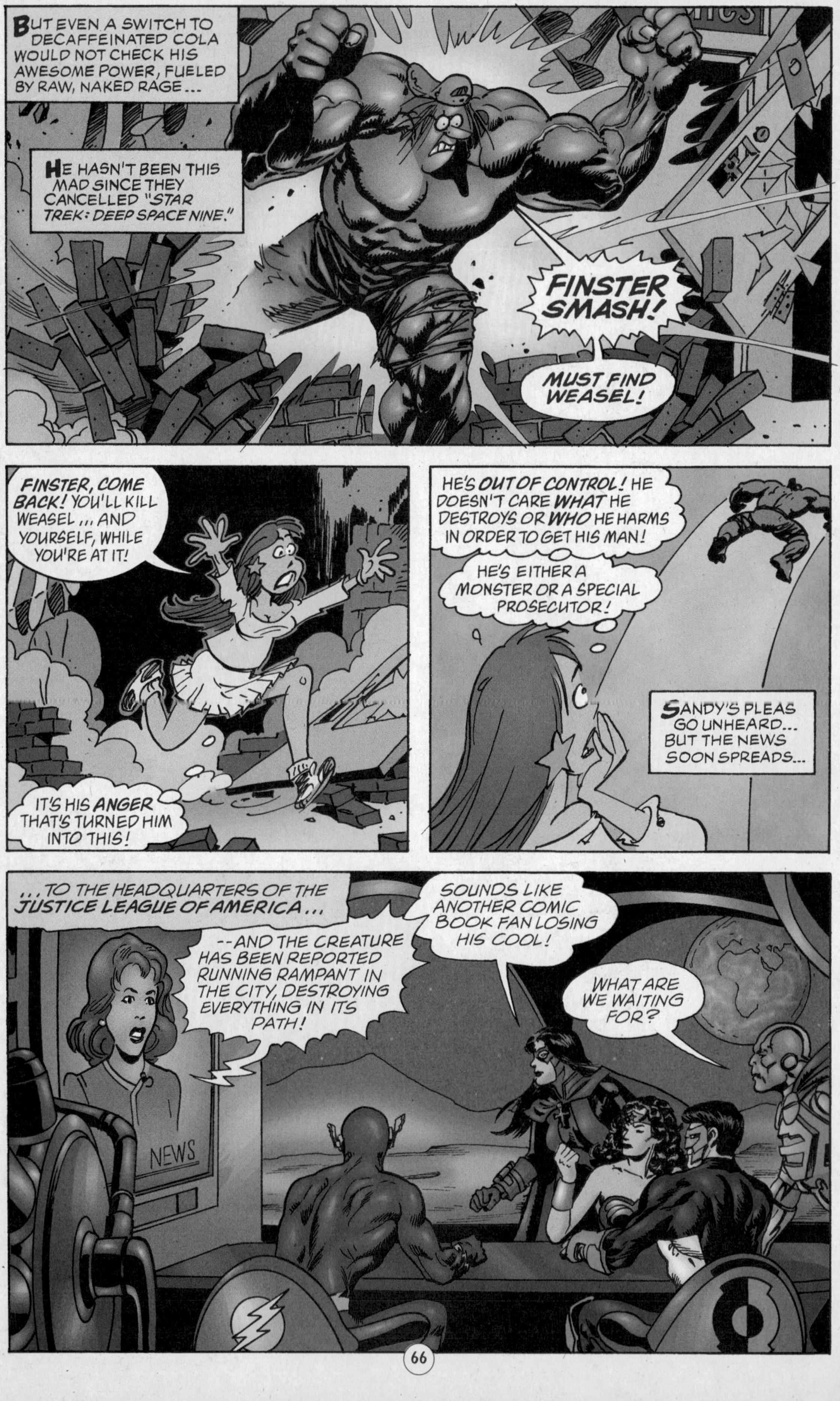

BUT EVEN A SWITCH TO DECAFFEINATED COLA WOULD NOT CHECK HIS AWESOME POWER, FUELED BY RAW, NAKED RAGE...
HE HASN'T BEEN THIS MAD SINCE THEY CANCELLED "STAR TREK: DEEP SPACE NINE."
FINSTER SMASH!
MUST FIND WEASEL!
FINSTER, COME BACK! YOU'LL KILL WEASEL ... AND YOURSELF, WHILE YOU'RE AT IT!
IT'S HIS ANGER THAT'S TURNED HIM INTO THIS!
HE'S OUT OF CONTROL! HE DOESN'T CARE WHAT HE DESTROYS OR WHO HE HARMS IN ORDER TO GET HIS MAN!
HE'S EITHER A MONSTER OR A SPECIAL PROSECUTOR!
SANDY'S PLEAS GO UNHEARD... BUT THE NEWS SOON SPREADS...
...TO THE HEADQUARTERS OF THE JUSTICE LEAGUE OF AMERICA...
--AND THE CREATURE HAS BEEN REPORTED RUNNING RAMPANT IN THE CITY, DESTROYING EVERYTHING IN ITS PATH!
NEWS
SOUNDS LIKE ANOTHER COMIC BOOK FAN LOSING HIS COOL!
WHAT ARE WE WAITING FOR?

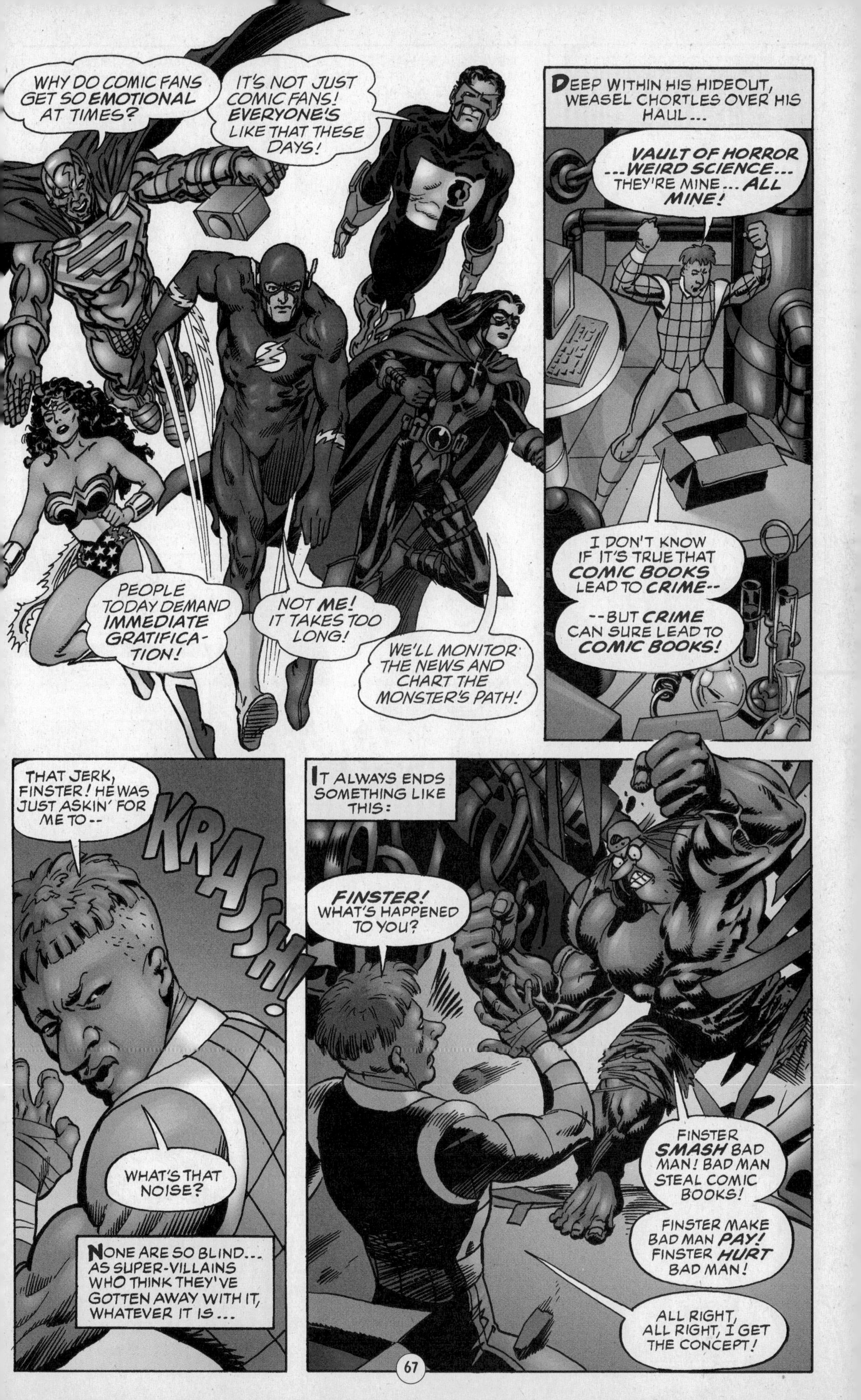
WHY DO COMIC FANS GET SO EMOTIONAL AT TIMES?
IT'S NOT JUST COMIC FANS! EVERYONE'S LIKE THAT THESE DAYS!
PEOPLE TODAY DEMAND IMMEDIATE GRATIFICA-TION!
NOT ME! IT TAKES TOO LONG!
WE'LL MONITOR THE NEWS AND CHART THE MONSTER'S PATH!
DEEP WITHIN HIS HIDEOUT, WEASEL CHORTLES OVER HIS HAUL...
VAULT OF HORROR ...WEIRD SCIENCE... THEY'RE MINE... ALL MINE!
I DON'T KNOW IF IT'S TRUE THAT COMIC BOOKS LEAD TO CRIME--
--BUT CRIME CAN SURE LEAD TO COMIC BOOKS!
THAT JERK, FINSTER! HE WAS JUST ASKIN' FOR ME TO--
KRASSH!
WHAT'S THAT NOISE?
NONE ARE SO BLIND... AS SUPER-VILLAINS WHO THINK THEY'VE GOTTEN AWAY WITH IT, WHATEVER IT IS...
IT ALWAYS ENDS SOMETHING LIKE THIS:
FINSTER! WHAT'S HAPPENED TO YOU?
FINSTER SMASH BAD MAN! BAD MAN STEAL COMIC BOOKS!
FINSTER MAKE BAD MAN PAY! FINSTER HURT BAD MAN!
ALL RIGHT, ALL RIGHT, I GET THE CONCEPT!

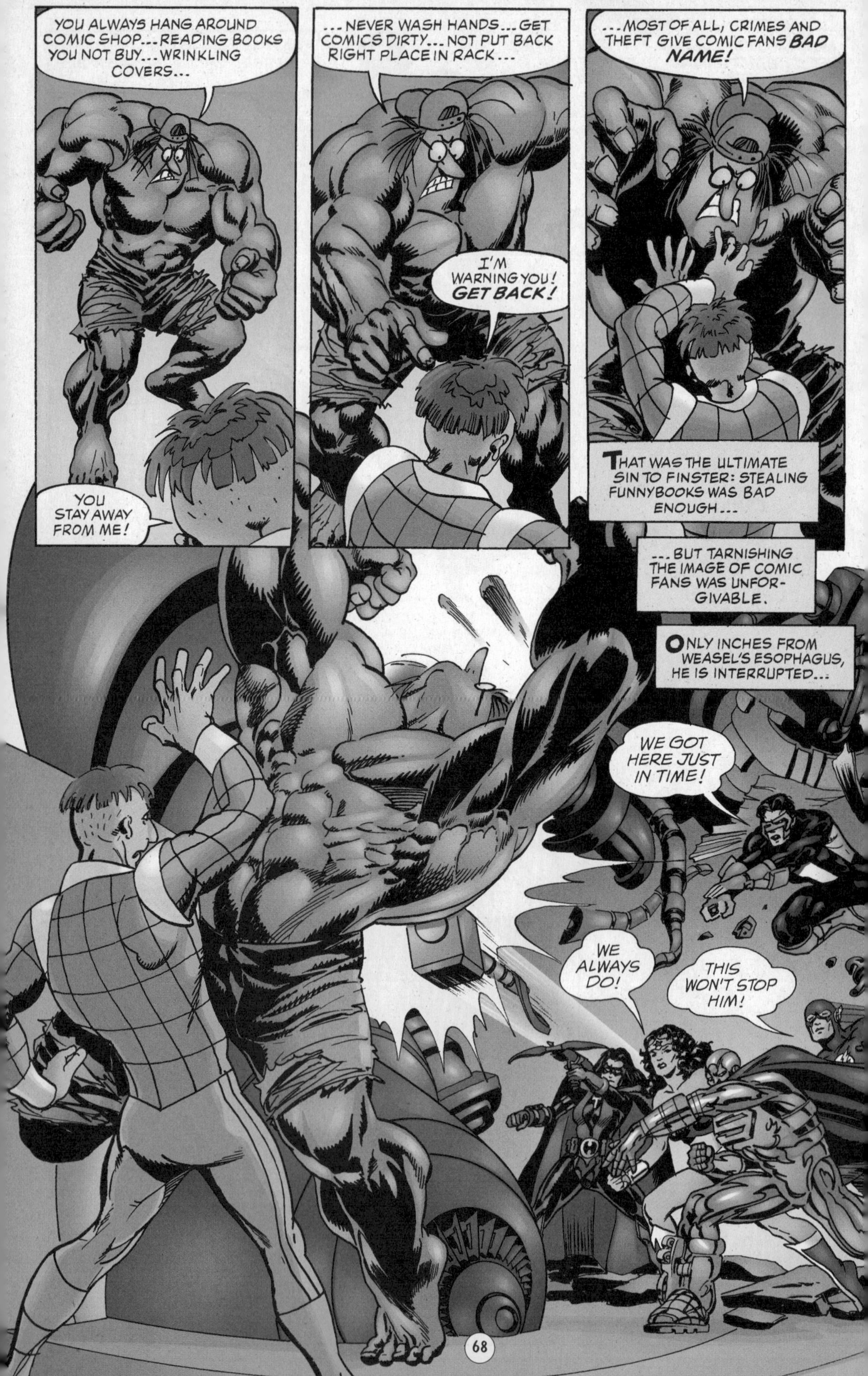

YOU ALWAYS HANG AROUND COMIC SHOP... READING BOOKS YOU NOT BUY... WRINKLING COVERS...
YOU STAY AWAY FROM ME!
...NEVER WASH HANDS...GET COMICS DIRTY... NOT PUT BACK RIGHT PLACE IN RACK...
I'M WARNING YOU! GET BACK!
...MOST OF ALL, CRIMES AND THEFT GIVE COMIC FANS BAD NAME!
THAT WAS THE ULTIMATE SIN TO FINSTER: STEALING FUNNYBOOKS WAS BAD ENOUGH...
...BUT TARNISHING THE IMAGE OF COMIC FANS WAS UNFORGIVABLE.
ONLY INCHES FROM WEASEL'S ESOPHAGUS, HE IS INTERRUPTED...
WE GOT HERE JUST IN TIME!
WE ALWAYS DO!
THIS WON'T STOP HIM!

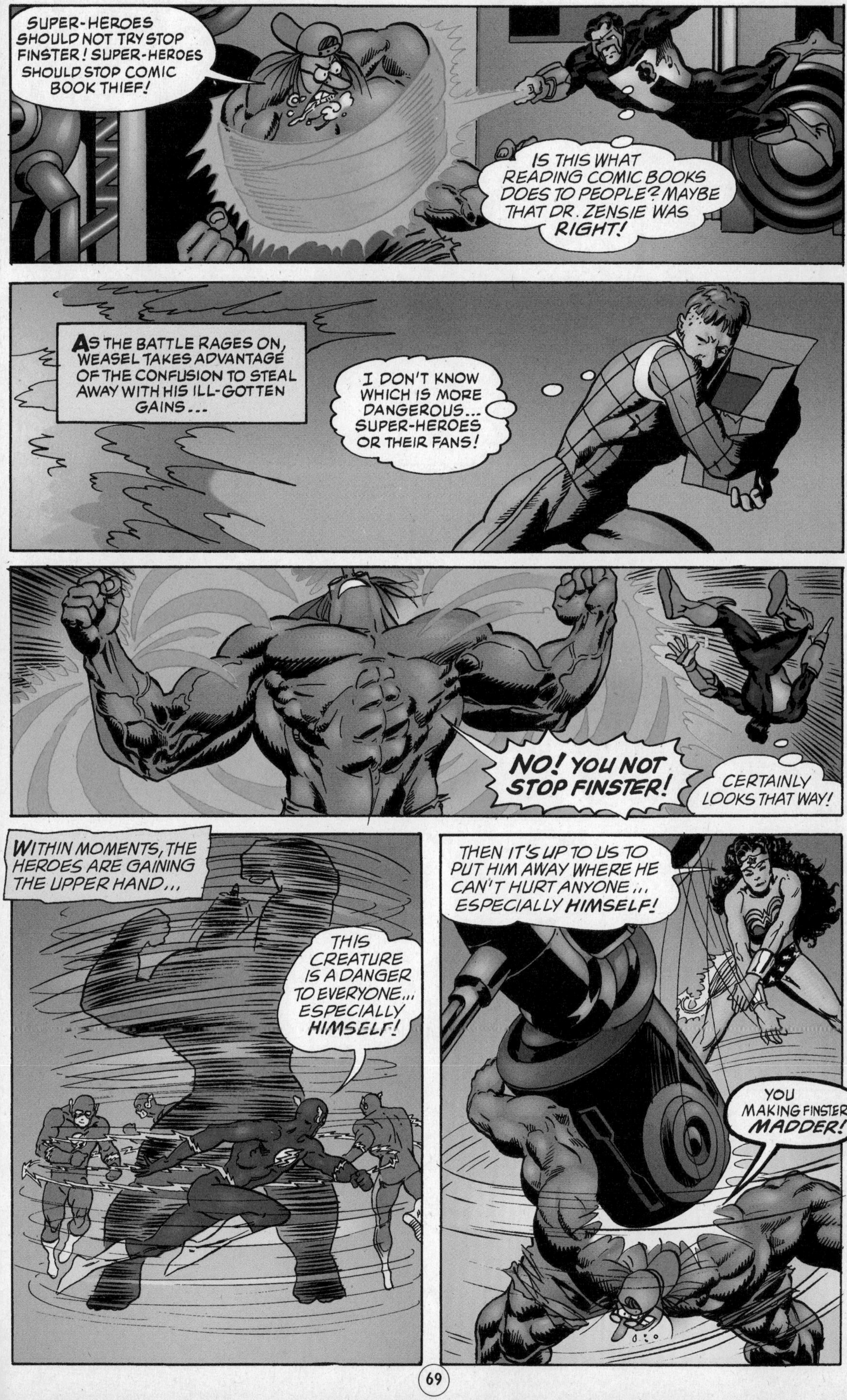

SUPER-HEROES SHOULD NOT TRY STOP FINSTER! SUPER-HEROES SHOULD STOP COMIC BOOK THIEF!
IS THIS WHAT READING COMIC BOOKS DOES TO PEOPLE? MAYBE THAT DR. ZENSIE WAS RIGHT!
AS THE BATTLE RAGES ON, WEASEL TAKES ADVANTAGE OF THE CONFUSION TO STEAL AWAY WITH HIS ILL-GOTTEN GAINS...
I DON'T KNOW WHICH IS MORE DANGEROUS... SUPER-HEROES OR THEIR FANS!
NO! YOU NOT STOP FINSTER!
CERTAINLY LOOKS THAT WAY!
WITHIN MOMENTS, THE HEROES ARE GAINING THE UPPER HAND...
THIS CREATURE IS A DANGER TO EVERYONE... ESPECIALLY HIMSELF!
THEN IT'S UP TO US TO PUT HIM AWAY WHERE HE CAN'T HURT ANYONE... ESPECIALLY HIMSELF!
YOU MAKING FINSTER MADDER!

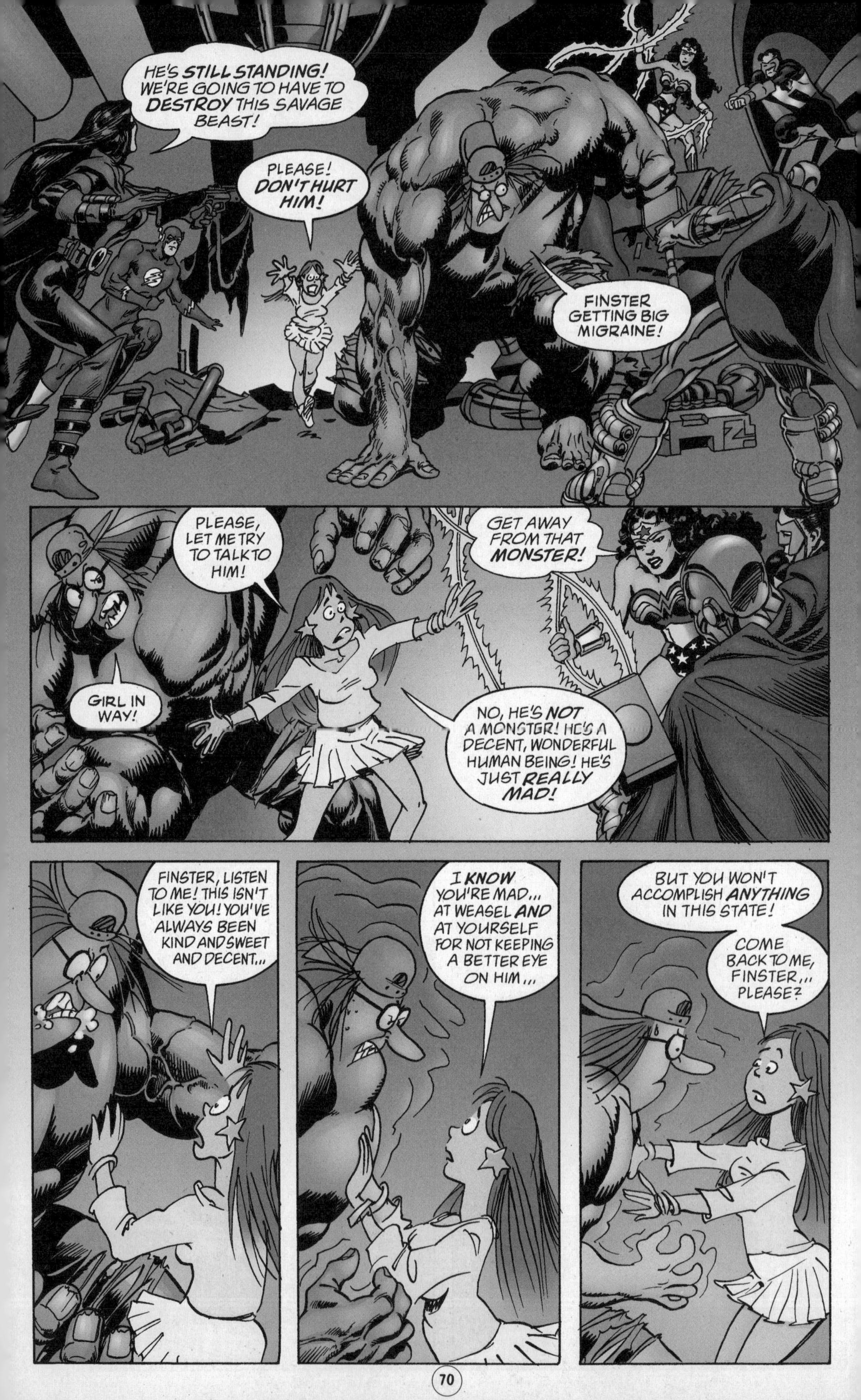

HE'S STILL STANDING! WE'RE GOING TO HAVE TO DESTROY THIS SAVAGE BEAST!
PLEASE! DON'T HURT HIM!
FINSTER GETTING BIG MIGRAINE!
PLEASE, LET ME TRY TO TALK TO HIM!
GET AWAY FROM THAT MONSTER!
GIRL IN WAY!
NO, HE'S NOT A MONSTER! HE'S A DECENT, WONDERFUL HUMAN BEING! HE'S JUST REALLY MAD!
FINSTER, LISTEN TO ME! THIS ISN'T LIKE YOU! YOU'VE ALWAYS BEEN KIND AND SWEET AND DECENT...
I KNOW YOU'RE MAD... AT WEASEL AND AT YOURSELF FOR NOT KEEPING A BETTER EYE ON HIM...
BUT YOU WON'T ACCOMPLISH ANYTHING IN THIS STATE!
COME BACK TO ME, FINSTER... PLEASE?

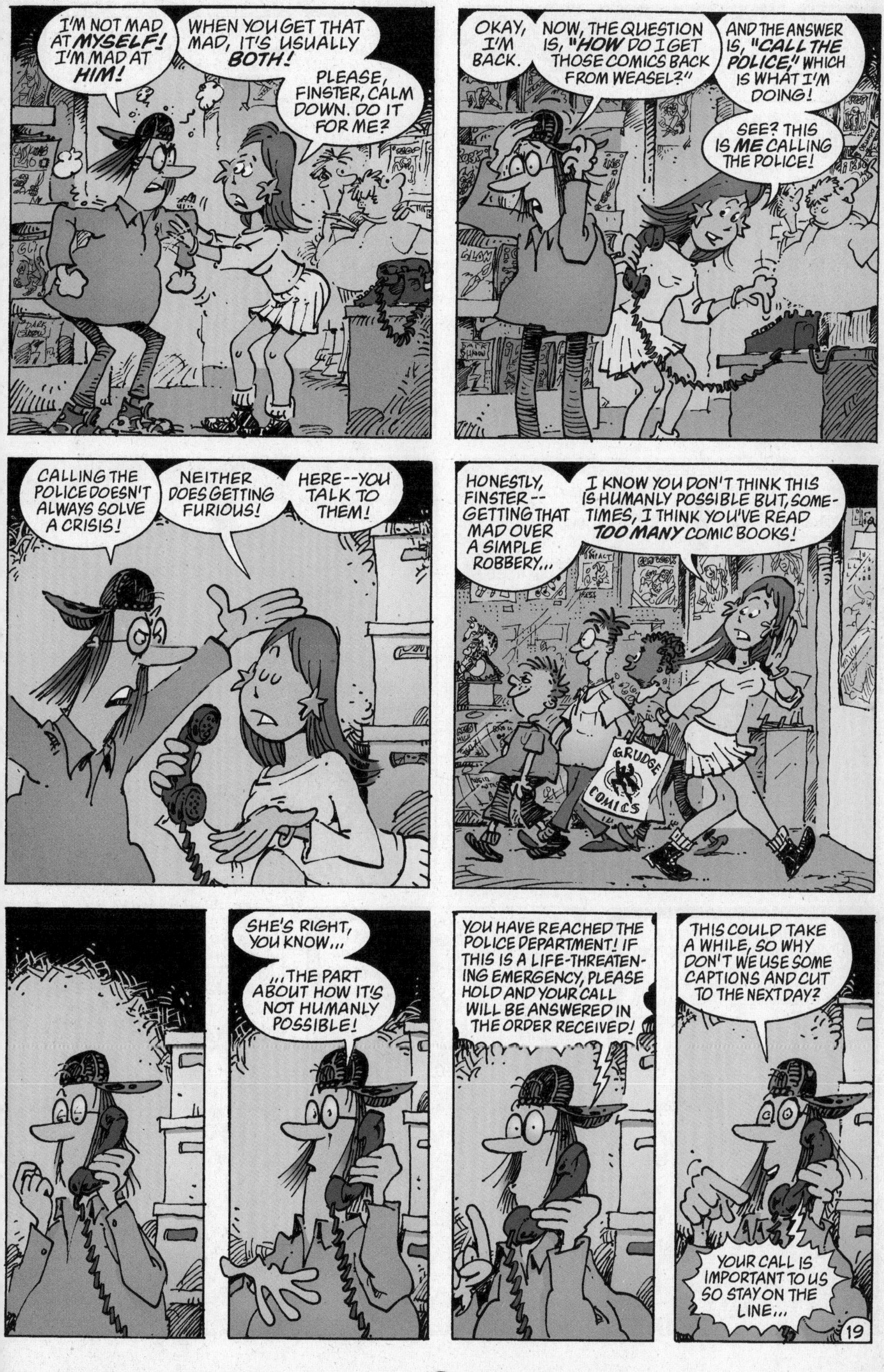

I'M NOT MAD AT MYSELF! I'M MAD AT HIM!
WHEN YOU GET THAT MAD, IT'S USUALLY BOTH!
PLEASE, FINSTER, CALM DOWN. DO IT FOR ME?
OKAY, I'M BACK.
NOW, THE QUESTION IS, "HOW DO I GET THOSE COMICS BACK FROM WEASEL?"
AND THE ANSWER IS, "CALL THE POLICE," WHICH IS WHAT I'M DOING!
SEE? THIS IS ME CALLING THE POLICE!
CALLING THE POLICE DOESN'T ALWAYS SOLVE A CRISIS!
NEITHER DOES GETTING FURIOUS!
HERE--YOU TALK TO THEM!
HONESTLY, FINSTER-- GETTING THAT MAD OVER A SIMPLE ROBBERY...
I KNOW YOU DON'T THINK THIS IS HUMANLY POSSIBLE BUT, SOMETIMES, I THINK YOU'VE READ TOO MANY COMIC BOOKS!
GRUDGE COMICS
SHE'S RIGHT, YOU KNOW...
...THE PART ABOUT HOW IT'S NOT HUMANLY POSSIBLE!
YOU HAVE REACHED THE POLICE DEPARTMENT! IF THIS IS A LIFE-THREATENING EMERGENCY, PLEASE HOLD AND YOUR CALL WILL BE ANSWERED IN THE ORDER RECEIVED!
THIS COULD TAKE A WHILE, SO WHY DON'T WE USE SOME CAPTIONS AND CUT TO THE NEXT DAY?
YOUR CALL IS IMPORTANT TO US SO STAY ON THE LINE...
19

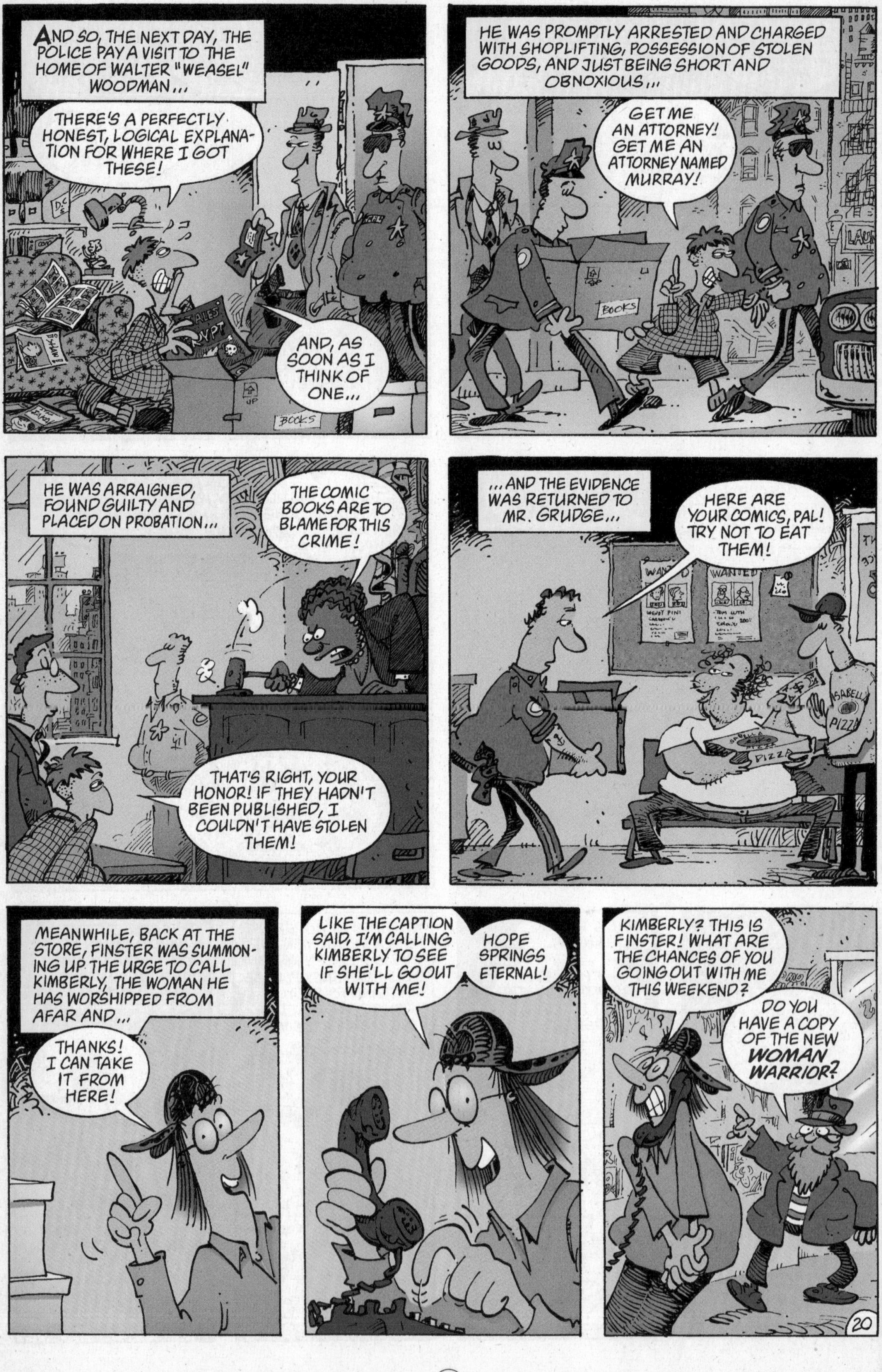
AND SO, THE NEXT DAY, THE POLICE PAY A VISIT TO THE HOME OF WALTER "WEASEL" WOODMAN...
THERE'S A PERFECTLY HONEST, LOGICAL EXPLANATION FOR WHERE I GOT THESE!
AND, AS SOON AS I THINK OF ONE...
BOOKS
HE WAS PROMPTLY ARRESTED AND CHARGED WITH SHOPLIFTING, POSSESSION OF STOLEN GOODS, AND JUST BEING SHORT AND OBNOXIOUS...
GET ME AN ATTORNEY! GET ME AN ATTORNEY NAMED MURRAY!
BOOKS
HE WAS ARRAIGNED, FOUND GUILTY AND PLACED ON PROBATION...
THE COMIC BOOKS ARE TO BLAME FOR THIS CRIME!
THAT'S RIGHT, YOUR HONOR! IF THEY HADN'T BEEN PUBLISHED, I COULDN'T HAVE STOLEN THEM!
...AND THE EVIDENCE WAS RETURNED TO MR. GRUDGE...
HERE ARE YOUR COMICS, PAL! TRY NOT TO EAT THEM!
WANTED
WANTED
PIZZA
MEANWHILE, BACK AT THE STORE, FINSTER WAS SUMMONING UP THE URGE TO CALL KIMBERLY, THE WOMAN HE HAS WORSHIPPED FROM AFAR AND...
THANKS! I CAN TAKE IT FROM HERE!
LIKE THE CAPTION SAID, I'M CALLING KIMBERLY TO SEE IF SHE'LL GO OUT WITH ME!
HOPE SPRINGS ETERNAL!
KIMBERLY? THIS IS FINSTER! WHAT ARE THE CHANCES OF YOU GOING OUT WITH ME THIS WEEKEND?
DO YOU HAVE A COPY OF THE NEW WOMAN WARRIOR?
20

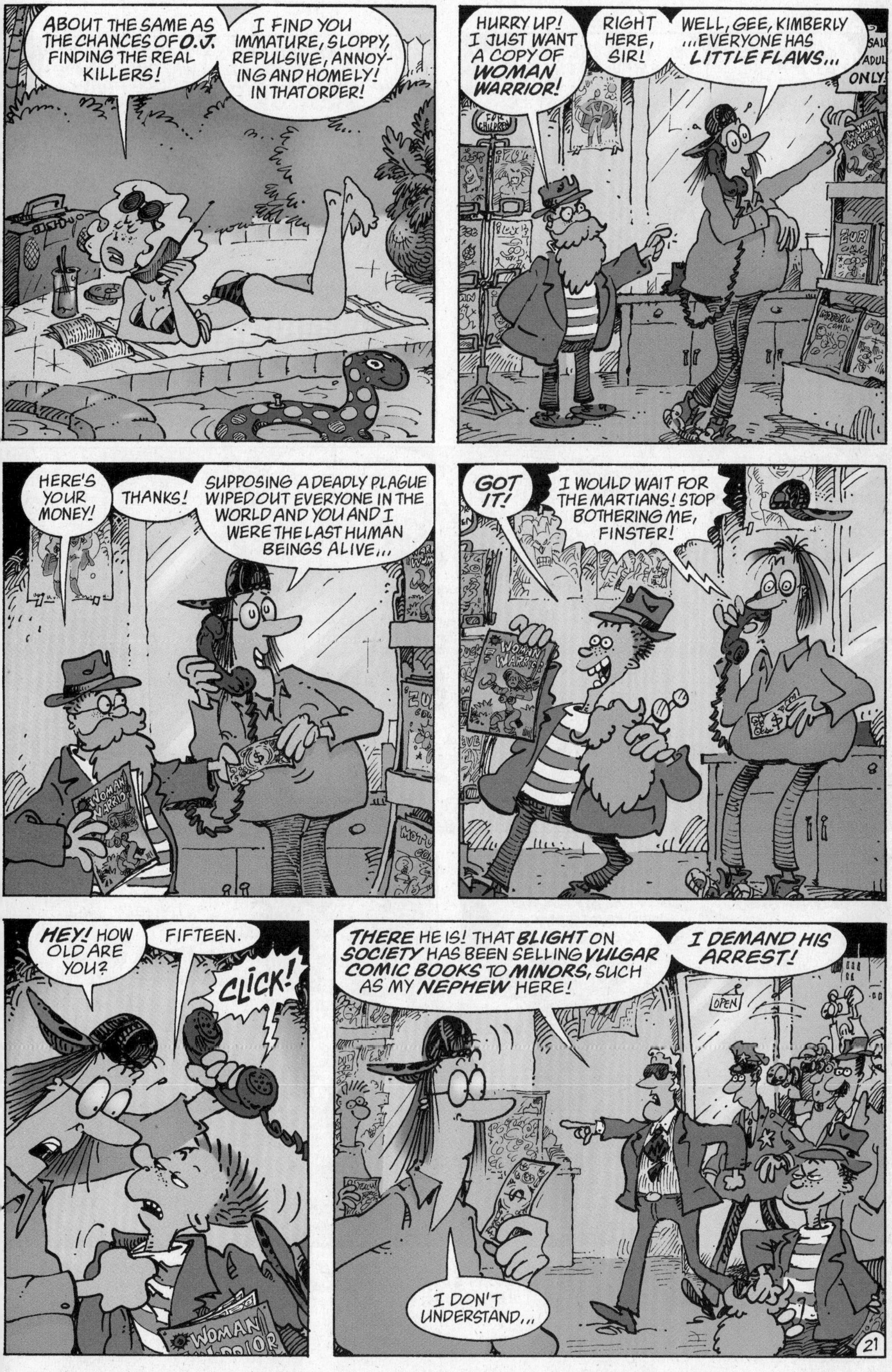
ABOUT THE SAME AS THE CHANCES OF O.J. FINDING THE REAL KILLERS!
I FIND YOU IMMATURE, SLOPPY, REPULSIVE, ANNOYING AND HOMELY! IN THAT ORDER!
HURRY UP! I JUST WANT A COPY OF WOMAN WARRIOR!
RIGHT HERE, SIR!
WELL, GEE, KIMBERLY ...EVERYONE HAS LITTLE FLAWS...
ADULTS ONLY
HERE'S YOUR MONEY!
THANKS!
SUPPOSING A DEADLY PLAGUE WIPED OUT EVERYONE IN THE WORLD AND YOU AND I WERE THE LAST HUMAN BEINGS ALIVE...
GOT IT!
I WOULD WAIT FOR THE MARTIANS! STOP BOTHERING ME, FINSTER!
HEY! HOW OLD ARE YOU?
FIFTEEN.
CLICK!
THERE HE IS! THAT BLIGHT ON SOCIETY HAS BEEN SELLING VULGAR COMIC BOOKS TO MINORS, SUCH AS MY NEPHEW HERE!
I DEMAND HIS ARREST!
OPEN
I DON'T UNDERSTAND...
21

THEY TRICKED ME! THAT KID HAD ON A FAKE BEARD AND HE--
YOU HAVE THE RIGHT TO REMAIN SILENT, AND ANYTHING YOU SAY MAY BE USED AGAINST YOU IN A COURT OF LAW...
YOU DID FINE, RENFREW! YOU HELPED ELIMINATE A PURVEYOR OF FILTH AND OBSCENITY!
"HANDCUFFS"? WHY DO YOU HAVE TO USE HAND-CUFFS?
STANDARD PROCEDURE...
NEAT! CAN I KEEP THE COMIC BOOK?
WOMAN WARRIO
CLAMP!
THEY LOOK DRAMATIC ON TELEVISION!
OPEN
MR. FINSTER, HOW DO YOU FEEL?
ARE YOU LOOKING FORWARD TO PRISON?
TV
HAVE YOU EVER MET MONICA LEWINSKY?
THIS, MY FRIENDS, IS JUST THE BEGINNING!
WE SHALL CLOSE EVERY COMIC BOOK SHOP IN TOWN OR MY NAME ISN'T JEREMIAH KREED!
THAT'S "KREED" WITH A "K!"
WOMAN WARRIOR
COMICS
BOY, I HOPE THIS IS A CONTINUED STORY!
POLICE

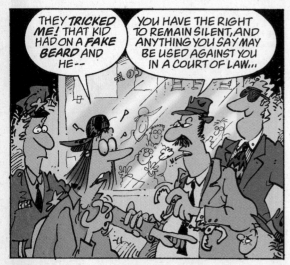

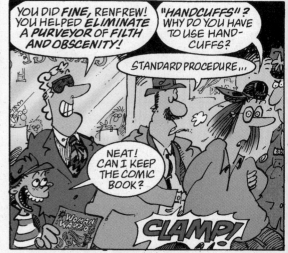

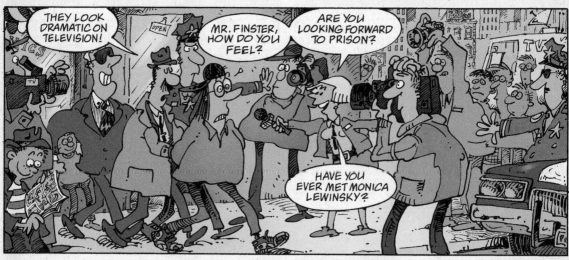

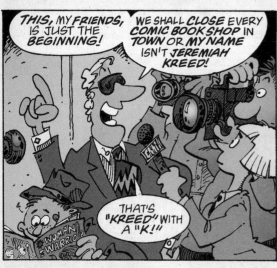

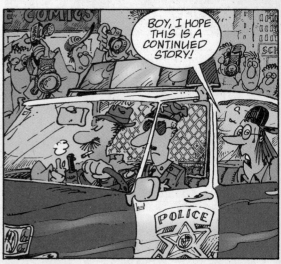

By **MARK EVANIER** and **SERGIO ARAGONÉS**

(PAGE 5 & 7) **BILL SIENKIEWICZ**
(PAGES 13-18) **BRENT ANDERSON**
- GUEST ARTISTS -

LETTERING: **TODD KLEIN**
COLORING: **TOM LUTH**
EDITING: **TONY BEDARD**

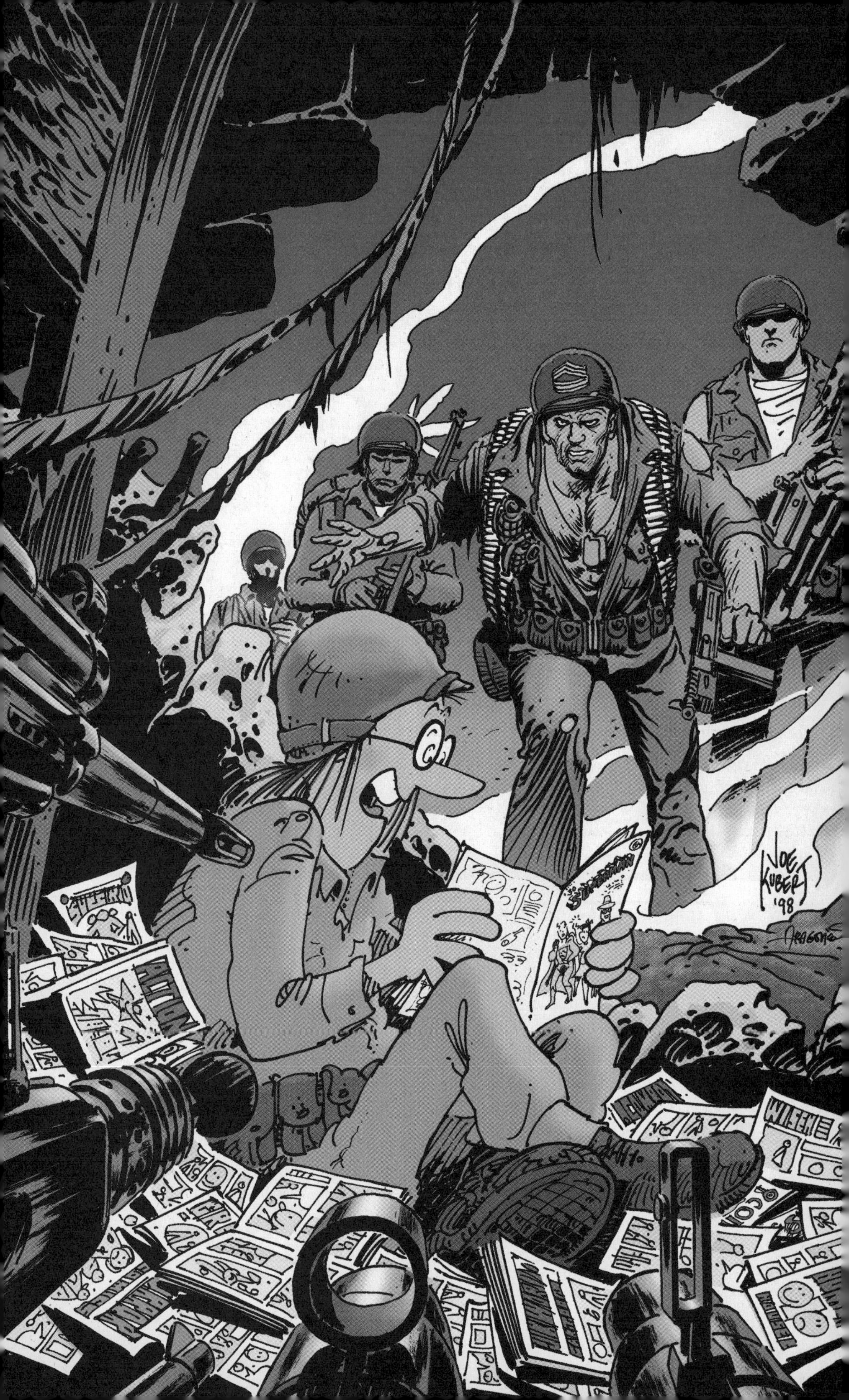
JOE KUBERT '98

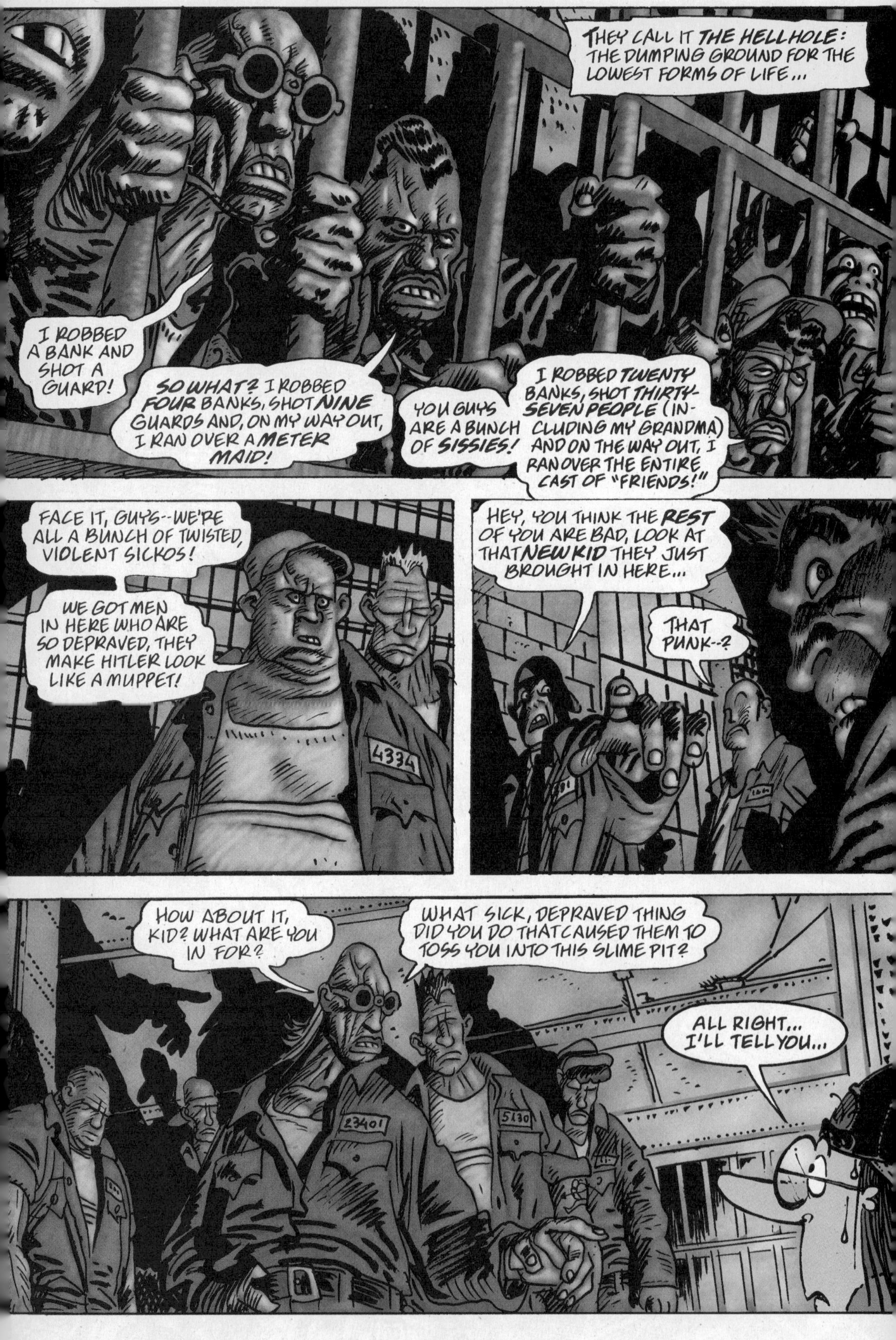
THEY CALL IT THE HELLHOLE: THE DUMPING GROUND FOR THE LOWEST FORMS OF LIFE...
I ROBBED A BANK AND SHOT A GUARD!
SO WHAT? I ROBBED FOUR BANKS, SHOT NINE GUARDS AND, ON MY WAY OUT, I RAN OVER A METER MAID!
YOU GUYS ARE A BUNCH OF SISSIES!
I ROBBED TWENTY BANKS, SHOT THIRTY-SEVEN PEOPLE (IN-CLUDING MY GRANDMA) AND ON THE WAY OUT, I RAN OVER THE ENTIRE CAST OF "FRIENDS!"
FACE IT, GUYS--WE'RE ALL A BUNCH OF TWISTED, VIOLENT SICKOS!
WE GOT MEN IN HERE WHO ARE SO DEPRAVED, THEY MAKE HITLER LOOK LIKE A MUPPET!
HEY, YOU THINK THE REST OF YOU ARE BAD, LOOK AT THAT NEW KID THEY JUST BROUGHT IN HERE...
THAT PUNK--?
4334
HOW ABOUT IT, KID? WHAT ARE YOU IN FOR?
WHAT SICK, DEPRAVED THING DID YOU DO THAT CAUSED THEM TO TOSS YOU INTO THIS SLIME PIT?
ALL RIGHT... I'LL TELL YOU...
23401
5130

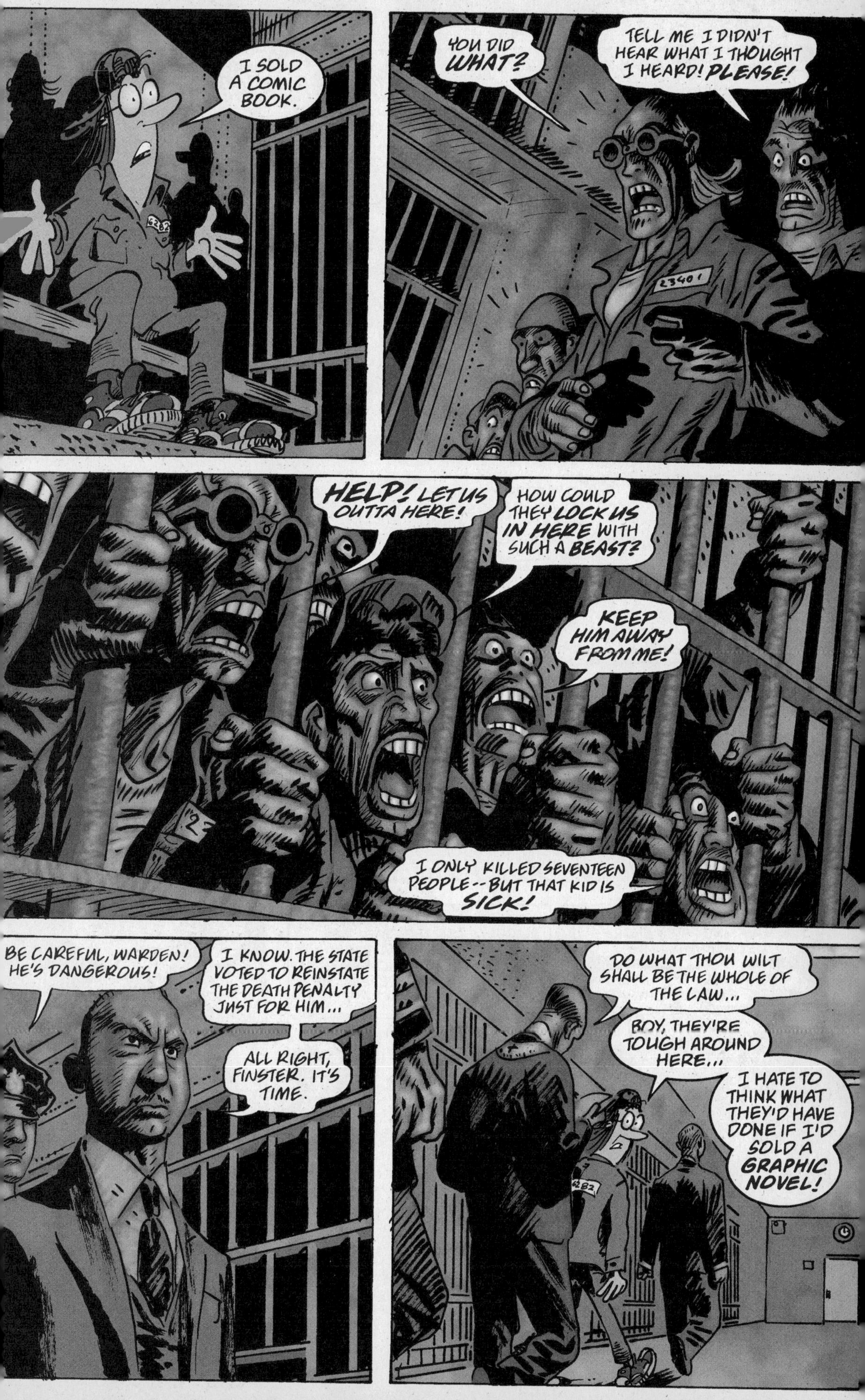
I SOLD A COMIC BOOK.
YOU DID WHAT?
TELL ME I DIDN'T HEAR WHAT I THOUGHT I HEARD! PLEASE!
HELP! LET US OUTTA HERE!
HOW COULD THEY LOCK US IN HERE WITH SUCH A BEAST?
KEEP HIM AWAY FROM ME!
I ONLY KILLED SEVENTEEN PEOPLE--BUT THAT KID IS SICK!
BE CAREFUL, WARDEN! HE'S DANGEROUS!
I KNOW. THE STATE VOTED TO REINSTATE THE DEATH PENALTY JUST FOR HIM...
ALL RIGHT, FINSTER. IT'S TIME.
DO WHAT THOU WILT SHALL BE THE WHOLE OF THE LAW...
BOY, THEY'RE TOUGH AROUND HERE...
I HATE TO THINK WHAT THEY'D HAVE DONE IF I'D SOLD A GRAPHIC NOVEL!

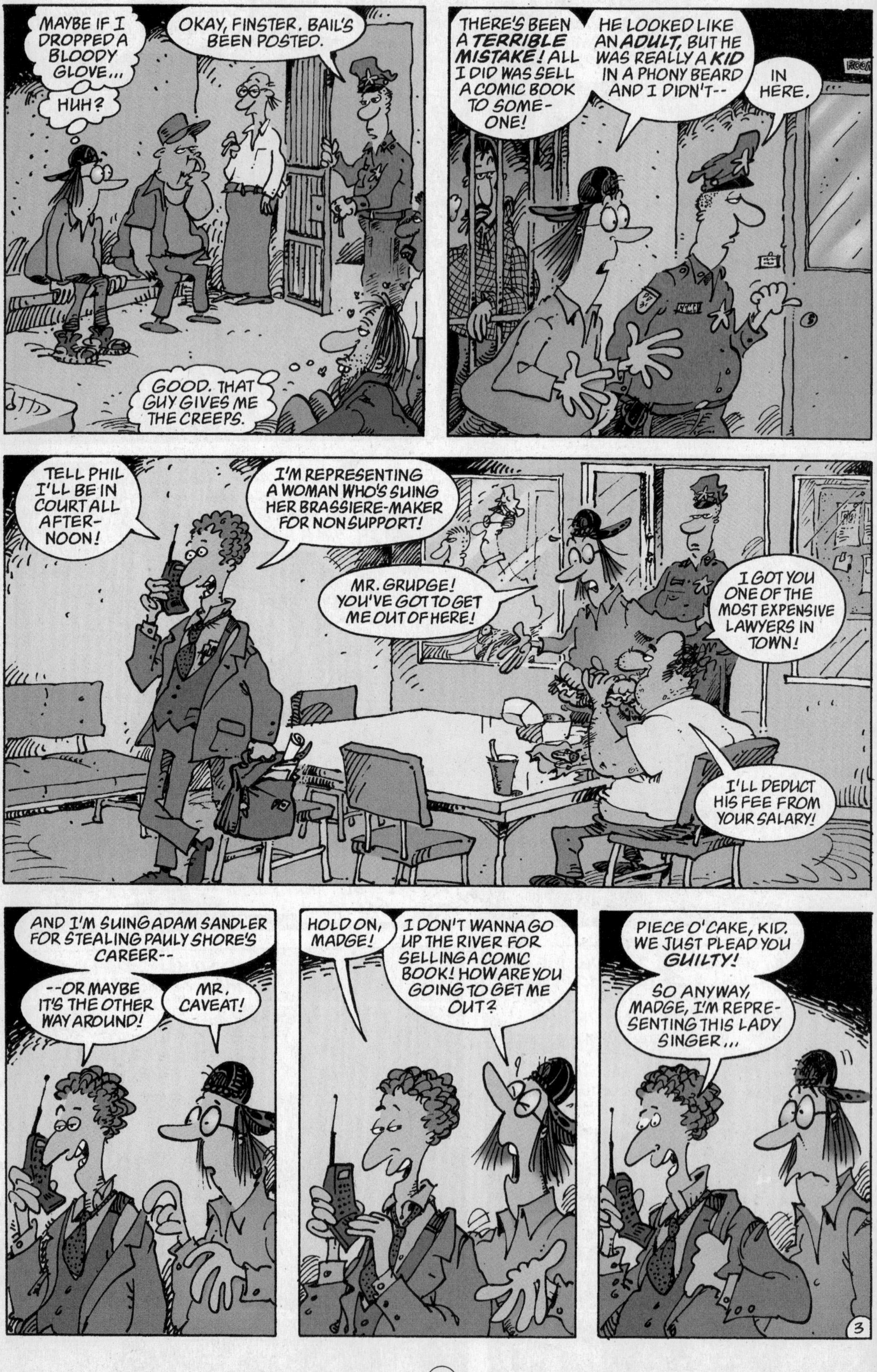
MAYBE IF I DROPPED A BLOODY GLOVE...
OKAY, FINSTER. BAIL'S BEEN POSTED.
HUH?
GOOD. THAT GUY GIVES ME THE CREEPS.
THERE'S BEEN A **TERRIBLE MISTAKE!** ALL I DID WAS SELL A COMIC BOOK TO SOMEONE!
HE LOOKED LIKE AN **ADULT,** BUT HE WAS REALLY A **KID** IN A PHONY BEARD AND I DIDN'T--
IN HERE.
TELL PHIL I'LL BE IN COURT ALL AFTERNOON!
I'M REPRESENTING A WOMAN WHO'S SUING HER BRASSIERE-MAKER FOR NON SUPPORT!
MR. GRUDGE! YOU'VE GOT TO GET ME OUT OF HERE!
I GOT YOU ONE OF THE MOST EXPENSIVE LAWYERS IN TOWN!
I'LL DEDUCT HIS FEE FROM YOUR SALARY!
AND I'M SUING ADAM SANDLER FOR STEALING PAULY SHORE'S CAREER--
--OR MAYBE IT'S THE OTHER WAY AROUND!
MR. CAVEAT!
HOLD ON, MADGE!
I DON'T WANNA GO UP THE RIVER FOR SELLING A COMIC BOOK! HOW ARE YOU GOING TO GET ME OUT?
PIECE O' CAKE, KID. WE JUST PLEAD YOU **GUILTY!**
SO ANYWAY, MADGE, I'M REPRESENTING THIS LADY SINGER...
3

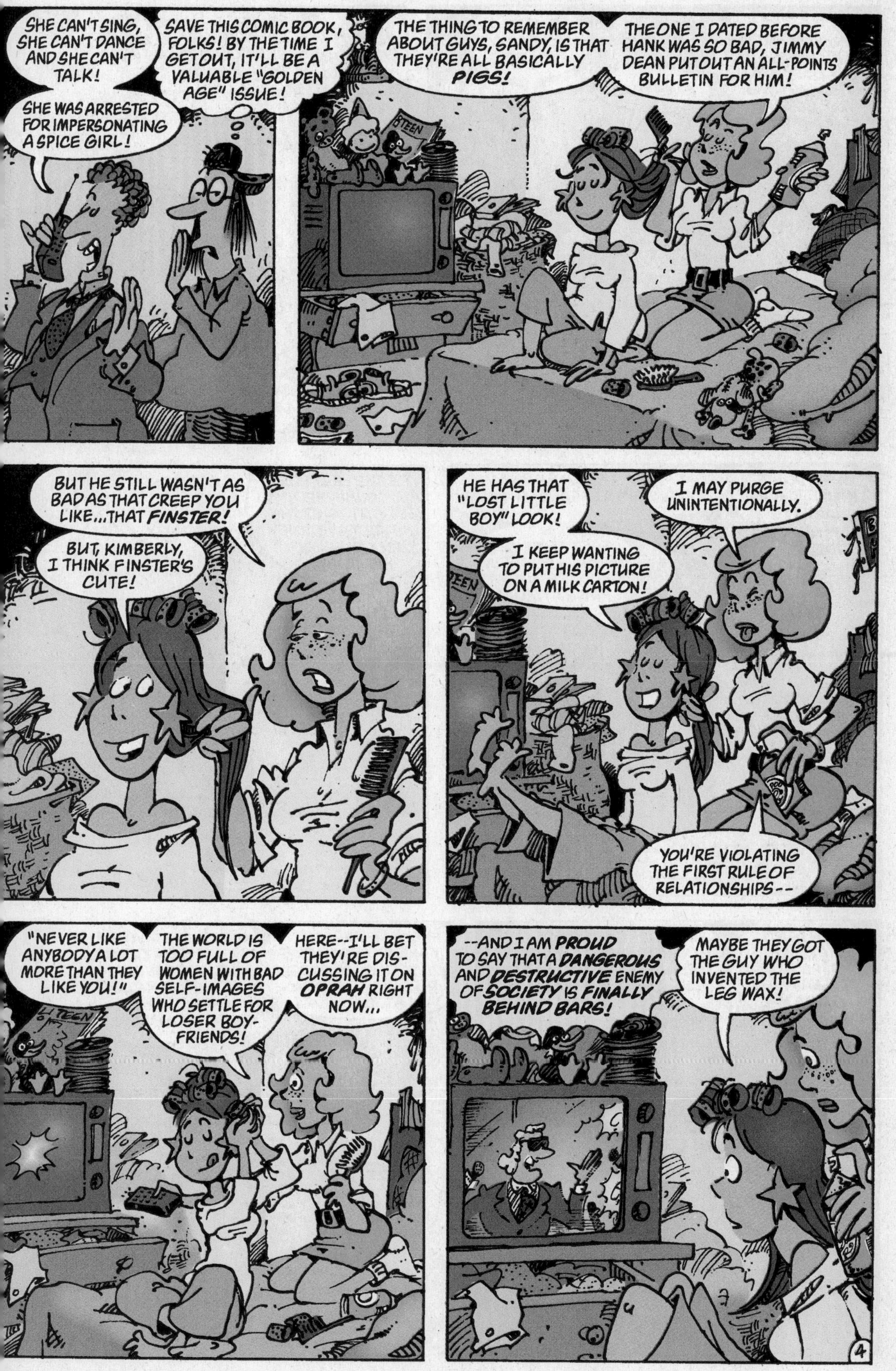
SHE CAN'T SING, SHE CAN'T DANCE AND SHE CAN'T TALK!
SHE WAS ARRESTED FOR IMPERSONATING A SPICE GIRL!
SAVE THIS COMIC BOOK, FOLKS! BY THE TIME I GET OUT, IT'LL BE A VALUABLE "GOLDEN AGE" ISSUE!
TEEN
THE THING TO REMEMBER ABOUT GUYS, SANDY, IS THAT THEY'RE ALL BASICALLY PIGS!
THE ONE I DATED BEFORE HANK WAS SO BAD, JIMMY DEAN PUT OUT AN ALL-POINTS BULLETIN FOR HIM!
BUT HE STILL WASN'T AS BAD AS THAT CREEP YOU LIKE... THAT FINSTER!
BUT, KIMBERLY, I THINK FINSTER'S CUTE!
HE HAS THAT "LOST LITTLE BOY" LOOK!
I KEEP WANTING TO PUT HIS PICTURE ON A MILK CARTON!
I MAY PURGE UNINTENTIONALLY.
YOU'RE VIOLATING THE FIRST RULE OF RELATIONSHIPS--
"NEVER LIKE ANYBODY A LOT MORE THAN THEY LIKE YOU!"
THE WORLD IS TOO FULL OF WOMEN WITH BAD SELF-IMAGES WHO SETTLE FOR LOSER BOY-FRIENDS!
HERE--I'LL BET THEY'RE DIS-CUSSING IT ON OPRAH RIGHT NOW...
--AND I AM PROUD TO SAY THAT A DANGEROUS AND DESTRUCTIVE ENEMY OF SOCIETY IS FINALLY BEHIND BARS!
MAYBE THEY GOT THE GUY WHO INVENTED THE LEG WAX!
4

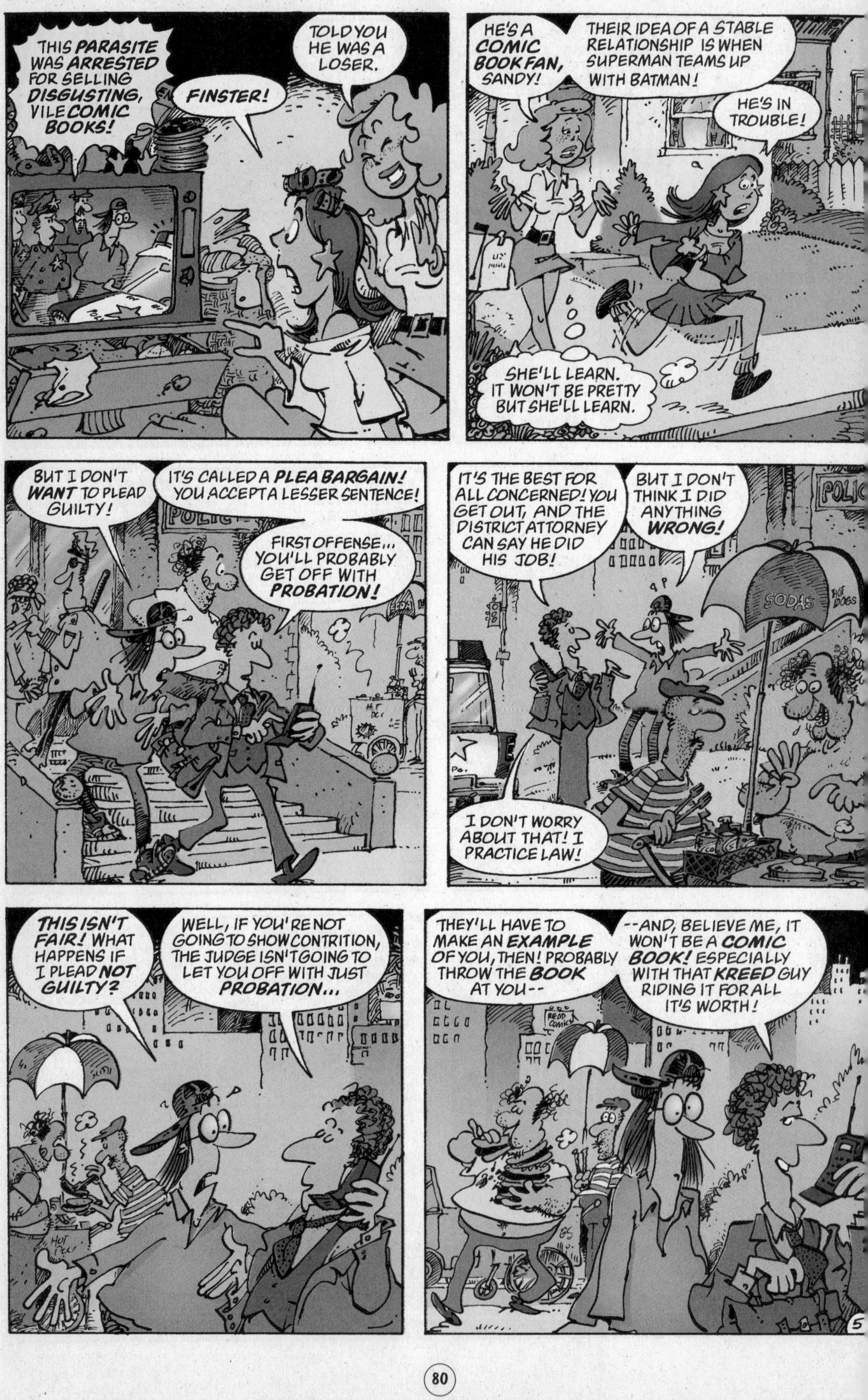

THIS PARASITE WAS ARRESTED FOR SELLING DISGUSTING, VILE COMIC BOOKS!
FINSTER!
TOLD YOU HE WAS A LOSER.
HE'S A COMIC BOOK FAN, SANDY!
THEIR IDEA OF A STABLE RELATIONSHIP IS WHEN SUPERMAN TEAMS UP WITH BATMAN!
HE'S IN TROUBLE!
SHE'LL LEARN. IT WON'T BE PRETTY BUT SHE'LL LEARN.
BUT I DON'T WANT TO PLEAD GUILTY!
IT'S CALLED A PLEA BARGAIN! YOU ACCEPT A LESSER SENTENCE!
FIRST OFFENSE... YOU'LL PROBABLY GET OFF WITH PROBATION!
IT'S THE BEST FOR ALL CONCERNED! YOU GET OUT, AND THE DISTRICT ATTORNEY CAN SAY HE DID HIS JOB!
BUT I DON'T THINK I DID ANYTHING WRONG!
SODAS
HOT DOGS
I DON'T WORRY ABOUT THAT! I PRACTICE LAW!
THIS ISN'T FAIR! WHAT HAPPENS IF I PLEAD NOT GUILTY?
WELL, IF YOU'RE NOT GOING TO SHOW CONTRITION, THE JUDGE ISN'T GOING TO LET YOU OFF WITH JUST PROBATION...
THEY'LL HAVE TO MAKE AN EXAMPLE OF YOU, THEN! PROBABLY THROW THE BOOK AT YOU--
--AND, BELIEVE ME, IT WON'T BE A COMIC BOOK! ESPECIALLY WITH THAT KREED GUY RIDING IT FOR ALL IT'S WORTH!
READ COMICS

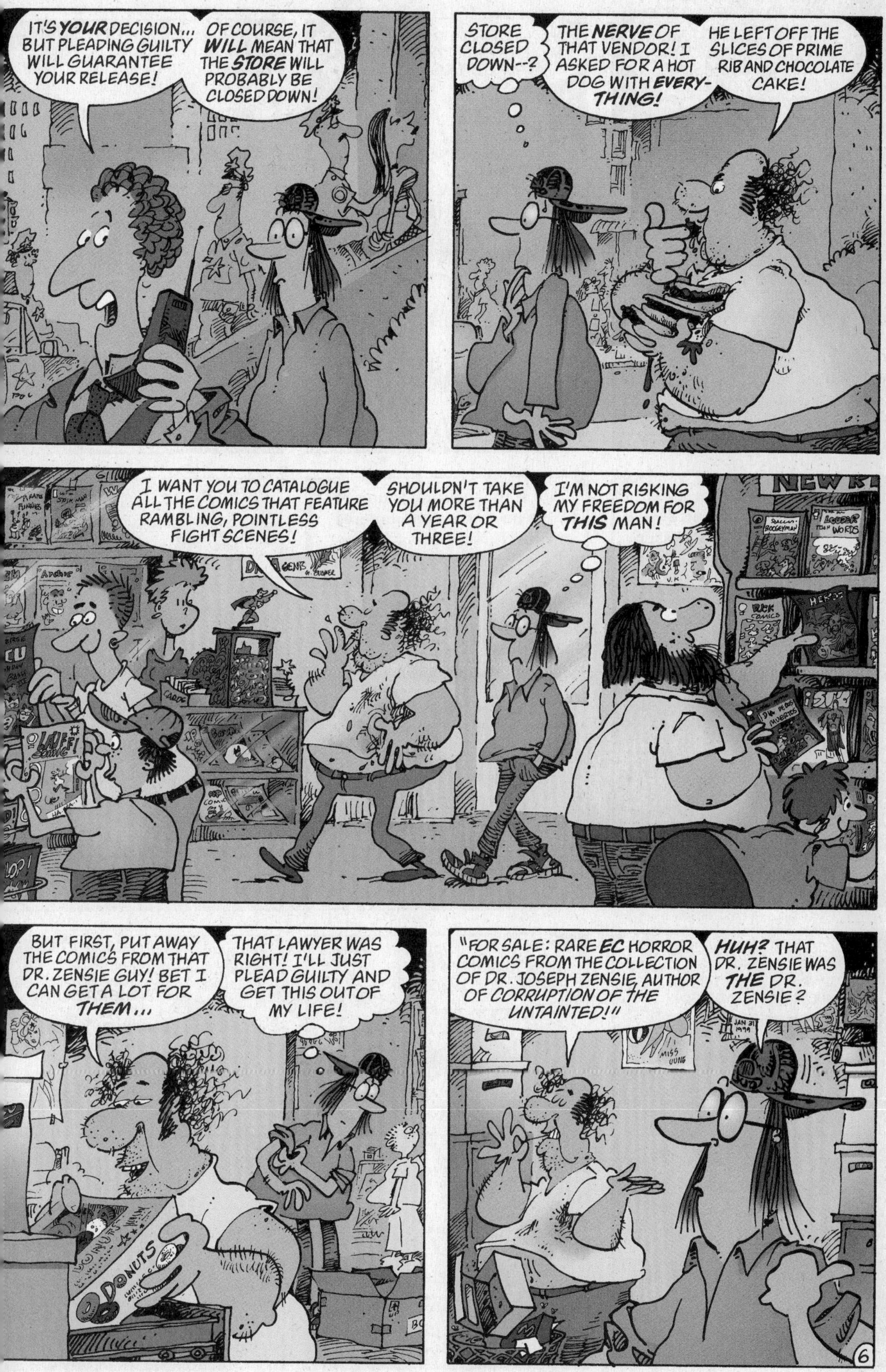
IT'S YOUR DECISION... BUT PLEADING GUILTY WILL GUARANTEE YOUR RELEASE!
OF COURSE, IT WILL MEAN THAT THE STORE WILL PROBABLY BE CLOSED DOWN!
STORE CLOSED DOWN--?
THE NERVE OF THAT VENDOR! I ASKED FOR A HOT DOG WITH EVERYTHING!
HE LEFT OFF THE SLICES OF PRIME RIB AND CHOCOLATE CAKE!
I WANT YOU TO CATALOGUE ALL THE COMICS THAT FEATURE RAMBLING, POINTLESS FIGHT SCENES!
SHOULDN'T TAKE YOU MORE THAN A YEAR OR THREE!
I'M NOT RISKING MY FREEDOM FOR THIS MAN!
BUT FIRST, PUT AWAY THE COMICS FROM THAT DR. ZENSIE GUY! BET I CAN GET A LOT FOR THEM...
THAT LAWYER WAS RIGHT! I'LL JUST PLEAD GUILTY AND GET THIS OUT OF MY LIFE!
DONUTS
"FOR SALE: RARE EC HORROR COMICS FROM THE COLLECTION OF DR. JOSEPH ZENSIE, AUTHOR OF CORRUPTION OF THE UNTAINTED!"
HUH? THAT DR. ZENSIE WAS THE DR. ZENSIE?
6

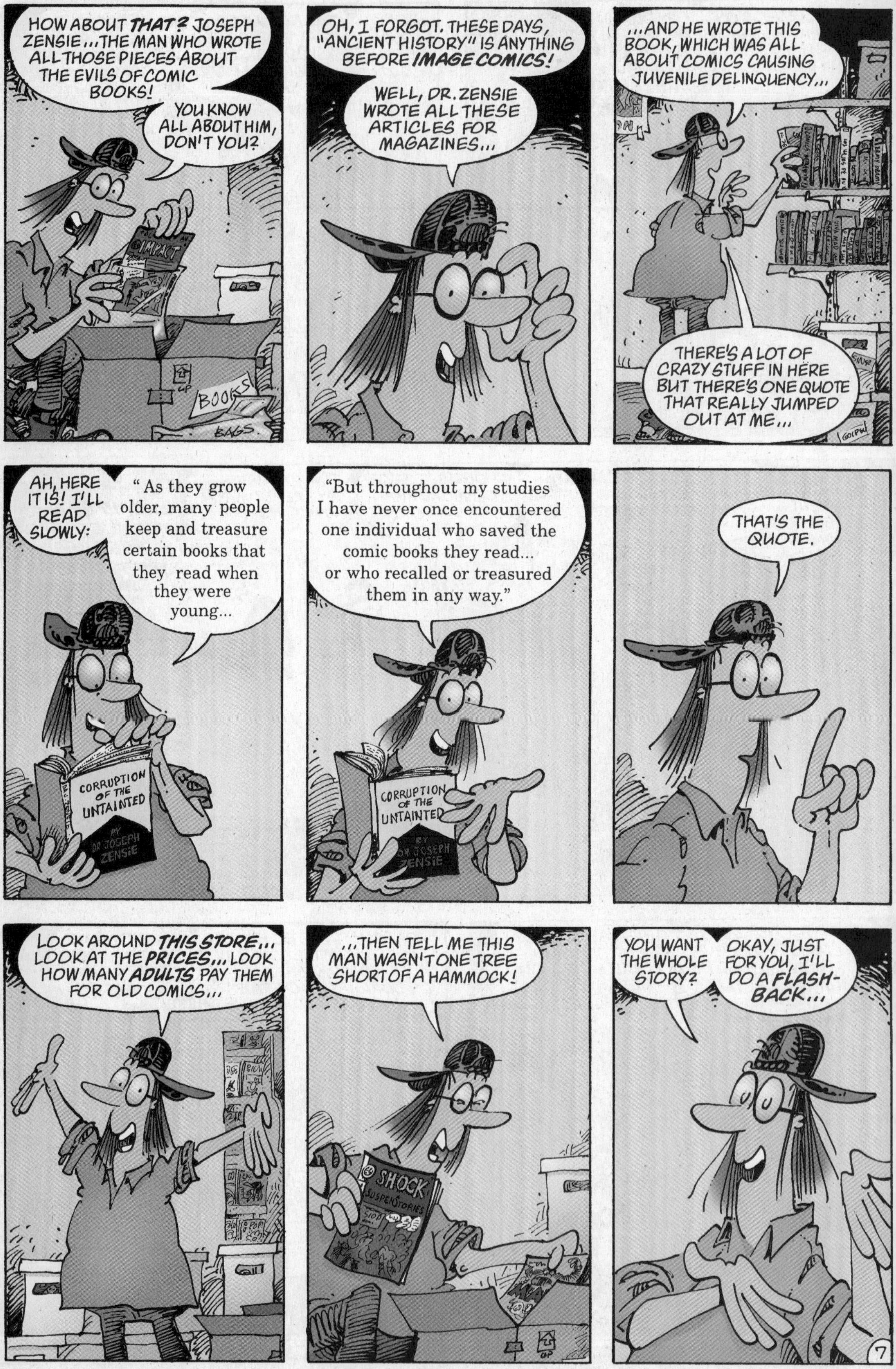
HOW ABOUT THAT? JOSEPH ZENSIE...THE MAN WHO WROTE ALL THOSE PIECES ABOUT THE EVILS OF COMIC BOOKS!
YOU KNOW ALL ABOUT HIM, DON'T YOU?
IMPACT
BOOKS
BAGS
OH, I FORGOT. THESE DAYS, "ANCIENT HISTORY" IS ANYTHING BEFORE IMAGE COMICS!
WELL, DR. ZENSIE WROTE ALL THESE ARTICLES FOR MAGAZINES...
...AND HE WROTE THIS BOOK, WHICH WAS ALL ABOUT COMICS CAUSING JUVENILE DELINQUENCY...
THERE'S A LOT OF CRAZY STUFF IN HERE BUT THERE'S ONE QUOTE THAT REALLY JUMPED OUT AT ME...
AH, HERE IT IS! I'LL READ SLOWLY:
" As they grow older, many people keep and treasure certain books that they read when they were young...
CORRUPTION OF THE UNTAINTED BY DR. JOSEPH ZENSIE
"But throughout my studies I have never once encountered one individual who saved the comic books they read... or who recalled or treasured them in any way."
CORRUPTION OF THE UNTAINTED BY DR. JOSEPH ZENSIE
THAT'S THE QUOTE.
LOOK AROUND THIS STORE... LOOK AT THE PRICES... LOOK HOW MANY ADULTS PAY THEM FOR OLD COMICS...
...THEN TELL ME THIS MAN WASN'T ONE TREE SHORT OF A HAMMOCK!
SHOCK SUSPENSTORIES
YOU WANT THE WHOLE STORY?
OKAY, JUST FOR YOU, I'LL DO A FLASH-BACK...
7

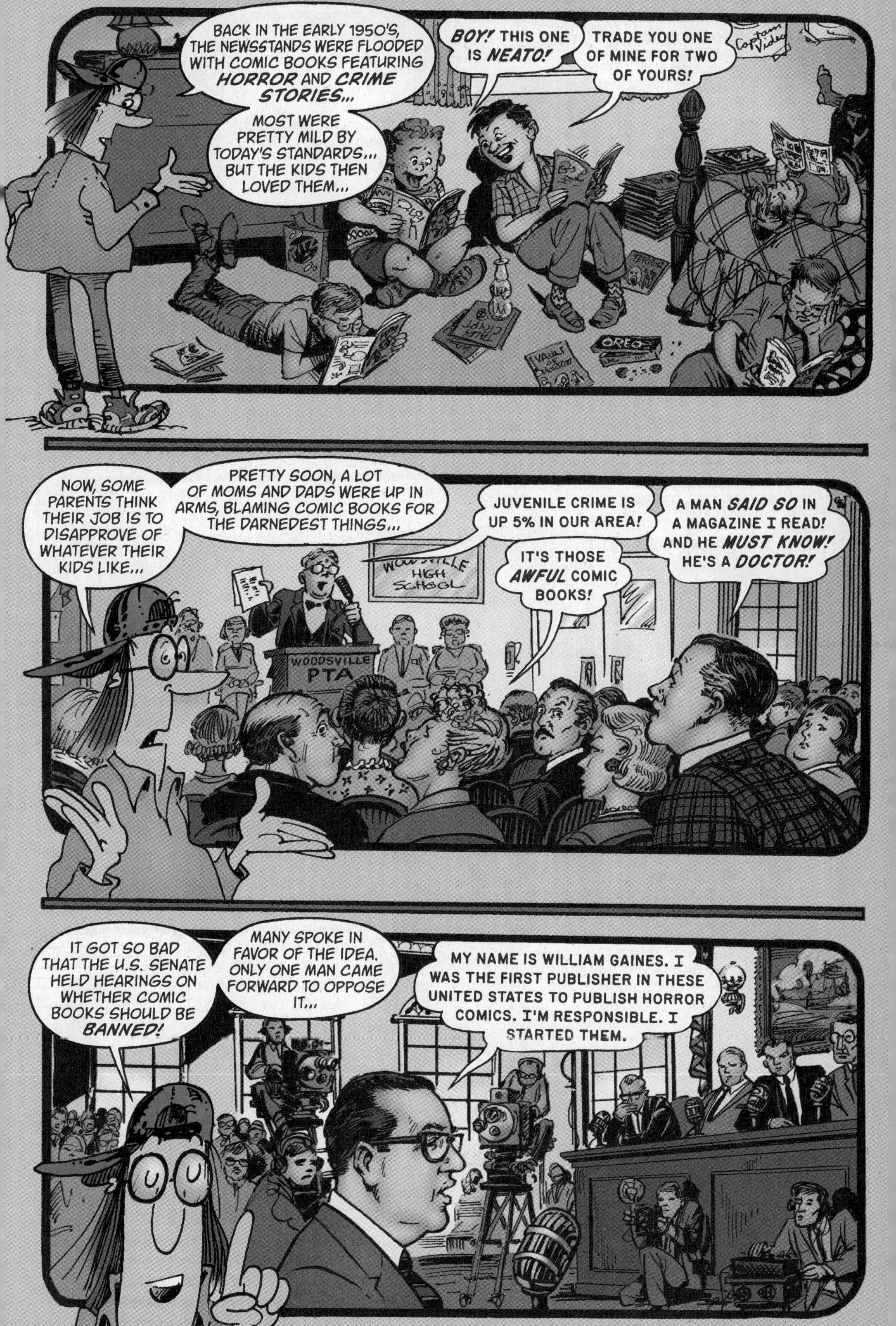
BACK IN THE EARLY 1950'S, THE NEWSSTANDS WERE FLOODED WITH COMIC BOOKS FEATURING *HORROR* AND *CRIME STORIES*...
MOST WERE PRETTY MILD BY TODAY'S STANDARDS... BUT THE KIDS THEN LOVED THEM...
BOY! THIS ONE IS *NEATO!*
TRADE YOU ONE OF MINE FOR TWO OF YOURS!
Captain Video
OREO
NOW, SOME PARENTS THINK THEIR JOB IS TO DISAPPROVE OF WHATEVER THEIR KIDS LIKE...
PRETTY SOON, A LOT OF MOMS AND DADS WERE UP IN ARMS, BLAMING COMIC BOOKS FOR THE DARNEDEST THINGS...
HIGH SCHOOL
WOODSVILLE PTA
JUVENILE CRIME IS UP 5% IN OUR AREA!
IT'S THOSE *AWFUL* COMIC BOOKS!
A MAN *SAID SO* IN A MAGAZINE I READ! AND HE *MUST KNOW!* HE'S A *DOCTOR!*
IT GOT SO BAD THAT THE U.S. SENATE HELD HEARINGS ON WHETHER COMIC BOOKS SHOULD BE *BANNED!*
MANY SPOKE IN FAVOR OF THE IDEA. ONLY ONE MAN CAME FORWARD TO OPPOSE IT...
MY NAME IS WILLIAM GAINES. I WAS THE FIRST PUBLISHER IN THESE UNITED STATES TO PUBLISH HORROR COMICS. I'M RESPONSIBLE. I STARTED THEM.

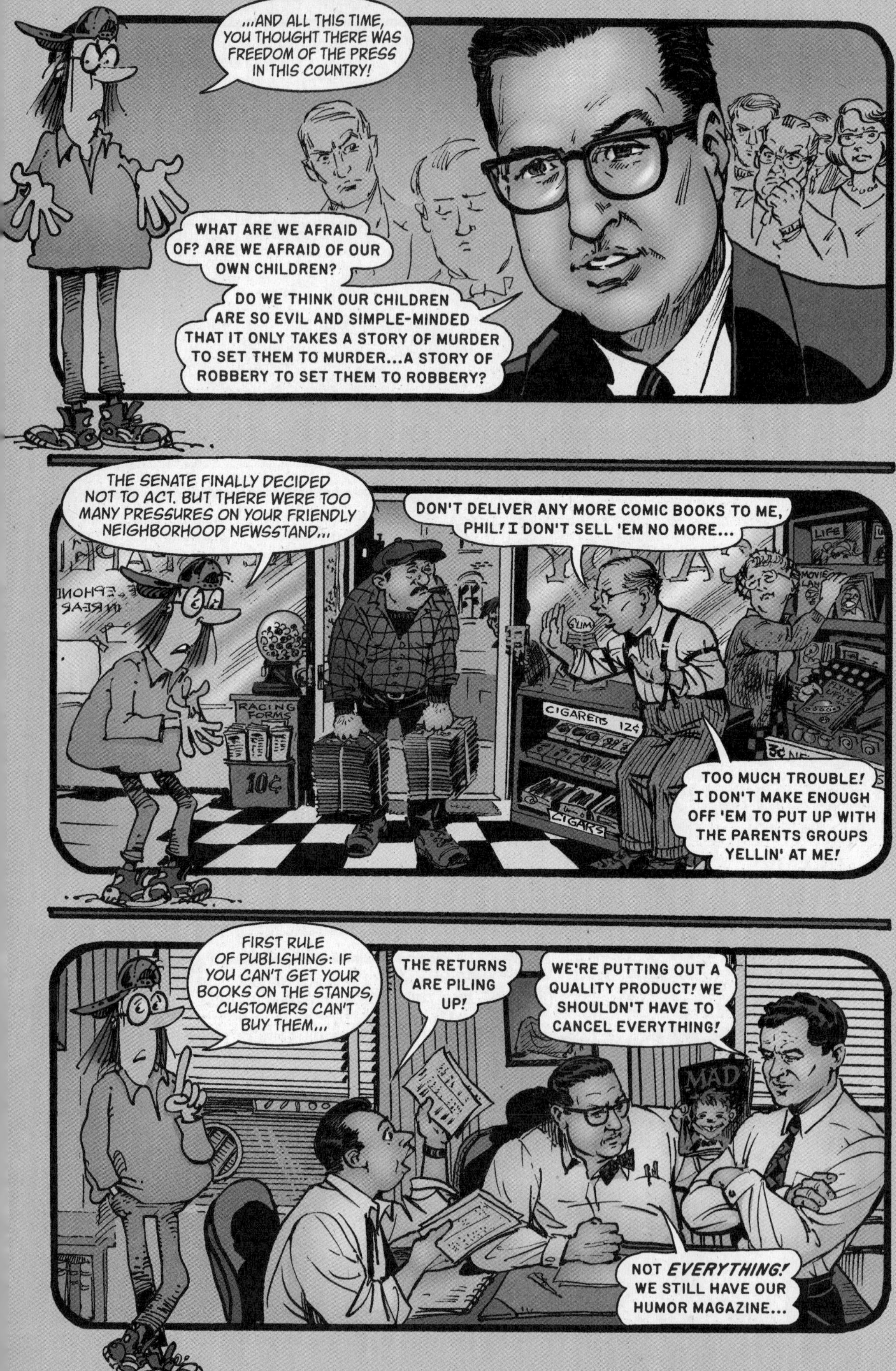
...AND ALL THIS TIME, YOU THOUGHT THERE WAS FREEDOM OF THE PRESS IN THIS COUNTRY!
WHAT ARE WE AFRAID OF? ARE WE AFRAID OF OUR OWN CHILDREN?
DO WE THINK OUR CHILDREN ARE SO EVIL AND SIMPLE-MINDED THAT IT ONLY TAKES A STORY OF MURDER TO SET THEM TO MURDER...A STORY OF ROBBERY TO SET THEM TO ROBBERY?
THE SENATE FINALLY DECIDED NOT TO ACT. BUT THERE WERE TOO MANY PRESSURES ON YOUR FRIENDLY NEIGHBORHOOD NEWSSTAND...
DON'T DELIVER ANY MORE COMIC BOOKS TO ME, PHIL! I DON'T SELL 'EM NO MORE...
RACING FORMS
10¢
LIFE
GUM
CIGARETS 12¢
CIGARS
TOO MUCH TROUBLE! I DON'T MAKE ENOUGH OFF 'EM TO PUT UP WITH THE PARENTS GROUPS YELLIN' AT ME!
FIRST RULE OF PUBLISHING: IF YOU CAN'T GET YOUR BOOKS ON THE STANDS, CUSTOMERS CAN'T BUY THEM...
THE RETURNS ARE PILING UP!
WE'RE PUTTING OUT A QUALITY PRODUCT! WE SHOULDN'T HAVE TO CANCEL EVERYTHING!
MAD
NOT *EVERYTHING!* WE STILL HAVE OUR HUMOR MAGAZINE...

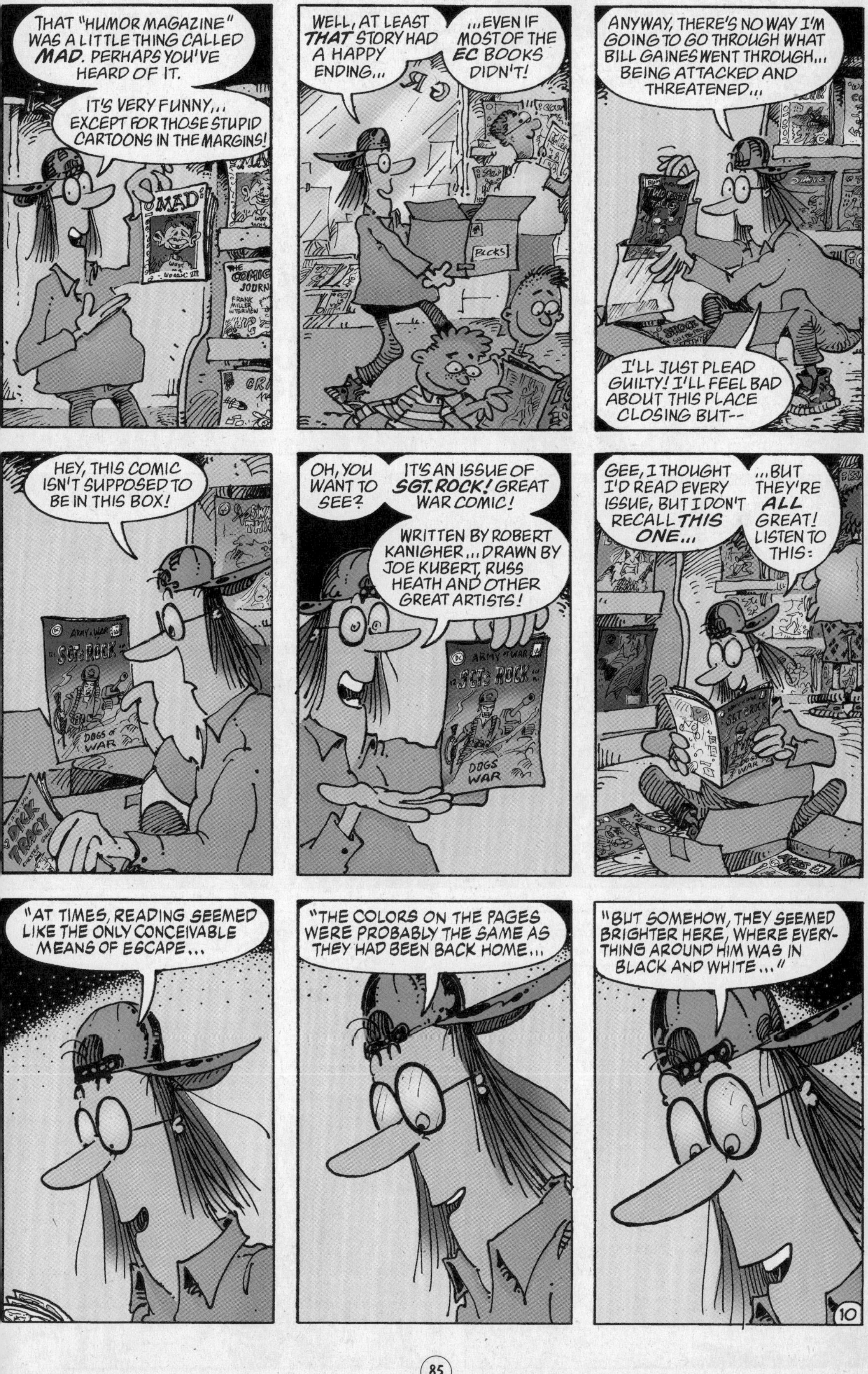
THAT "HUMOR MAGAZINE" WAS A LITTLE THING CALLED MAD. PERHAPS YOU'VE HEARD OF IT.
IT'S VERY FUNNY... EXCEPT FOR THOSE STUPID CARTOONS IN THE MARGINS!
MAD
THE COMICS JOURNAL
FRANK MILLER INTERVIEW
WELL, AT LEAST THAT STORY HAD A HAPPY ENDING...
...EVEN IF MOST OF THE EC BOOKS DIDN'T!
BOOKS
ANYWAY, THERE'S NO WAY I'M GOING TO GO THROUGH WHAT BILL GAINES WENT THROUGH... BEING ATTACKED AND THREATENED...
I'LL JUST PLEAD GUILTY! I'LL FEEL BAD ABOUT THIS PLACE CLOSING BUT--
HEY, THIS COMIC ISN'T SUPPOSED TO BE IN THIS BOX!
ARMY AT WAR
SGT. ROCK
DOGS OF WAR
DICK TRACY
OH, YOU WANT TO SEE?
IT'S AN ISSUE OF SGT. ROCK! GREAT WAR COMIC!
WRITTEN BY ROBERT KANIGHER... DRAWN BY JOE KUBERT, RUSS HEATH AND OTHER GREAT ARTISTS!
GEE, I THOUGHT I'D READ EVERY ISSUE, BUT I DON'T RECALL THIS ONE...
...BUT THEY'RE ALL GREAT! LISTEN TO THIS:
"AT TIMES, READING SEEMED LIKE THE ONLY CONCEIVABLE MEANS OF ESCAPE...
"THE COLORS ON THE PAGES WERE PROBABLY THE SAME AS THEY HAD BEEN BACK HOME...
"BUT SOMEHOW, THEY SEEMED BRIGHTER HERE, WHERE EVERYTHING AROUND HIM WAS IN BLACK AND WHITE..."
10

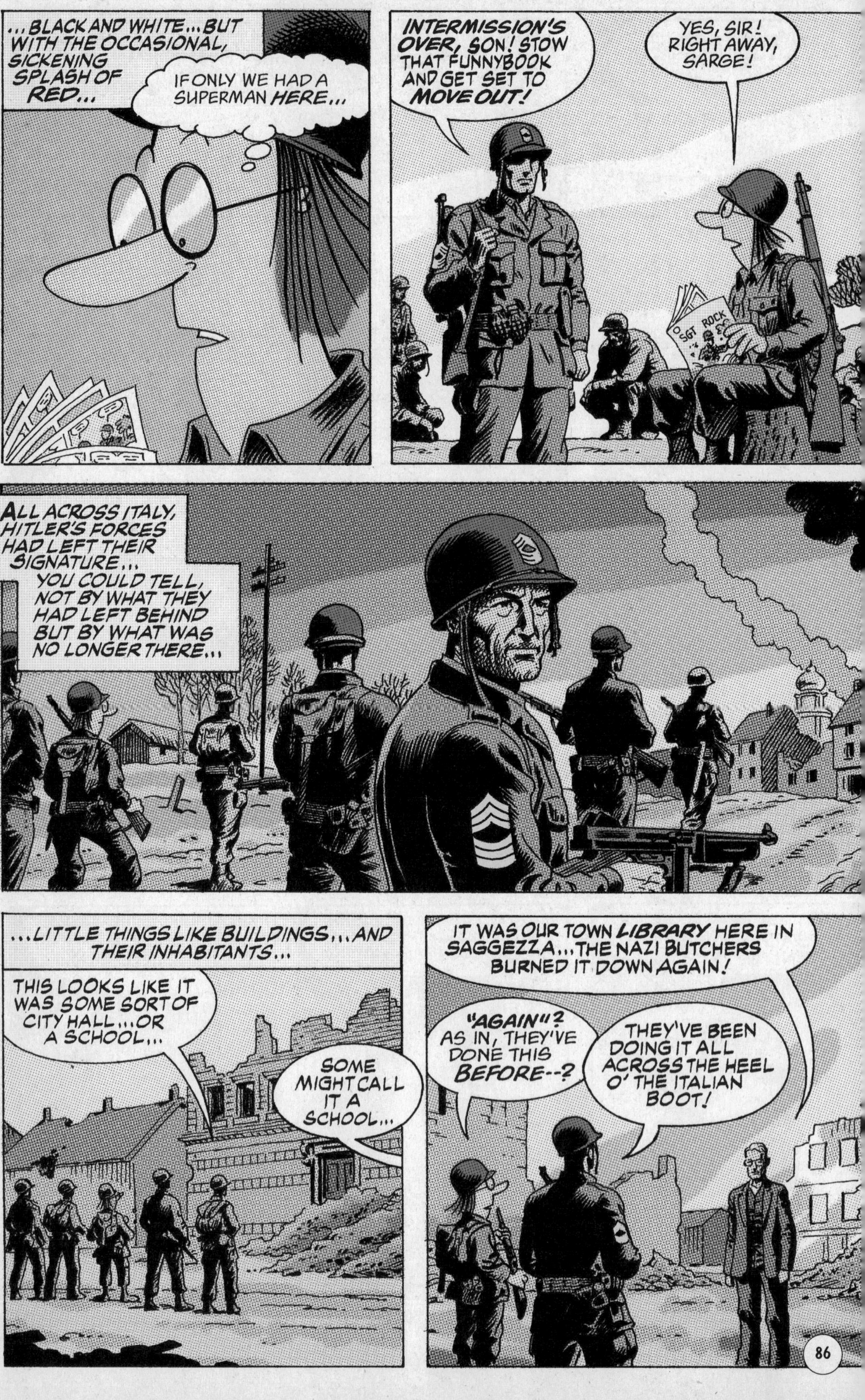
...BLACK AND WHITE...BUT WITH THE OCCASIONAL, SICKENING SPLASH OF RED...
IF ONLY WE HAD A SUPERMAN HERE...
INTERMISSION'S OVER, SON! STOW THAT FUNNYBOOK AND GET SET TO MOVE OUT!
YES, SIR! RIGHT AWAY, SARGE!
SGT ROCK
ALL ACROSS ITALY, HITLER'S FORCES HAD LEFT THEIR SIGNATURE... YOU COULD TELL, NOT BY WHAT THEY HAD LEFT BEHIND BUT BY WHAT WAS NO LONGER THERE...
...LITTLE THINGS LIKE BUILDINGS...AND THEIR INHABITANTS...
THIS LOOKS LIKE IT WAS SOME SORT OF CITY HALL...OR A SCHOOL...
SOME MIGHT CALL IT A SCHOOL...
IT WAS OUR TOWN LIBRARY HERE IN SAGGEZZA...THE NAZI BUTCHERS BURNED IT DOWN AGAIN!
"AGAIN"? AS IN, THEY'VE DONE THIS BEFORE--?
THEY'VE BEEN DOING IT ALL ACROSS THE HEEL O' THE ITALIAN BOOT!

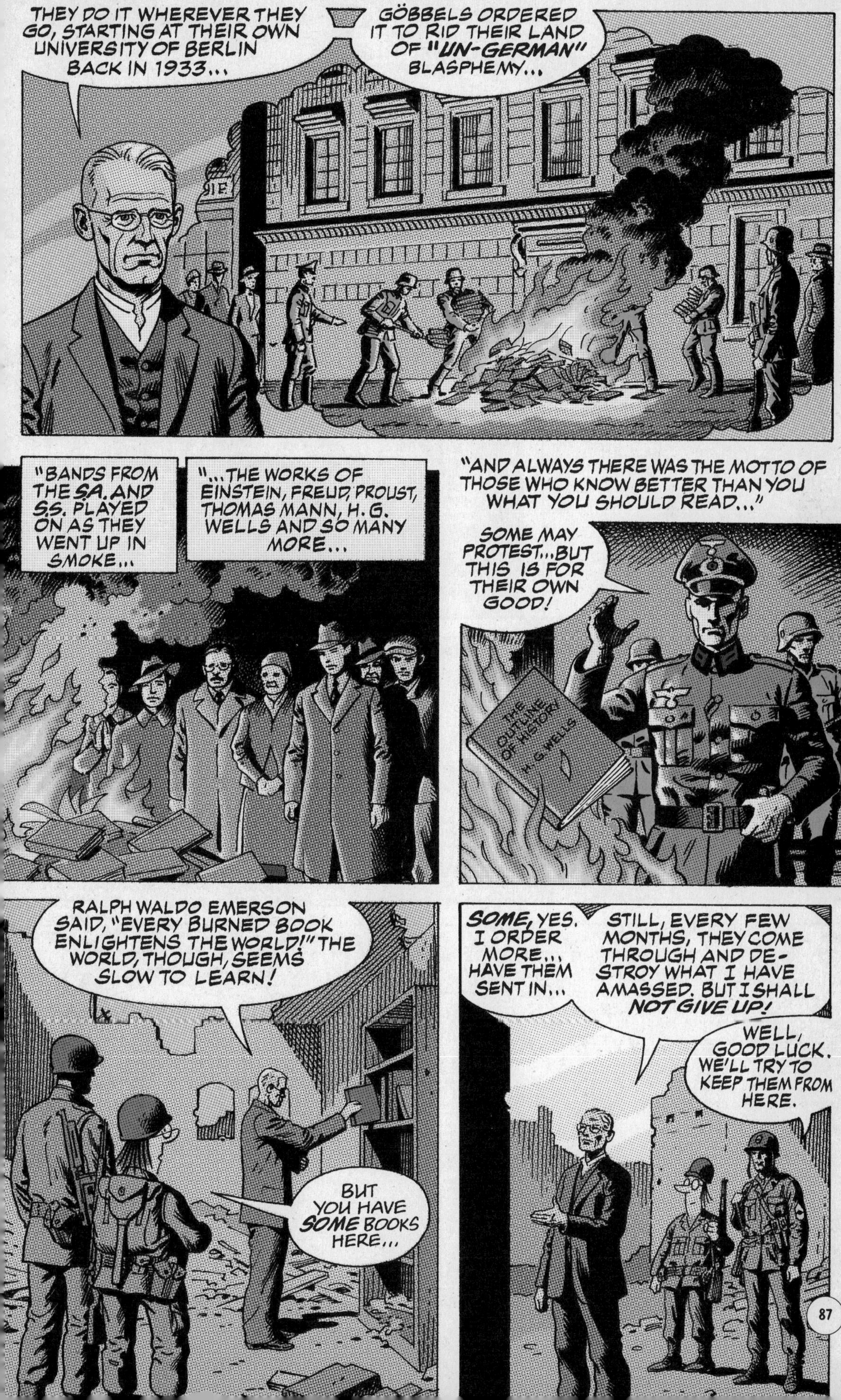

THEY DO IT WHEREVER THEY GO, STARTING AT THEIR OWN UNIVERSITY OF BERLIN BACK IN 1933...
GÖBBELS ORDERED IT TO RID THEIR LAND OF "UN-GERMAN" BLASPHEMY...
"BANDS FROM THE SA. AND S.S. PLAYED ON AS THEY WENT UP IN SMOKE...
"...THE WORKS OF EINSTEIN, FREUD, PROUST, THOMAS MANN, H.G. WELLS AND SO MANY MORE...
"AND ALWAYS THERE WAS THE MOTTO OF THOSE WHO KNOW BETTER THAN YOU WHAT YOU SHOULD READ..."
SOME MAY PROTEST...BUT THIS IS FOR THEIR OWN GOOD!
THE OUTLINE OF HISTORY H. G. WELLS
RALPH WALDO EMERSON SAID, "EVERY BURNED BOOK ENLIGHTENS THE WORLD!" THE WORLD, THOUGH, SEEMS SLOW TO LEARN!
BUT YOU HAVE SOME BOOKS HERE...
SOME, YES. I ORDER MORE... HAVE THEM SENT IN...
STILL, EVERY FEW MONTHS, THEY COME THROUGH AND DESTROY WHAT I HAVE AMASSED. BUT I SHALL NOT GIVE UP!
WELL, GOOD LUCK. WE'LL TRY TO KEEP THEM FROM HERE.

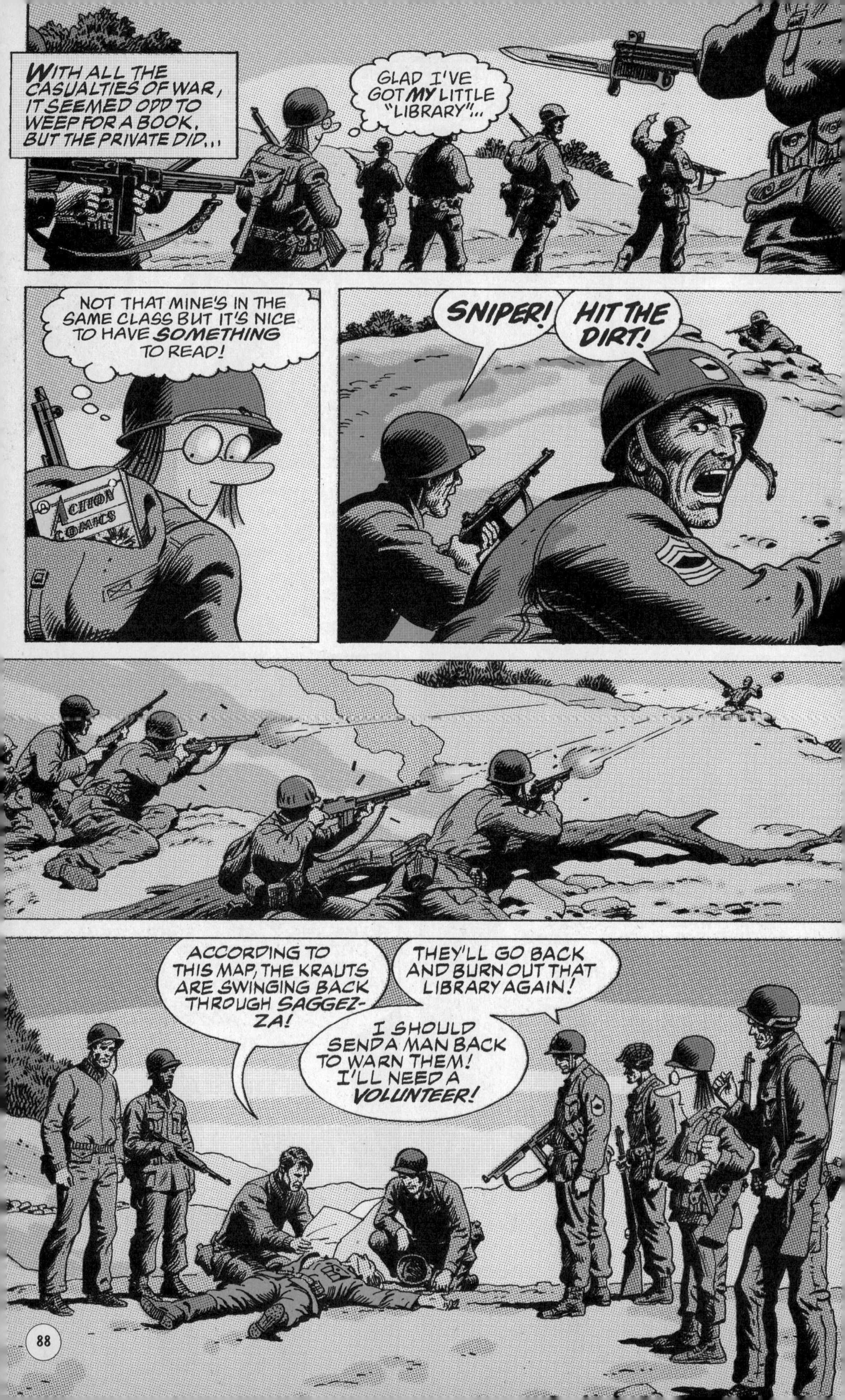
WITH ALL THE CASUALTIES OF WAR, IT SEEMED ODD TO WEEP FOR A BOOK, BUT THE PRIVATE DID...
GLAD I'VE GOT MY LITTLE "LIBRARY"...
NOT THAT MINE'S IN THE SAME CLASS BUT IT'S NICE TO HAVE SOMETHING TO READ!
ACTION COMICS
SNIPER!
HIT THE DIRT!
ACCORDING TO THIS MAP, THE KRAUTS ARE SWINGING BACK THROUGH SAGGEZ-ZA!
THEY'LL GO BACK AND BURN OUT THAT LIBRARY AGAIN!
I SHOULD SEND A MAN BACK TO WARN THEM! I'LL NEED A VOLUNTEER!

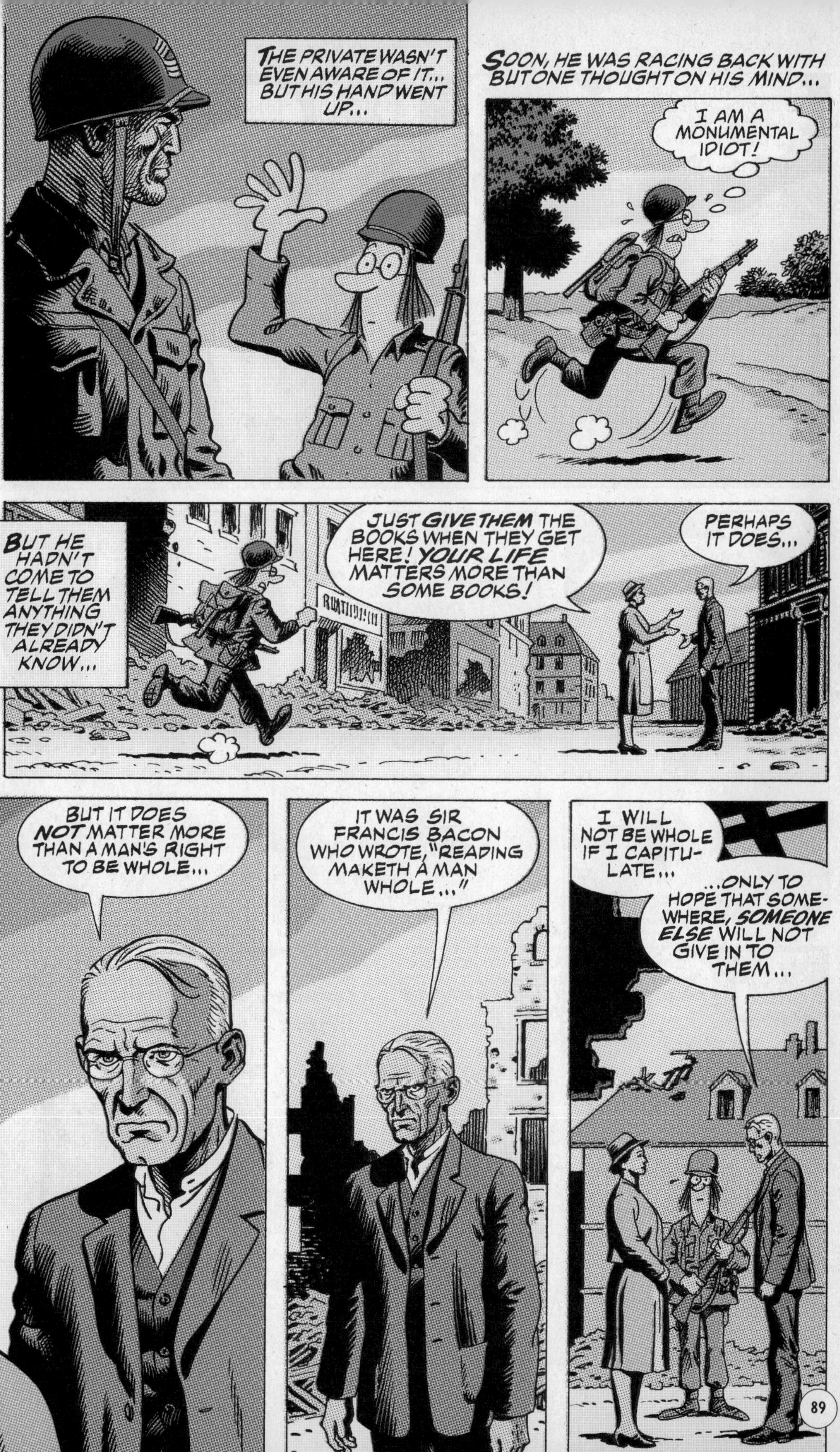
THE PRIVATE WASN'T EVEN AWARE OF IT... BUT HIS HAND WENT UP...
SOON, HE WAS RACING BACK WITH BUT ONE THOUGHT ON HIS MIND...
I AM A MONUMENTAL IDIOT!
BUT HE HADN'T COME TO TELL THEM ANYTHING THEY DIDN'T ALREADY KNOW...
JUST GIVE THEM THE BOOKS WHEN THEY GET HERE! YOUR LIFE MATTERS MORE THAN SOME BOOKS!
PERHAPS IT DOES...
BUT IT DOES NOT MATTER MORE THAN A MAN'S RIGHT TO BE WHOLE...
IT WAS SIR FRANCIS BACON WHO WROTE, "READING MAKETH A MAN WHOLE..."
I WILL NOT BE WHOLE IF I CAPITU-LATE...
...ONLY TO HOPE THAT SOME-WHERE, SOMEONE ELSE WILL NOT GIVE IN TO THEM...

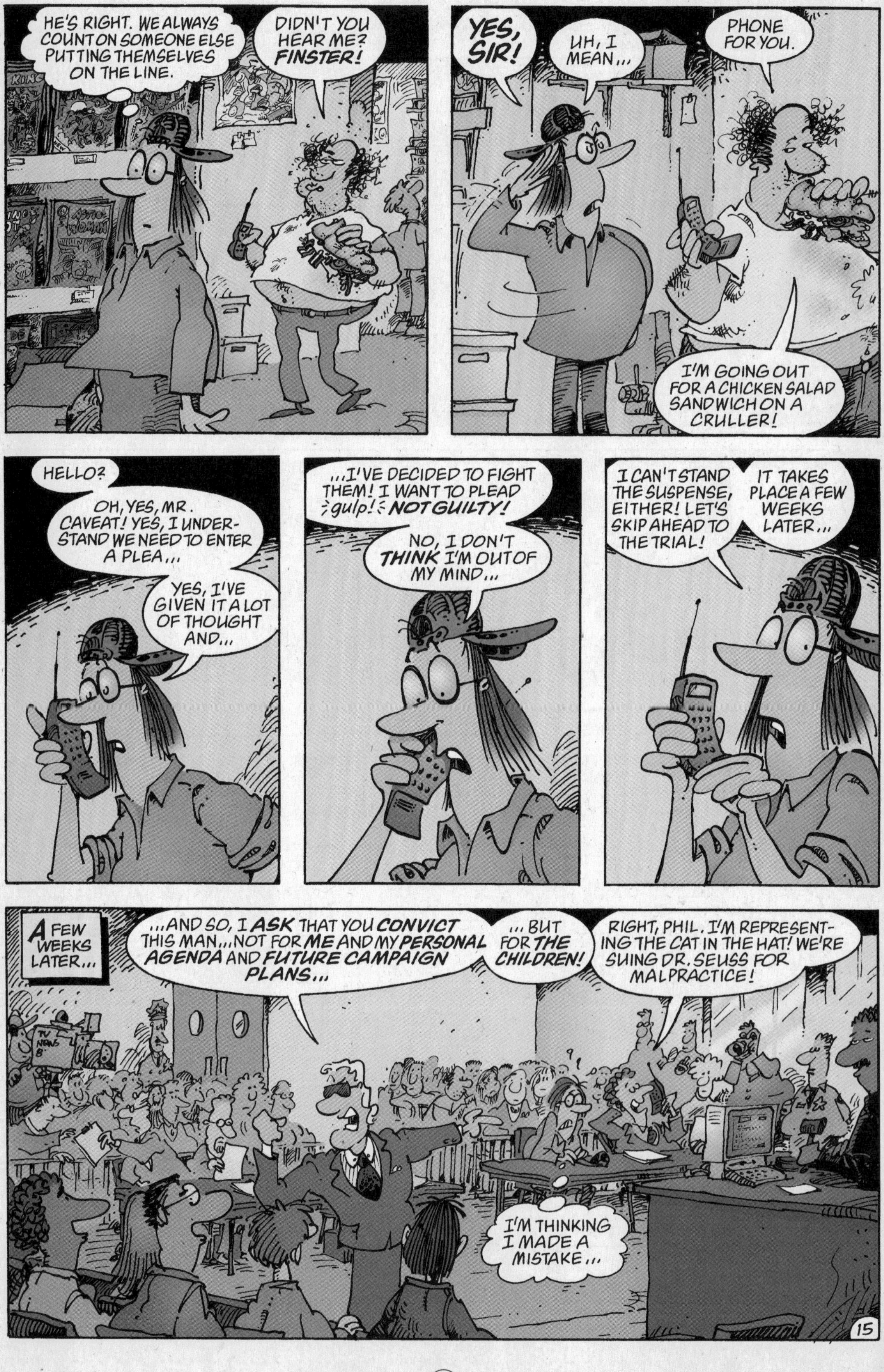
HE'S RIGHT. WE ALWAYS COUNT ON SOMEONE ELSE PUTTING THEMSELVES ON THE LINE.
DIDN'T YOU HEAR ME? FINSTER!
YES, SIR!
UH, I MEAN...
PHONE FOR YOU.
I'M GOING OUT FOR A CHICKEN SALAD SANDWICH ON A CRULLER!
HELLO?
OH, YES, MR. CAVEAT! YES, I UNDERSTAND WE NEED TO ENTER A PLEA...
YES, I'VE GIVEN IT A LOT OF THOUGHT AND...
...I'VE DECIDED TO FIGHT THEM! I WANT TO PLEAD gulp! NOT GUILTY!
NO, I DON'T THINK I'M OUT OF MY MIND...
I CAN'T STAND THE SUSPENSE, EITHER! LET'S SKIP AHEAD TO THE TRIAL!
IT TAKES PLACE A FEW WEEKS LATER...
A FEW WEEKS LATER...
...AND SO, I ASK THAT YOU CONVICT THIS MAN...NOT FOR ME AND MY PERSONAL AGENDA AND FUTURE CAMPAIGN PLANS...
...BUT FOR THE CHILDREN!
RIGHT, PHIL. I'M REPRESENTING THE CAT IN THE HAT! WE'RE SUING DR. SEUSS FOR MALPRACTICE!
TV NEWS 8
I'M THINKING I MADE A MISTAKE...
15

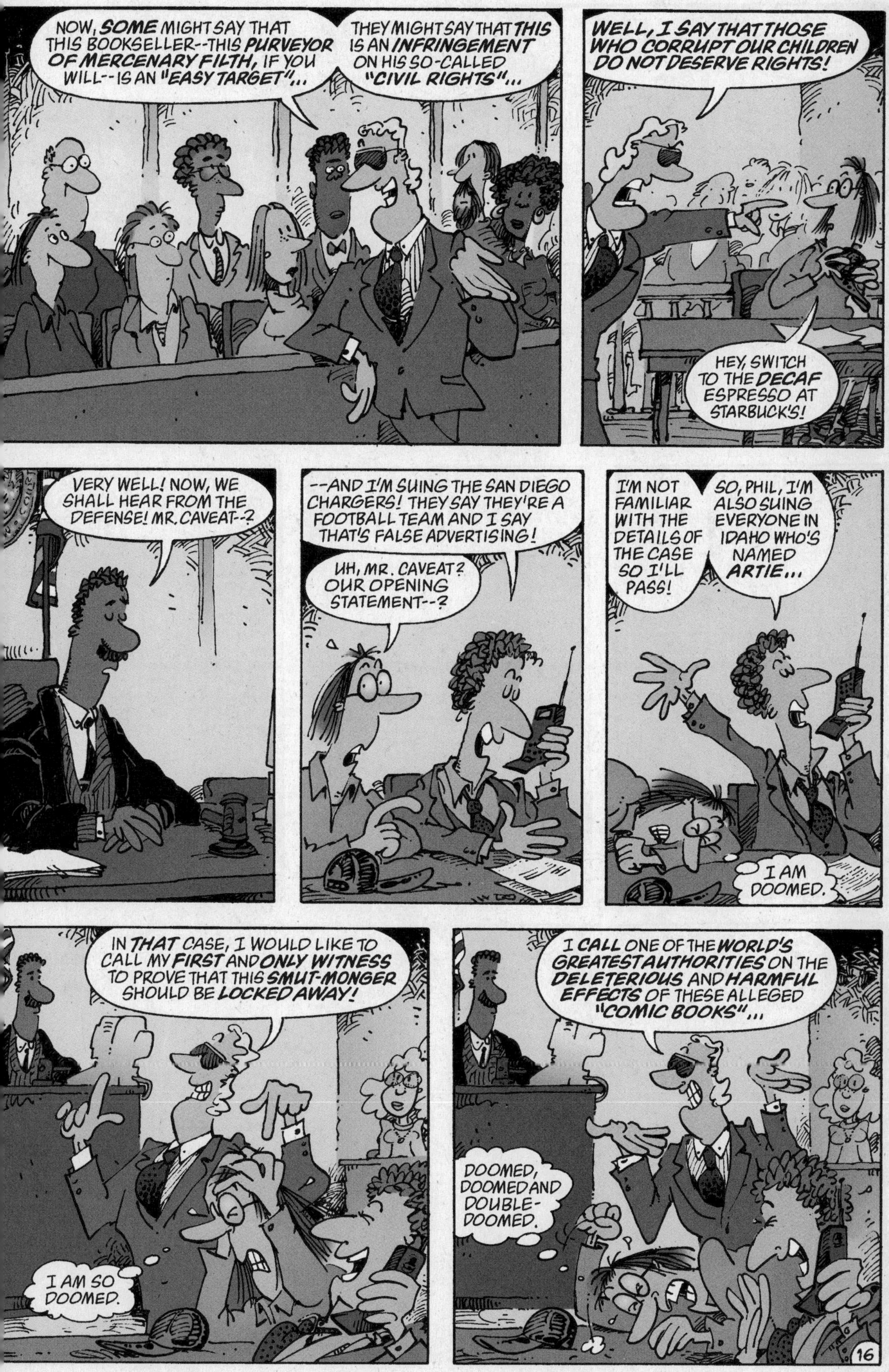
NOW, SOME MIGHT SAY THAT THIS BOOKSELLER--THIS PURVEYOR OF MERCENARY FILTH, IF YOU WILL--IS AN "EASY TARGET"...
THEY MIGHT SAY THAT THIS IS AN INFRINGEMENT ON HIS SO-CALLED "CIVIL RIGHTS"...
WELL, I SAY THAT THOSE WHO CORRUPT OUR CHILDREN DO NOT DESERVE RIGHTS!
HEY, SWITCH TO THE DECAF ESPRESSO AT STARBUCK'S!
VERY WELL! NOW, WE SHALL HEAR FROM THE DEFENSE! MR. CAVEAT--?
--AND I'M SUING THE SAN DIEGO CHARGERS! THEY SAY THEY'RE A FOOTBALL TEAM AND I SAY THAT'S FALSE ADVERTISING!
UH, MR. CAVEAT? OUR OPENING STATEMENT--?
I'M NOT FAMILIAR WITH THE DETAILS OF THE CASE SO I'LL PASS!
SO, PHIL, I'M ALSO SUING EVERYONE IN IDAHO WHO'S NAMED ARTIE...
I AM DOOMED.
IN THAT CASE, I WOULD LIKE TO CALL MY FIRST AND ONLY WITNESS TO PROVE THAT THIS SMUT-MONGER SHOULD BE LOCKED AWAY!
I AM SO DOOMED.
I CALL ONE OF THE WORLD'S GREATEST AUTHORITIES ON THE DELETERIOUS AND HARMFUL EFFECTS OF THESE ALLEGED "COMIC BOOKS"...
DOOMED, DOOMED AND DOUBLE-DOOMED.
16

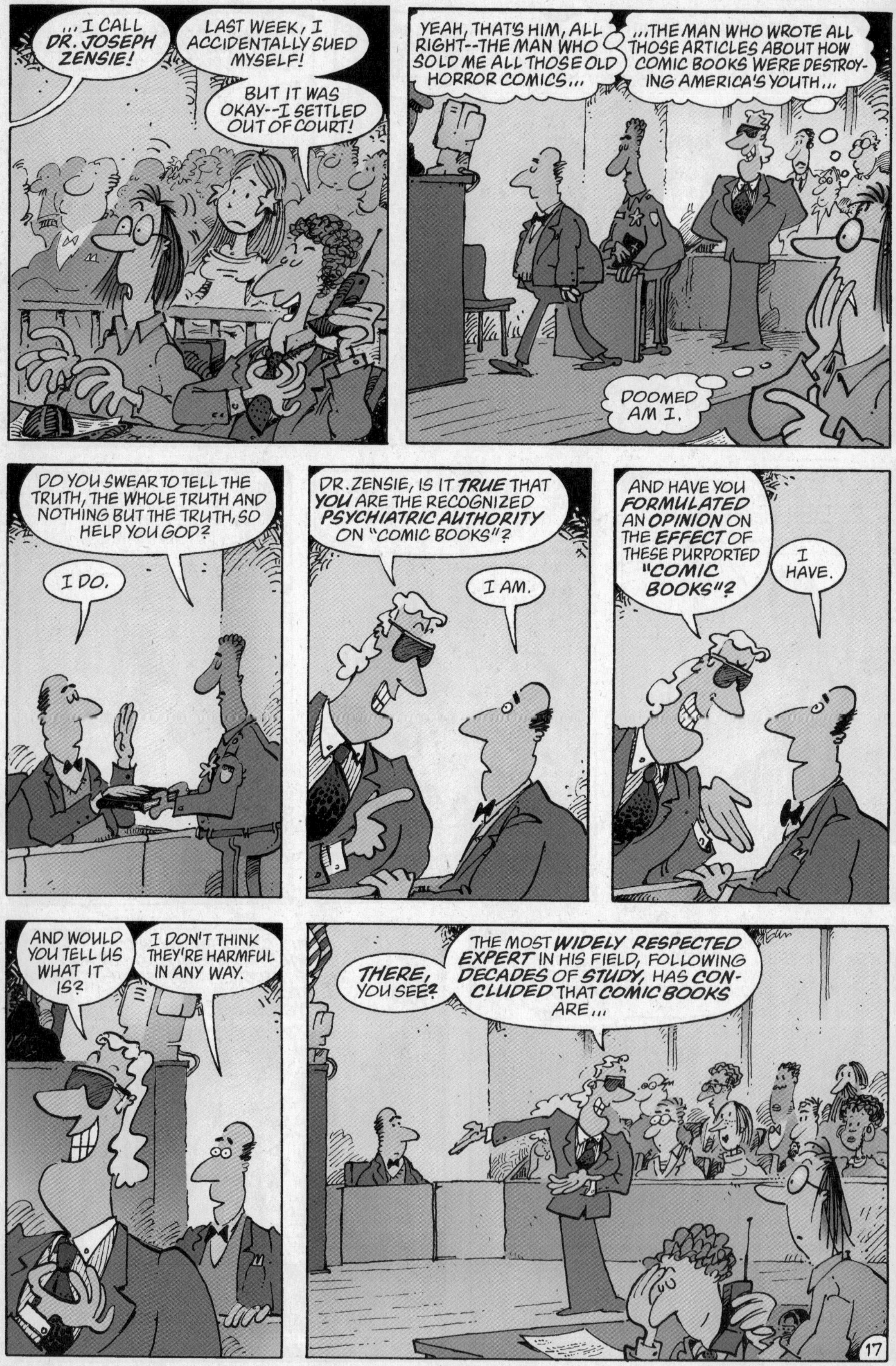
...I CALL DR. JOSEPH ZENSIE!
LAST WEEK, I ACCIDENTALLY SUED MYSELF!
BUT IT WAS OKAY--I SETTLED OUT OF COURT!
YEAH, THAT'S HIM, ALL RIGHT--THE MAN WHO SOLD ME ALL THOSE OLD HORROR COMICS...
...THE MAN WHO WROTE ALL THOSE ARTICLES ABOUT HOW COMIC BOOKS WERE DESTROYING AMERICA'S YOUTH...
DOOMED AM I.
DO YOU SWEAR TO TELL THE TRUTH, THE WHOLE TRUTH AND NOTHING BUT THE TRUTH, SO HELP YOU GOD?
I DO.
DR. ZENSIE, IS IT TRUE THAT YOU ARE THE RECOGNIZED PSYCHIATRIC AUTHORITY ON "COMIC BOOKS"?
I AM.
AND HAVE YOU FORMULATED AN OPINION ON THE EFFECT OF THESE PURPORTED "COMIC BOOKS"?
I HAVE.
AND WOULD YOU TELL US WHAT IT IS?
I DON'T THINK THEY'RE HARMFUL IN ANY WAY.
THERE, YOU SEE?
THE MOST WIDELY RESPECTED EXPERT IN HIS FIELD, FOLLOWING DECADES OF STUDY, HAS CONCLUDED THAT COMIC BOOKS ARE...
17

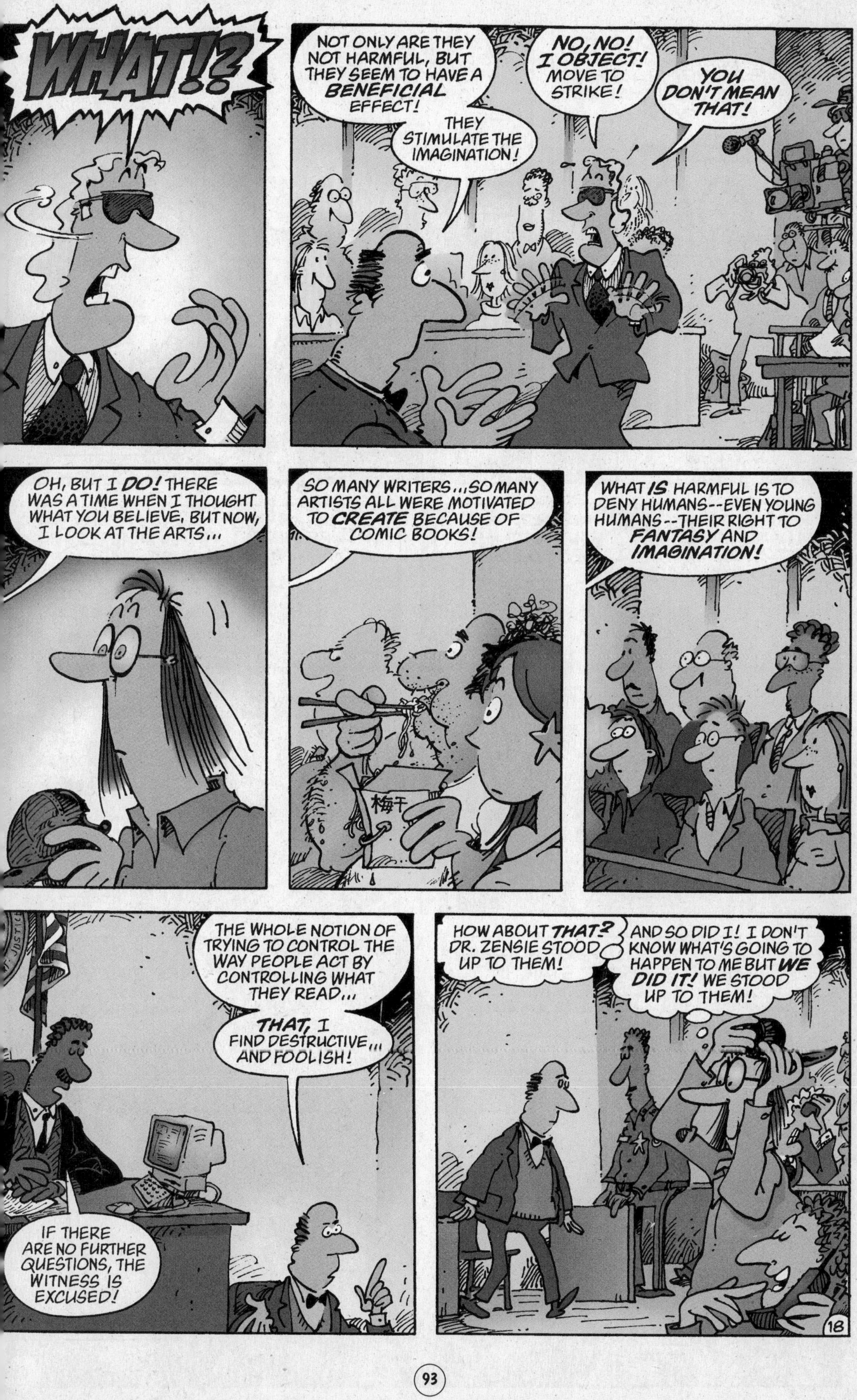
WHAT!?
NOT ONLY ARE THEY NOT HARMFUL, BUT THEY SEEM TO HAVE A BENEFICIAL EFFECT!
THEY STIMULATE THE IMAGINATION!
NO, NO! I OBJECT! MOVE TO STRIKE!
YOU DON'T MEAN THAT!
OH, BUT I DO! THERE WAS A TIME WHEN I THOUGHT WHAT YOU BELIEVE, BUT NOW, I LOOK AT THE ARTS...
SO MANY WRITERS...SO MANY ARTISTS ALL WERE MOTIVATED TO CREATE BECAUSE OF COMIC BOOKS!
梅干
WHAT IS HARMFUL IS TO DENY HUMANS--EVEN YOUNG HUMANS--THEIR RIGHT TO FANTASY AND IMAGINATION!
THE WHOLE NOTION OF TRYING TO CONTROL THE WAY PEOPLE ACT BY CONTROLLING WHAT THEY READ...
THAT, I FIND DESTRUCTIVE... AND FOOLISH!
IF THERE ARE NO FURTHER QUESTIONS, THE WITNESS IS EXCUSED!
HOW ABOUT THAT? DR. ZENSIE STOOD UP TO THEM!
AND SO DID I! I DON'T KNOW WHAT'S GOING TO HAPPEN TO ME BUT WE DID IT! WE STOOD UP TO THEM!
18

IF SOMEONE DOESN'T STAND UP TO THESE PEOPLE, THEY'LL KEEP ON DOING WHAT THEY'RE DOING AND...

UH, I WAS JUST THINKING ...YOU'RE PUTTING YOUR *LIFE* ON THE LINE FOR THIS LIBRARY!

IN THE WORDS OF LORD BYRON, "THEY NEVER FAIL WHO DIE IN A GREAT CAUSE."

I WILL PROTECT YOU AND YOUR BOOKS WITH MY LIFE!

NO! NO, THAT WILL NOT BE NECESSARY...

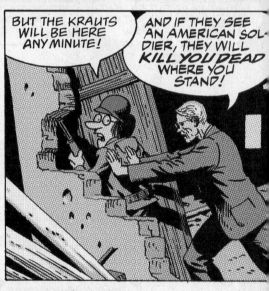

BUT THE KRAUTS WILL BE HERE ANY MINUTE!

AND IF THEY SEE AN AMERICAN SOLDIER, THEY WILL *KILL YOU DEAD* WHERE YOU STAND!

NEIN, NEIN, BIBLIOTHEKAR!

YOU WERE *WARNED* ABOUT STARTING YOUR FORBIDDEN LIBRARY AGAIN...

PLEASE...THEY ARE JUST *BOOKS* ...EVEN HITLER WRITES BOOKS...

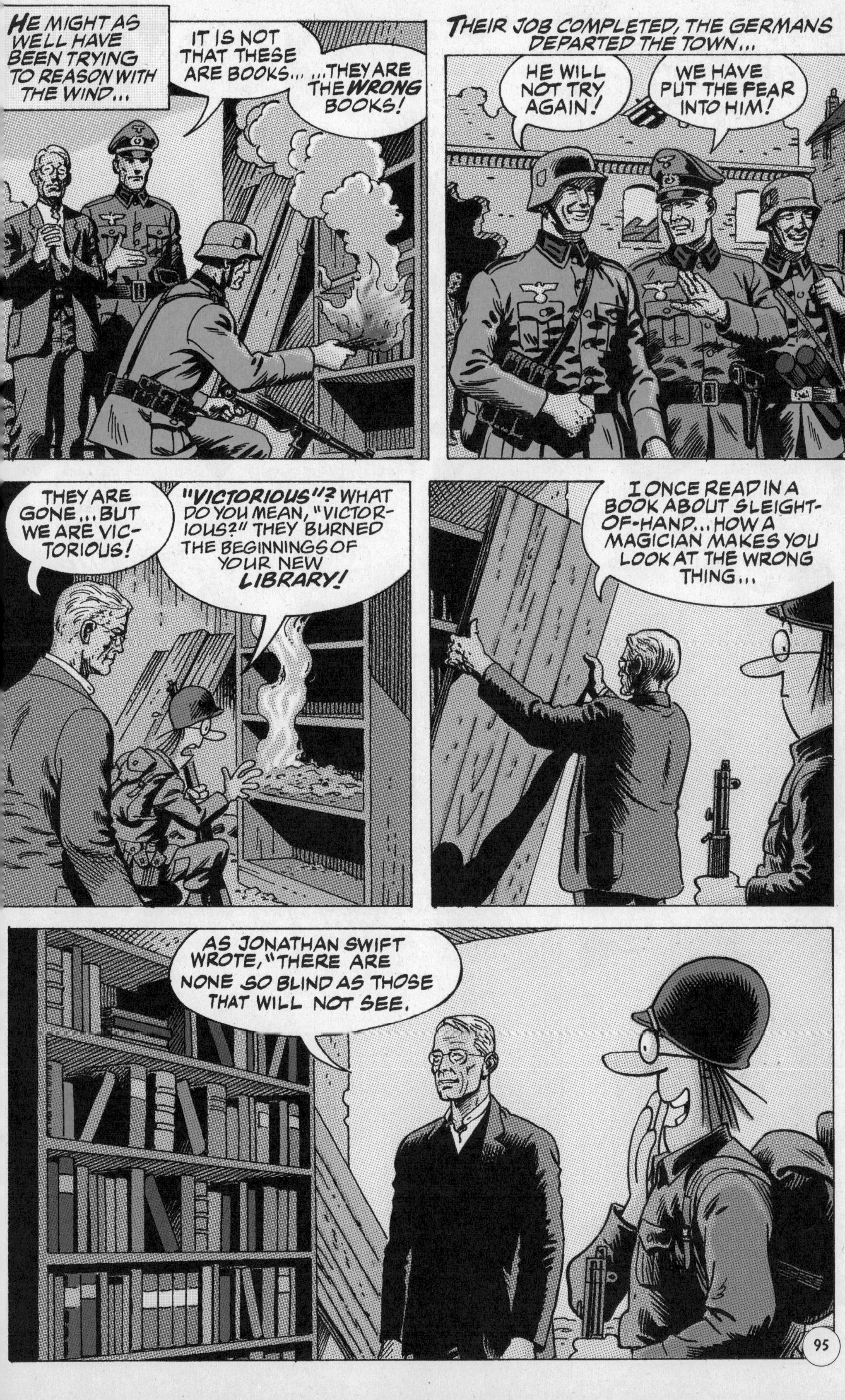

HE MIGHT AS WELL HAVE BEEN TRYING TO REASON WITH THE WIND...
IT IS NOT THAT THESE ARE BOOKS...
...THEY ARE THE WRONG BOOKS!
THEIR JOB COMPLETED, THE GERMANS DEPARTED THE TOWN...
HE WILL NOT TRY AGAIN!
WE HAVE PUT THE FEAR INTO HIM!
THEY ARE GONE... BUT WE ARE VICTORIOUS!
"VICTORIOUS"? WHAT DO YOU MEAN, "VICTORIOUS?" THEY BURNED THE BEGINNINGS OF YOUR NEW LIBRARY!
I ONCE READ IN A BOOK ABOUT SLEIGHT-OF-HAND... HOW A MAGICIAN MAKES YOU LOOK AT THE WRONG THING...
AS JONATHAN SWIFT WROTE, "THERE ARE NONE SO BLIND AS THOSE THAT WILL NOT SEE.

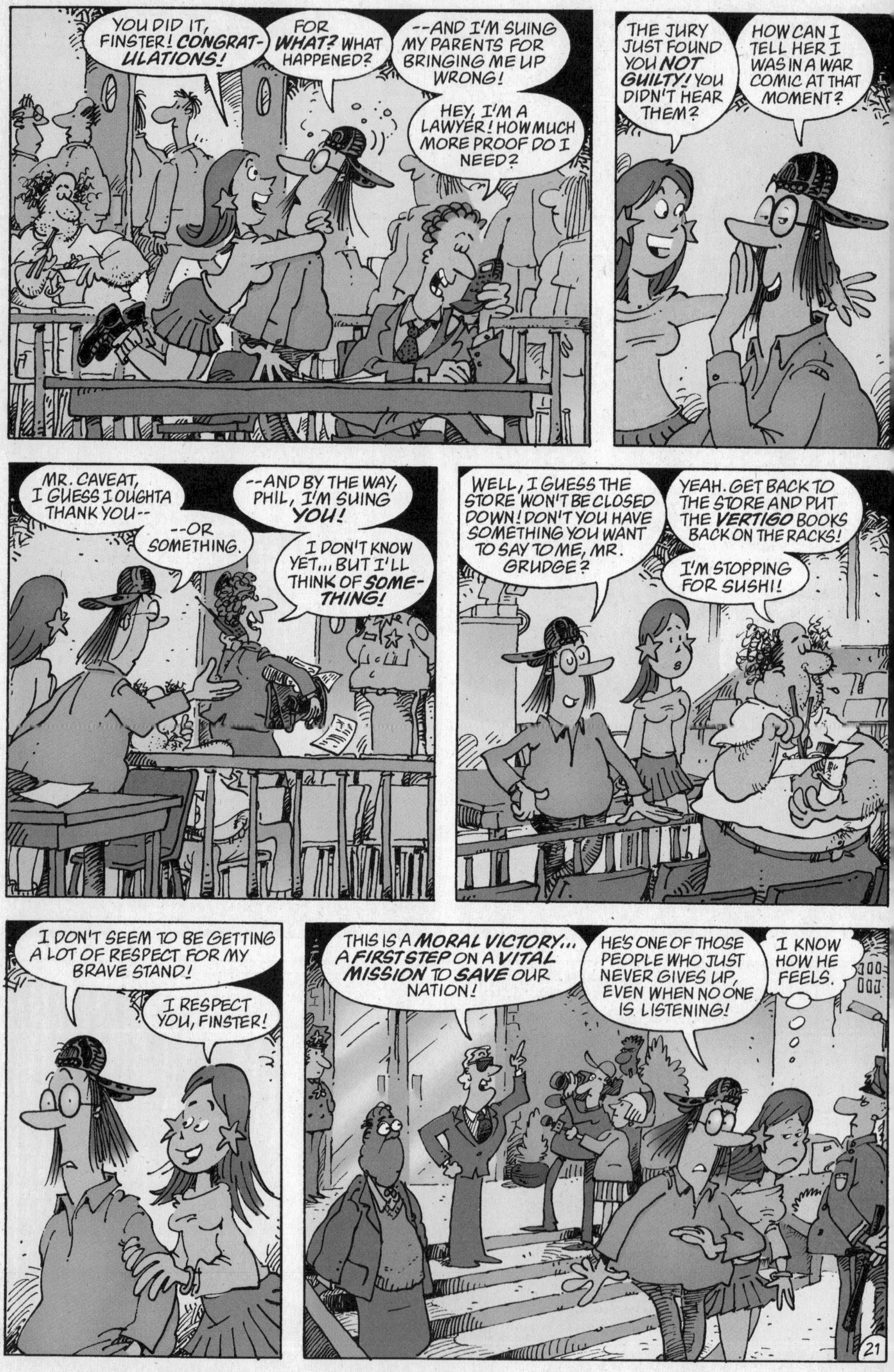
YOU DID IT, FINSTER! CONGRAT-ULATIONS!
FOR WHAT? WHAT HAPPENED?
--AND I'M SUING MY PARENTS FOR BRINGING ME UP WRONG!
HEY, I'M A LAWYER! HOW MUCH MORE PROOF DO I NEED?
THE JURY JUST FOUND YOU NOT GUILTY! YOU DIDN'T HEAR THEM?
HOW CAN I TELL HER I WAS IN A WAR COMIC AT THAT MOMENT?
MR. CAVEAT, I GUESS I OUGHTA THANK YOU--
--OR SOMETHING.
--AND BY THE WAY, PHIL, I'M SUING YOU!
I DON'T KNOW YET... BUT I'LL THINK OF SOME-THING!
WELL, I GUESS THE STORE WON'T BE CLOSED DOWN! DON'T YOU HAVE SOMETHING YOU WANT TO SAY TO ME, MR. GRUDGE?
YEAH. GET BACK TO THE STORE AND PUT THE VERTIGO BOOKS BACK ON THE RACKS!
I'M STOPPING FOR SUSHI!
I DON'T SEEM TO BE GETTING A LOT OF RESPECT FOR MY BRAVE STAND!
I RESPECT YOU, FINSTER!
THIS IS A MORAL VICTORY... A FIRST STEP ON A VITAL MISSION TO SAVE OUR NATION!
HE'S ONE OF THOSE PEOPLE WHO JUST NEVER GIVES UP, EVEN WHEN NO ONE IS LISTENING!
I KNOW HOW HE FEELS.
21

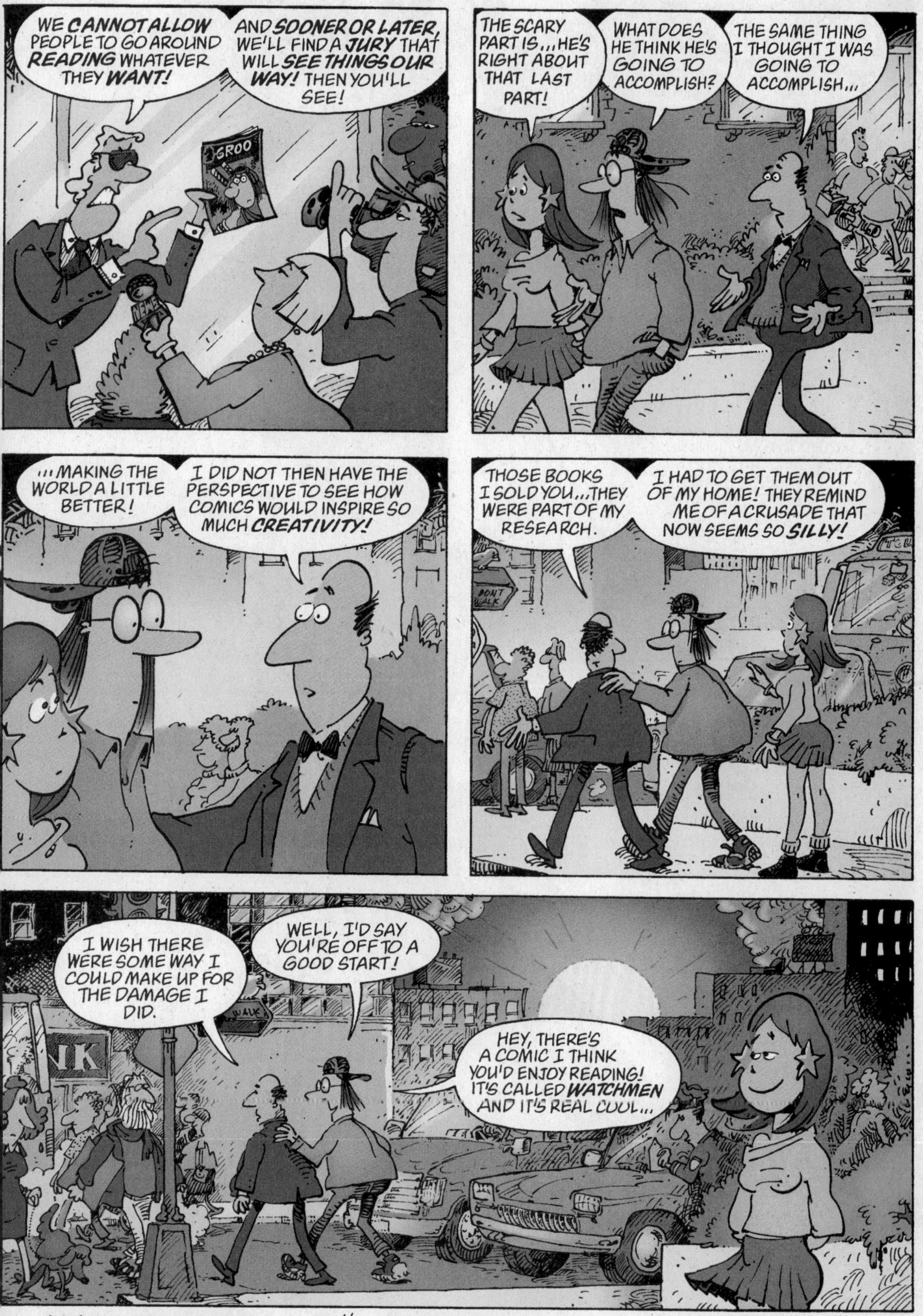
WE CANNOT ALLOW PEOPLE TO GO AROUND READING WHATEVER THEY WANT!
AND SOONER OR LATER, WE'LL FIND A JURY THAT WILL SEE THINGS OUR WAY! THEN YOU'LL SEE!
GROO
NEWS
THE SCARY PART IS... HE'S RIGHT ABOUT THAT LAST PART!
WHAT DOES HE THINK HE'S GOING TO ACCOMPLISH?
THE SAME THING I THOUGHT I WAS GOING TO ACCOMPLISH...
...MAKING THE WORLD A LITTLE BETTER!
I DID NOT THEN HAVE THE PERSPECTIVE TO SEE HOW COMICS WOULD INSPIRE SO MUCH CREATIVITY!
THOSE BOOKS I SOLD YOU... THEY WERE PART OF MY RESEARCH.
I HAD TO GET THEM OUT OF MY HOME! THEY REMIND ME OF A CRUSADE THAT NOW SEEMS SO SILLY!
DON'T WALK
I WISH THERE WERE SOME WAY I COULD MAKE UP FOR THE DAMAGE I DID.
WELL, I'D SAY YOU'RE OFF TO A GOOD START!
HEY, THERE'S A COMIC I THINK YOU'D ENJOY READING! IT'S CALLED WATCHMEN AND IT'S REAL COOL...

By **MARK EVANIER** and **SERGIO ARAGONÉS** with guest artists: **JORDI BERNET** (p.1-2) **MARIE SEVERIN** (p.8-9) **RUSS HEATH** (p.11-14, 19-20)

LETTERING: **TODD KLEIN**
COLORING: **TOM LUTH**
EDITOR: **TONY BEDARD**

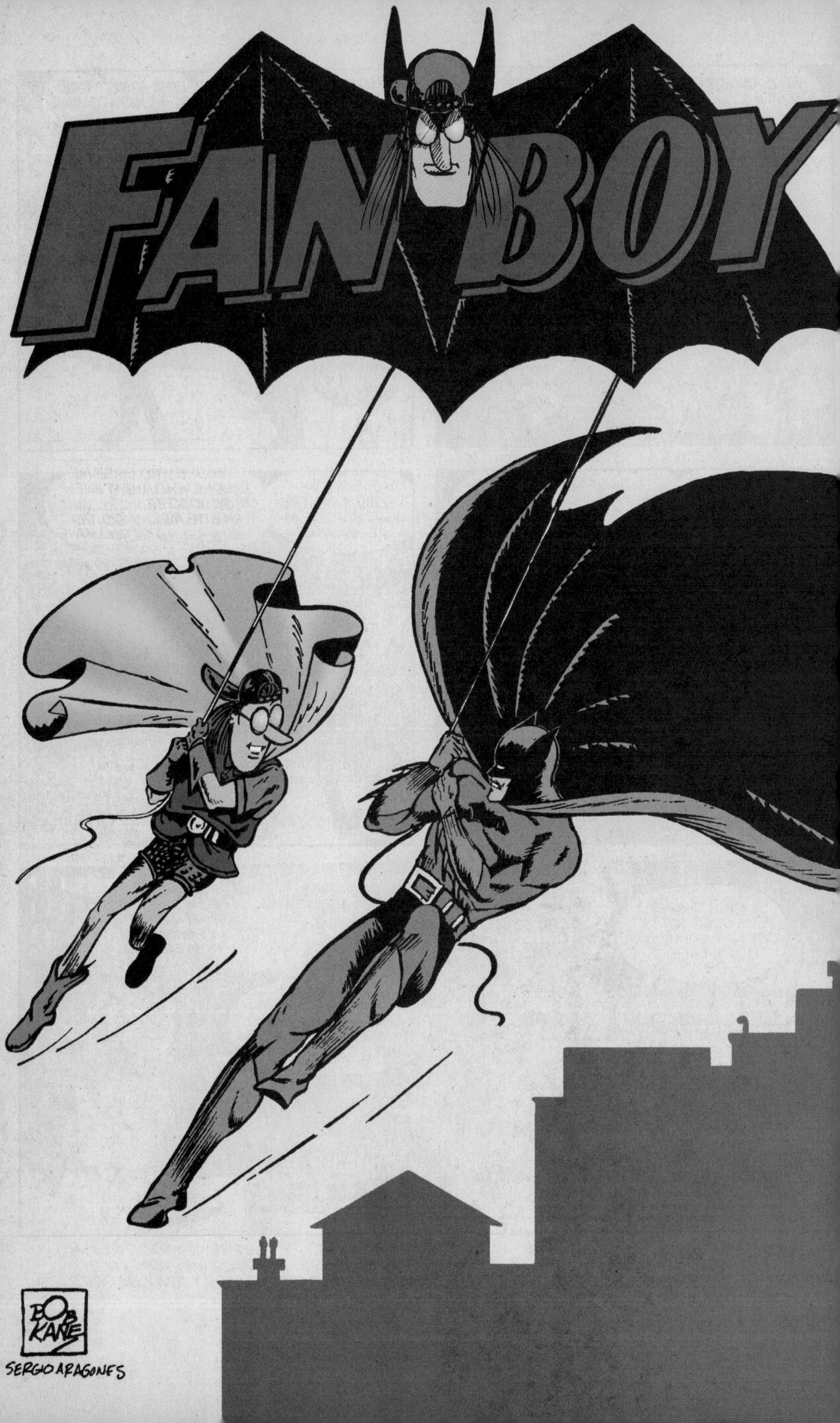
FAN BOY
BOB KANE
SERGIO ARAGONES

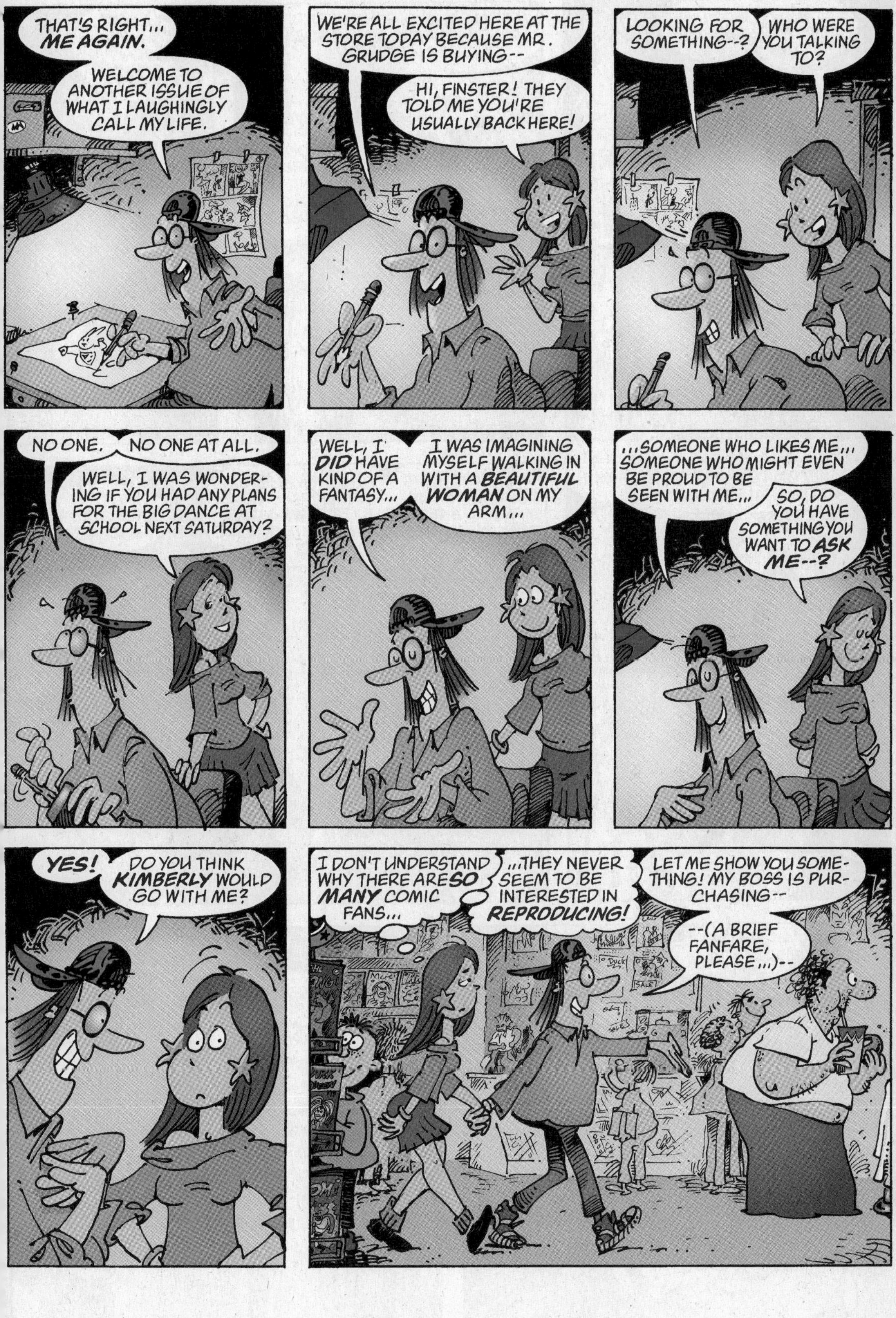
THAT'S RIGHT... ME AGAIN.
WELCOME TO ANOTHER ISSUE OF WHAT I LAUGHINGLY CALL MY LIFE.
WE'RE ALL EXCITED HERE AT THE STORE TODAY BECAUSE MR. GRUDGE IS BUYING--
HI, FINSTER! THEY TOLD ME YOU'RE USUALLY BACK HERE!
LOOKING FOR SOMETHING--?
WHO WERE YOU TALKING TO?
NO ONE.
NO ONE AT ALL.
WELL, I WAS WONDERING IF YOU HAD ANY PLANS FOR THE BIG DANCE AT SCHOOL NEXT SATURDAY?
WELL, I DID HAVE KIND OF A FANTASY...
I WAS IMAGINING MYSELF WALKING IN WITH A BEAUTIFUL WOMAN ON MY ARM...
...SOMEONE WHO LIKES ME... SOMEONE WHO MIGHT EVEN BE PROUD TO BE SEEN WITH ME...
SO, DO YOU HAVE SOMETHING YOU WANT TO ASK ME--?
YES!
DO YOU THINK KIMBERLY WOULD GO WITH ME?
I DON'T UNDERSTAND WHY THERE ARE SO MANY COMIC FANS...
...THEY NEVER SEEM TO BE INTERESTED IN REPRODUCING!
LET ME SHOW YOU SOMETHING! MY BOSS IS PURCHASING--
--(A BRIEF FANFARE, PLEASE...)--

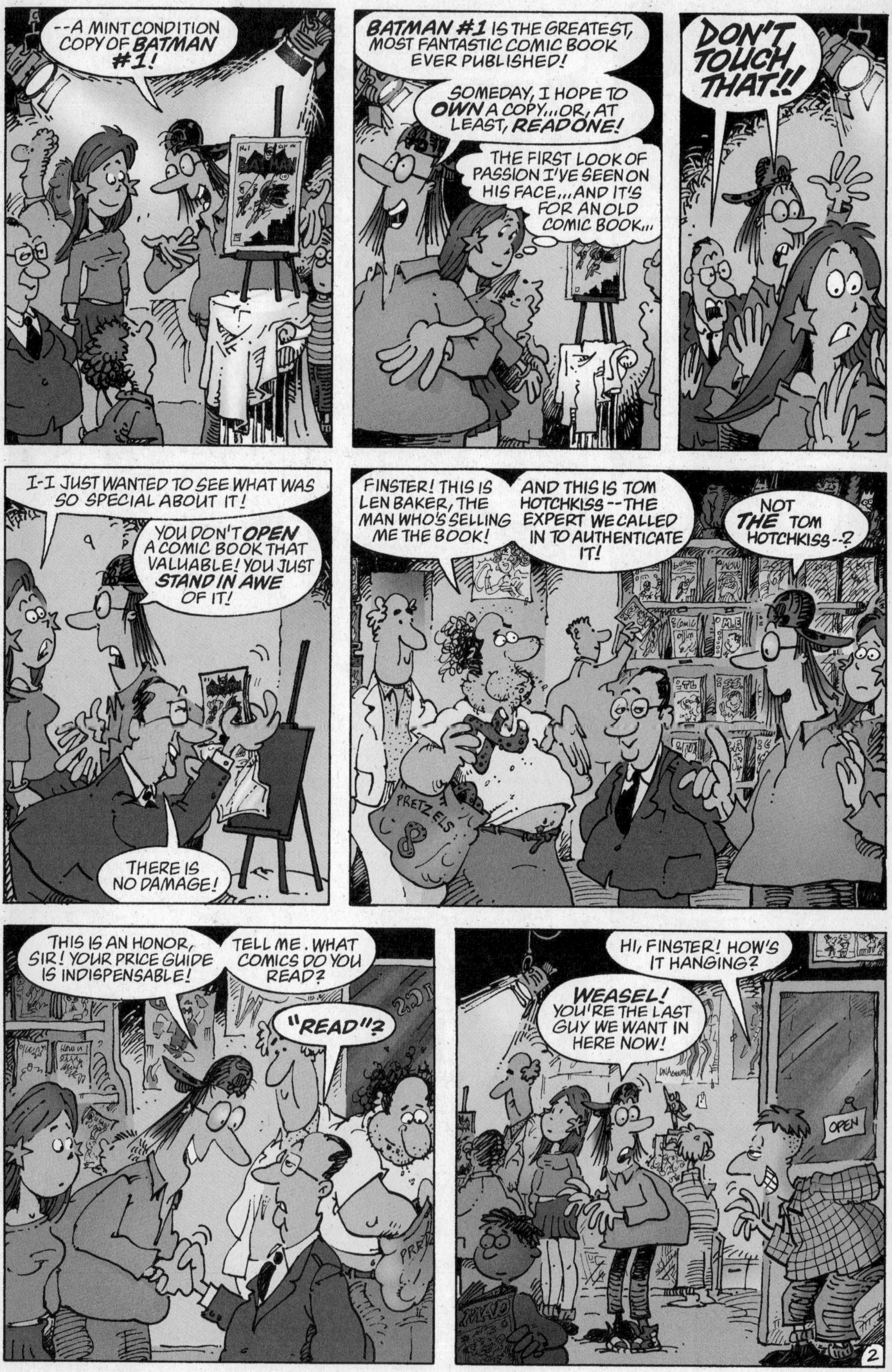
--A MINT CONDITION COPY OF BATMAN #1!
BATMAN #1 IS THE GREATEST, MOST FANTASTIC COMIC BOOK EVER PUBLISHED!
SOMEDAY, I HOPE TO OWN A COPY...OR, AT LEAST, READ ONE!
THE FIRST LOOK OF PASSION I'VE SEEN ON HIS FACE...AND IT'S FOR AN OLD COMIC BOOK...
DON'T TOUCH THAT!!
I-I JUST WANTED TO SEE WHAT WAS SO SPECIAL ABOUT IT!
YOU DON'T OPEN A COMIC BOOK THAT VALUABLE! YOU JUST STAND IN AWE OF IT!
THERE IS NO DAMAGE!
FINSTER! THIS IS LEN BAKER, THE MAN WHO'S SELLING ME THE BOOK!
AND THIS IS TOM HOTCHKISS--THE EXPERT WE CALLED IN TO AUTHENTICATE IT!
NOT THE TOM HOTCHKISS--?
PRETZELS
THIS IS AN HONOR, SIR! YOUR PRICE GUIDE IS INDISPENSABLE!
TELL ME. WHAT COMICS DO YOU READ?
"READ"?
HI, FINSTER! HOW'S IT HANGING?
WEASEL! YOU'RE THE LAST GUY WE WANT IN HERE NOW!
OPEN
2

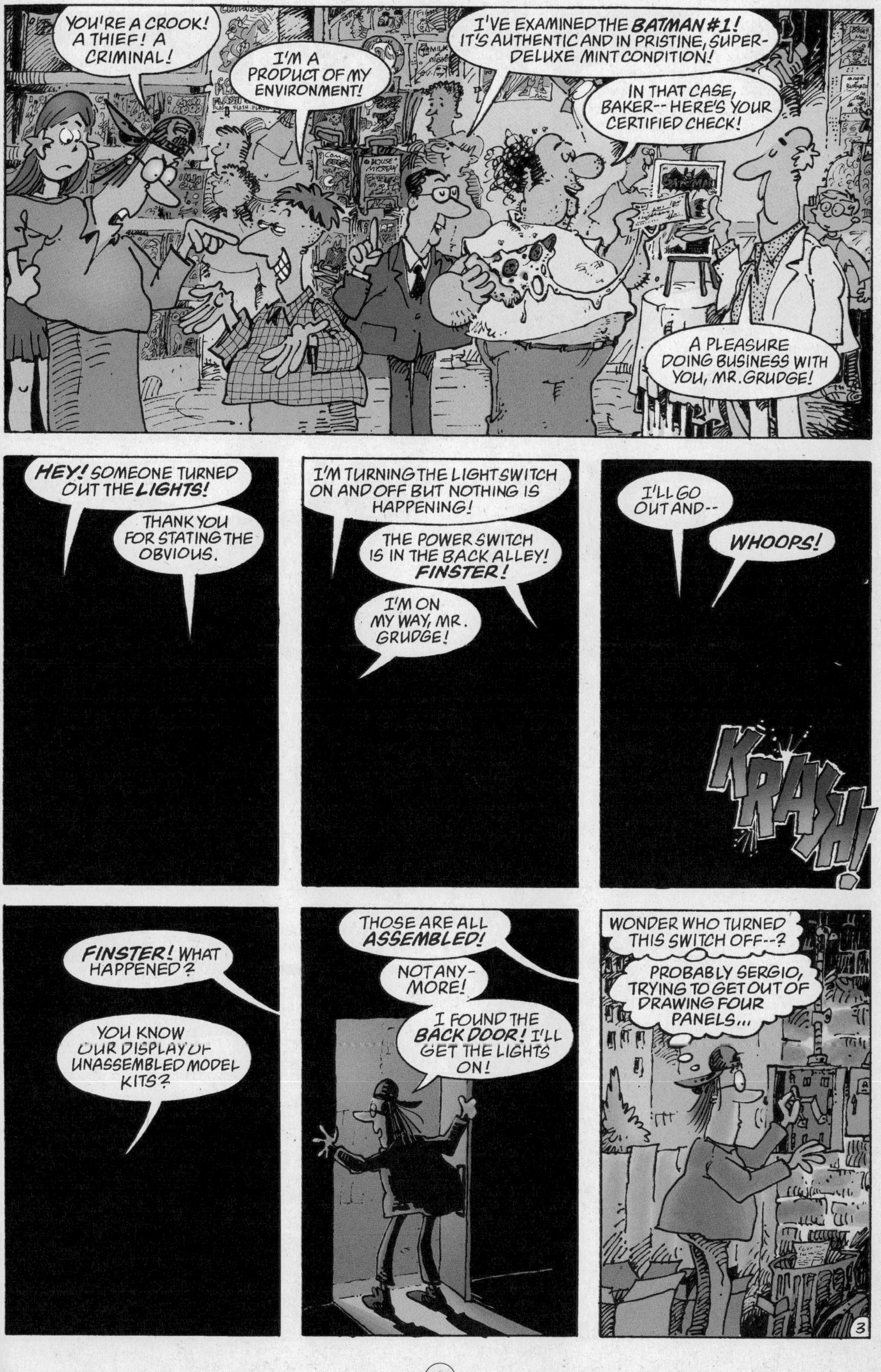

YOU'RE A CROOK! A THIEF! A CRIMINAL!
I'M A PRODUCT OF MY ENVIRONMENT!
I'VE EXAMINED THE BATMAN #1! IT'S AUTHENTIC AND IN PRISTINE, SUPER-DELUXE MINT CONDITION!
IN THAT CASE, BAKER-- HERE'S YOUR CERTIFIED CHECK!
A PLEASURE DOING BUSINESS WITH YOU, MR. GRUDGE!
HEY! SOMEONE TURNED OUT THE LIGHTS!
THANK YOU FOR STATING THE OBVIOUS.
I'M TURNING THE LIGHT SWITCH ON AND OFF BUT NOTHING IS HAPPENING!
THE POWER SWITCH IS IN THE BACK ALLEY! FINSTER!
I'M ON MY WAY, MR. GRUDGE!
I'LL GO OUT AND--
WHOOPS!
KRASH!
FINSTER! WHAT HAPPENED?
YOU KNOW OUR DISPLAY OF UNASSEMBLED MODEL KITS?
THOSE ARE ALL ASSEMBLED!
NOT ANY-MORE!
I FOUND THE BACK DOOR! I'LL GET THE LIGHTS ON!
WONDER WHO TURNED THIS SWITCH OFF--?
PROBABLY SERGIO, TRYING TO GET OUT OF DRAWING FOUR PANELS...
3

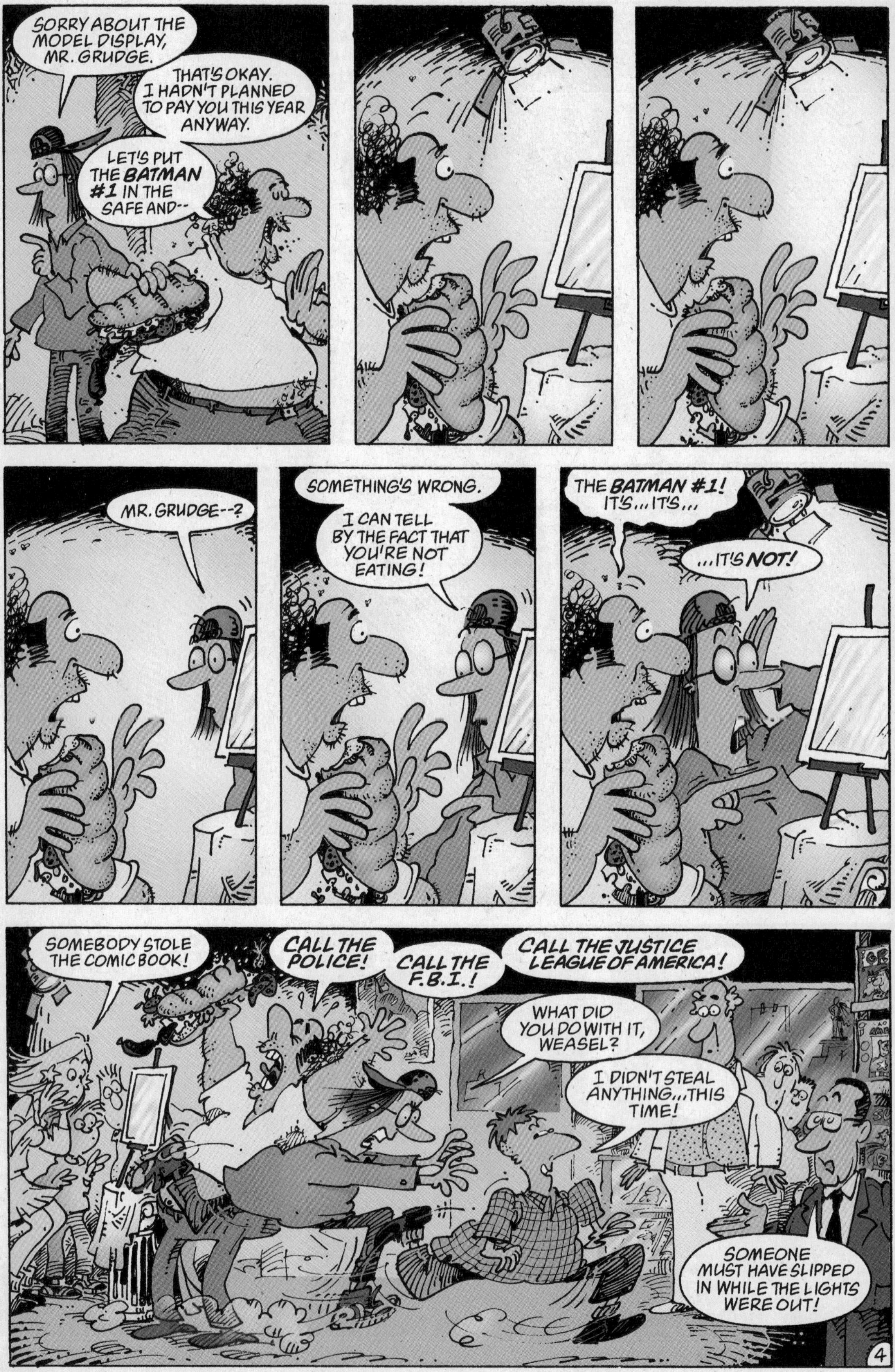
SORRY ABOUT THE MODEL DISPLAY, MR. GRUDGE.
THAT'S OKAY. I HADN'T PLANNED TO PAY YOU THIS YEAR ANYWAY.
LET'S PUT THE BATMAN #1 IN THE SAFE AND--
MR. GRUDGE--?
SOMETHING'S WRONG.
I CAN TELL BY THE FACT THAT YOU'RE NOT EATING!
THE BATMAN #1! IT'S... IT'S...
...IT'S NOT!
SOMEBODY STOLE THE COMIC BOOK!
CALL THE POLICE!
CALL THE F.B.I.!
CALL THE JUSTICE LEAGUE OF AMERICA!
WHAT DID YOU DO WITH IT, WEASEL?
I DIDN'T STEAL ANYTHING... THIS TIME!
SOMEONE MUST HAVE SLIPPED IN WHILE THE LIGHTS WERE OUT!
4

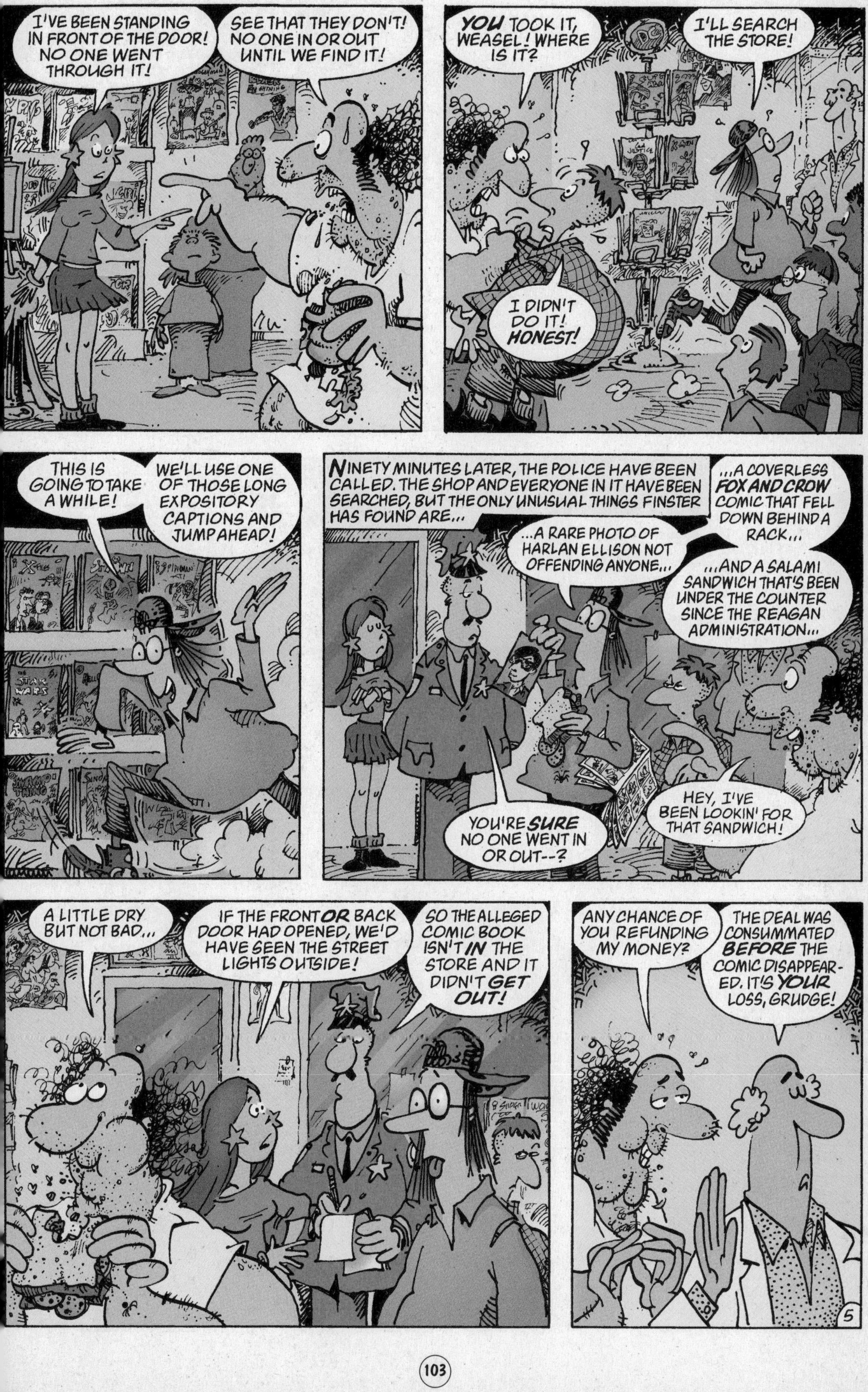
I'VE BEEN STANDING IN FRONT OF THE DOOR! NO ONE WENT THROUGH IT!
SEE THAT THEY DON'T! NO ONE IN OR OUT UNTIL WE FIND IT!
YOU TOOK IT, WEASEL! WHERE IS IT?
I'LL SEARCH THE STORE!
I DIDN'T DO IT! HONEST!
THIS IS GOING TO TAKE A WHILE!
WE'LL USE ONE OF THOSE LONG EXPOSITORY CAPTIONS AND JUMP AHEAD!
NINETY MINUTES LATER, THE POLICE HAVE BEEN CALLED. THE SHOP AND EVERYONE IN IT HAVE BEEN SEARCHED, BUT THE ONLY UNUSUAL THINGS FINSTER HAS FOUND ARE...
...A RARE PHOTO OF HARLAN ELLISON NOT OFFENDING ANYONE...
...A COVERLESS FOX AND CROW COMIC THAT FELL DOWN BEHIND A RACK...
...AND A SALAMI SANDWICH THAT'S BEEN UNDER THE COUNTER SINCE THE REAGAN ADMINISTRATION...
YOU'RE SURE NO ONE WENT IN OR OUT--?
HEY, I'VE BEEN LOOKIN' FOR THAT SANDWICH!
A LITTLE DRY BUT NOT BAD...
IF THE FRONT OR BACK DOOR HAD OPENED, WE'D HAVE SEEN THE STREET LIGHTS OUTSIDE!
SO THE ALLEGED COMIC BOOK ISN'T IN THE STORE AND IT DIDN'T GET OUT!
ANY CHANCE OF YOU REFUNDING MY MONEY?
THE DEAL WAS CONSUMMATED BEFORE THE COMIC DISAPPEARED. IT'S YOUR LOSS, GRUDGE!
5

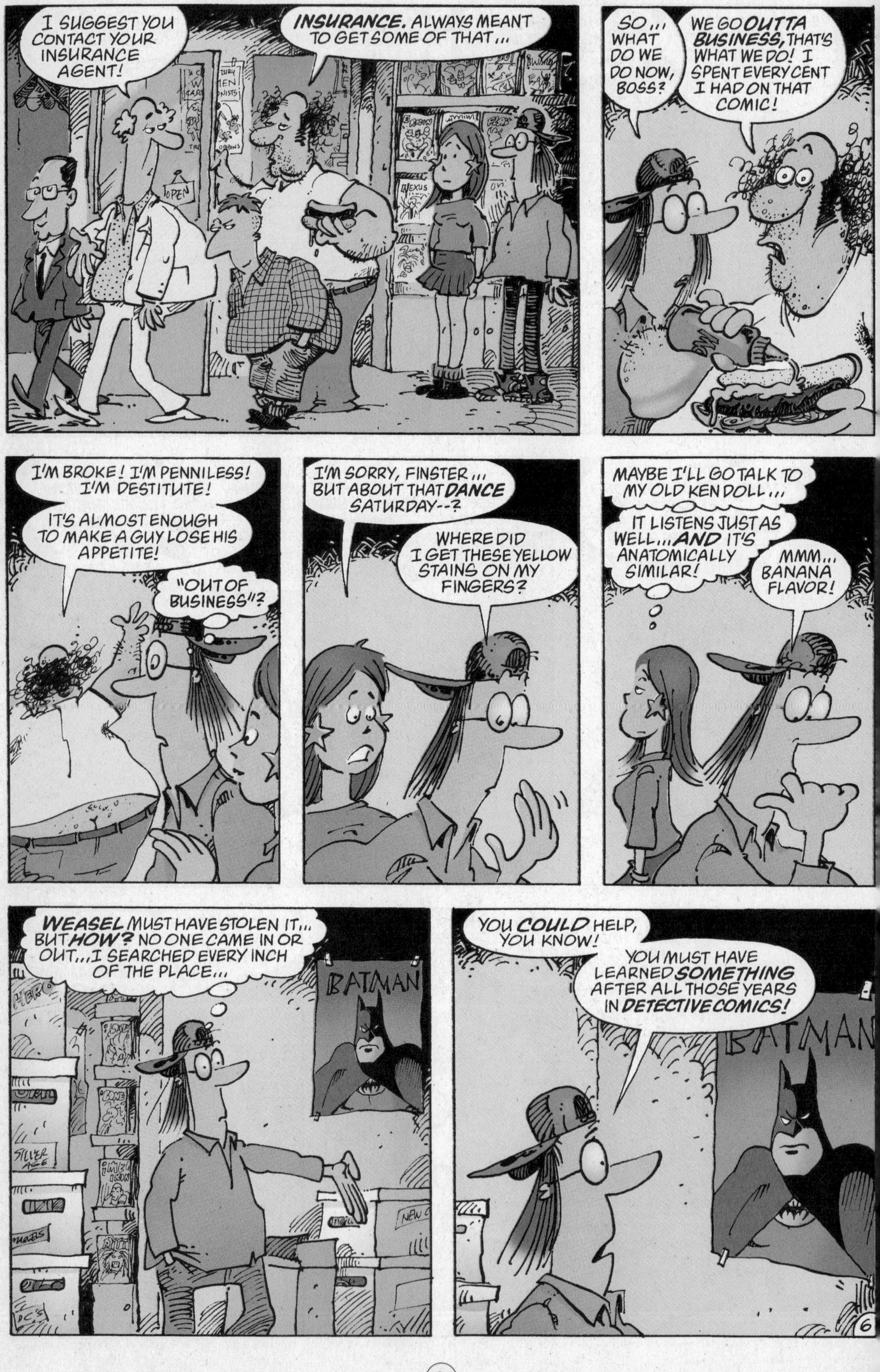
I SUGGEST YOU CONTACT YOUR INSURANCE AGENT!
INSURANCE. ALWAYS MEANT TO GET SOME OF THAT...
OPEN
SO... WHAT DO WE DO NOW, BOSS?
WE GO OUTTA BUSINESS, THAT'S WHAT WE DO! I SPENT EVERY CENT I HAD ON THAT COMIC!
I'M BROKE! I'M PENNILESS! I'M DESTITUTE!
IT'S ALMOST ENOUGH TO MAKE A GUY LOSE HIS APPETITE!
"OUT OF BUSINESS"?
I'M SORRY, FINSTER... BUT ABOUT THAT DANCE SATURDAY--?
WHERE DID I GET THESE YELLOW STAINS ON MY FINGERS?
MAYBE I'LL GO TALK TO MY OLD KEN DOLL...
IT LISTENS JUST AS WELL...AND IT'S ANATOMICALLY SIMILAR!
MMM... BANANA FLAVOR!
WEASEL MUST HAVE STOLEN IT... BUT HOW? NO ONE CAME IN OR OUT...I SEARCHED EVERY INCH OF THE PLACE...
BATMAN
SILVER AGE
YOU COULD HELP, YOU KNOW!
YOU MUST HAVE LEARNED SOMETHING AFTER ALL THOSE YEARS IN DETECTIVE COMICS!
BATMAN
6

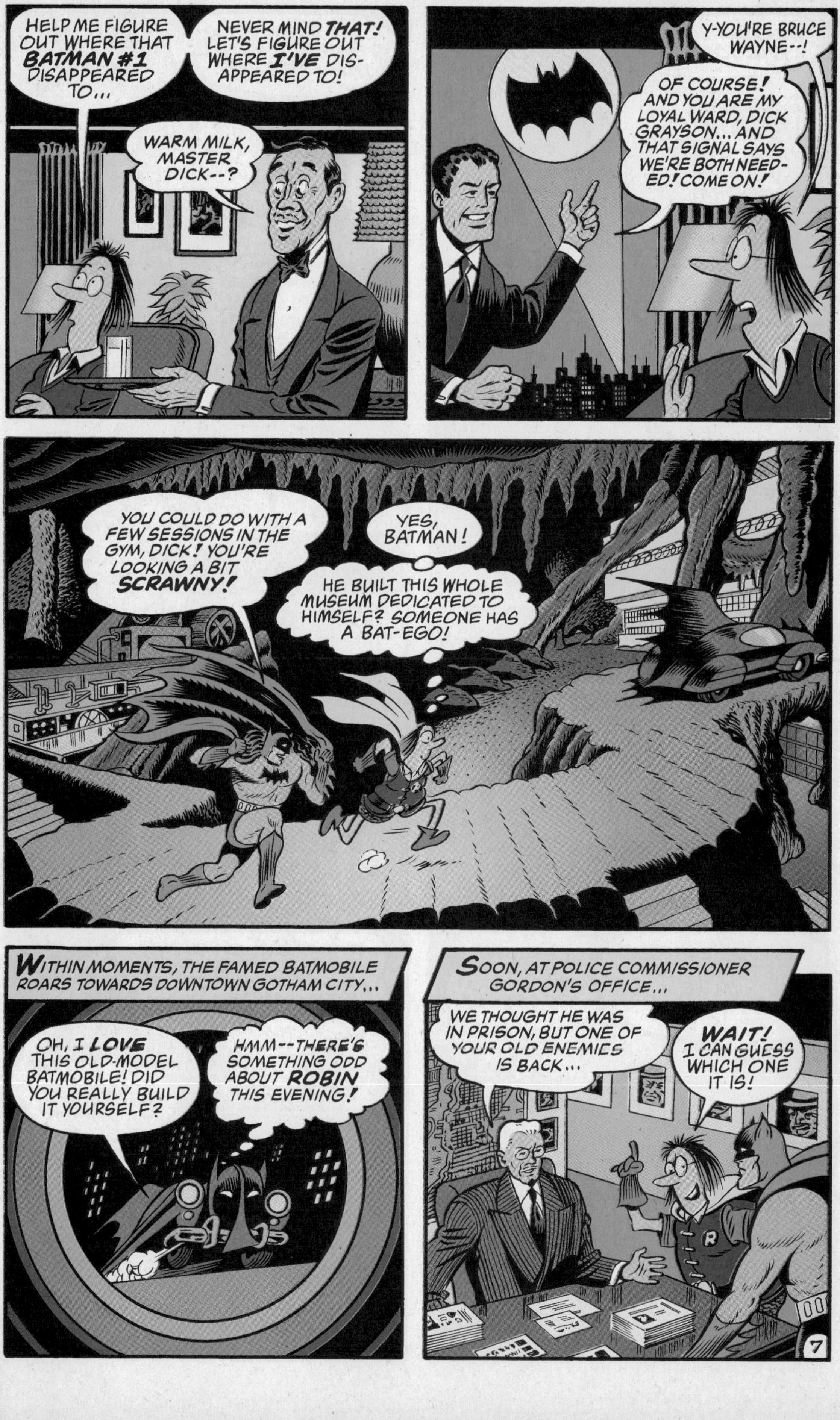
HELP ME FIGURE OUT WHERE THAT BATMAN #1 DISAPPEARED TO...
NEVER MIND THAT! LET'S FIGURE OUT WHERE I'VE DIS-APPEARED TO!
WARM MILK, MASTER DICK--?
Y-YOU'RE BRUCE WAYNE--!
OF COURSE! AND YOU ARE MY LOYAL WARD, DICK GRAYSON... AND THAT SIGNAL SAYS WE'RE BOTH NEED-ED! COME ON!
YOU COULD DO WITH A FEW SESSIONS IN THE GYM, DICK! YOU'RE LOOKING A BIT SCRAWNY!
YES, BATMAN!
HE BUILT THIS WHOLE MUSEUM DEDICATED TO HIMSELF? SOMEONE HAS A BAT-EGO!
WITHIN MOMENTS, THE FAMED BATMOBILE ROARS TOWARDS DOWNTOWN GOTHAM CITY...
OH, I LOVE THIS OLD-MODEL BATMOBILE! DID YOU REALLY BUILD IT YOURSELF?
HMM--THERE'S SOMETHING ODD ABOUT ROBIN THIS EVENING!
SOON, AT POLICE COMMISSIONER GORDON'S OFFICE...
WE THOUGHT HE WAS IN PRISON, BUT ONE OF YOUR OLD ENEMIES IS BACK...
WAIT! I CAN GUESS WHICH ONE IT IS!

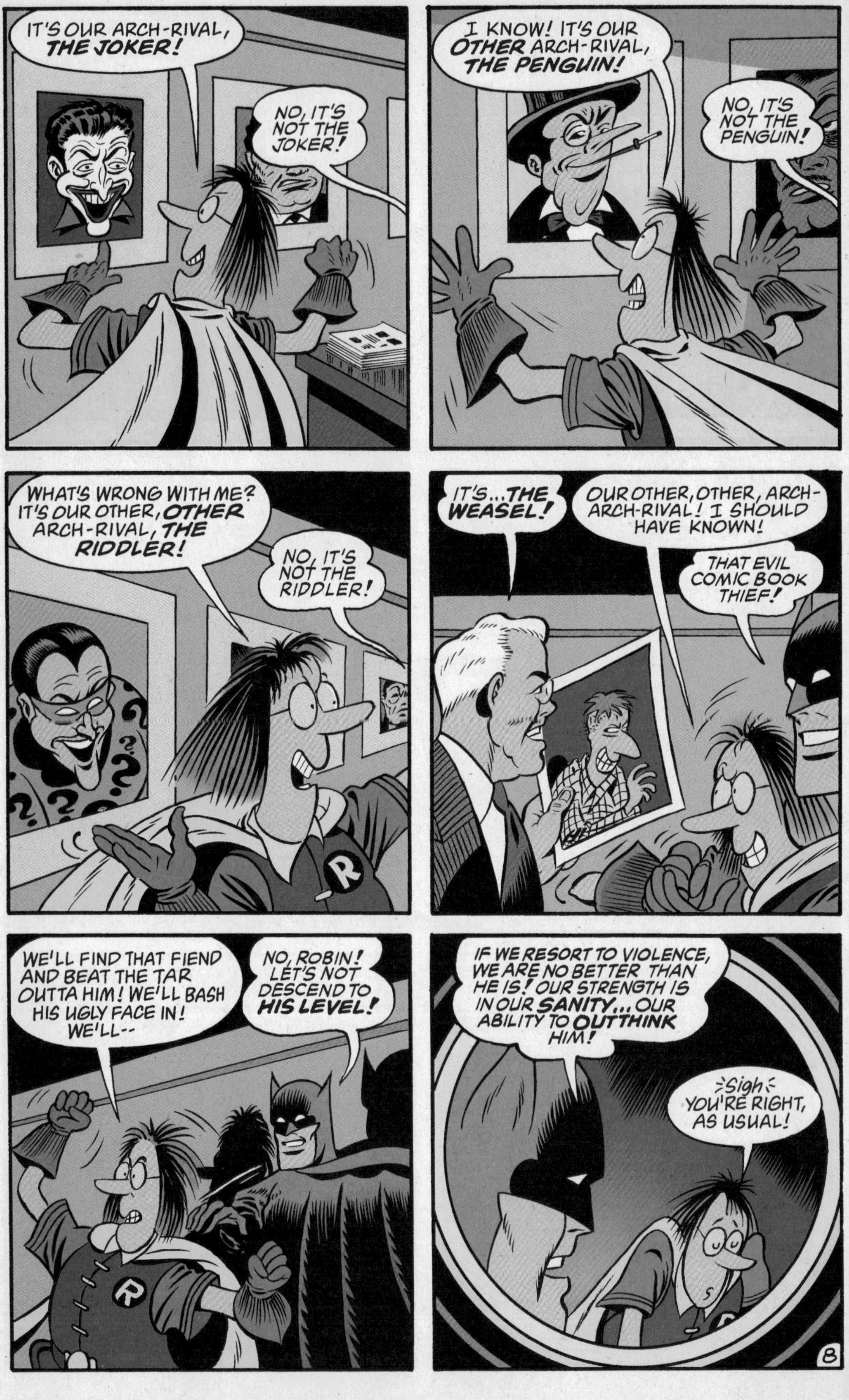

IT'S OUR ARCH-RIVAL, THE JOKER!
NO, IT'S NOT THE JOKER!
I KNOW! IT'S OUR OTHER ARCH-RIVAL, THE PENGUIN!
NO, IT'S NOT THE PENGUIN!
WHAT'S WRONG WITH ME? IT'S OUR OTHER, OTHER ARCH-RIVAL, THE RIDDLER!
NO, IT'S NOT THE RIDDLER!
IT'S...THE WEASEL!
OUR OTHER, OTHER, ARCH-ARCH-RIVAL! I SHOULD HAVE KNOWN!
THAT EVIL COMIC BOOK THIEF!
WE'LL FIND THAT FIEND AND BEAT THE TAR OUTTA HIM! WE'LL BASH HIS UGLY FACE IN! WE'LL--
NO, ROBIN! LET'S NOT DESCEND TO HIS LEVEL!
IF WE RESORT TO VIOLENCE, WE ARE NO BETTER THAN HE IS! OUR STRENGTH IS IN OUR SANITY... OUR ABILITY TO OUTTHINK HIM!
Sigh YOU'RE RIGHT, AS USUAL!
8

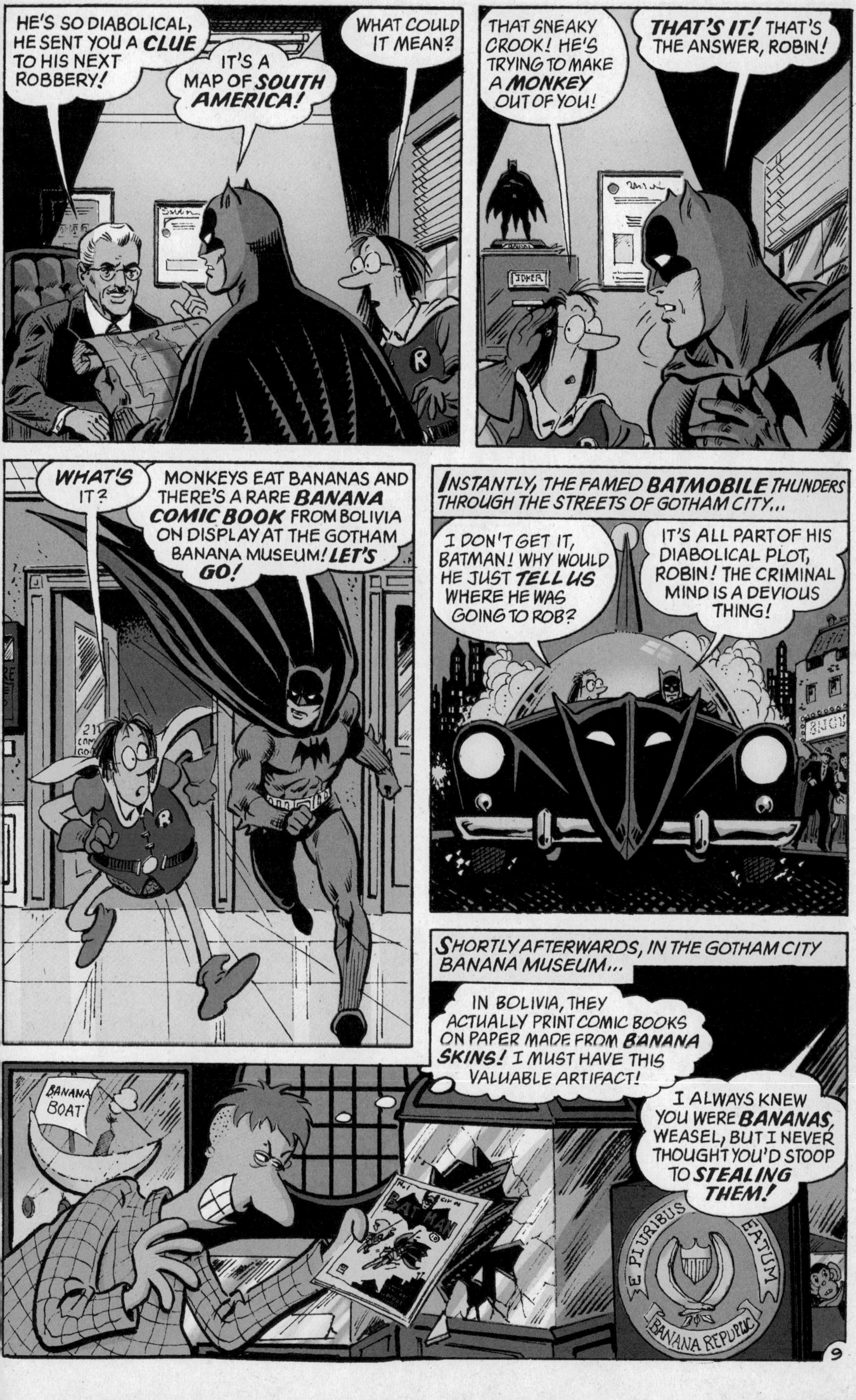
HE'S SO DIABOLICAL, HE SENT YOU A CLUE TO HIS NEXT ROBBERY!
IT'S A MAP OF SOUTH AMERICA!
WHAT COULD IT MEAN?
THAT SNEAKY CROOK! HE'S TRYING TO MAKE A MONKEY OUT OF YOU!
THAT'S IT! THAT'S THE ANSWER, ROBIN!
JOKER
WHAT'S IT?
MONKEYS EAT BANANAS AND THERE'S A RARE BANANA COMIC BOOK FROM BOLIVIA ON DISPLAY AT THE GOTHAM BANANA MUSEUM! LET'S GO!
INSTANTLY, THE FAMED BATMOBILE THUNDERS THROUGH THE STREETS OF GOTHAM CITY...
I DON'T GET IT, BATMAN! WHY WOULD HE JUST TELL US WHERE HE WAS GOING TO ROB?
IT'S ALL PART OF HIS DIABOLICAL PLOT, ROBIN! THE CRIMINAL MIND IS A DEVIOUS THING!
SHORTLY AFTERWARDS, IN THE GOTHAM CITY BANANA MUSEUM...
IN BOLIVIA, THEY ACTUALLY PRINT COMIC BOOKS ON PAPER MADE FROM BANANA SKINS! I MUST HAVE THIS VALUABLE ARTIFACT!
I ALWAYS KNEW YOU WERE BANANAS, WEASEL, BUT I NEVER THOUGHT YOU'D STOOP TO STEALING THEM!
BANANA BOAT
BATMAN
E PLURIBUS EATUM
BANANA REPUBLIC

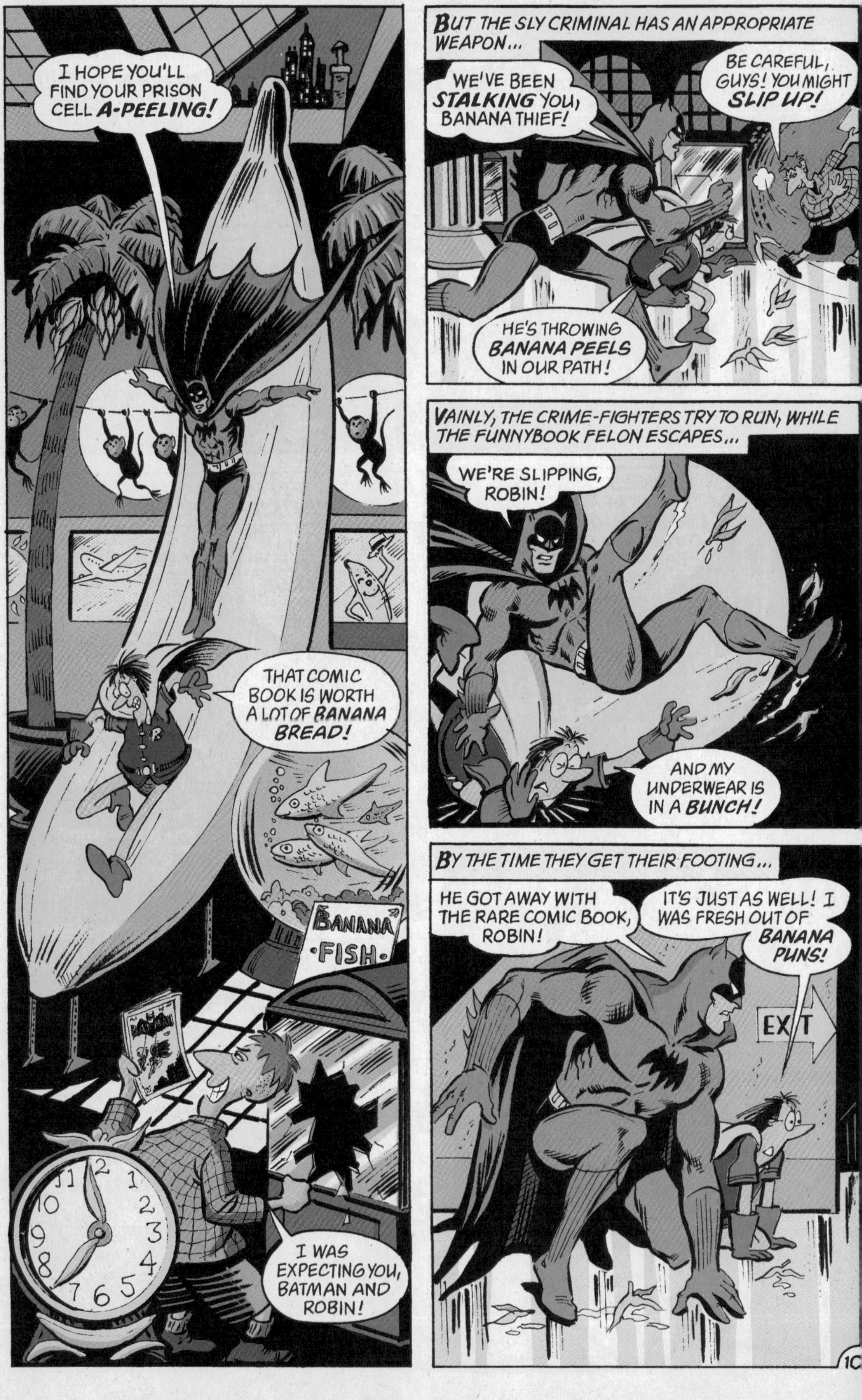
I HOPE YOU'LL FIND YOUR PRISON CELL A-PEELING!
THAT COMIC BOOK IS WORTH A LOT OF BANANA BREAD!
BANANA FISH
I WAS EXPECTING YOU, BATMAN AND ROBIN!
BUT THE SLY CRIMINAL HAS AN APPROPRIATE WEAPON...
WE'VE BEEN STALKING YOU, BANANA THIEF!
BE CAREFUL, GUYS! YOU MIGHT SLIP UP!
HE'S THROWING BANANA PEELS IN OUR PATH!
VAINLY, THE CRIME-FIGHTERS TRY TO RUN, WHILE THE FUNNYBOOK FELON ESCAPES...
WE'RE SLIPPING, ROBIN!
AND MY UNDERWEAR IS IN A BUNCH!
BY THE TIME THEY GET THEIR FOOTING...
HE GOT AWAY WITH THE RARE COMIC BOOK, ROBIN!
IT'S JUST AS WELL! I WAS FRESH OUT OF BANANA PUNS!
EXIT

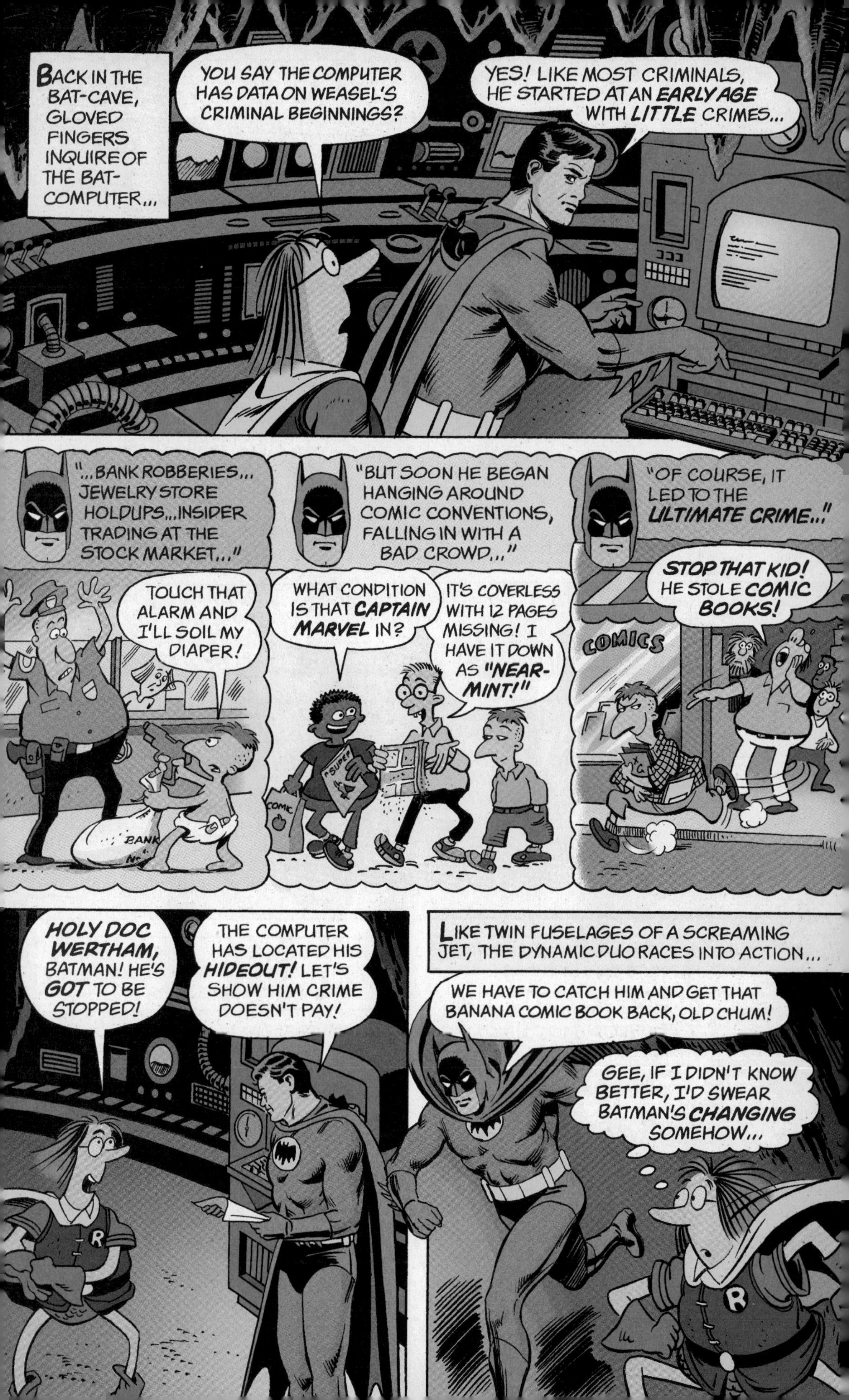
BACK IN THE BAT-CAVE, GLOVED FINGERS INQUIRE OF THE BAT-COMPUTER...
YOU SAY THE COMPUTER HAS DATA ON WEASEL'S CRIMINAL BEGINNINGS?
YES! LIKE MOST CRIMINALS, HE STARTED AT AN EARLY AGE WITH LITTLE CRIMES...
"...BANK ROBBERIES... JEWELRY STORE HOLDUPS...INSIDER TRADING AT THE STOCK MARKET..."
TOUCH THAT ALARM AND I'LL SOIL MY DIAPER!
BANK
"BUT SOON HE BEGAN HANGING AROUND COMIC CONVENTIONS, FALLING IN WITH A BAD CROWD..."
WHAT CONDITION IS THAT CAPTAIN MARVEL IN?
IT'S COVERLESS WITH 12 PAGES MISSING! I HAVE IT DOWN AS "NEAR-MINT!"
SUPER
COMIC
"OF COURSE, IT LED TO THE ULTIMATE CRIME..."
STOP THAT KID! HE STOLE COMIC BOOKS!
COMICS
HOLY DOC WERTHAM, BATMAN! HE'S GOT TO BE STOPPED!
THE COMPUTER HAS LOCATED HIS HIDEOUT! LET'S SHOW HIM CRIME DOESN'T PAY!
LIKE TWIN FUSELAGES OF A SCREAMING JET, THE DYNAMIC DUO RACES INTO ACTION...
WE HAVE TO CATCH HIM AND GET THAT BANANA COMIC BOOK BACK, OLD CHUM!
GEE, IF I DIDN'T KNOW BETTER, I'D SWEAR BATMAN'S CHANGING SOMEHOW...

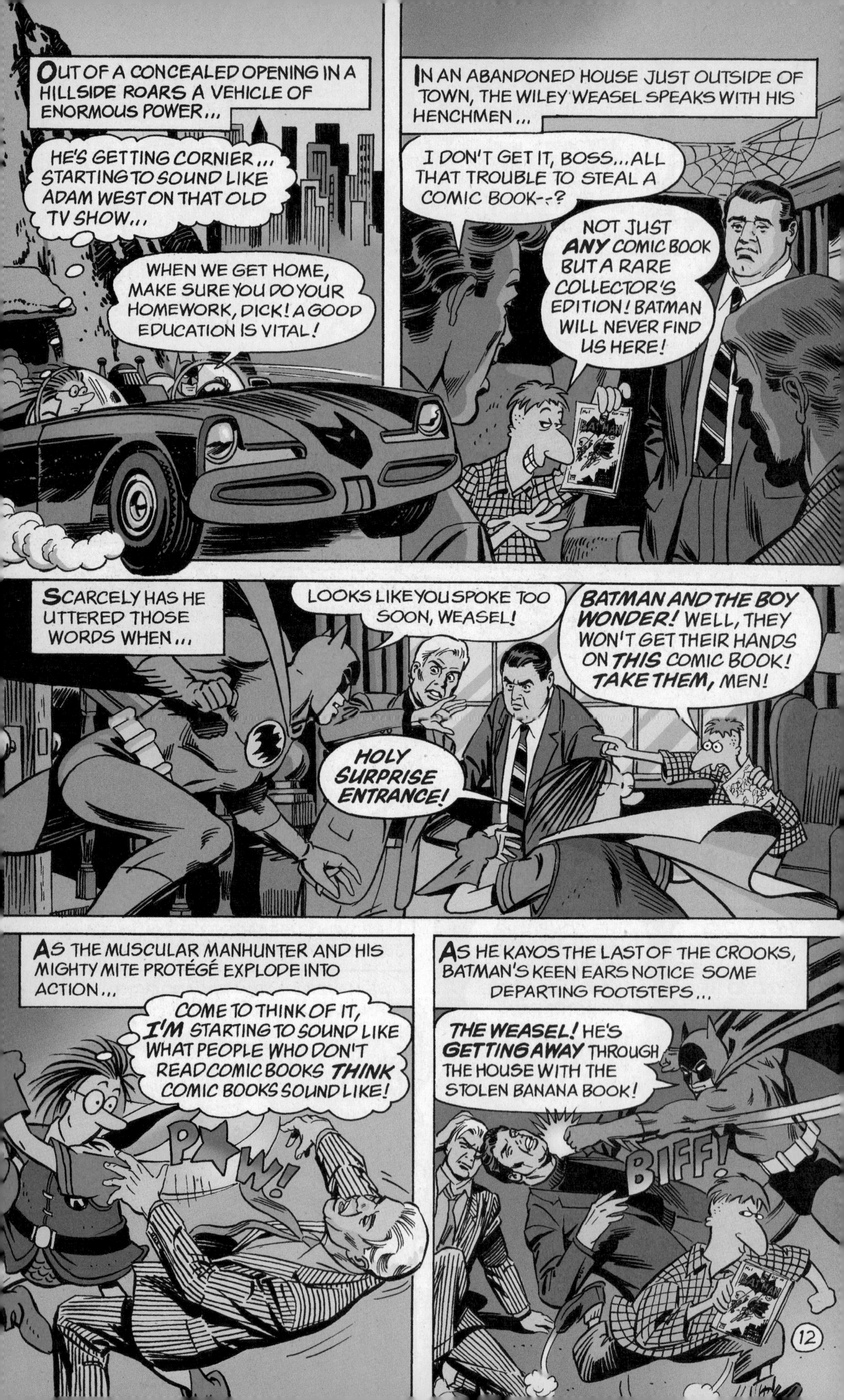
OUT OF A CONCEALED OPENING IN A HILLSIDE ROARS A VEHICLE OF ENORMOUS POWER...
HE'S GETTING CORNIER... STARTING TO SOUND LIKE ADAM WEST ON THAT OLD TV SHOW...
WHEN WE GET HOME, MAKE SURE YOU DO YOUR HOMEWORK, DICK! A GOOD EDUCATION IS VITAL!
IN AN ABANDONED HOUSE JUST OUTSIDE OF TOWN, THE WILEY WEASEL SPEAKS WITH HIS HENCHMEN...
I DON'T GET IT, BOSS... ALL THAT TROUBLE TO STEAL A COMIC BOOK--?
NOT JUST ANY COMIC BOOK BUT A RARE COLLECTOR'S EDITION! BATMAN WILL NEVER FIND US HERE!
SCARCELY HAS HE UTTERED THOSE WORDS WHEN...
LOOKS LIKE YOU SPOKE TOO SOON, WEASEL!
BATMAN AND THE BOY WONDER! WELL, THEY WON'T GET THEIR HANDS ON THIS COMIC BOOK! TAKE THEM, MEN!
HOLY SURPRISE ENTRANCE!
AS THE MUSCULAR MANHUNTER AND HIS MIGHTY MITE PROTÉGÉ EXPLODE INTO ACTION...
COME TO THINK OF IT, I'M STARTING TO SOUND LIKE WHAT PEOPLE WHO DON'T READ COMIC BOOKS THINK COMIC BOOKS SOUND LIKE!
POW!
AS HE KAYOS THE LAST OF THE CROOKS, BATMAN'S KEEN EARS NOTICE SOME DEPARTING FOOTSTEPS...
THE WEASEL! HE'S GETTING AWAY THROUGH THE HOUSE WITH THE STOLEN BANANA BOOK!
BIFF!

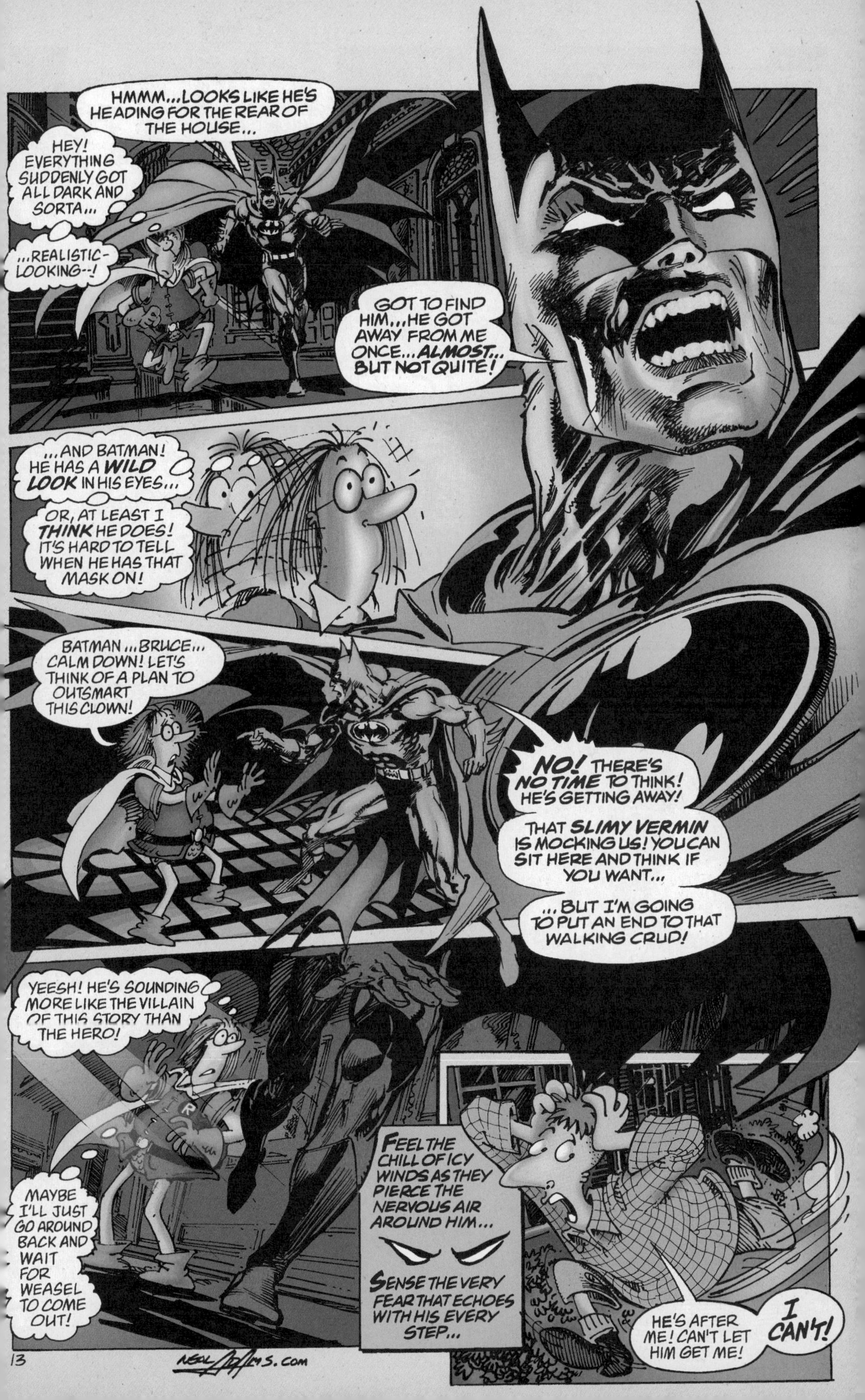
HMMM...LOOKS LIKE HE'S HEADING FOR THE REAR OF THE HOUSE...
HEY! EVERYTHING SUDDENLY GOT ALL DARK AND SORTA...
...REALISTIC-LOOKING--!
GOT TO FIND HIM...HE GOT AWAY FROM ME ONCE...ALMOST... BUT NOT QUITE!
...AND BATMAN! HE HAS A WILD LOOK IN HIS EYES...
OR, AT LEAST I THINK HE DOES! IT'S HARD TO TELL WHEN HE HAS THAT MASK ON!
BATMAN...BRUCE... CALM DOWN! LET'S THINK OF A PLAN TO OUTSMART THIS CLOWN!
NO! THERE'S NO TIME TO THINK! HE'S GETTING AWAY!
THAT SLIMY VERMIN IS MOCKING US! YOU CAN SIT HERE AND THINK IF YOU WANT...
...BUT I'M GOING TO PUT AN END TO THAT WALKING CRUD!
YEESH! HE'S SOUNDING MORE LIKE THE VILLAIN OF THIS STORY THAN THE HERO!
MAYBE I'LL JUST GO AROUND BACK AND WAIT FOR WEASEL TO COME OUT!
FEEL THE CHILL OF ICY WINDS AS THEY PIERCE THE NERVOUS AIR AROUND HIM...
SENSE THE VERY FEAR THAT ECHOES WITH HIS EVERY STEP...
HE'S AFTER ME! CAN'T LET HIM GET ME!
I CAN'T!

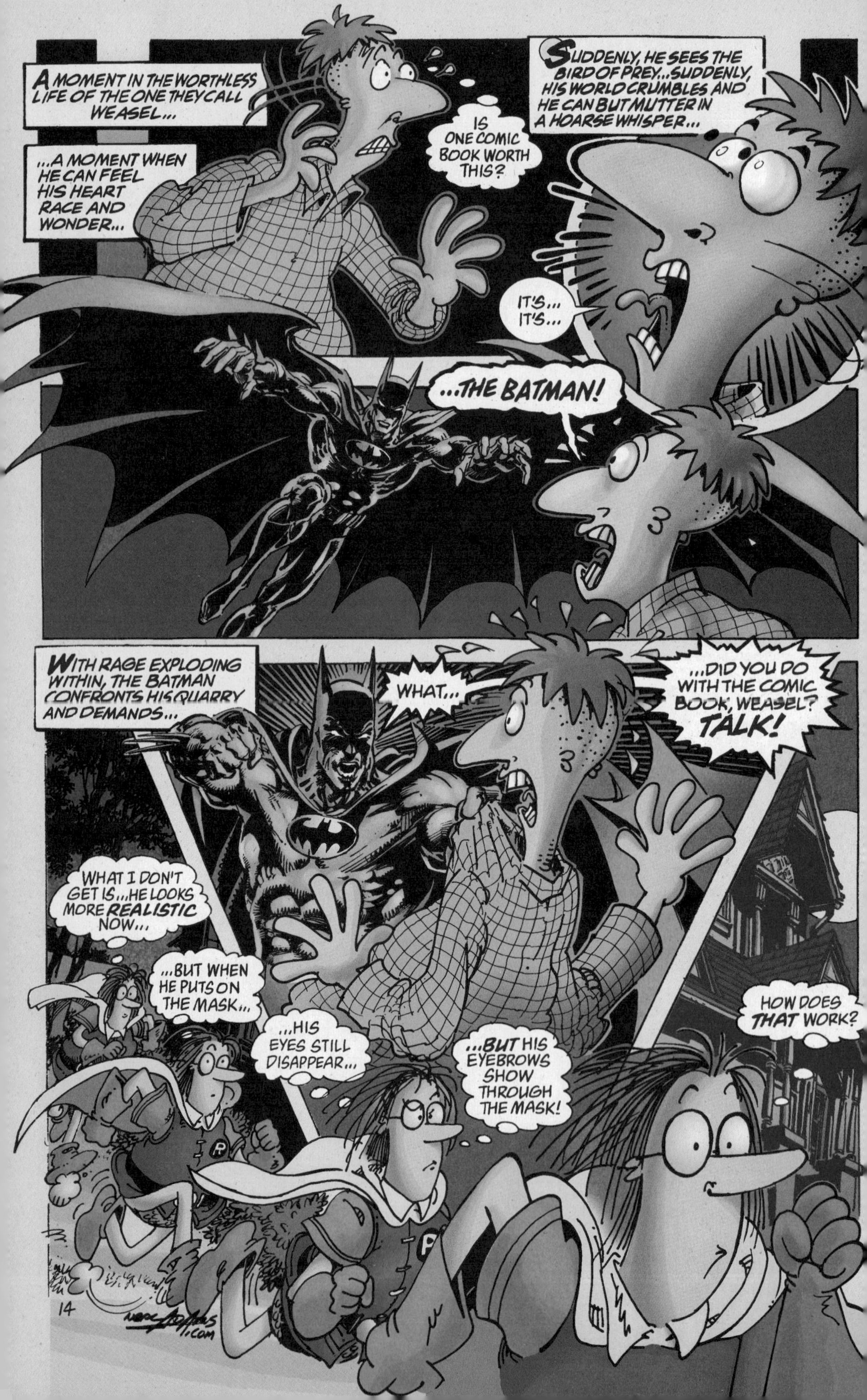
A MOMENT IN THE WORTHLESS LIFE OF THE ONE THEY CALL WEASEL...
...A MOMENT WHEN HE CAN FEEL HIS HEART RACE AND WONDER...
IS ONE COMIC BOOK WORTH THIS?
SUDDENLY, HE SEES THE BIRD OF PREY... SUDDENLY, HIS WORLD CRUMBLES AND HE CAN BUT MUTTER IN A HOARSE WHISPER...
IT'S... IT'S...
...THE BATMAN!
WITH RAGE EXPLODING WITHIN, THE BATMAN CONFRONTS HIS QUARRY AND DEMANDS...
WHAT...
...DID YOU DO WITH THE COMIC BOOK, WEASEL? TALK!
WHAT I DON'T GET IS... HE LOOKS MORE REALISTIC NOW...
...BUT WHEN HE PUTS ON THE MASK...
...HIS EYES STILL DISAPPEAR...
...BUT HIS EYEBROWS SHOW THROUGH THE MASK!
HOW DOES THAT WORK?

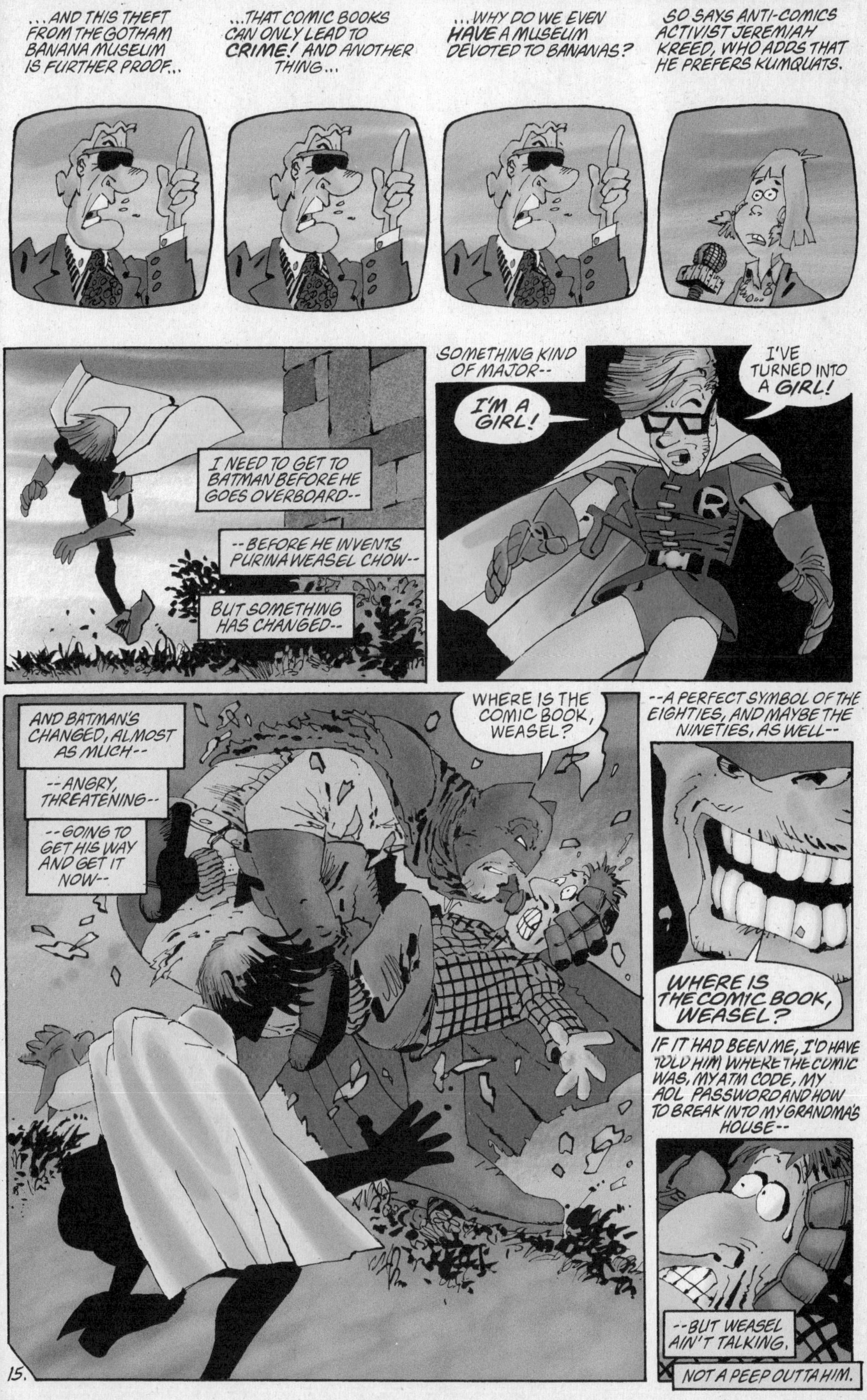
...AND THIS THEFT FROM THE GOTHAM BANANA MUSEUM IS FURTHER PROOF...
...THAT COMIC BOOKS CAN ONLY LEAD TO CRIME! AND ANOTHER THING...
...WHY DO WE EVEN HAVE A MUSEUM DEVOTED TO BANANAS?
SO SAYS ANTI-COMICS ACTIVIST JEREMIAH KREED, WHO ADDS THAT HE PREFERS KUMQUATS.
I NEED TO GET TO BATMAN BEFORE HE GOES OVERBOARD--
--BEFORE HE INVENTS PURINA WEASEL CHOW--
BUT SOMETHING HAS CHANGED--
SOMETHING KIND OF MAJOR--
I'M A GIRL!
I'VE TURNED INTO A GIRL!
AND BATMAN'S CHANGED, ALMOST AS MUCH--
--ANGRY, THREATENING--
--GOING TO GET HIS WAY AND GET IT NOW--
WHERE IS THE COMIC BOOK, WEASEL?
--A PERFECT SYMBOL OF THE EIGHTIES, AND MAYBE THE NINETIES, AS WELL--
WHERE IS THE COMIC BOOK, WEASEL?
IF IT HAD BEEN ME, I'D HAVE TOLD HIM WHERE THE COMIC WAS, MY ATM CODE, MY AOL PASSWORD AND HOW TO BREAK INTO MY GRANDMA'S HOUSE--
--BUT WEASEL AIN'T TALKING.
NOT A PEEP OUTTA HIM.

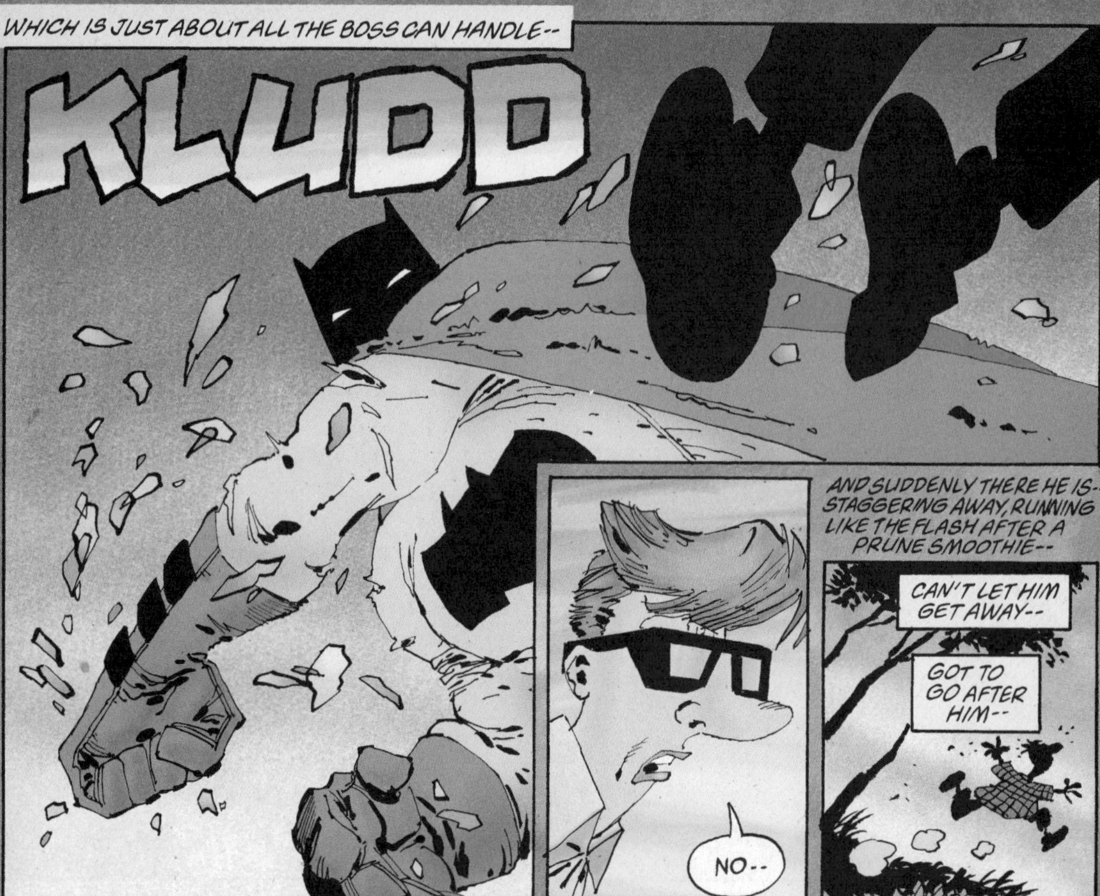
WHICH IS JUST ABOUT ALL THE BOSS CAN HANDLE--
KLUDD
AND SUDDENLY THERE HE IS-- STAGGERING AWAY, RUNNING LIKE THE FLASH AFTER A PRUNE SMOOTHIE--
NO--
CAN'T LET HIM GET AWAY--
GOT TO GO AFTER HIM--

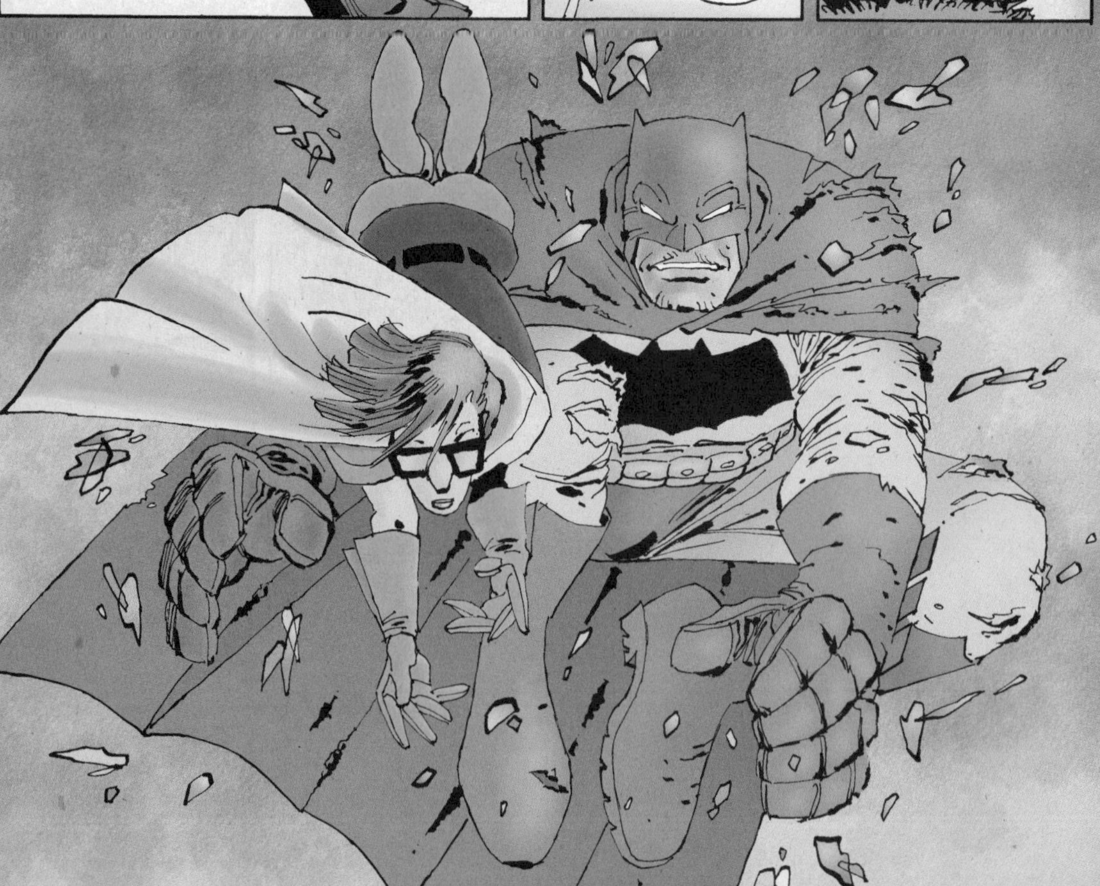

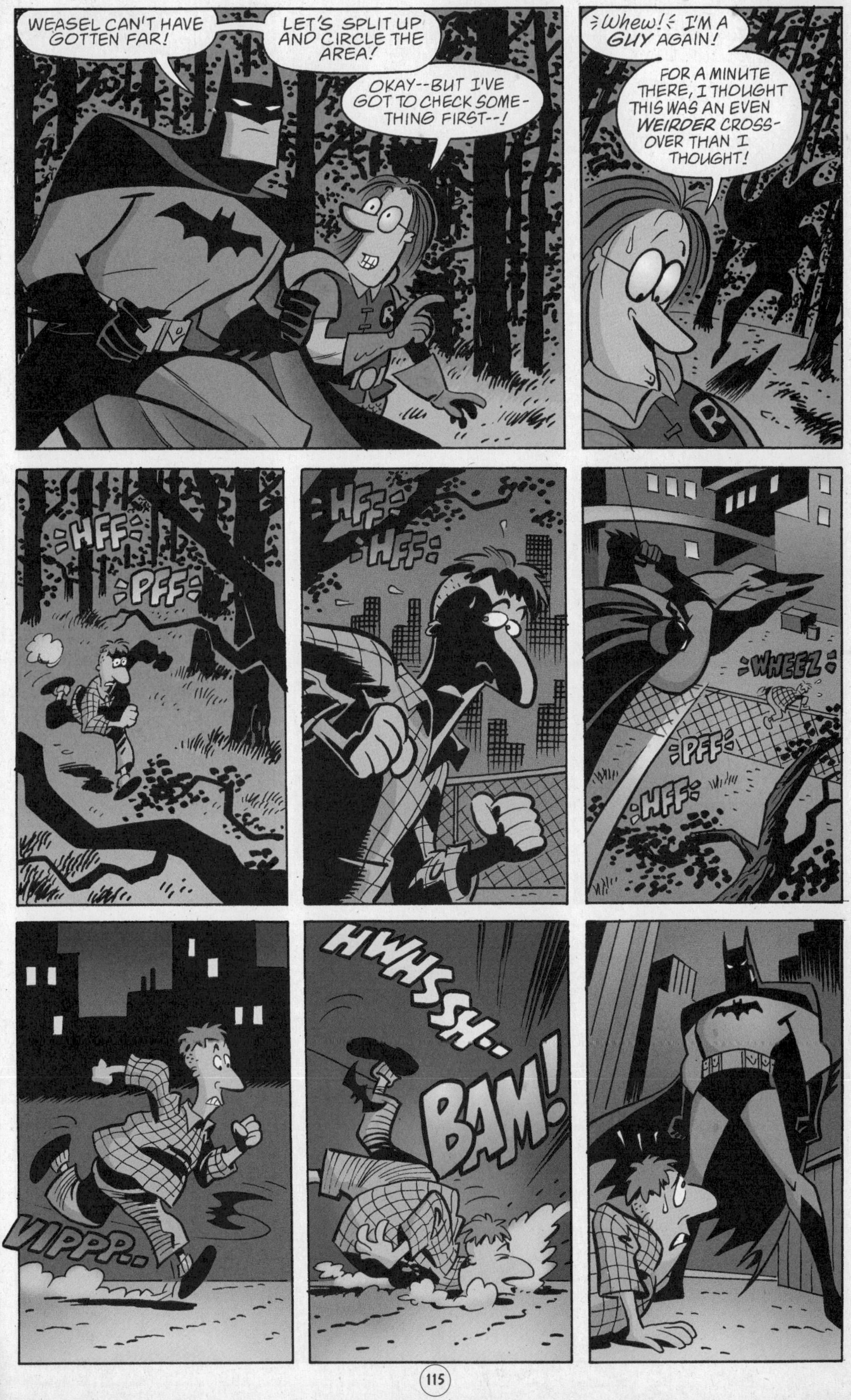

WEASEL CAN'T HAVE GOTTEN FAR!
LET'S SPLIT UP AND CIRCLE THE AREA!
OKAY--BUT I'VE GOT TO CHECK SOME-THING FIRST--!
Whew! I'M A GUY AGAIN!
FOR A MINUTE THERE, I THOUGHT THIS WAS AN EVEN WEIRDER CROSS-OVER THAN I THOUGHT!
HFF
PFF
HFF
HFF
WHEEZ
PFF
HFF
VIPPP..
HWHSSH..
BAM!

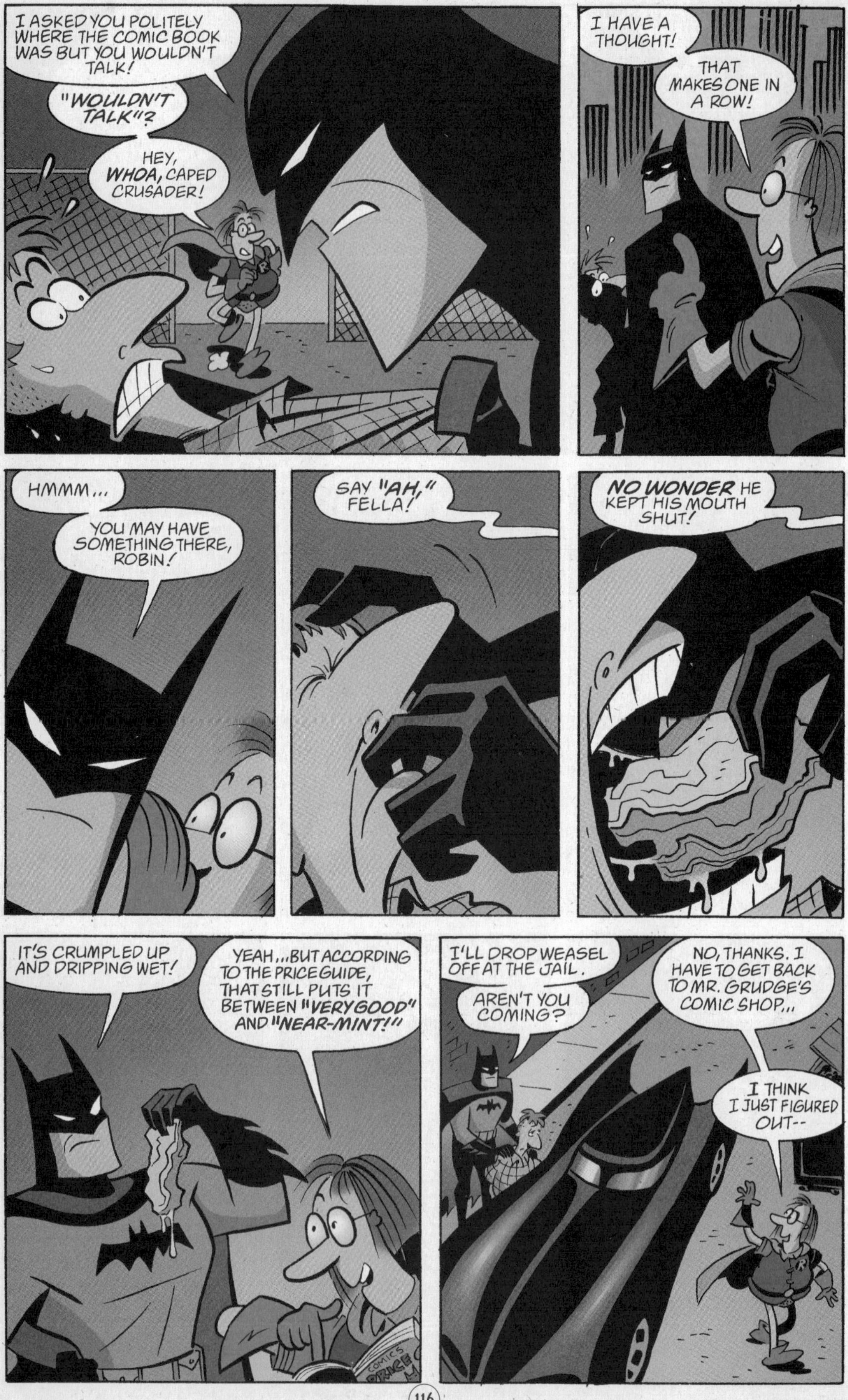
I ASKED YOU POLITELY WHERE THE COMIC BOOK WAS BUT YOU WOULDN'T TALK!
"WOULDN'T TALK"?
HEY, WHOA, CAPED CRUSADER!
I HAVE A THOUGHT!
THAT MAKES ONE IN A ROW!
HMMM...
YOU MAY HAVE SOMETHING THERE, ROBIN!
SAY "AH," FELLA!
NO WONDER HE KEPT HIS MOUTH SHUT!
IT'S CRUMPLED UP AND DRIPPING WET!
YEAH...BUT ACCORDING TO THE PRICE GUIDE, THAT STILL PUTS IT BETWEEN "VERY GOOD" AND "NEAR-MINT!"
I'LL DROP WEASEL OFF AT THE JAIL.
AREN'T YOU COMING?
NO, THANKS. I HAVE TO GET BACK TO MR. GRUDGE'S COMIC SHOP...
I THINK I JUST FIGURED OUT--

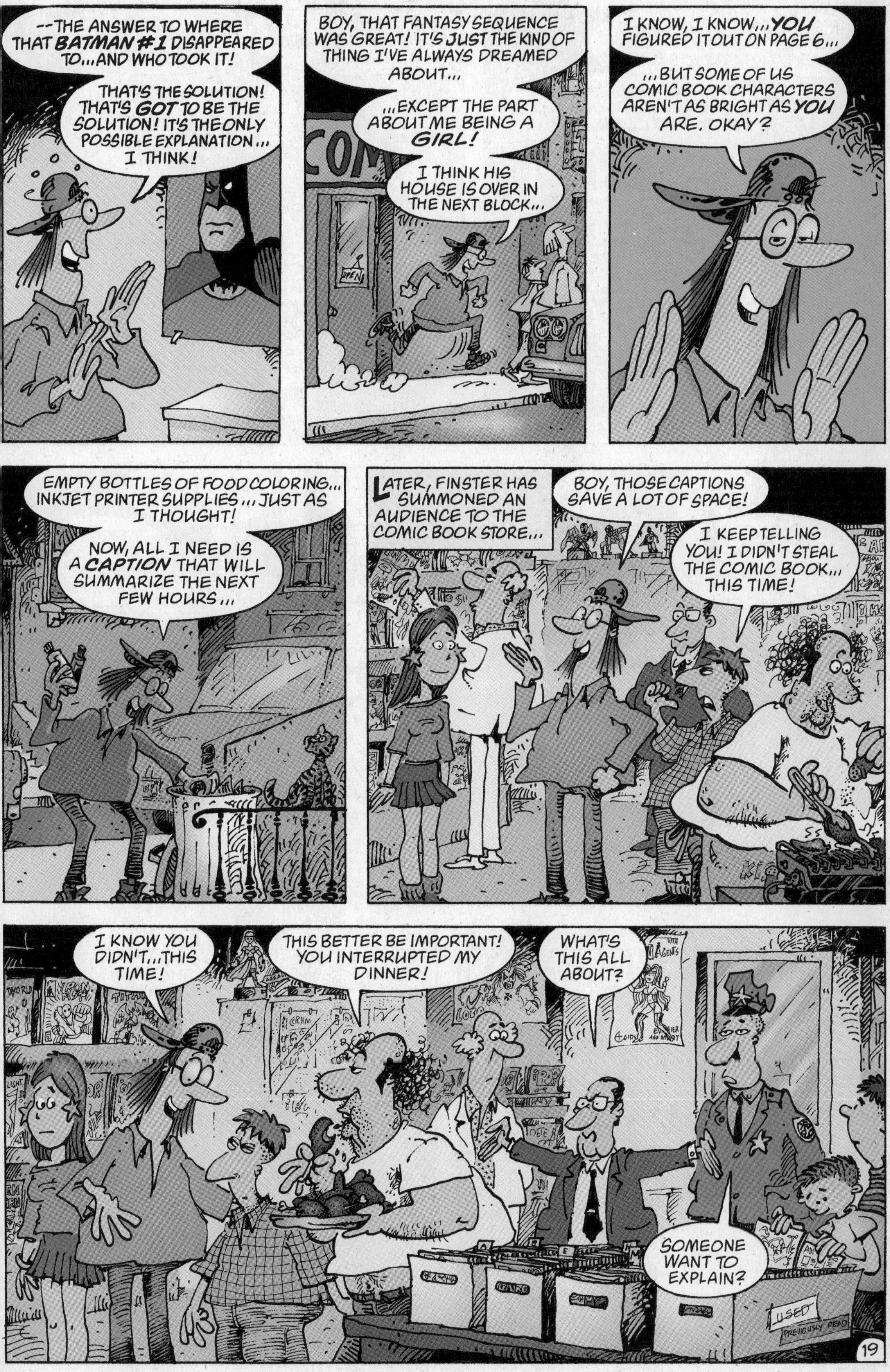
--THE ANSWER TO WHERE THAT BATMAN #1 DISAPPEARED TO... AND WHO TOOK IT!
THAT'S THE SOLUTION! THAT'S GOT TO BE THE SOLUTION! IT'S THE ONLY POSSIBLE EXPLANATION... I THINK!
BOY, THAT FANTASY SEQUENCE WAS GREAT! IT'S JUST THE KIND OF THING I'VE ALWAYS DREAMED ABOUT...
...EXCEPT THE PART ABOUT ME BEING A GIRL!
I THINK HIS HOUSE IS OVER IN THE NEXT BLOCK...
OPEN
I KNOW, I KNOW... YOU FIGURED IT OUT ON PAGE 6...
...BUT SOME OF US COMIC BOOK CHARACTERS AREN'T AS BRIGHT AS YOU ARE. OKAY?
EMPTY BOTTLES OF FOOD COLORING... INKJET PRINTER SUPPLIES... JUST AS I THOUGHT!
NOW, ALL I NEED IS A CAPTION THAT WILL SUMMARIZE THE NEXT FEW HOURS...
LATER, FINSTER HAS SUMMONED AN AUDIENCE TO THE COMIC BOOK STORE...
BOY, THOSE CAPTIONS SAVE A LOT OF SPACE!
I KEEP TELLING YOU! I DIDN'T STEAL THE COMIC BOOK... THIS TIME!
I KNOW YOU DIDN'T... THIS TIME!
THIS BETTER BE IMPORTANT! YOU INTERRUPTED MY DINNER!
WHAT'S THIS ALL ABOUT?
SOMEONE WANT TO EXPLAIN?
USED
PREVIOUSLY READ
19

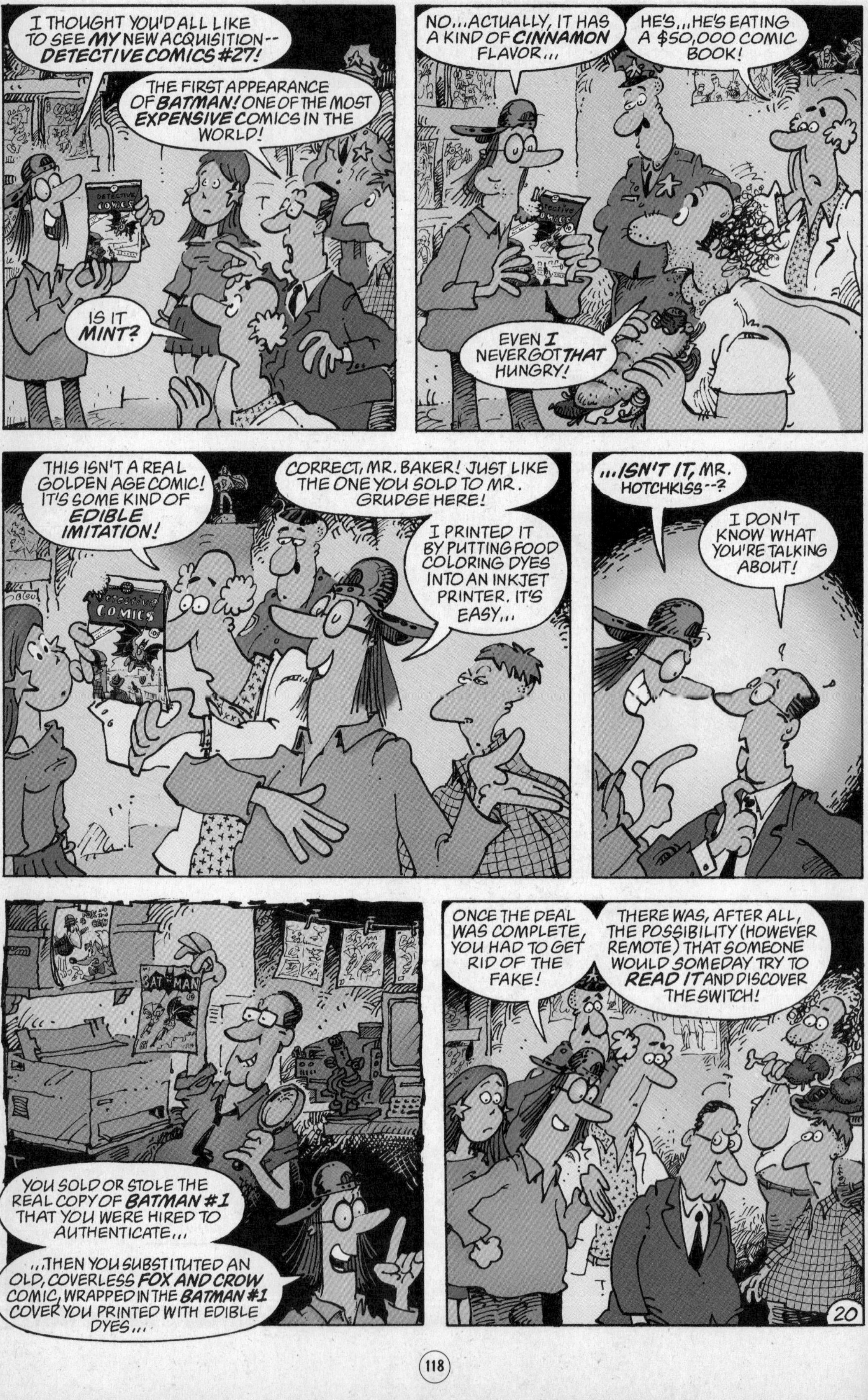
I THOUGHT YOU'D ALL LIKE TO SEE MY NEW ACQUISITION-- DETECTIVE COMICS #27!
THE FIRST APPEARANCE OF BATMAN! ONE OF THE MOST EXPENSIVE COMICS IN THE WORLD!
IS IT MINT?
NO... ACTUALLY, IT HAS A KIND OF CINNAMON FLAVOR...
HE'S... HE'S EATING A $50,000 COMIC BOOK!
EVEN I NEVER GOT THAT HUNGRY!
THIS ISN'T A REAL GOLDEN AGE COMIC! IT'S SOME KIND OF EDIBLE IMITATION!
CORRECT, MR. BAKER! JUST LIKE THE ONE YOU SOLD TO MR. GRUDGE HERE!
I PRINTED IT BY PUTTING FOOD COLORING DYES INTO AN INKJET PRINTER. IT'S EASY...
...ISN'T IT, MR. HOTCHKISS--?
I DON'T KNOW WHAT YOU'RE TALKING ABOUT!
BATMAN
YOU SOLD OR STOLE THE REAL COPY OF BATMAN #1 THAT YOU WERE HIRED TO AUTHENTICATE...
...THEN YOU SUBSTITUTED AN OLD, COVERLESS FOX AND CROW COMIC, WRAPPED IN THE BATMAN #1 COVER YOU PRINTED WITH EDIBLE DYES...
ONCE THE DEAL WAS COMPLETE, YOU HAD TO GET RID OF THE FAKE!
THERE WAS, AFTER ALL, THE POSSIBILITY (HOWEVER REMOTE) THAT SOMEONE WOULD SOMEDAY TRY TO READ IT AND DISCOVER THE SWITCH!
20

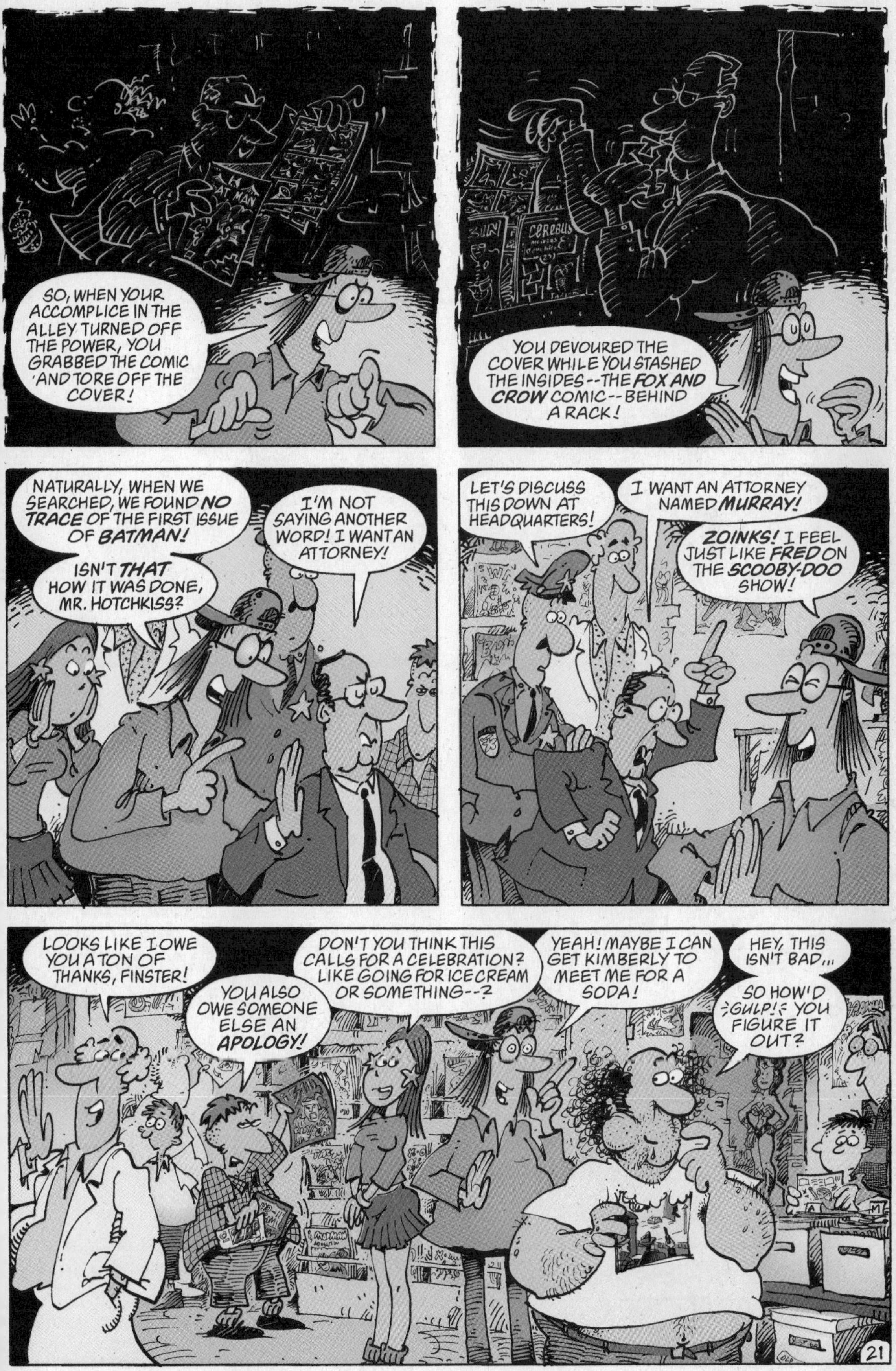
SO, WHEN YOUR ACCOMPLICE IN THE ALLEY TURNED OFF THE POWER, YOU GRABBED THE COMIC AND TORE OFF THE COVER!
YOU DEVOURED THE COVER WHILE YOU STASHED THE INSIDES--THE FOX AND CROW COMIC--BEHIND A RACK!
NATURALLY, WHEN WE SEARCHED, WE FOUND NO TRACE OF THE FIRST ISSUE OF BATMAN!
ISN'T THAT HOW IT WAS DONE, MR. HOTCHKISS?
I'M NOT SAYING ANOTHER WORD! I WANT AN ATTORNEY!
LET'S DISCUSS THIS DOWN AT HEADQUARTERS!
I WANT AN ATTORNEY NAMED MURRAY!
ZOINKS! I FEEL JUST LIKE FRED ON THE SCOOBY-DOO SHOW!
LOOKS LIKE I OWE YOU A TON OF THANKS, FINSTER!
YOU ALSO OWE SOMEONE ELSE AN APOLOGY!
DON'T YOU THINK THIS CALLS FOR A CELEBRATION? LIKE GOING FOR ICE CREAM OR SOMETHING--?
YEAH! MAYBE I CAN GET KIMBERLY TO MEET ME FOR A SODA!
HEY, THIS ISN'T BAD...
SO HOW'D *GULP!* YOU FIGURE IT OUT?
21

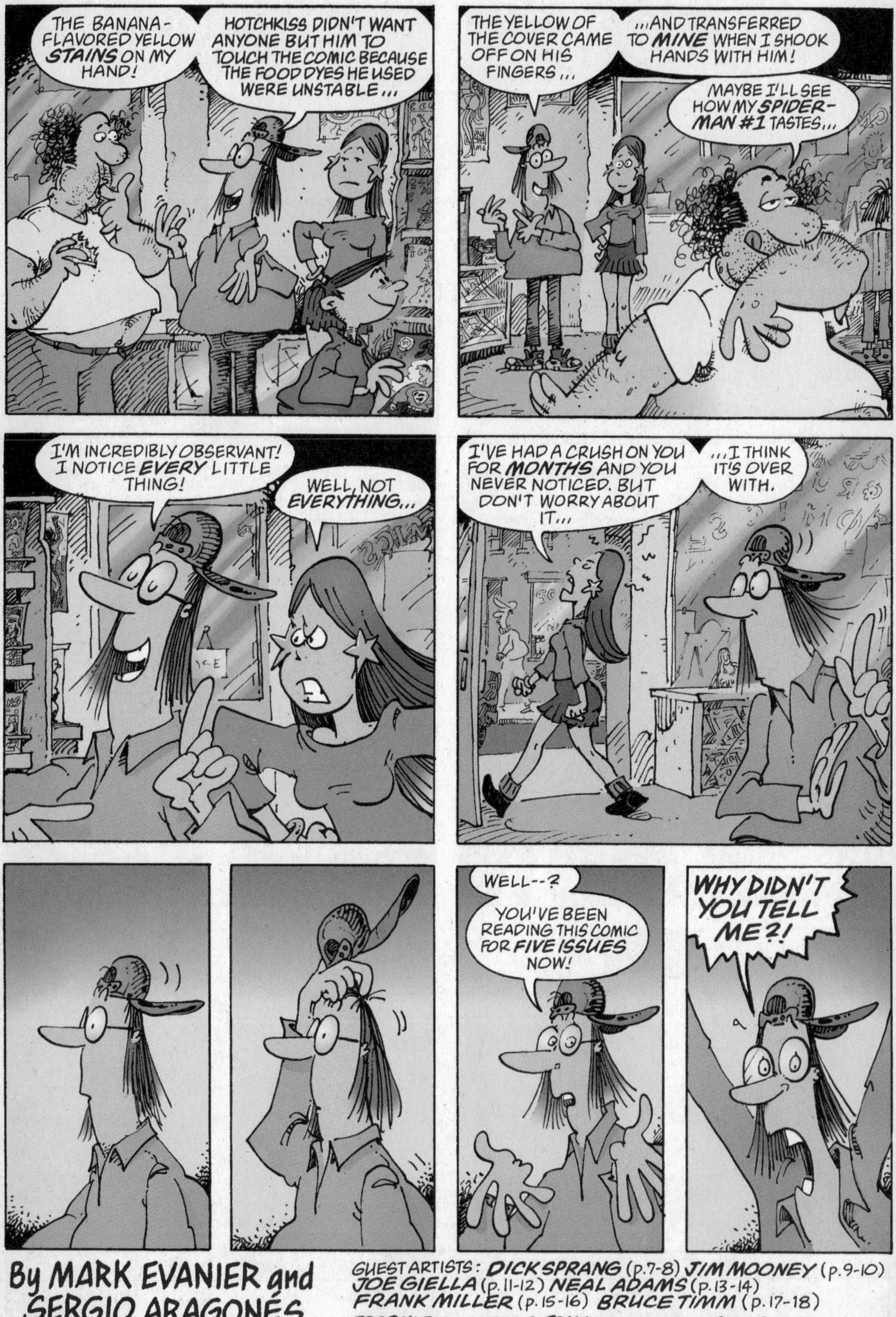
THE BANANA-FLAVORED YELLOW STAINS ON MY HAND!
HOTCHKISS DIDN'T WANT ANYONE BUT HIM TO TOUCH THE COMIC BECAUSE THE FOOD DYES HE USED WERE UNSTABLE...
THE YELLOW OF THE COVER CAME OFF ON HIS FINGERS...
...AND TRANSFERRED TO MINE WHEN I SHOOK HANDS WITH HIM!
MAYBE I'LL SEE HOW MY SPIDER-MAN #1 TASTES...
I'M INCREDIBLY OBSERVANT! I NOTICE EVERY LITTLE THING!
WELL, NOT EVERYTHING...
I'VE HAD A CRUSH ON YOU FOR MONTHS AND YOU NEVER NOTICED. BUT DON'T WORRY ABOUT IT...
...I THINK IT'S OVER WITH.
WELL--?
YOU'VE BEEN READING THIS COMIC FOR FIVE ISSUES NOW!
WHY DIDN'T YOU TELL ME?!

By MARK EVANIER and SERGIO ARAGONÉS

GUEST ARTISTS: DICK SPRANG (p.7-8) JIM MOONEY (p.9-10) JOE GIELLA (p.11-12) NEAL ADAMS (p.13-14) FRANK MILLER (p.15-16) BRUCE TIMM (p.17-18)

TODD KLEIN: LETTERING TOM LUTH: COLORING TONY BEDARD: EDITOR

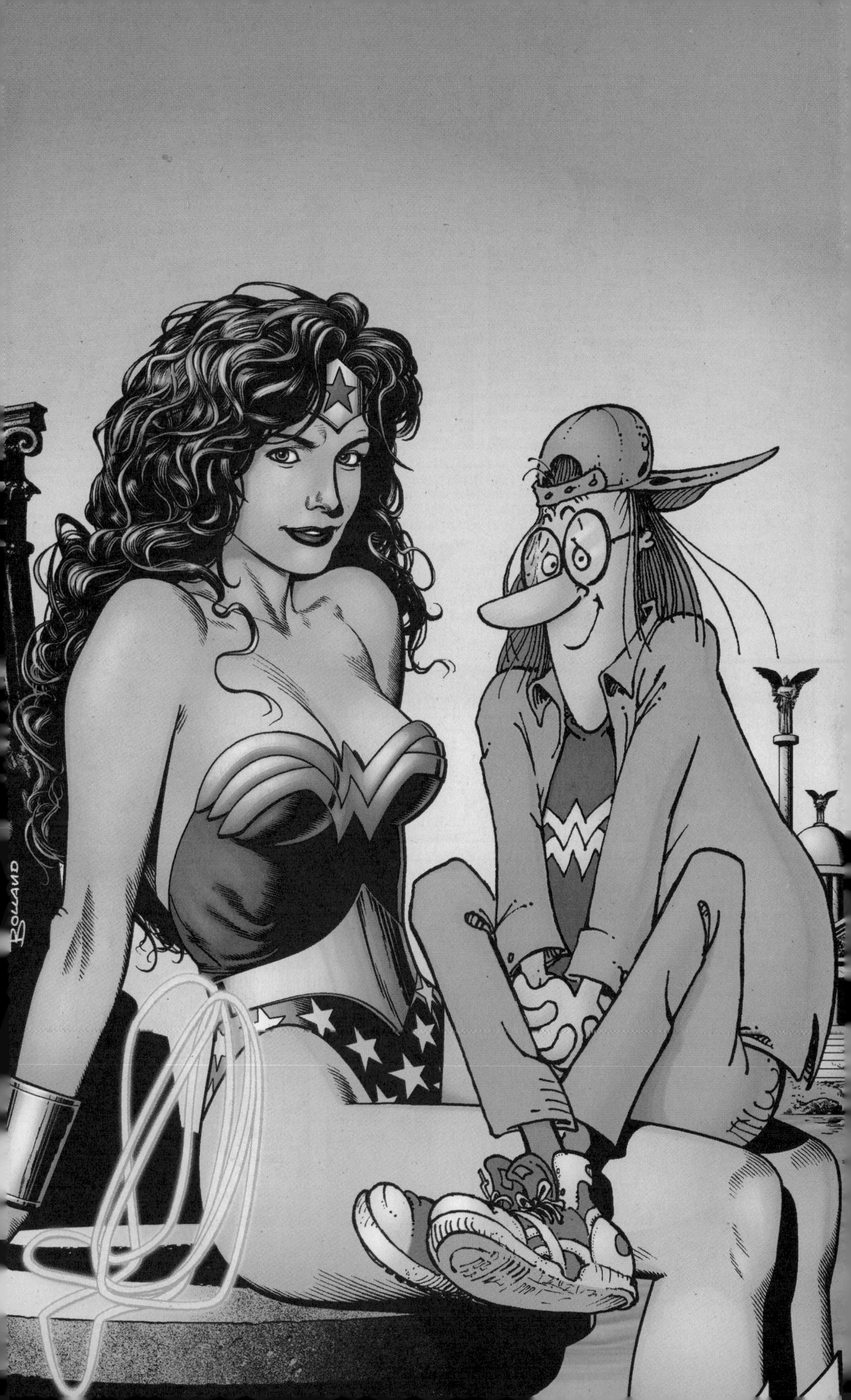
BOLLAND

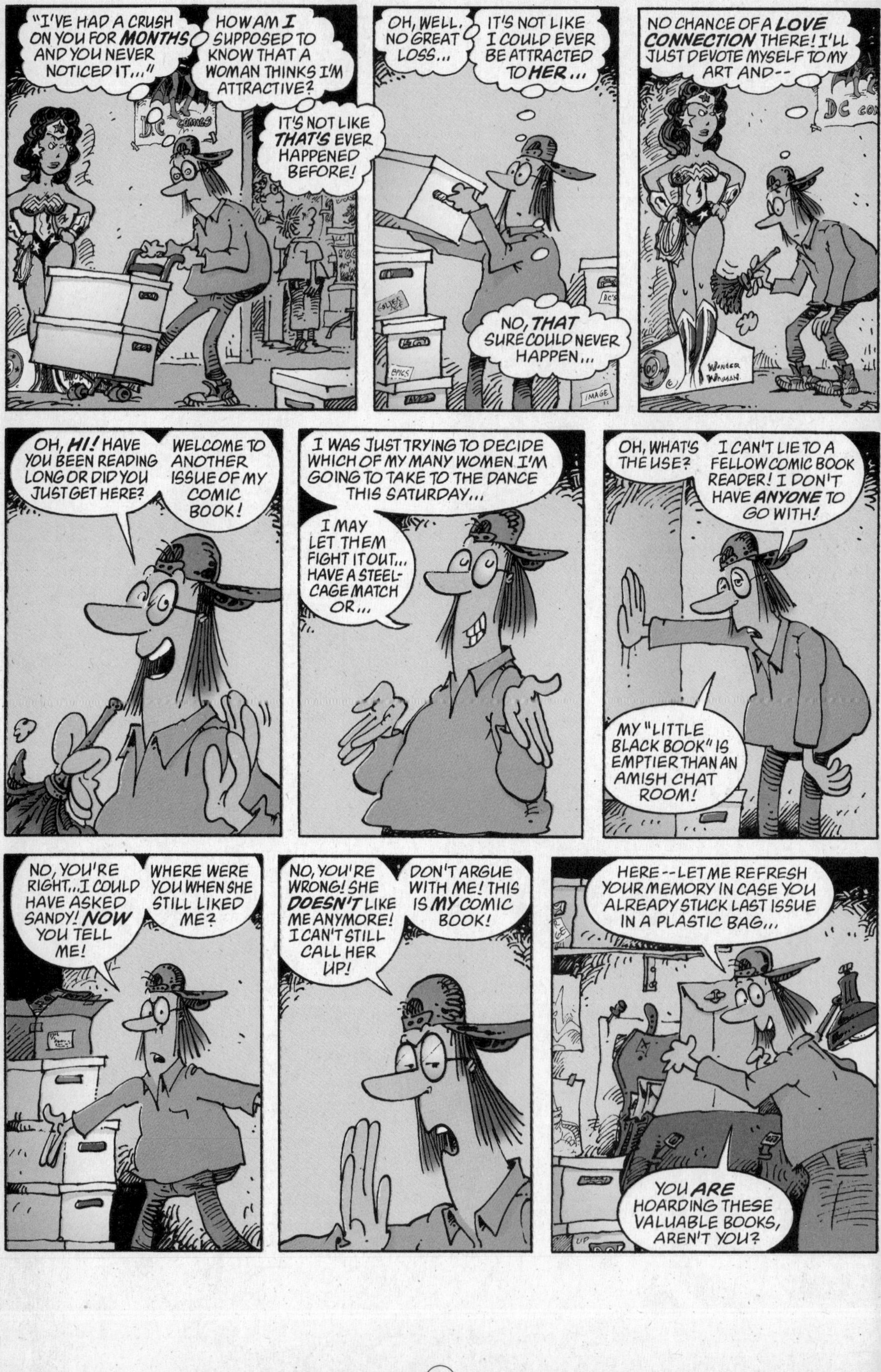
"I'VE HAD A CRUSH ON YOU FOR MONTHS AND YOU NEVER NOTICED IT..."
HOW AM I SUPPOSED TO KNOW THAT A WOMAN THINKS I'M ATTRACTIVE?
IT'S NOT LIKE THAT'S EVER HAPPENED BEFORE!
OH, WELL. NO GREAT LOSS...
IT'S NOT LIKE I COULD EVER BE ATTRACTED TO HER...
NO, THAT SURE COULD NEVER HAPPEN...
NO CHANCE OF A LOVE CONNECTION THERE! I'LL JUST DEVOTE MYSELF TO MY ART AND--
OH, HI! HAVE YOU BEEN READING LONG OR DID YOU JUST GET HERE?
WELCOME TO ANOTHER ISSUE OF MY COMIC BOOK!
I WAS JUST TRYING TO DECIDE WHICH OF MY MANY WOMEN I'M GOING TO TAKE TO THE DANCE THIS SATURDAY...
I MAY LET THEM FIGHT IT OUT... HAVE A STEEL-CAGE MATCH OR...
OH, WHAT'S THE USE?
I CAN'T LIE TO A FELLOW COMIC BOOK READER! I DON'T HAVE ANYONE TO GO WITH!
MY "LITTLE BLACK BOOK" IS EMPTIER THAN AN AMISH CHAT ROOM!
NO, YOU'RE RIGHT...I COULD HAVE ASKED SANDY! NOW YOU TELL ME!
WHERE WERE YOU WHEN SHE STILL LIKED ME?
NO, YOU'RE WRONG! SHE DOESN'T LIKE ME ANYMORE! I CAN'T STILL CALL HER UP!
DON'T ARGUE WITH ME! THIS IS MY COMIC BOOK!
HERE--LET ME REFRESH YOUR MEMORY IN CASE YOU ALREADY STUCK LAST ISSUE IN A PLASTIC BAG...
YOU ARE HOARDING THESE VALUABLE BOOKS, AREN'T YOU?

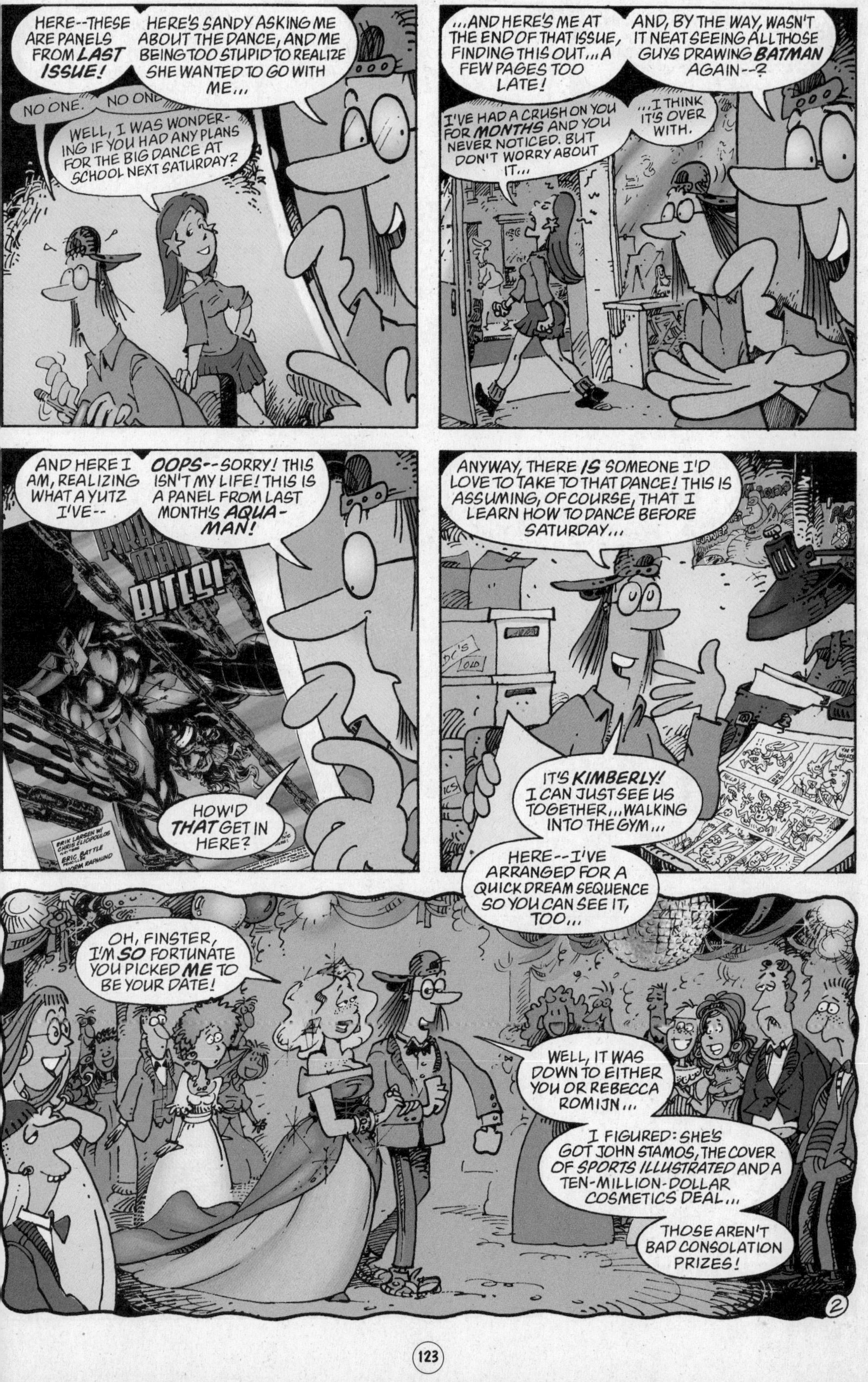
HERE--THESE ARE PANELS FROM LAST ISSUE!
HERE'S SANDY ASKING ME ABOUT THE DANCE, AND ME BEING TOO STUPID TO REALIZE SHE WANTED TO GO WITH ME...
NO ONE.
WELL, I WAS WONDERING IF YOU HAD ANY PLANS FOR THE BIG DANCE AT SCHOOL NEXT SATURDAY?
...AND HERE'S ME AT THE END OF THAT ISSUE, FINDING THIS OUT... A FEW PAGES TOO LATE!
AND, BY THE WAY, WASN'T IT NEAT SEEING ALL THOSE GUYS DRAWING BATMAN AGAIN--?
I'VE HAD A CRUSH ON YOU FOR MONTHS AND YOU NEVER NOTICED. BUT DON'T WORRY ABOUT IT...
...I THINK IT'S OVER WITH.
AND HERE I AM, REALIZING WHAT A YUTZ I'VE--
OOPS--SORRY! THIS ISN'T MY LIFE! THIS IS A PANEL FROM LAST MONTH'S AQUAMAN!
BITES!
HOW'D THAT GET IN HERE?
ANYWAY, THERE IS SOMEONE I'D LOVE TO TAKE TO THAT DANCE! THIS IS ASSUMING, OF COURSE, THAT I LEARN HOW TO DANCE BEFORE SATURDAY...
IT'S KIMBERLY! I CAN JUST SEE US TOGETHER... WALKING INTO THE GYM...
HERE--I'VE ARRANGED FOR A QUICK DREAM SEQUENCE SO YOU CAN SEE IT, TOO...
OH, FINSTER, I'M SO FORTUNATE YOU PICKED ME TO BE YOUR DATE!
WELL, IT WAS DOWN TO EITHER YOU OR REBECCA ROMIJN...
I FIGURED: SHE'S GOT JOHN STAMOS, THE COVER OF SPORTS ILLUSTRATED AND A TEN-MILLION-DOLLAR COSMETICS DEAL...
THOSE AREN'T BAD CONSOLATION PRIZES!
2

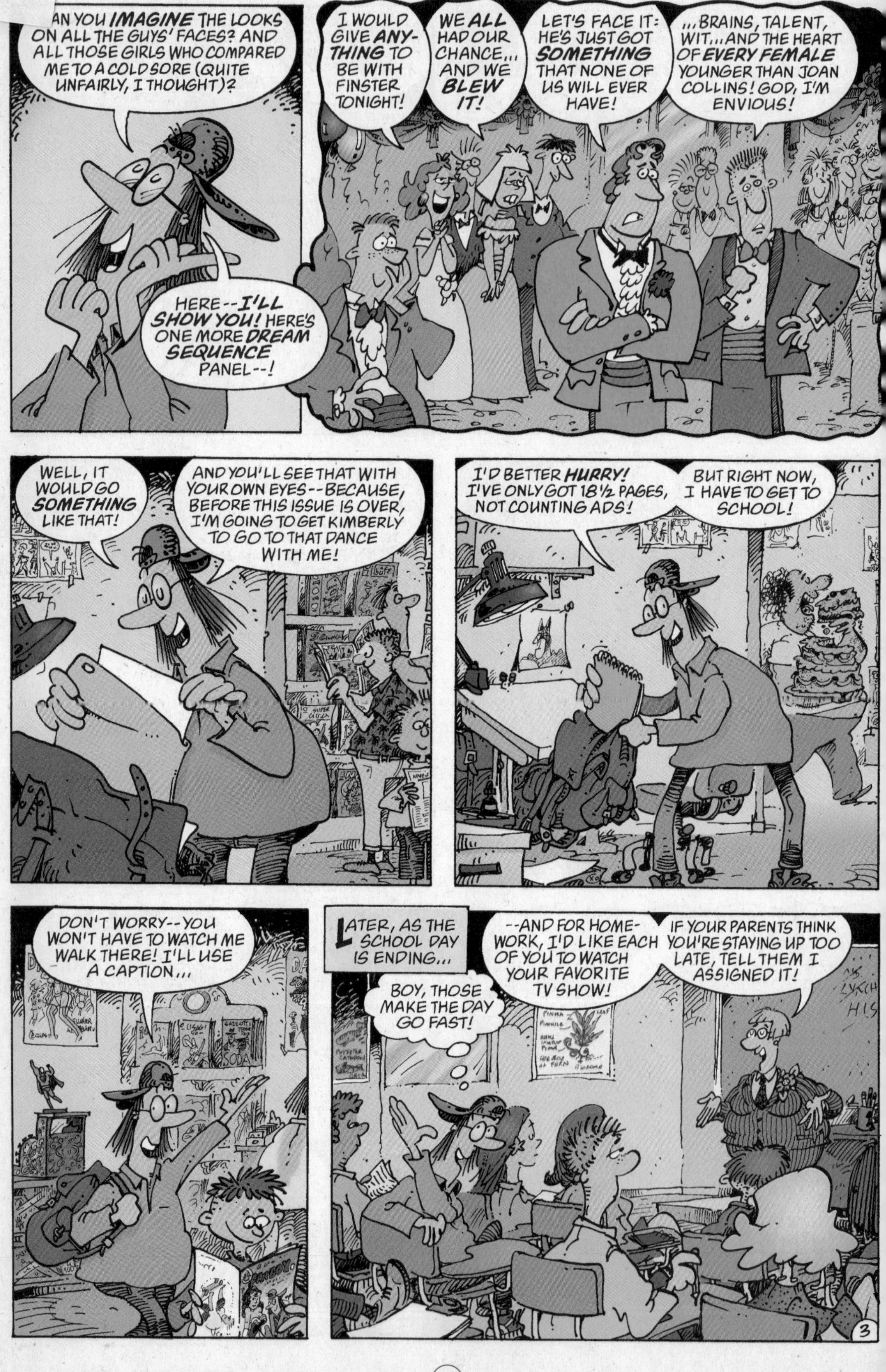
AN YOU IMAGINE THE LOOKS ON ALL THE GUYS' FACES? AND ALL THOSE GIRLS WHO COMPARED ME TO A COLD SORE (QUITE UNFAIRLY, I THOUGHT)?
HERE--I'LL SHOW YOU! HERE'S ONE MORE DREAM SEQUENCE PANEL--!
I WOULD GIVE ANYTHING TO BE WITH FINSTER TONIGHT!
WE ALL HAD OUR CHANCE... AND WE BLEW IT!
LET'S FACE IT: HE'S JUST GOT SOMETHING THAT NONE OF US WILL EVER HAVE!
...BRAINS, TALENT, WIT...AND THE HEART OF EVERY FEMALE YOUNGER THAN JOAN COLLINS! GOD, I'M ENVIOUS!
WELL, IT WOULD GO SOMETHING LIKE THAT!
AND YOU'LL SEE THAT WITH YOUR OWN EYES--BECAUSE, BEFORE THIS ISSUE IS OVER, I'M GOING TO GET KIMBERLY TO GO TO THAT DANCE WITH ME!
I'D BETTER HURRY! I'VE ONLY GOT 18½ PAGES, NOT COUNTING ADS!
BUT RIGHT NOW, I HAVE TO GET TO SCHOOL!
DON'T WORRY--YOU WON'T HAVE TO WATCH ME WALK THERE! I'LL USE A CAPTION...
LATER, AS THE SCHOOL DAY IS ENDING...
BOY, THOSE MAKE THE DAY GO FAST!
--AND FOR HOMEWORK, I'D LIKE EACH OF YOU TO WATCH YOUR FAVORITE TV SHOW!
IF YOUR PARENTS THINK YOU'RE STAYING UP TOO LATE, TELL THEM I ASSIGNED IT!
3

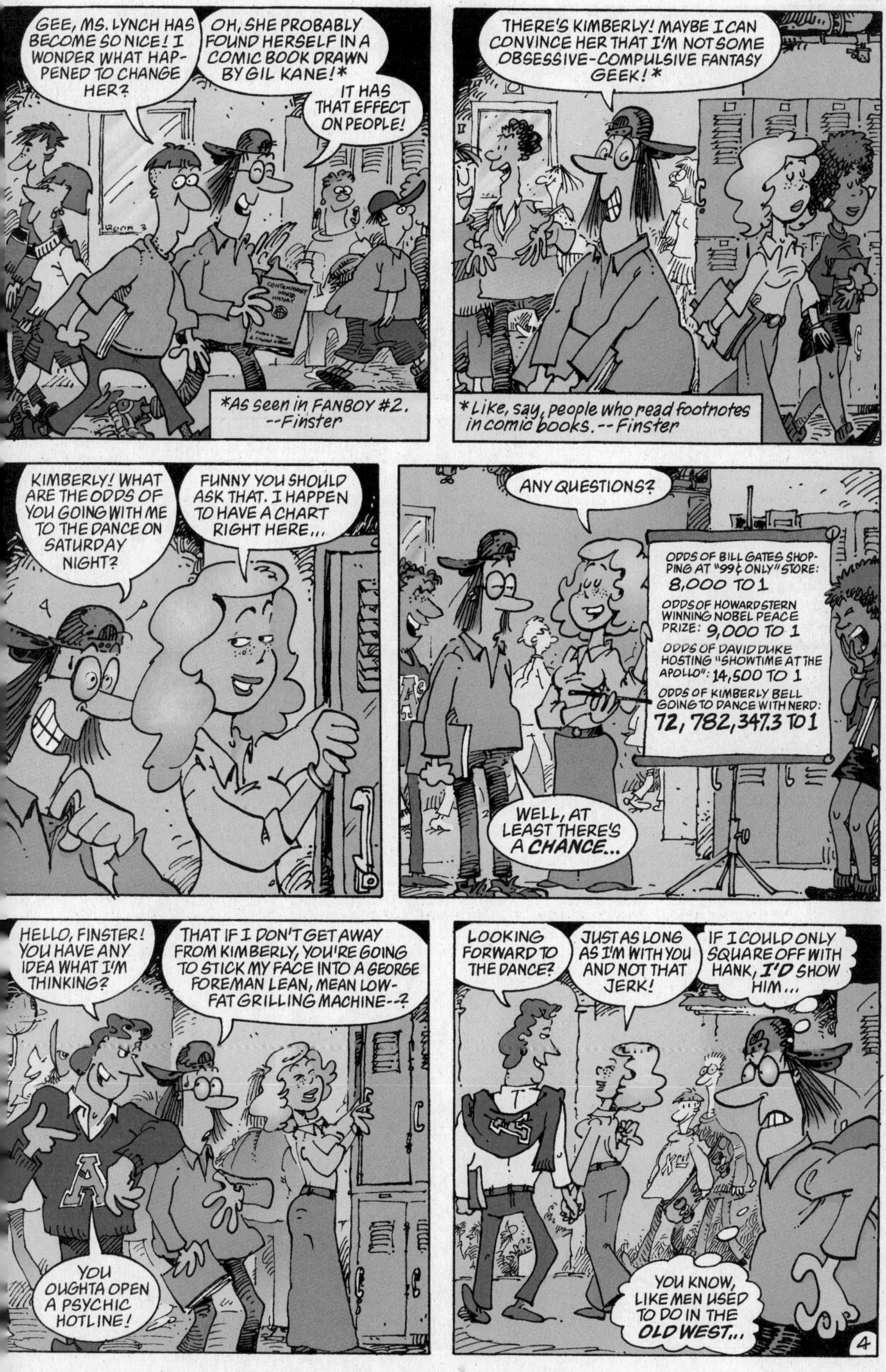
GEE, MS. LYNCH HAS BECOME SO NICE! I WONDER WHAT HAPPENED TO CHANGE HER?
OH, SHE PROBABLY FOUND HERSELF IN A COMIC BOOK DRAWN BY GIL KANE!*
IT HAS THAT EFFECT ON PEOPLE!
*As seen in FANBOY #2. --Finster
THERE'S KIMBERLY! MAYBE I CAN CONVINCE HER THAT I'M NOT SOME OBSESSIVE-COMPULSIVE FANTASY GEEK!*
*Like, say, people who read footnotes in comic books. --Finster
KIMBERLY! WHAT ARE THE ODDS OF YOU GOING WITH ME TO THE DANCE ON SATURDAY NIGHT?
FUNNY YOU SHOULD ASK THAT. I HAPPEN TO HAVE A CHART RIGHT HERE...
ANY QUESTIONS?
ODDS OF BILL GATES SHOPPING AT "99¢ ONLY" STORE: 8,000 TO 1
ODDS OF HOWARD STERN WINNING NOBEL PEACE PRIZE: 9,000 TO 1
ODDS OF DAVID DUKE HOSTING "SHOWTIME AT THE APOLLO": 14,500 TO 1
ODDS OF KIMBERLY BELL GOING TO DANCE WITH NERD: 72,782,347.3 TO 1
WELL, AT LEAST THERE'S A CHANCE...
HELLO, FINSTER! YOU HAVE ANY IDEA WHAT I'M THINKING?
THAT IF I DON'T GET AWAY FROM KIMBERLY, YOU'RE GOING TO STICK MY FACE INTO A GEORGE FOREMAN LEAN, MEAN LOW-FAT GRILLING MACHINE--?
YOU OUGHTA OPEN A PSYCHIC HOTLINE!
LOOKING FORWARD TO THE DANCE?
JUST AS LONG AS I'M WITH YOU AND NOT THAT JERK!
IF I COULD ONLY SQUARE OFF WITH HANK, I'D SHOW HIM...
YOU KNOW, LIKE MEN USED TO DO IN THE OLD WEST...
4

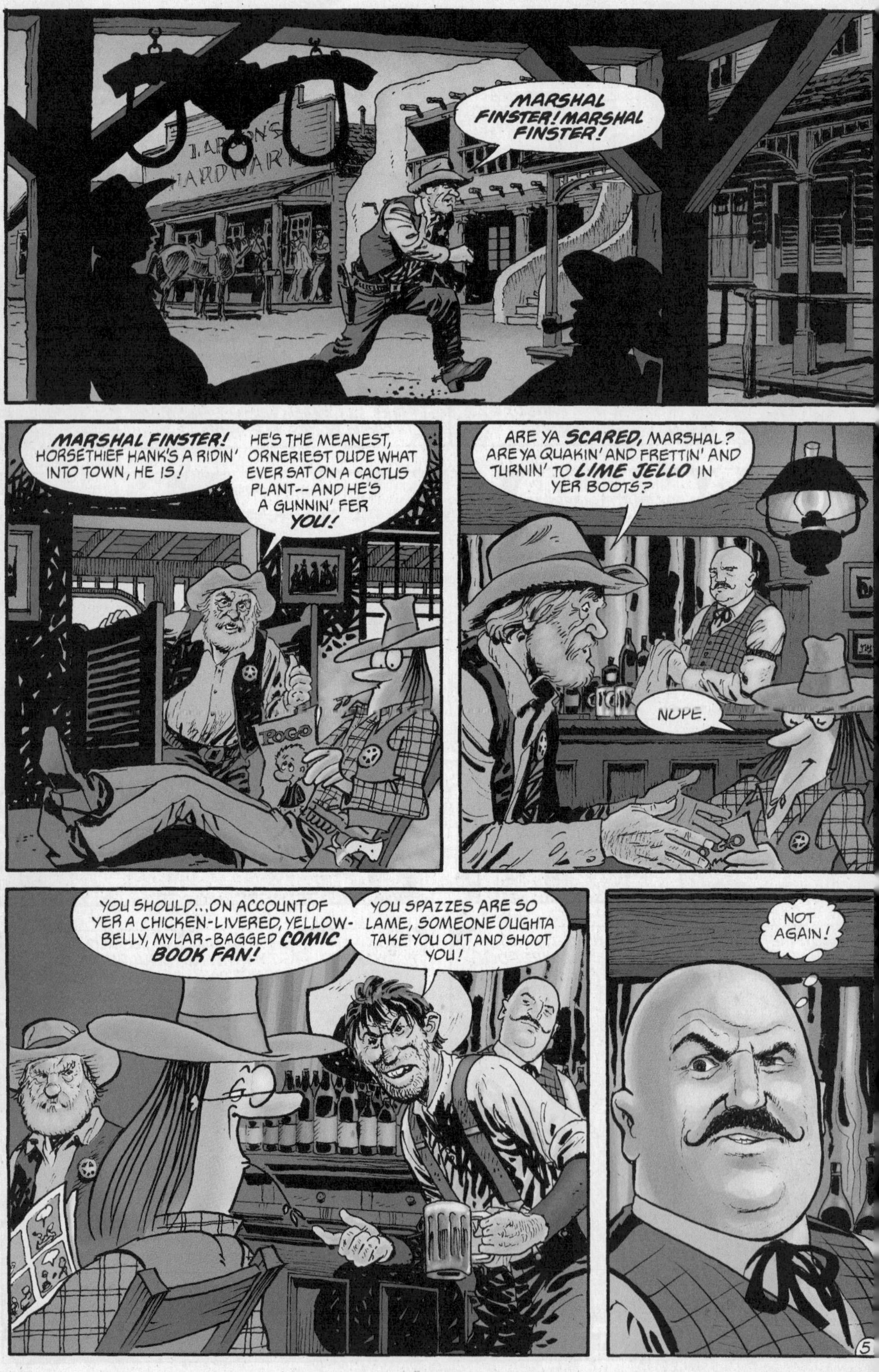
MARSHAL FINSTER! MARSHAL FINSTER!
MARSHAL FINSTER! HORSETHIEF HANK'S A RIDIN' INTO TOWN, HE IS!
HE'S THE MEANEST, ORNERIEST DUDE WHAT EVER SAT ON A CACTUS PLANT--AND HE'S A GUNNIN' FER YOU!
POGO
ARE YA SCARED, MARSHAL? ARE YA QUAKIN' AND FRETTIN' AND TURNIN' TO LIME JELLO IN YER BOOTS?
NOPE.
YOU SHOULD...ON ACCOUNT OF YER A CHICKEN-LIVERED, YELLOW-BELLY, MYLAR-BAGGED COMIC BOOK FAN!
YOU SPAZZES ARE SO LAME, SOMEONE OUGHTA TAKE YOU OUT AND SHOOT YOU!
NOT AGAIN!
5

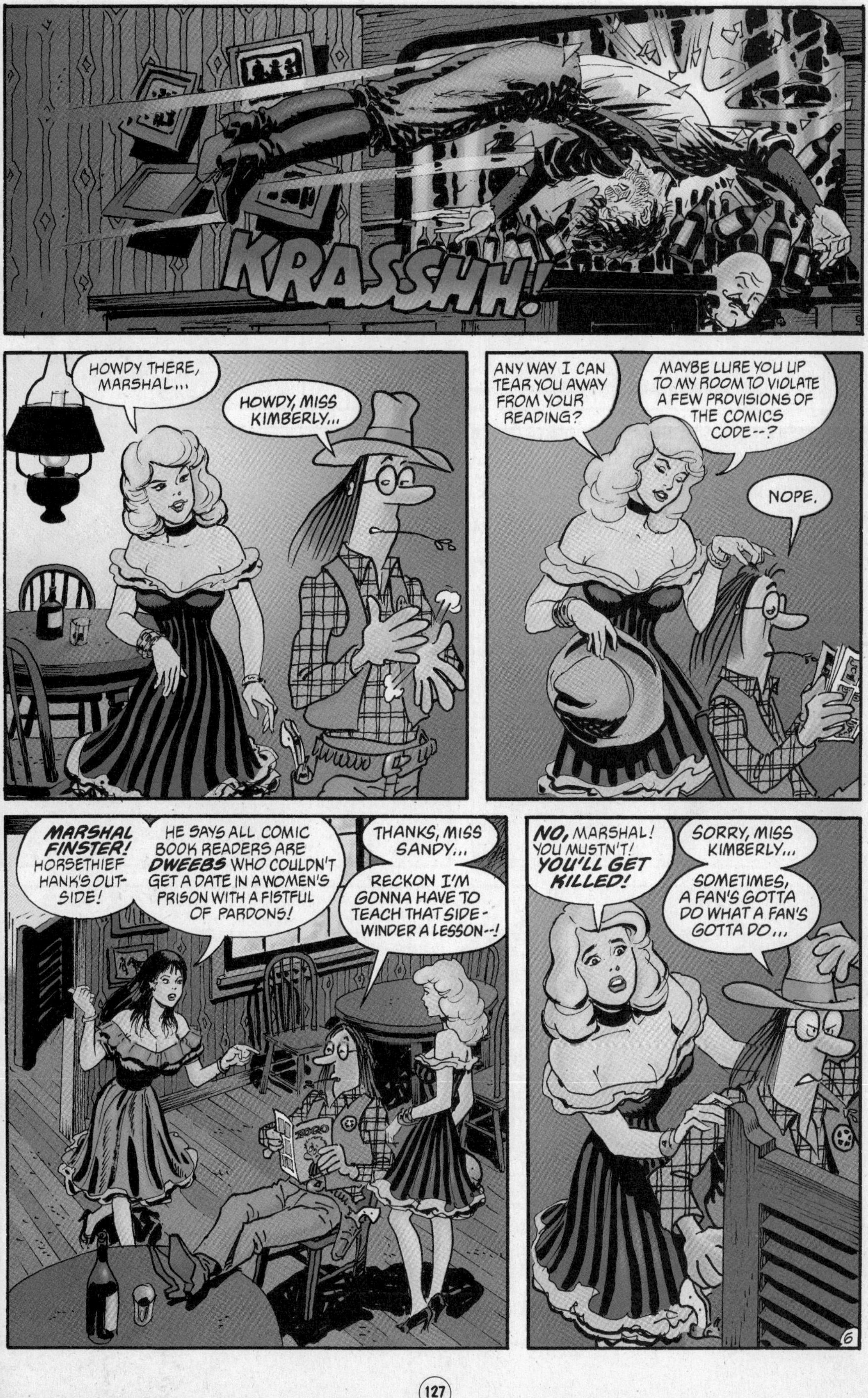
KRASSHH!
HOWDY THERE, MARSHAL...
HOWDY, MISS KIMBERLY...
ANY WAY I CAN TEAR YOU AWAY FROM YOUR READING?
MAYBE LURE YOU UP TO MY ROOM TO VIOLATE A FEW PROVISIONS OF THE COMICS CODE--?
NOPE.
MARSHAL FINSTER! HORSETHIEF HANK'S OUTSIDE!
HE SAYS ALL COMIC BOOK READERS ARE DWEEBS WHO COULDN'T GET A DATE IN A WOMEN'S PRISON WITH A FISTFUL OF PARDONS!
THANKS, MISS SANDY...
RECKON I'M GONNA HAVE TO TEACH THAT SIDEWINDER A LESSON--!
NO, MARSHAL! YOU MUSTN'T! YOU'LL GET KILLED!
SORRY, MISS KIMBERLY...
SOMETIMES, A FAN'S GOTTA DO WHAT A FAN'S GOTTA DO...
6

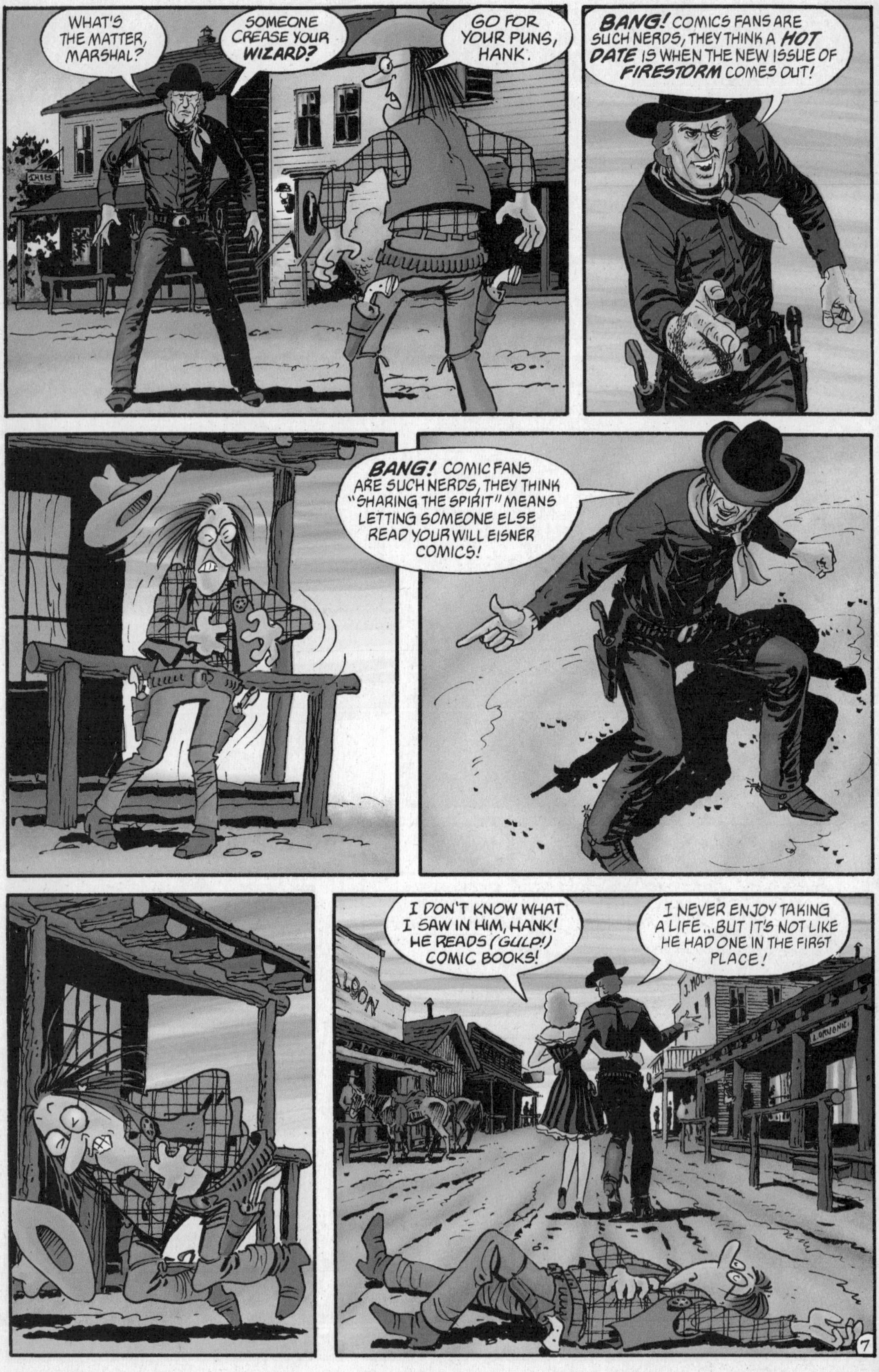
WHAT'S THE MATTER, MARSHAL?
SOMEONE CREASE YOUR WIZARD?
GO FOR YOUR PUNS, HANK.
BANG! COMICS FANS ARE SUCH NERDS, THEY THINK A HOT DATE IS WHEN THE NEW ISSUE OF FIRESTORM COMES OUT!
BANG! COMIC FANS ARE SUCH NERDS, THEY THINK "SHARING THE SPIRIT" MEANS LETTING SOMEONE ELSE READ YOUR WILL EISNER COMICS!
I DON'T KNOW WHAT I SAW IN HIM, HANK! HE READS (GULP!) COMIC BOOKS!
I NEVER ENJOY TAKING A LIFE... BUT IT'S NOT LIKE HE HAD ONE IN THE FIRST PLACE!
7

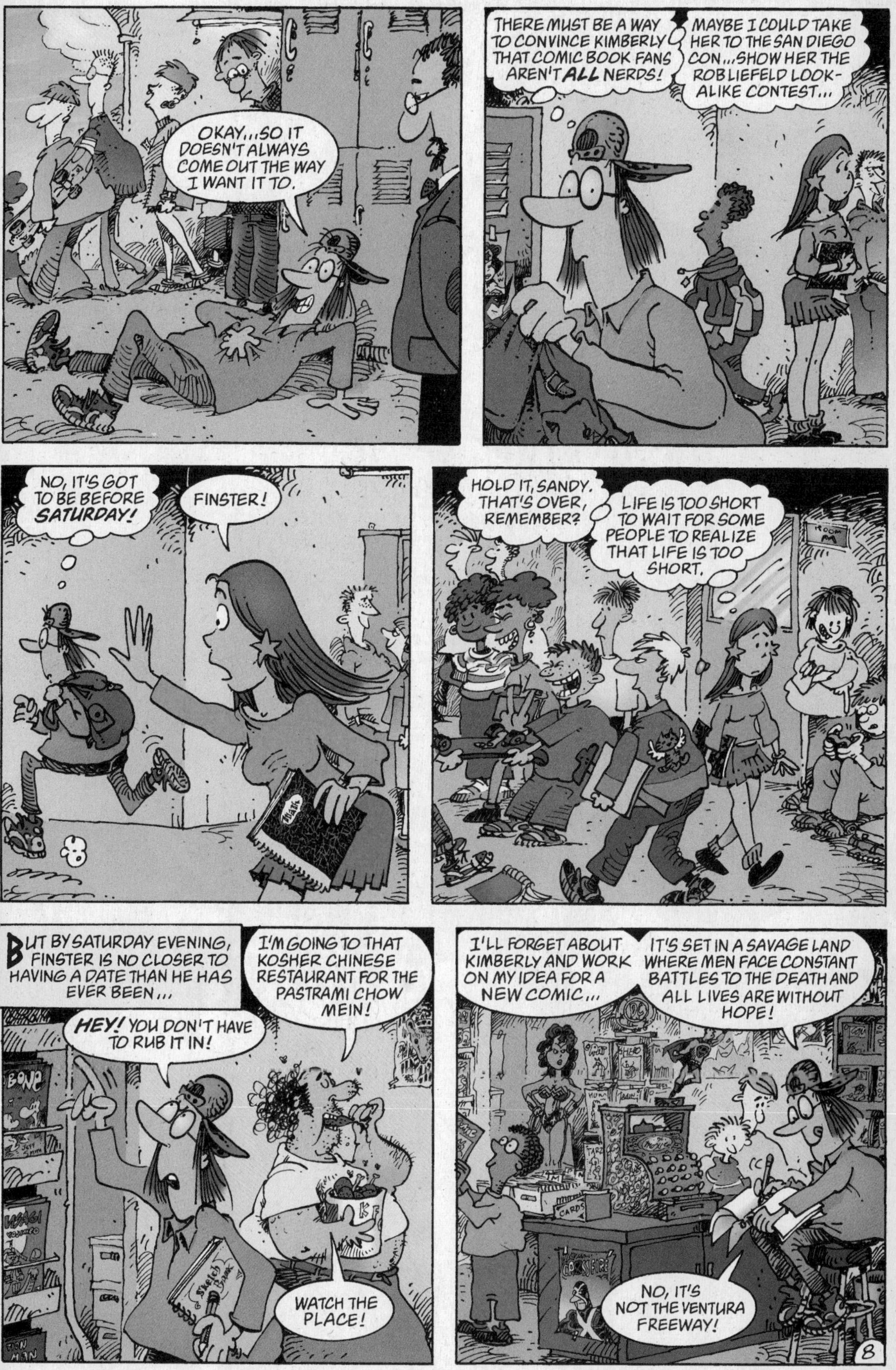
OKAY...SO IT DOESN'T ALWAYS COME OUT THE WAY I WANT IT TO.
THERE MUST BE A WAY TO CONVINCE KIMBERLY THAT COMIC BOOK FANS AREN'T **ALL** NERDS!
MAYBE I COULD TAKE HER TO THE SAN DIEGO CON...SHOW HER THE ROB LIEFELD LOOK-ALIKE CONTEST...
NO, IT'S GOT TO BE BEFORE **SATURDAY!**
FINSTER!
HOLD IT, SANDY. THAT'S OVER, REMEMBER?
LIFE IS TOO SHORT TO WAIT FOR SOME PEOPLE TO REALIZE THAT LIFE IS TOO SHORT.
BUT BY SATURDAY EVENING, FINSTER IS NO CLOSER TO HAVING A DATE THAN HE HAS EVER BEEN...
I'M GOING TO THAT KOSHER CHINESE RESTAURANT FOR THE PASTRAMI CHOW MEIN!
HEY! YOU DON'T HAVE TO RUB IT IN!
WATCH THE PLACE!
I'LL FORGET ABOUT KIMBERLY AND WORK ON MY IDEA FOR A NEW COMIC...
IT'S SET IN A SAVAGE LAND WHERE MEN FACE CONSTANT BATTLES TO THE DEATH AND ALL LIVES ARE WITHOUT HOPE!
NO, IT'S NOT THE VENTURA FREEWAY!
8

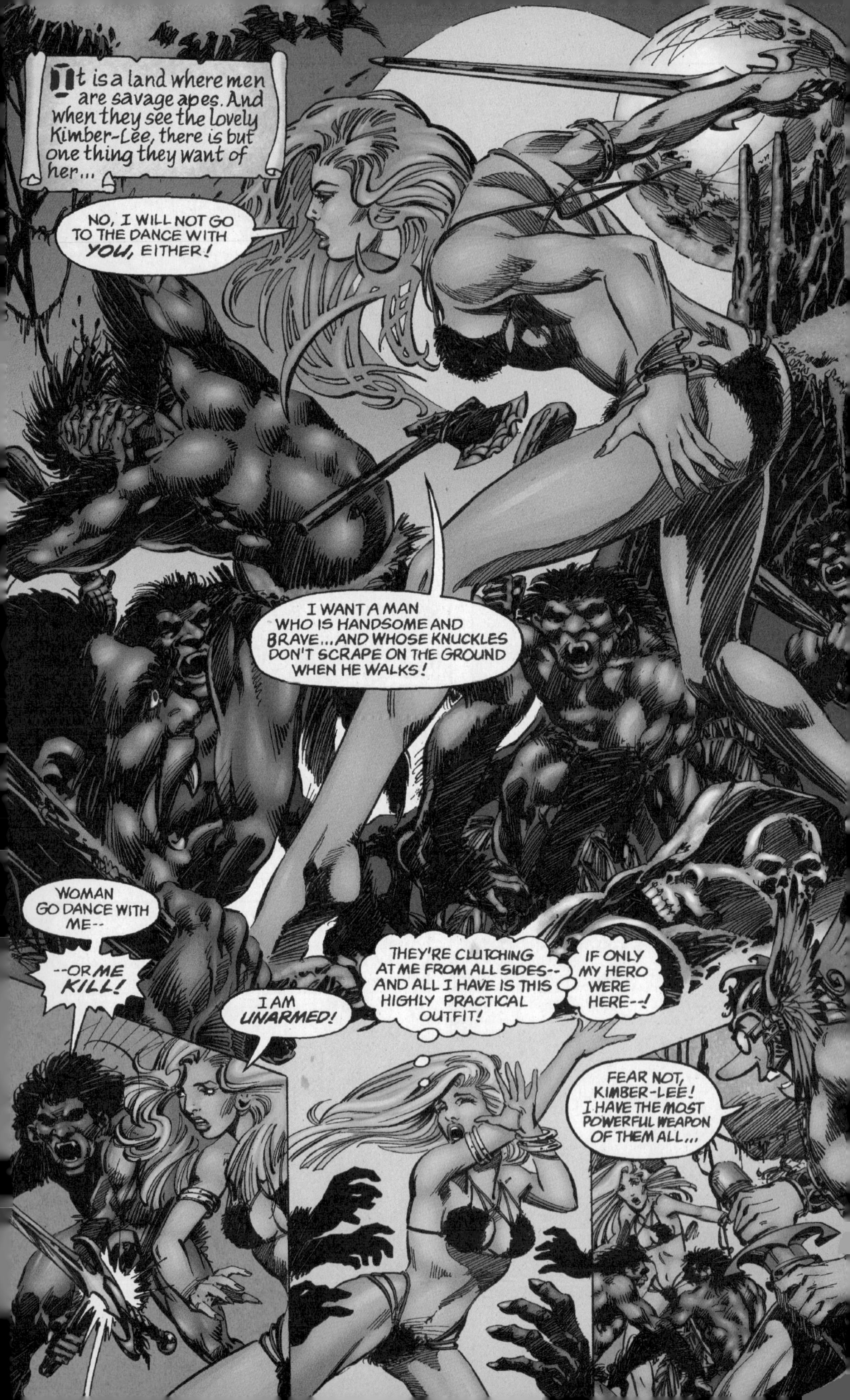
It is a land where men are savage apes. And when they see the lovely Kimber-Lee, there is but one thing they want of her...
NO, I WILL NOT GO TO THE DANCE WITH YOU, EITHER!
I WANT A MAN WHO IS HANDSOME AND BRAVE... AND WHOSE KNUCKLES DON'T SCRAPE ON THE GROUND WHEN HE WALKS!
WOMAN GO DANCE WITH ME--
--OR ME KILL!
I AM UNARMED!
THEY'RE CLUTCHING AT ME FROM ALL SIDES-- AND ALL I HAVE IS THIS HIGHLY PRACTICAL OUTFIT!
IF ONLY MY HERO WERE HERE--!
FEAR NOT, KIMBER-LEE! I HAVE THE MOST POWERFUL WEAPON OF THEM ALL...

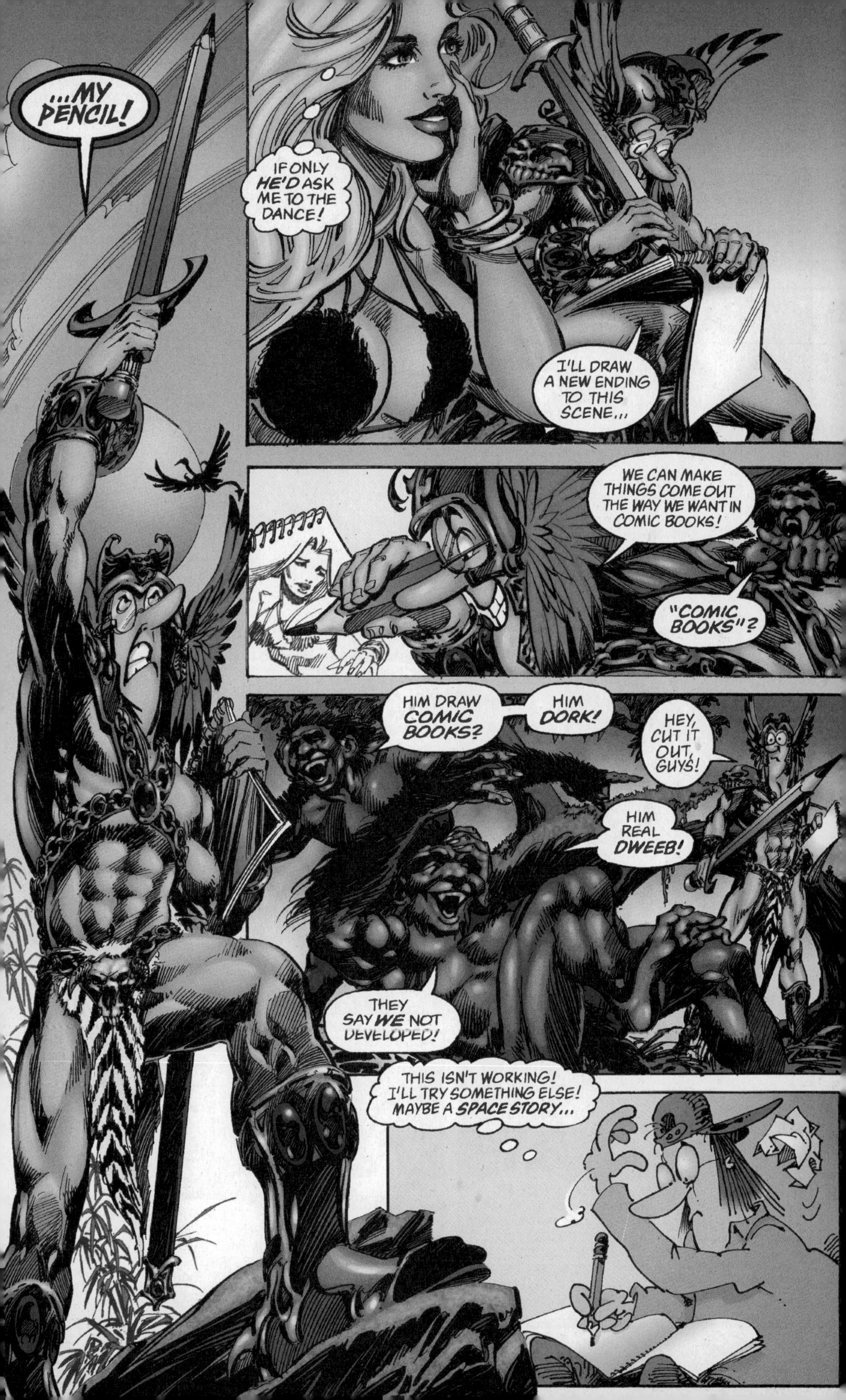
...MY PENCIL!
IF ONLY HE'D ASK ME TO THE DANCE!
I'LL DRAW A NEW ENDING TO THIS SCENE...
WE CAN MAKE THINGS COME OUT THE WAY WE WANT IN COMIC BOOKS!
"COMIC BOOKS"?
HIM DRAW COMIC BOOKS?
HIM DORK!
HEY, CUT IT OUT, GUYS!
HIM REAL DWEEB!
THEY SAY WE NOT DEVELOPED!
THIS ISN'T WORKING! I'LL TRY SOMETHING ELSE! MAYBE A SPACE STORY...

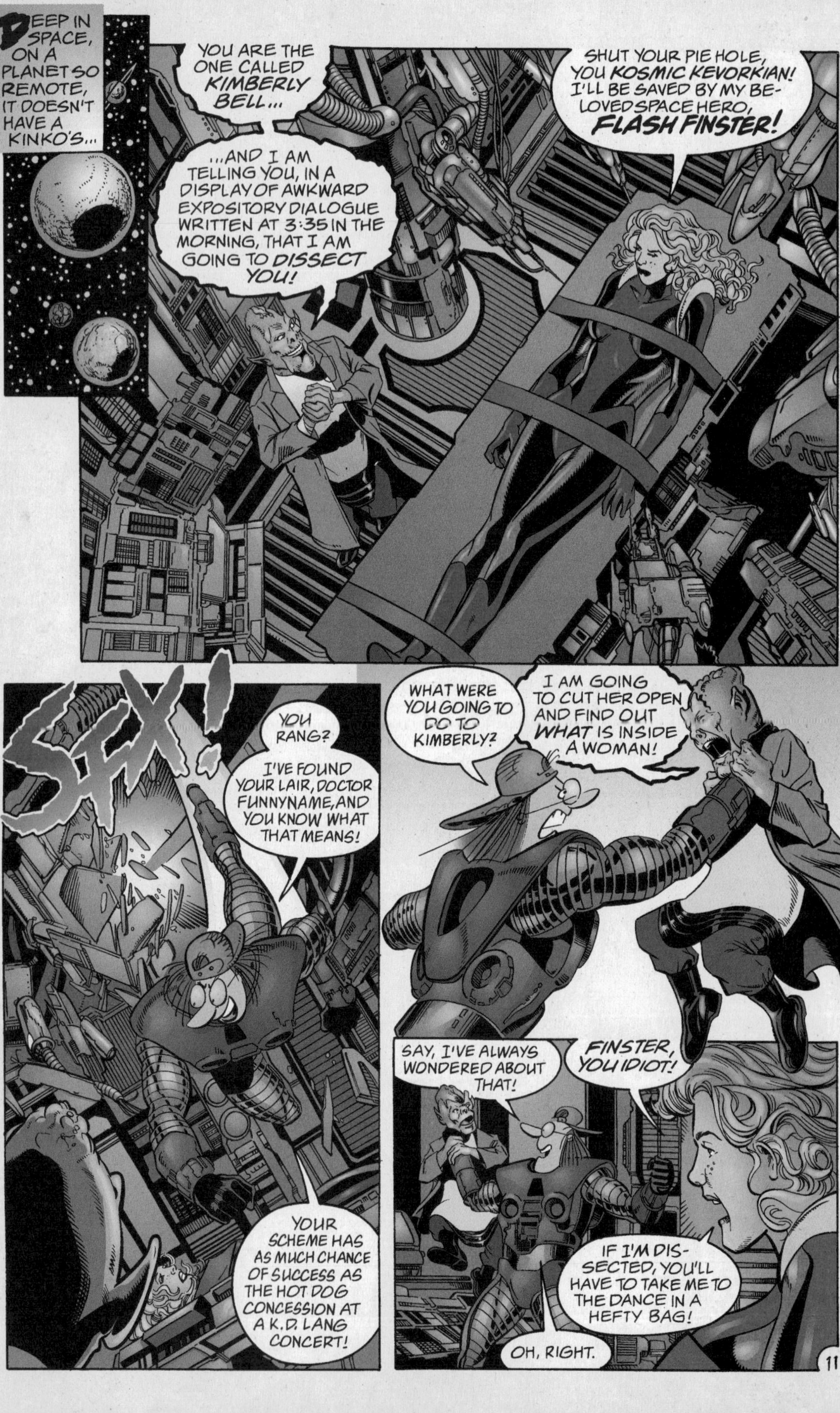
DEEP IN SPACE, ON A PLANET SO REMOTE, IT DOESN'T HAVE A KINKO'S...
YOU ARE THE ONE CALLED KIMBERLY BELL...
...AND I AM TELLING YOU, IN A DISPLAY OF AWKWARD EXPOSITORY DIALOGUE WRITTEN AT 3:35 IN THE MORNING, THAT I AM GOING TO DISSECT YOU!
SHUT YOUR PIE HOLE, YOU KOSMIC KEVORKIAN! I'LL BE SAVED BY MY BE-LOVED SPACE HERO, FLASH FINSTER!
SFX!
YOU RANG?
I'VE FOUND YOUR LAIR, DOCTOR FUNNYNAME, AND YOU KNOW WHAT THAT MEANS!
YOUR SCHEME HAS AS MUCH CHANCE OF SUCCESS AS THE HOT DOG CONCESSION AT A K.D. LANG CONCERT!
WHAT WERE YOU GOING TO DO TO KIMBERLY?
I AM GOING TO CUT HER OPEN AND FIND OUT WHAT IS INSIDE A WOMAN!
SAY, I'VE ALWAYS WONDERED ABOUT THAT!
FINSTER, YOU IDIOT!
IF I'M DIS-SECTED, YOU'LL HAVE TO TAKE ME TO THE DANCE IN A HEFTY BAG!
OH, RIGHT.

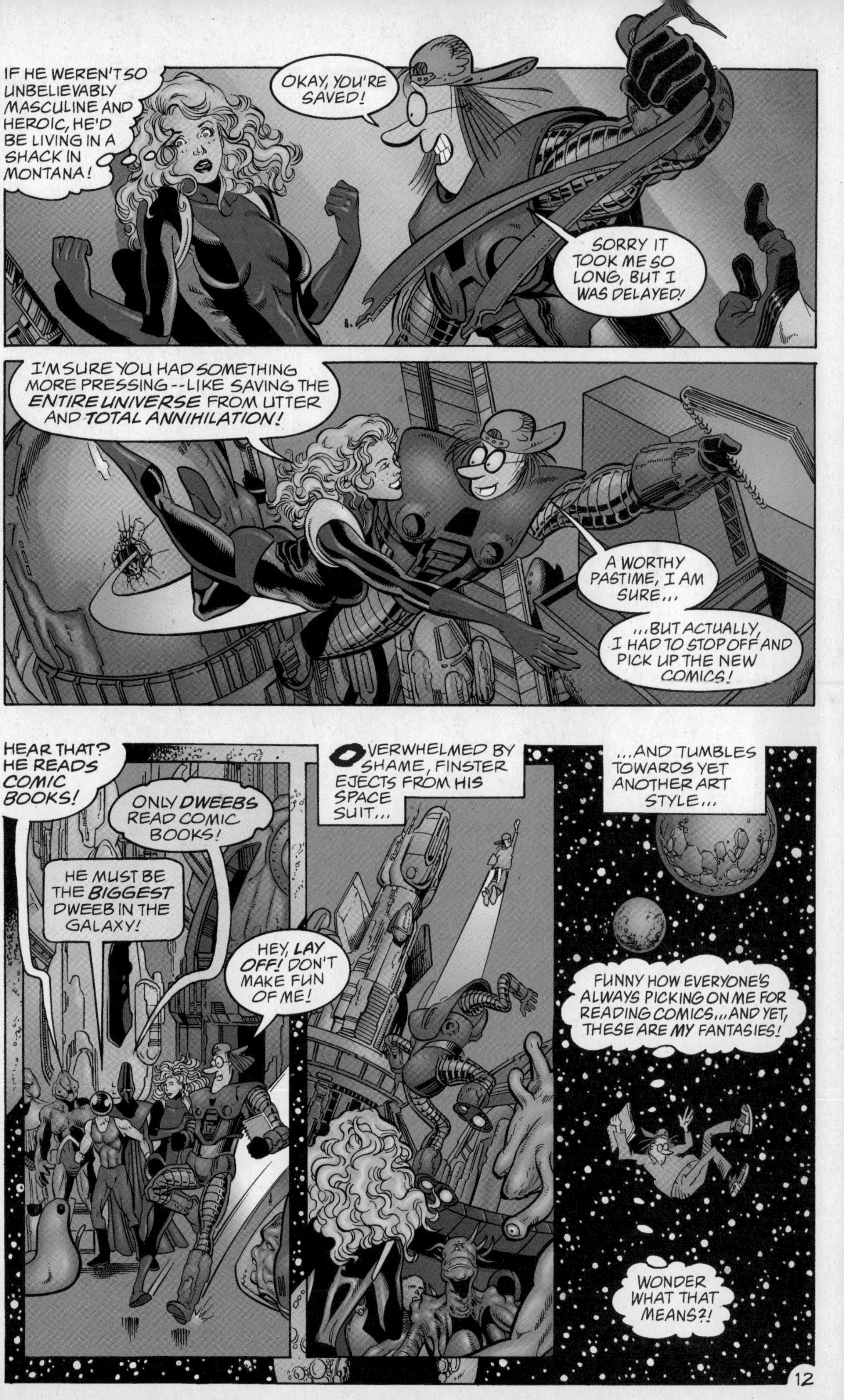
IF HE WEREN'T SO UNBELIEVABLY MASCULINE AND HEROIC, HE'D BE LIVING IN A SHACK IN MONTANA!
OKAY, YOU'RE SAVED!
SORRY IT TOOK ME SO LONG, BUT I WAS DELAYED!
I'M SURE YOU HAD SOMETHING MORE PRESSING--LIKE SAVING THE ENTIRE UNIVERSE FROM UTTER AND TOTAL ANNIHILATION!
A WORTHY PASTIME, I AM SURE...
...BUT ACTUALLY, I HAD TO STOP OFF AND PICK UP THE NEW COMICS!
HEAR THAT? HE READS COMIC BOOKS!
ONLY DWEEBS READ COMIC BOOKS!
HE MUST BE THE BIGGEST DWEEB IN THE GALAXY!
HEY, LAY OFF! DON'T MAKE FUN OF ME!
OVERWHELMED BY SHAME, FINSTER EJECTS FROM HIS SPACE SUIT...
...AND TUMBLES TOWARDS YET ANOTHER ART STYLE...
FUNNY HOW EVERYONE'S ALWAYS PICKING ON ME FOR READING COMICS... AND YET, THESE ARE MY FANTASIES!
WONDER WHAT THAT MEANS?!

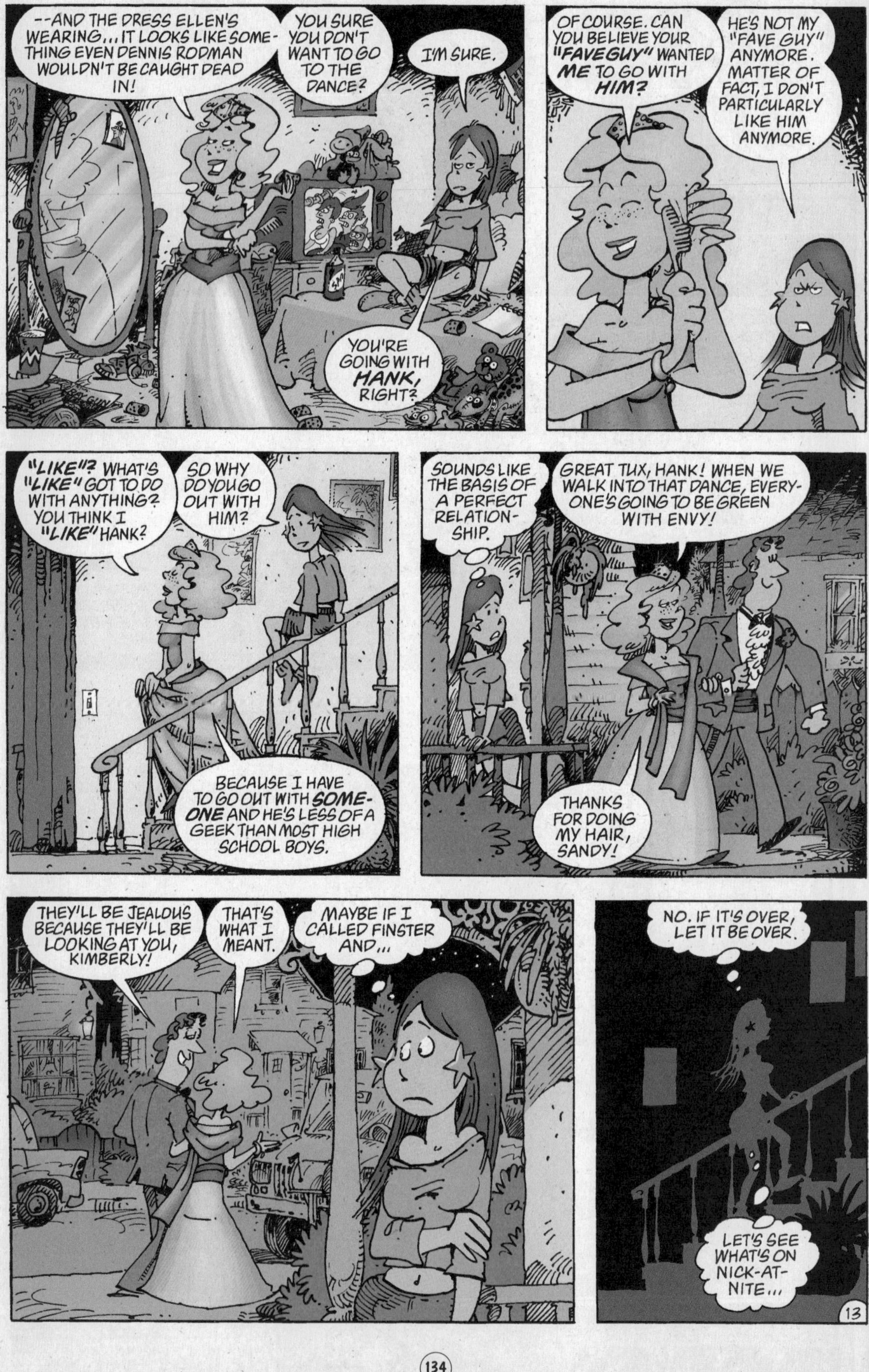
--AND THE DRESS ELLEN'S WEARING... IT LOOKS LIKE SOMETHING EVEN DENNIS RODMAN WOULDN'T BE CAUGHT DEAD IN!
YOU SURE YOU DON'T WANT TO GO TO THE DANCE?
I'M SURE.
YOU'RE GOING WITH HANK, RIGHT?
OF COURSE. CAN YOU BELIEVE YOUR "FAVE GUY" WANTED ME TO GO WITH HIM?
HE'S NOT MY "FAVE GUY" ANYMORE. MATTER OF FACT, I DON'T PARTICULARLY LIKE HIM ANYMORE.
"LIKE"? WHAT'S "LIKE" GOT TO DO WITH ANYTHING? YOU THINK I "LIKE" HANK?
SO WHY DO YOU GO OUT WITH HIM?
BECAUSE I HAVE TO GO OUT WITH SOMEONE AND HE'S LESS OF A GEEK THAN MOST HIGH SCHOOL BOYS.
SOUNDS LIKE THE BASIS OF A PERFECT RELATIONSHIP.
GREAT TUX, HANK! WHEN WE WALK INTO THAT DANCE, EVERYONE'S GOING TO BE GREEN WITH ENVY!
THANKS FOR DOING MY HAIR, SANDY!
THEY'LL BE JEALOUS BECAUSE THEY'LL BE LOOKING AT YOU, KIMBERLY!
THAT'S WHAT I MEANT.
MAYBE IF I CALLED FINSTER AND...
NO. IF IT'S OVER, LET IT BE OVER.
LET'S SEE WHAT'S ON NICK-AT-NITE...
13

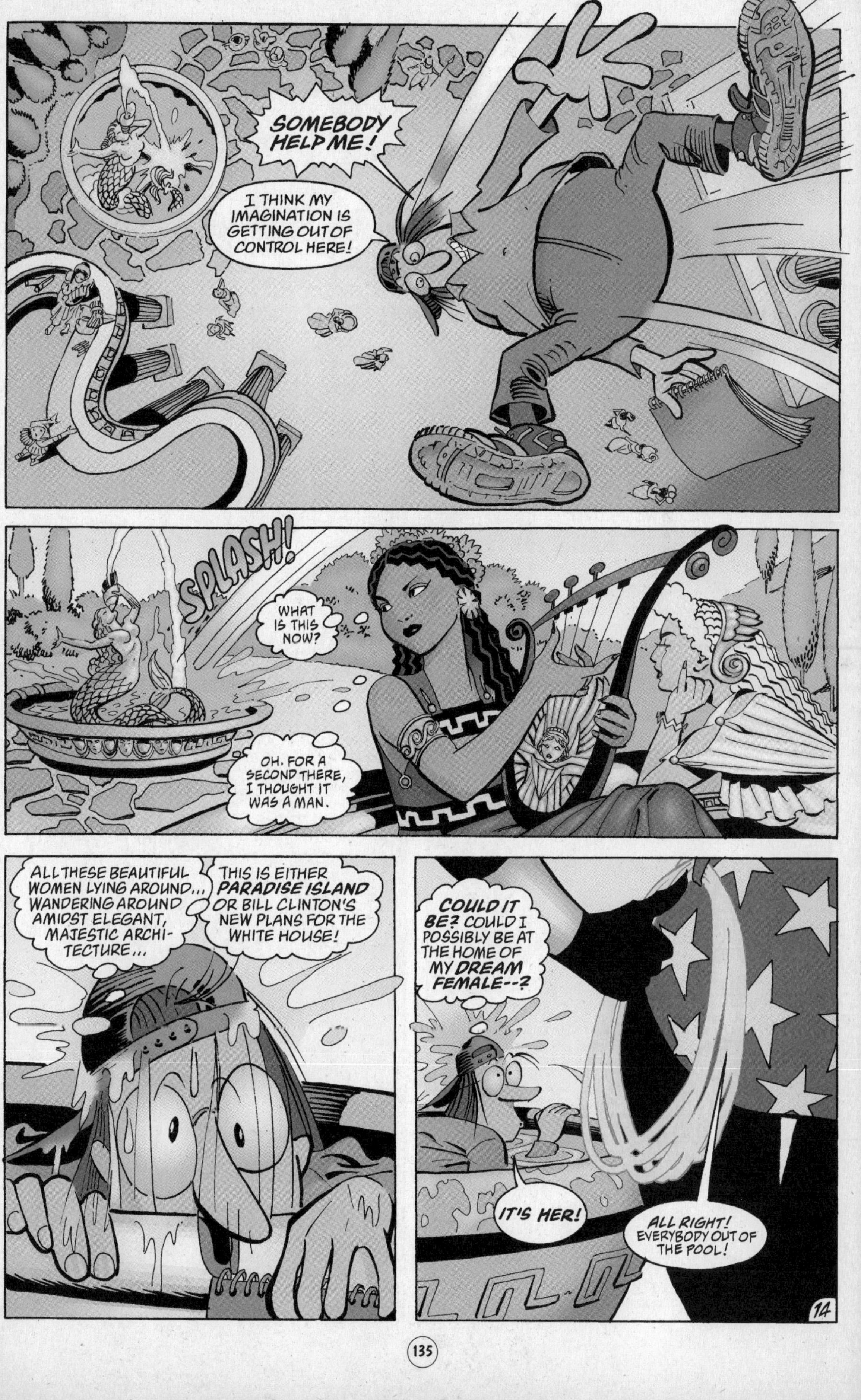
SOMEBODY HELP ME!
I THINK MY IMAGINATION IS GETTING OUT OF CONTROL HERE!
SPLASH!
WHAT IS THIS NOW?
OH. FOR A SECOND THERE, I THOUGHT IT WAS A MAN.
ALL THESE BEAUTIFUL WOMEN LYING AROUND... WANDERING AROUND AMIDST ELEGANT, MAJESTIC ARCHI-TECTURE...
THIS IS EITHER PARADISE ISLAND OR BILL CLINTON'S NEW PLANS FOR THE WHITE HOUSE!
COULD IT BE? COULD I POSSIBLY BE AT THE HOME OF MY DREAM FEMALE--?
IT'S HER!
ALL RIGHT! EVERYBODY OUT OF THE POOL!
14

THIS ONE'S PROBABLY UNDER THE LEGAL MINIMUM SIZE! I'LL HAVE TO THROW HIM BACK!

WONDER WOMAN! I'M YOUR BIGGEST FAN IN THE WHOLE WIDE WORLD! I HAVE EVERY COMIC BOOK YOU'VE EVER BEEN IN!

I'VE EVEN READ SOME OF THEM! EVEN DURING ALL THOSE YEARS WHEN IT WAS REALLY CRUMMY!

IF THAT DOESN'T PROVE TRUE LOVE, I DON'T KNOW WHAT DOES!

HEY,...ISN'T THERE SOME RULE THAT SAYS NO MAN CAN SET FOOT HERE ON PARADISE ISLAND?

YES...MAN! IT DOESN'T APPLY TO COMIC BOOK READERS OR OTHER GUYS WHO DON'T DATE!

THAT'S NOT TRUE! I HAVE WOMEN SURROUNDING ME, NIGHT AND DAY!

YEAH. ME, SUPERGIRL, CATWOMAN, BLACK CANARY...

SHE'S EVERYTHING I DREAMED OF IN A WOMAN... AND MORE! SHE'S EVEN INKED WELL!

IF I COULD GET HER TO GO TO THE DANCE WITH ME...

OH, WOULDN'T THAT BE SOMETHING? I CAN SEE IT ALL NOW--

--ALL THAT ENVY... EVERYONE'S EYES POPPING OUT LIKE A TEX AVERY CARTOON STARRING MARTY FELDMAN...

15

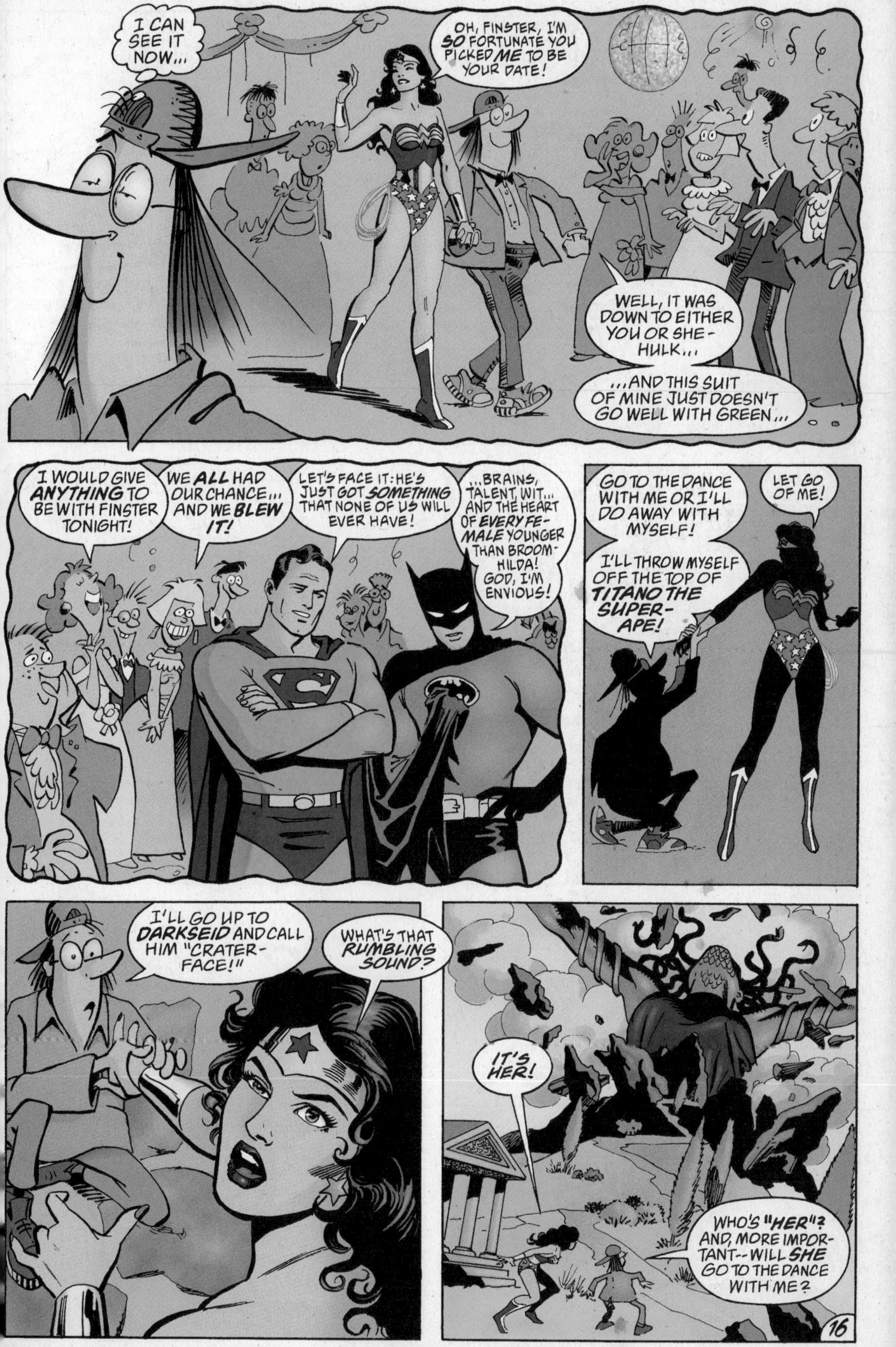
I CAN SEE IT NOW...
OH, FINSTER, I'M **SO** FORTUNATE YOU PICKED **ME** TO BE YOUR DATE!
WELL, IT WAS DOWN TO EITHER YOU OR SHE-HULK...
...AND THIS SUIT OF MINE JUST DOESN'T GO WELL WITH GREEN...
I WOULD GIVE **ANYTHING** TO BE WITH FINSTER TONIGHT!
WE **ALL** HAD OUR CHANCE... AND WE **BLEW IT!**
LET'S FACE IT: HE'S JUST GOT **SOMETHING** THAT NONE OF US WILL EVER HAVE!
...BRAINS, TALENT, WIT... AND THE HEART OF **EVERY FEMALE** YOUNGER THAN BROOM-HILDA! GOD, I'M ENVIOUS!
GO TO THE DANCE WITH ME OR I'LL DO AWAY WITH MYSELF!
LET GO OF ME!
I'LL THROW MYSELF OFF THE TOP OF **TITANO THE SUPER-APE!**
I'LL GO UP TO **DARKSEID** AND CALL HIM "CRATER-FACE!"
WHAT'S THAT **RUMBLING SOUND?**
IT'S HER!
WHO'S **"HER"**? AND, MORE IMPORTANT--WILL **SHE** GO TO THE DANCE WITH ME?
16

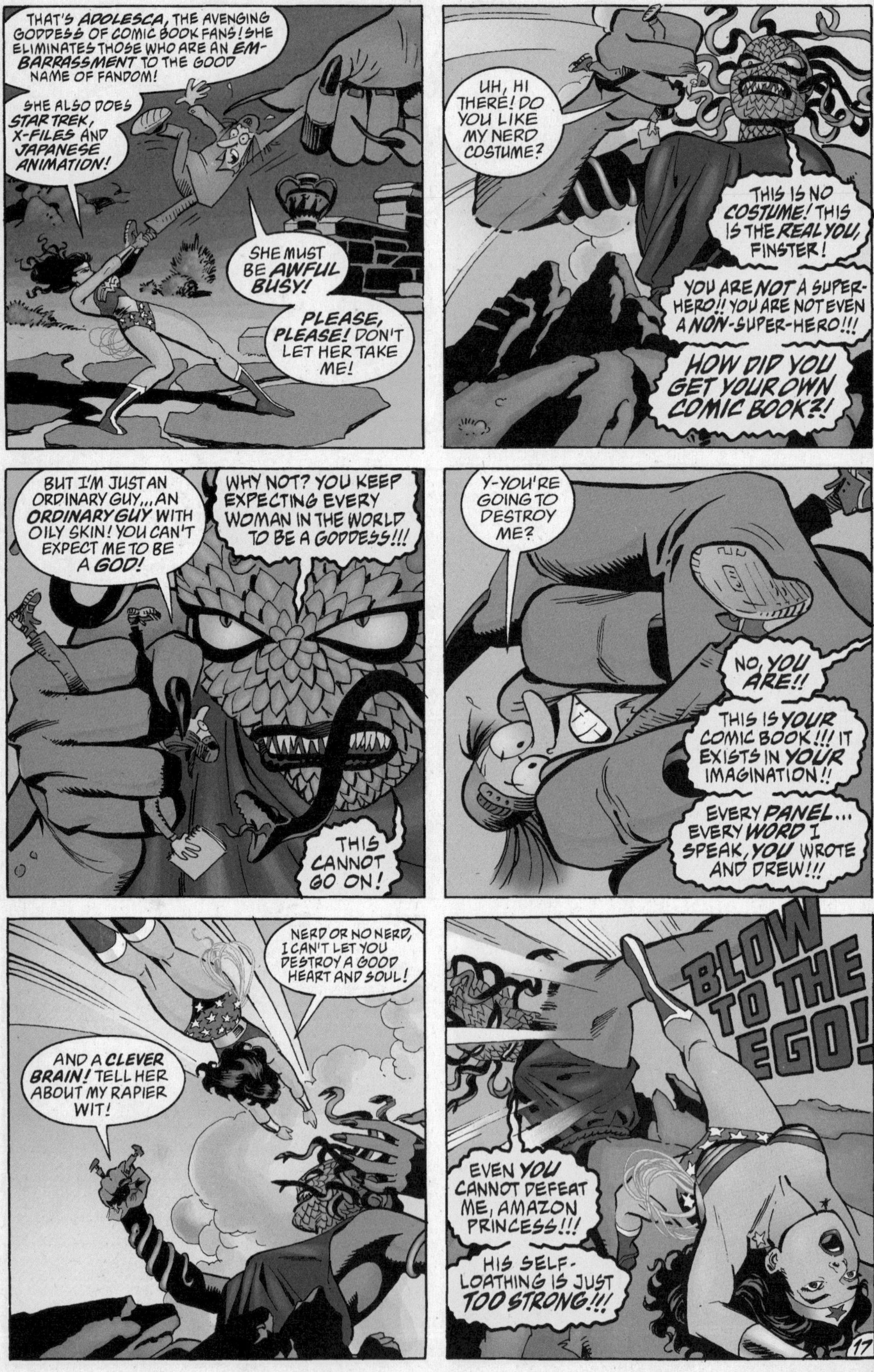
THAT'S ADOLESCA, THE AVENGING GODDESS OF COMIC BOOK FANS! SHE ELIMINATES THOSE WHO ARE AN EMBARRASSMENT TO THE GOOD NAME OF FANDOM!
SHE ALSO DOES STAR TREK, X-FILES AND JAPANESE ANIMATION!
SHE MUST BE AWFUL BUSY!
PLEASE, PLEASE! DON'T LET HER TAKE ME!
UH, HI THERE! DO YOU LIKE MY NERD COSTUME?
THIS IS NO COSTUME! THIS IS THE REAL YOU, FINSTER!
YOU ARE NOT A SUPER-HERO!! YOU ARE NOT EVEN A NON-SUPER-HERO!!!
HOW DID YOU GET YOUR OWN COMIC BOOK?!
BUT I'M JUST AN ORDINARY GUY... AN ORDINARY GUY WITH OILY SKIN! YOU CAN'T EXPECT ME TO BE A GOD!
WHY NOT? YOU KEEP EXPECTING EVERY WOMAN IN THE WORLD TO BE A GODDESS!!!
THIS CANNOT GO ON!
Y-YOU'RE GOING TO DESTROY ME?
NO, YOU ARE!!
THIS IS YOUR COMIC BOOK!!! IT EXISTS IN YOUR IMAGINATION!!
EVERY PANEL... EVERY WORD I SPEAK, YOU WROTE AND DREW!!!
NERD OR NO NERD, I CAN'T LET YOU DESTROY A GOOD HEART AND SOUL!
AND A CLEVER BRAIN! TELL HER ABOUT MY RAPIER WIT!
BLOW TO THE EGO!
EVEN YOU CANNOT DEFEAT ME, AMAZON PRINCESS!!!
HIS SELF-LOATHING IS JUST TOO STRONG!!!
17

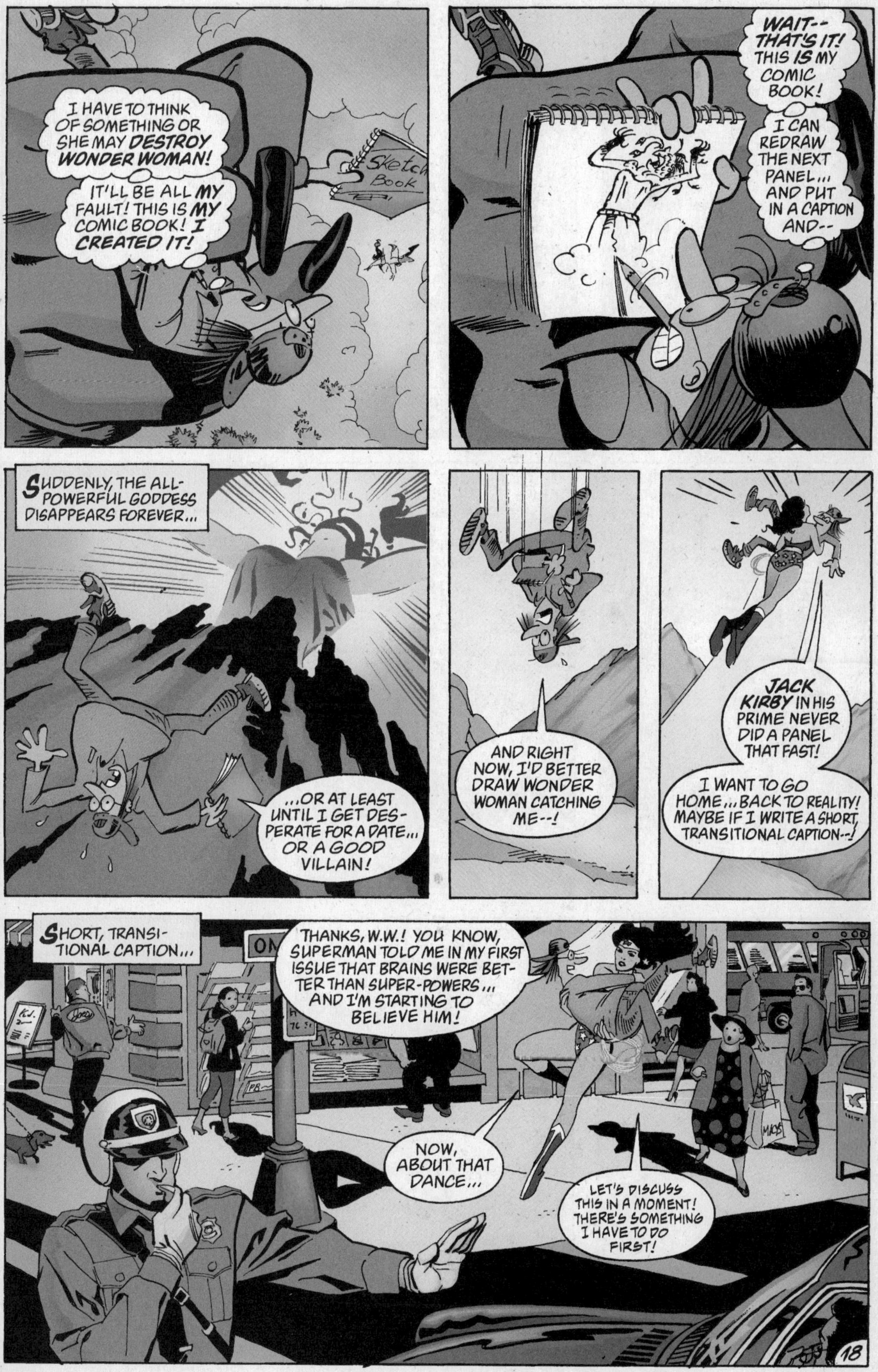
I HAVE TO THINK OF SOMETHING OR SHE MAY DESTROY WONDER WOMAN!
IT'LL BE ALL MY FAULT! THIS IS MY COMIC BOOK! I CREATED IT!
Sketch Book
WAIT-- THAT'S IT! THIS IS MY COMIC BOOK!
I CAN REDRAW THE NEXT PANEL... AND PUT IN A CAPTION AND--
SUDDENLY, THE ALL-POWERFUL GODDESS DISAPPEARS FOREVER...
...OR AT LEAST UNTIL I GET DESPERATE FOR A DATE... OR A GOOD VILLAIN!
AND RIGHT NOW, I'D BETTER DRAW WONDER WOMAN CATCHING ME--!
JACK KIRBY IN HIS PRIME NEVER DID A PANEL THAT FAST!
I WANT TO GO HOME... BACK TO REALITY! MAYBE IF I WRITE A SHORT, TRANSITIONAL CAPTION--!
SHORT, TRANSITIONAL CAPTION...
THANKS, W.W.! YOU KNOW, SUPERMAN TOLD ME IN MY FIRST ISSUE THAT BRAINS WERE BETTER THAN SUPER-POWERS... AND I'M STARTING TO BELIEVE HIM!
NOW, ABOUT THAT DANCE...
LET'S DISCUSS THIS IN A MOMENT! THERE'S SOMETHING I HAVE TO DO FIRST!
18

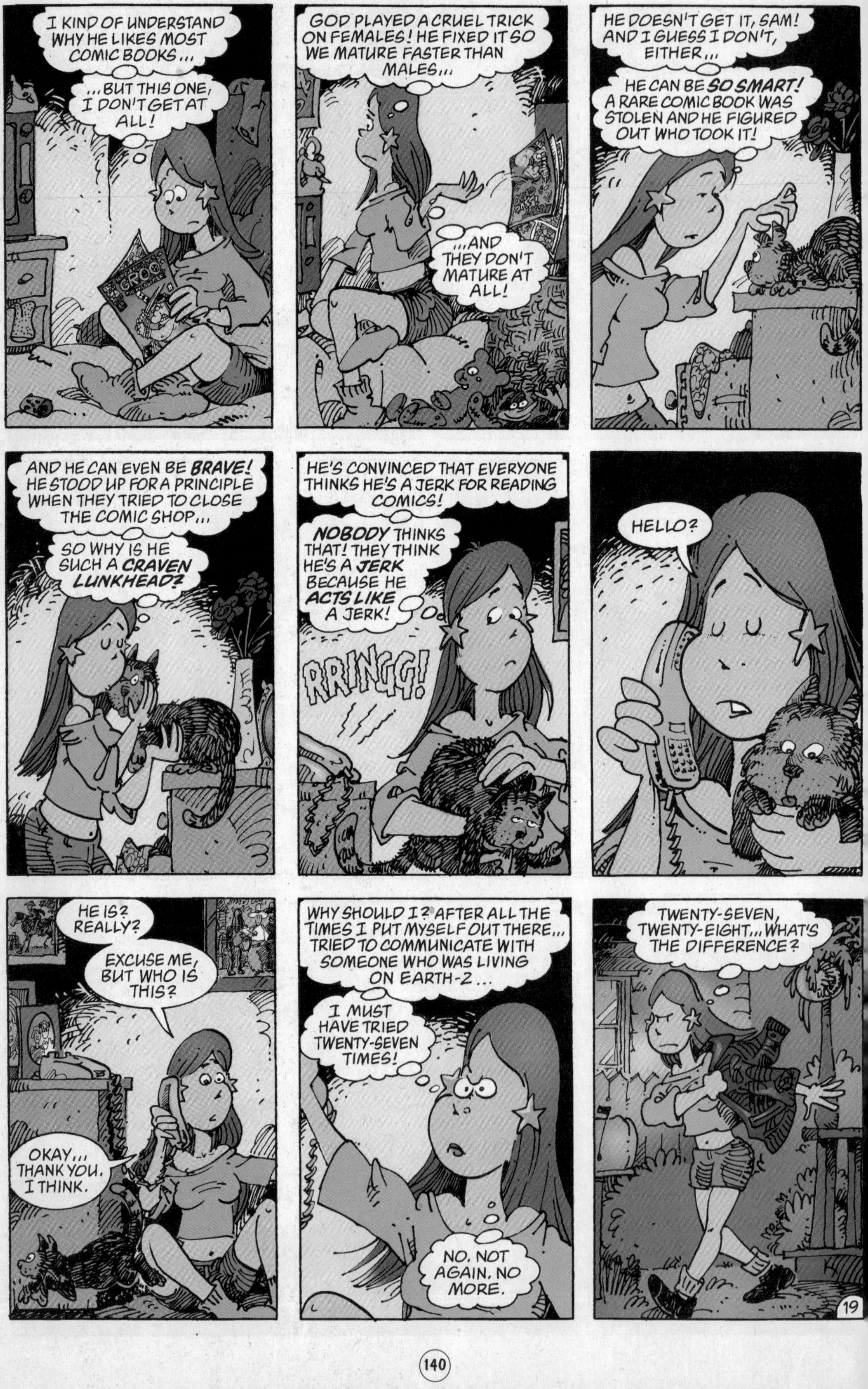
I KIND OF UNDERSTAND WHY HE LIKES MOST COMIC BOOKS...
...BUT THIS ONE, I DON'T GET AT ALL!
GOD PLAYED A CRUEL TRICK ON FEMALES! HE FIXED IT SO WE MATURE FASTER THAN MALES...
...AND THEY DON'T MATURE AT ALL!
HE DOESN'T GET IT, SAM! AND I GUESS I DON'T, EITHER...
HE CAN BE SO SMART! A RARE COMIC BOOK WAS STOLEN AND HE FIGURED OUT WHO TOOK IT!
AND HE CAN EVEN BE BRAVE! HE STOOD UP FOR A PRINCIPLE WHEN THEY TRIED TO CLOSE THE COMIC SHOP...
SO WHY IS HE SUCH A CRAVEN LUNKHEAD?
HE'S CONVINCED THAT EVERYONE THINKS HE'S A JERK FOR READING COMICS!
NOBODY THINKS THAT! THEY THINK HE'S A JERK BECAUSE HE ACTS LIKE A JERK!
RRINGG!
HELLO?
HE IS? REALLY?
EXCUSE ME, BUT WHO IS THIS?
OKAY... THANK YOU. I THINK.
WHY SHOULD I? AFTER ALL THE TIMES I PUT MYSELF OUT THERE... TRIED TO COMMUNICATE WITH SOMEONE WHO WAS LIVING ON EARTH-2...
I MUST HAVE TRIED TWENTY-SEVEN TIMES!
NO. NOT AGAIN. NO MORE.
TWENTY-SEVEN, TWENTY-EIGHT... WHAT'S THE DIFFERENCE?
19

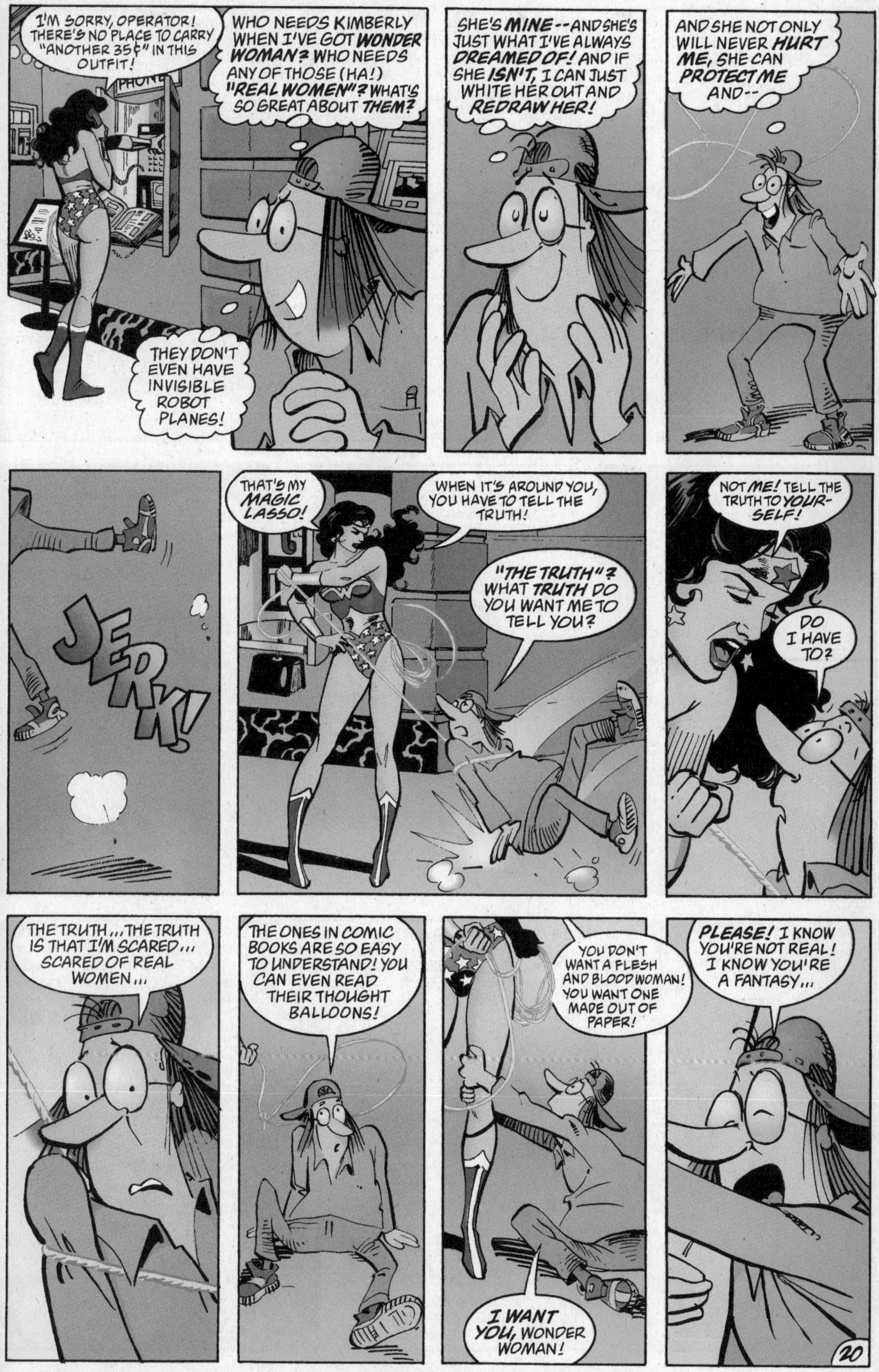

I'M SORRY, OPERATOR! THERE'S NO PLACE TO CARRY "ANOTHER 35¢" IN THIS OUTFIT!
PHONE
WHO NEEDS KIMBERLY WHEN I'VE GOT WONDER WOMAN? WHO NEEDS ANY OF THOSE (HA!) "REAL WOMEN"? WHAT'S SO GREAT ABOUT THEM?
THEY DON'T EVEN HAVE INVISIBLE ROBOT PLANES!
SHE'S MINE--AND SHE'S JUST WHAT I'VE ALWAYS DREAMED OF! AND IF SHE ISN'T, I CAN JUST WHITE HER OUT AND REDRAW HER!
AND SHE NOT ONLY WILL NEVER HURT ME, SHE CAN PROTECT ME AND--
JERK!
THAT'S MY MAGIC LASSO!
WHEN IT'S AROUND YOU, YOU HAVE TO TELL THE TRUTH!
"THE TRUTH"? WHAT TRUTH DO YOU WANT ME TO TELL YOU?
NOT ME! TELL THE TRUTH TO YOURSELF!
DO I HAVE TO?
THE TRUTH... THE TRUTH IS THAT I'M SCARED... SCARED OF REAL WOMEN...
THE ONES IN COMIC BOOKS ARE SO EASY TO UNDERSTAND! YOU CAN EVEN READ THEIR THOUGHT BALLOONS!
YOU DON'T WANT A FLESH AND BLOOD WOMAN! YOU WANT ONE MADE OUT OF PAPER!
I WANT YOU, WONDER WOMAN!
PLEASE! I KNOW YOU'RE NOT REAL! I KNOW YOU'RE A FANTASY...
20

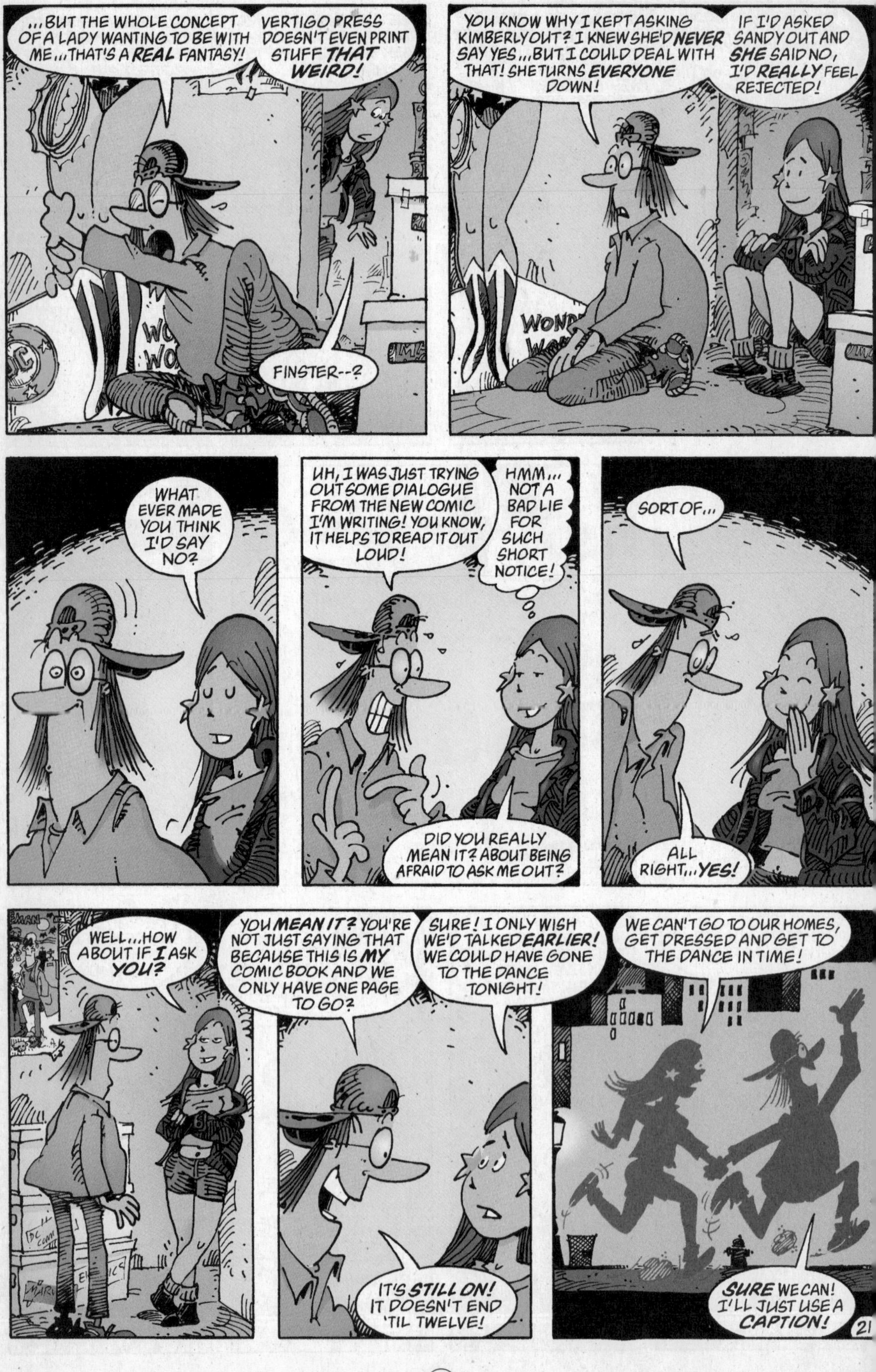
...BUT THE WHOLE CONCEPT OF A LADY WANTING TO BE WITH ME...THAT'S A REAL FANTASY!
VERTIGO PRESS DOESN'T EVEN PRINT STUFF THAT WEIRD!
FINSTER--?
YOU KNOW WHY I KEPT ASKING KIMBERLY OUT? I KNEW SHE'D NEVER SAY YES...BUT I COULD DEAL WITH THAT! SHE TURNS EVERYONE DOWN!
IF I'D ASKED SANDY OUT AND SHE SAID NO, I'D REALLY FEEL REJECTED!
WHAT EVER MADE YOU THINK I'D SAY NO?
UH, I WAS JUST TRYING OUT SOME DIALOGUE FROM THE NEW COMIC I'M WRITING! YOU KNOW, IT HELPS TO READ IT OUT LOUD!
HMM... NOT A BAD LIE FOR SUCH SHORT NOTICE!
DID YOU REALLY MEAN IT? ABOUT BEING AFRAID TO ASK ME OUT?
SORT OF...
ALL RIGHT...YES!
WELL...HOW ABOUT IF I ASK YOU?
YOU MEAN IT? YOU'RE NOT JUST SAYING THAT BECAUSE THIS IS MY COMIC BOOK AND WE ONLY HAVE ONE PAGE TO GO?
SURE! I ONLY WISH WE'D TALKED EARLIER! WE COULD HAVE GONE TO THE DANCE TONIGHT!
IT'S STILL ON! IT DOESN'T END 'TIL TWELVE!
WE CAN'T GO TO OUR HOMES, GET DRESSED AND GET TO THE DANCE IN TIME!
SURE WE CAN! I'LL JUST USE A CAPTION!
21

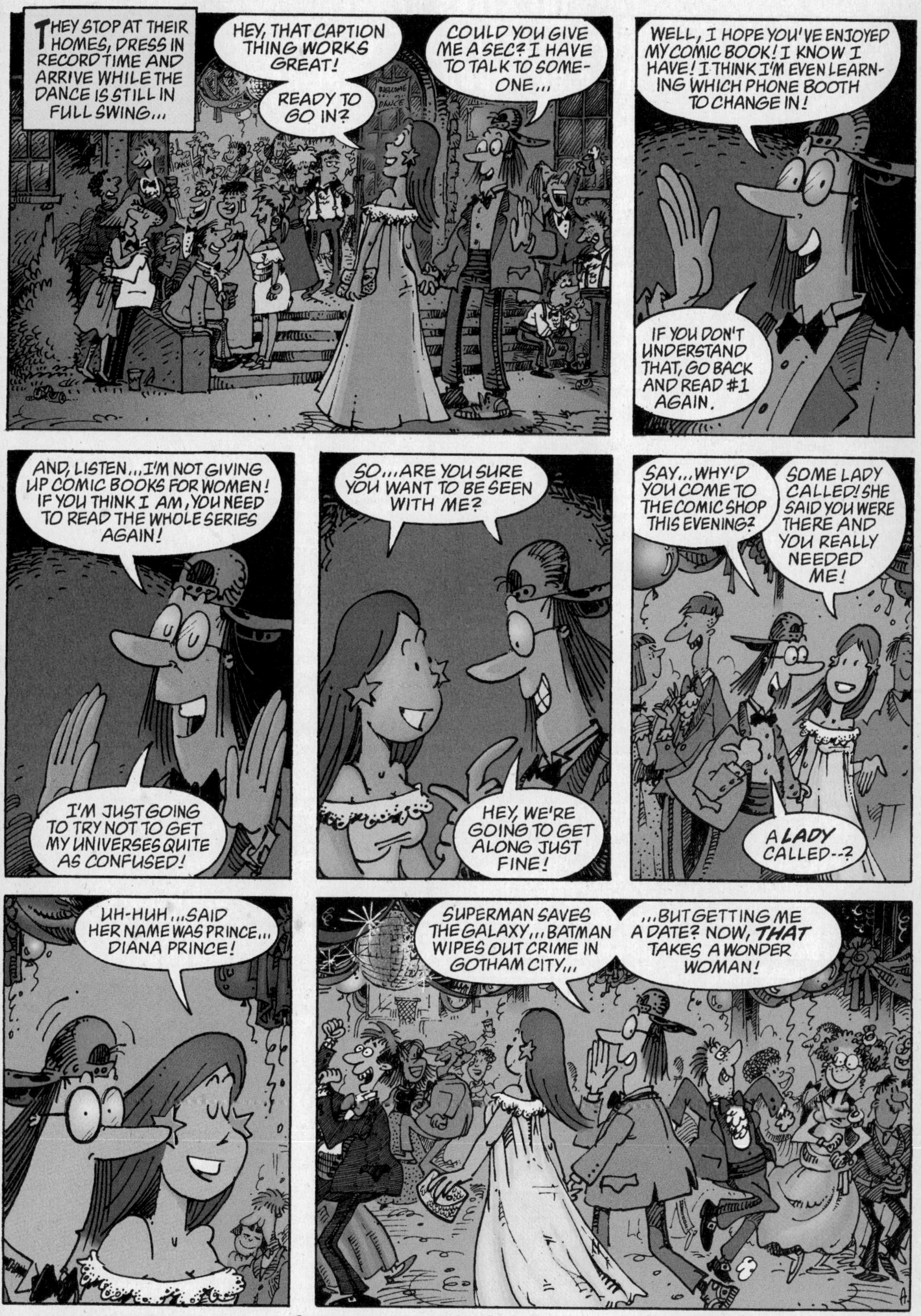
THEY STOP AT THEIR HOMES, DRESS IN RECORD TIME AND ARRIVE WHILE THE DANCE IS STILL IN FULL SWING...
HEY, THAT CAPTION THING WORKS GREAT!
READY TO GO IN?
COULD YOU GIVE ME A SEC? I HAVE TO TALK TO SOMEONE...
WELL, I HOPE YOU'VE ENJOYED MY COMIC BOOK! I KNOW I HAVE! I THINK I'M EVEN LEARNING WHICH PHONE BOOTH TO CHANGE IN!
IF YOU DON'T UNDERSTAND THAT, GO BACK AND READ #1 AGAIN.
AND, LISTEN...I'M NOT GIVING UP COMIC BOOKS FOR WOMEN! IF YOU THINK I AM, YOU NEED TO READ THE WHOLE SERIES AGAIN!
I'M JUST GOING TO TRY NOT TO GET MY UNIVERSES QUITE AS CONFUSED!
SO...ARE YOU SURE YOU WANT TO BE SEEN WITH ME?
HEY, WE'RE GOING TO GET ALONG JUST FINE!
SAY...WHY'D YOU COME TO THE COMIC SHOP THIS EVENING?
SOME LADY CALLED! SHE SAID YOU WERE THERE AND YOU REALLY NEEDED ME!
A LADY CALLED--?
UH-HUH...SAID HER NAME WAS PRINCE... DIANA PRINCE!
SUPERMAN SAVES THE GALAXY... BATMAN WIPES OUT CRIME IN GOTHAM CITY...
...BUT GETTING ME A DATE? NOW, THAT TAKES A WONDER WOMAN!

by **MARK EVANIER** and **SERGIO ARAGONÉS**

GUEST ARTISTS: **DAN SPIEGLE** (pg. 5-7) **MIKE GRELL** (pg. 9-10) **PHIL JIMENEZ** (pencils, pg. 11-12) **STEVE RUDE** (pencils, pg. 14-18, 20) **MARK McKENNA** (inks, pg. 11-12) **DICK GIORDANO** (inks, pg. 14-18, 20)
LETTERING: **TODD KLEIN** COLORING: **TOM LUTH** EDITOR: **TONY BEDARD**

THE STARS OF THE
DC UNIVERSE
CAN ALSO BE FOUND IN THESE BOOKS:

TO FIND MORE COLLECTED EDITIONS AND MONTHLY COMIC BOOKS FROM DC COMICS,
CALL 1-888-COMIC BOOK FOR THE NEAREST COMICS SHOP OR GO TO YOUR LOCAL BOOK STORE.

Visit us at www.dccomics.com